COMMITMENT

to the

Covenant

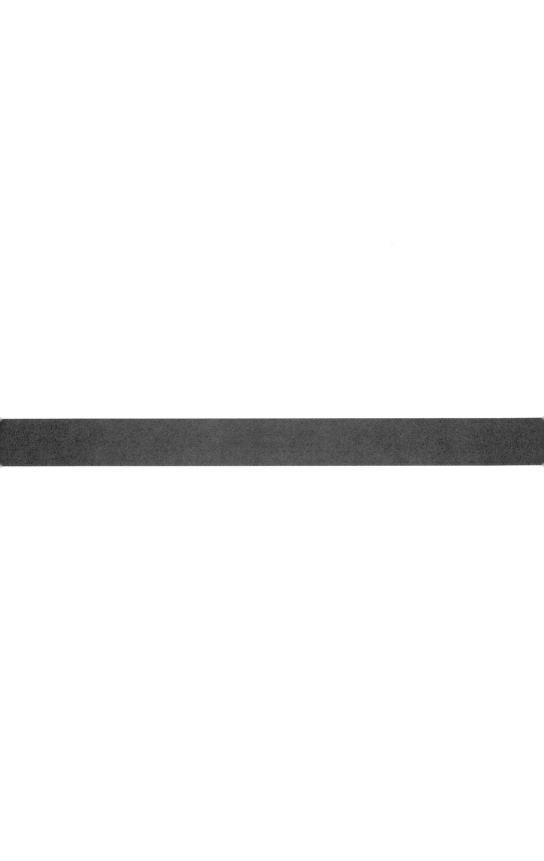

COMMITMENT

to the

Covenant

STRENGTHENING THE ME, WE, AND THEE OF MARRIAGE

DEBRA THEOBALD McCLENDON, PhD
RICHARD J. McCLENDON, PhD

RSC
BYU

DESERET
BOOK

Published by the Religious Studies Center, Brigham Young University, Provo, Utah, in cooperation with Deseret Book Company, Salt Lake City. Visit us at rsc.byu.edu.

Printed in the United States of America by Sheridan Books, Inc.

DESERET BOOK is a registered trademark of Deseret Book Company. Visit us at DeseretBook.com.

ISBN 978-1-9443-9431-8

Library of Congress Cataloging-in-Publication Data

Names: McClendon, Debra Theobald, 1975- author. | McClendon, Richard J. (Richard Jennings), 1962- author.
Title: Commitment to the covenant : strengthening the me, we, and thee of marriage / Debra Theobald McClendon, PhD & Richard J. McClendon, PhD.
Description: Utah : Religious Studies Center, Brigham Young University, [2018] | Includes bibliographical references.
Identifiers: LCCN 2017049434 | ISBN 9781944394318
Subjects: LCSH: Marriage--Religious aspects--Church of Jesus Christ of Latter-day Saints. | Marriage--Religious aspects--Mormon Church.
Classification: LCC BX8643.M36 M33 2018 | DDC 248.8/44--dc23
LC record available at https://lccn.loc.gov/2017049434

FOR
OUR CHILDREN

Contents

Preface ix

Chapter 1. Commitment to the Covenant 1

PART 1: THE *ME* IN MARRIAGE 25

Chapter 2. The Power of Commitment: Prioritizing
Our Marriage Covenant 27

Chapter 3. Bounce Back and Move Forward:
Resilience and Posttraumatic Growth . . . 61

Chapter 4. "I Forgive You": The Freedom
of Forgiveness 97

PART 2: THE *WE* IN MARRIAGE 129

Chapter 5. Close to You: Fostering
Emotional Intimacy 131

Chapter 6. "They Twain Shall Be One Flesh": Marital
Unity in the Sexual Relationship . . . 167

Chapter 7. "The Spirit of Contention Is Not of Me":
Working through Differences 193

Chapter 8. For Richer or for Poorer:
Working Together on Finances. . . . 231

PART 3: THE *THEE* IN MARRIAGE 259

Chapter 9. "Holding Fast to the Rod of Iron":
God's Word in Marriage 261

Chapter 10. "Safety in Counsel": Heeding
Prophets and Apostles 299

Chapter 11. "We Are a Covenant-Making People":
Gospel Principles and Ordinances
in Marriage 327

Appendix: In Sickness and in Health: Mental Health
Issues and Access to Treatment . . . 363

Bibliography 401

Index 419

About the Authors 431

Preface

Commitment to the Covenant: Strengthening the Me, We, and Thee of Marriage is a work of scholarly nonfiction strengthening marriage from three broad content areas—the things we need to do personally to improve our marriage (Me), the things we need to do together as a couple to strengthen our marital relationship (We), and the things we need to do personally and together as a couple to invite God into our marriage (Thee). While other publications focus either on religion or a particular academic discipline separately, we combine social science research with scripture, doctrine, and the counsel of latter-day prophets and apostles. We do this by drawing upon Richard's sociological training and his work in the Church Educational System, as well as Debra's training in marriage and family therapy and clinical psychology and her experiences as a psychotherapist. We believe that this multifaceted approach provides a rich perspective that can help a wide audience of LDS couples along their own marital journeys.

This book is a reflection of our professional and personal testimonies of the truthfulness of these principles. Writing this book has blessed our marriage as we have strengthened our own commitment to the covenant. We pray that you, too, may be blessed as you read from its pages.

We feel that Heavenly Father has been intimately involved in the process of writing and publishing this book. We are grateful for His guidance; He has continually prompted us as we have sought His direction. We would also like to express gratitude to all contributors who offered their personal stories to enrich this book. We are grateful to Bruce Chadwick for his many hours of editing. Finally, we appreciate the assistance of Brigham Young University's Religious Studies Center staff: Thomas A. Wayment, Joany O. Pinegar, R. Devan Jensen, Brent R. Nordgren, Tyler Balli, Carmen Durland Cole, Mandi Diaz, Emily Strong, and Shannon Taylor.

—Debra Theobald McClendon and Richard J. McClendon

CHAPTER 1

Commitment to the Covenant

DEBRA: *Richard and I are very different. The first couple of years of our marriage were difficult and painful. We had a lot of adjustments to make in order to be able to get along, become unified, and find happiness together. When I met Richard, I was a divorced, single mom with two very young daughters, most of the way through a clinical psychology PhD program. Working toward finishing my academic and professional training as a single mom was already difficult, but dating Richard, a longtime bachelor, upped the intensity of this period significantly.*

As the relationship progressed, the thought of being married again created a lot of fear of rejection for me, yet I moved forward in faith because I loved and respected Richard and knew he loved God and took seriously his role in God's plan. I sensed that Richard and I would be very good together, and I felt that God sanctioned the union. I also felt strongly that my daughters needed to be raised in a home with both a mother and a father who loved each other. Yet there were issues.

By the time we married, Richard had lived as a bachelor for twenty-four years post–LDS mission. Needless to say, he had anxiety about getting married, wasn't very flexible, and knew how things "should" be done (and I wasn't doing them that way). As a result, he was sometimes critical of me. We had arguments during our early relationship as I tried to defend my own worth and value to him while struggling with very real personal insecurities. I feared rejection, and Richard's actions intensified those fears through his unaccepting stance on a variety of personality issues. To be honest, I wasn't sure whether he was committed to me or to our marriage.

RICHARD: *I was a bachelor until I was forty-five years old. I had accumulated years of formal education and work experience, looking forward to the day when I could be a husband and father. However, many years of bachelorhood had rooted me in a comfortably settled lifestyle. I had some uncertainties, inflexibility, and a lot of anxiety when it came time to finally tying the knot. I had some major adjustments to make being married to a real woman with her own personality with unique strengths and flaws, rather than being married to the imagined, perfect wife that I had spent so many years hoping for. I made a lot of mistakes with Debra, trying to make her what I thought she should be rather than accepting her for who she was. This created a lot of conflict in our early relationship. She was not always patient with me in these situations, but thankfully she was forgiving of my self-righteousness and kept working with me. (I have often joked that it finally took a psychologist to get me married, but perhaps there is some truth to that!)*

Through the Lord's help, and our determination to make our marriage work, we weathered through those difficult early years, holding on to a hope that we could find greater happiness together. We learned critical lessons that, as we implemented them, set our relationship on a more positive course. Years later our marriage is thriving and wonderful. There are times that we still have disagreements, but we have learned to avoid the type of painful arguments we had in the early years. This has come as a result of our commitment to the covenant, which has created a daily, purposeful commitment to each other and to our marital relationship. We work hard to love each other, and we enjoy those marvelous benefits.

Commitment to the Covenant

*P*resident Dallin H. Oaks observed that "a good marriage does not require a perfect man or a perfect woman. It only requires a man and a woman committed to strive together toward perfection."[1] This book is born from that prophetic counsel. Marriage is an eternal principle in the plan of salvation. Marriage is the institution God established to bring a man and a woman together in order to support and sustain each other while traveling the mortal road toward perfection. Marriage is the workshop or factory where imperfect people join their efforts and synergize their unique individual gifts to build unifying celestial characteristics and find joy. Spouses are often very different from each other. Sometimes this creates misunderstanding and frustration that leads to arguments, resentment, or discord. President Oaks reminds us that regardless of differences, a good marriage is one in which both spouses are highly committed to each other and highly committed to working to improve their marriage.

Commitment to the Covenant seeks to strengthen marriage as a fundamental unit of society, as well as strengthen our individual relationships between husband and wife as a fundamental unit of eternity. We utilize social science research, particularly from the areas of sociology and psychology, as well as doctrines of the gospel of Jesus Christ to present key principles that, if applied, will help a marriage thrive. To illustrate these various principles, we share many stories. This tripartite approach (religion, science, and personal narrative) is intended to create a comprehensive discussion that is not only theoretical in nature but explicitly practical.

Throughout the book, we include several different types of personal narratives to illustrate principles. We share stories from our marriage that breach the barriers of "proper" social discourse; we go beyond the superficial aspects of marriage to openly share many of our personal triumphs, misunderstandings, arguments, struggles, and moments of clarity, revelation, and closeness. In addition, we provide anonymous stories from others who generously and courageously share their closed-door experiences relative to their personal histories, marriages, and mental health in hope that their stories will be of service. Our hope is that these narratives will provide a wide variety of experiences and perspectives to supplement the principles shared in this book.

DEBRA: *Lastly, throughout the text I share several client stories from my work as a psychologist. Please note that I highly value client confidentiality. Each of these clients has very generously and courageously given me permission to share their personal stories.*

Our prayer is that this book will be a valuable resource for couples in their efforts to strengthen their relationship and progress in the quest for eternal, celestial marriage. As an introduction, this chapter frames up *Commitment to the Covenant* by examining how the institution of marriage is currently doing in society as a whole as well as within The Church of Jesus Christ of Latter-day Saints. We will also introduce the layout and approach for the rest of the book.

The Current State of Marriage

In 2017, Elder David A. Bednar of the Quorum of the Twelve Apostles spoke at the Humanum Colloquium in New York City among a gathering of interreligious leaders. There he raised a warning voice against what he termed as a "skewed conception of marriage" currently being accepted in society. He explained that "increasing numbers of people are giving up on the very idea of marriage, believing that relationships are inherently unstable and transitory, thereby avoiding in their view the unnecessary commitments of formal marriage and pain of the inevitable divorce."[2]

Elder Bednar's observation and warning is both insightful and clear. The institution of marriage is struggling. Indeed, during the past several decades, we have seen the weakening of public support for the marriage vow in the United States and across the world. As prophets and Church leaders have noted this trend, social science researchers have also identified symptoms of this decline in marriage. For example, in the United States (US) alone, the marriage rate has dropped by about one-third since the 1970s and is at a historic low (see figure 1). This trend is also true in most countries across the world (see figure 2). In the US, millennials are five times less likely to marry by age twenty-five than when baby boomers were the same age.

Divorce rates are another way to measure marital health. When using the crude divorce rate (the number of divorces occurring in a particular geographical area in a given year, per 1,000 population), divorce rates are shown to have actually declined in the United States since the 1980s (see figure 1). Some argue that this is evidence that the health of marriage isn't as bad as some would suggest. We disagree. The problem is that even with such a turnaround, the most current divorce to marriage

Reflections

I have been married for twenty years, but the majority of it I have struggled with feelings of not wanting to stay married. Though I felt completely in love when we were dating and when we got married, I soon discovered that being married wasn't what I was expecting it would be. I thought it would be happiness, togetherness, and unity, but instead for us it became disagreement, stress, criticism, and unhappiness. I constantly felt marriage wasn't worth it. Several times we talked about divorce. I seriously wanted it, desperately wanted it. And several times I left for short periods of time. But I've always tried to rely on God for direction. Many times I prayed and prayed that He would just say I could leave, but He never did. The more I prayed about it and turned to Him in this very trying matter in my life, the clearer it became to me that He wanted me to stay married. I know that's not the case for everyone, but for me it was. So I fought through it, trying as hard as I could and clinging to my relationship with God to provide the love and support I was lacking at home. And He gave that to me. And much to my astonishment, things have gotten better—really, truly better, to the point that I actually feel happy and feel love again. It has been years of struggle and there are still major challenges, but slowly my heart has been changed. The challenges in marriage refine us as nothing else can, but it can take years and years. I'm so grateful that my marriage was preserved and that I have the opportunity to keep working on it, because it truly is worth it.

U.S. Marriage and Divorce Rates, 1870-2015 (per 1000 population)

FIGURE 1. CENTERS FOR DISEASE CONTROL (CDC), (2017). LINE GRAPH ILLUSTRATION: US MARRIAGE AND DIVORCE RATES, 1870–2015 (PER 1,000 POP.), ROBSLINK.COM/SAS/DEMOCD80/US_DIVORCE_AND_MARRIAGE.HTM.

ratio (.45 in 2015), is still far away from what it was in 1970 (.33) when the divorce rate began to climb (see figure 1). The institution of marriage has been hit hard by decades of the divorce culture and has not really recovered. This trend can also be found in other countries across the world (see figure 3). As a side note, some demographers aren't convinced that the crude divorce rate is even the most accurate measure. Instead, they argue that by using other statistical methods, divorce rates are in fact increasing.[3]

Marriage decline is also revealed by looking at the delay of first marriages. In the United States, the median age at first marriage for women has gone from around age 20 up to 27 since the 1970s. For men, the median age at first marriage has increased from age 23 to almost 30 (see figure 4). Researchers have found that 80 percent of young adults in the 1970s were married by the time they were 30, whereas today 80 percent of young adults

Crude marriage rate, 1970, 1995 and 2014 or latest available year[a]
Marriages per 1000 people

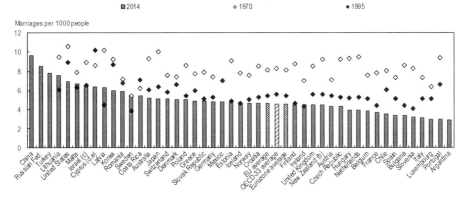

FIGURE 2. OECD FAMILY DATABASE (4 MARCH 2017). BAR GRAPH ILLUSTRATION: CRUDE MARRIAGE RATES, 1970, 1995, AND 2014 OR LATEST AVAILABLE YEAR. *SF3.1: Marriage and Divorce Rates*, HTTP://WWW.OECD.ORG/ELS/FAMILY/SF_3_1_MARRIAGE_ AND_DIVORCE_RATES.PDF.

Crude divorce rate, 1970, 1995 and 2014 or latest available year[a]
Divorces per 1000 people

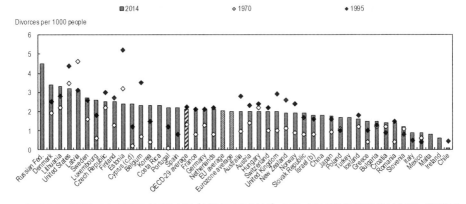

FIGURE 3. OECD FAMILY DATABASE (4 MARCH 2017). BAR GRAPH ILLUSTRATION: CRUDE DIVORCE RATES, 1970, 1995, AND 2014 OR LATEST AVAILABLE YEAR. *SF3.1: Marriage and Divorce Rates*, HTTP://WWW.OECD.ORG/ELS/FAMILY/SF_3_1_MARRIAGE_AND_DIVORCE_ RATES.PDF.

aren't married until age 45.[4] The delay of marriage is widespread in many countries across the world as well. Some have proposed that this increase in age at first marriage is a healthy trend because divorce rates are often lower for those who marry later in life. Yet we see this delay as a reflection of our culture's failure to prioritize or value the institution of marriage.

The increase of cohabitation, which is closely tied to the delay of marriage, is also a strong indicator of marriage decline. Since 1975, cohabitation in the US has increased more than twelve times among young adults (ages 18 to 34).[5] This change is a clear sign of the lack of interest the rising generation has in formalizing a conjugal relationship. Cohabiters enter into relationships in which they live and have sexual relations with a chosen partner, living together in a similar state as husband and wife, without the actual legal obligations and benefits of marriage. The hope of many is that they can see how the relationship works out while living together, as a trial period per se, and then if all goes as hoped, they may later marry to make the commitment to their love and their relationship official. If the relationship does not go as planned, by cohabitating they have maintained the freedom to separate without any of the legal inconveniences or expense of a divorce and certainly without the stigmatic societal label of being divorced.

Another major element that contributes to the erosion of marriage, at least in the US, is the wide acceptance of no-fault divorce laws. Back in the 1960s, no-fault divorce became popular in America through the lobbying efforts of lawyers to make divorce a faster and less judgmental legal process. Unfortunately, it has created a legal culture relative to marriage and divorce that has spilled over into general societal attitudes toward marriage. As one researcher put it, "Thanks to no-fault, the marriage contract is no longer enforceable. It takes two to marry but only one to divorce at any time, for any reason, as fast as the courts can sort out property and custody issues."[6]

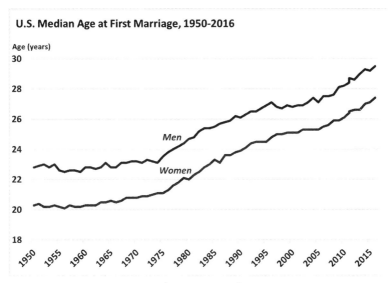

U.S. Median Age at First Marriage, 1950-2016

FIGURE 4. US CENSUS BUREAU (4 MARCH 2017). LINE GRAPH ILLUSTRATION: MEDIAN AGE AT FIRST MARRIAGE: 1950 TO 2016, HTTPS://WWW.CENSUS .GOV/HHES/FAMILIES/FILES/GRAPHICS/MS-2.PDF.

Selfishness Leads to Poor Marital Commitment

So what's behind these unfortunate trends leading to the decay of marriage? In his Humanum Colloquium address Elder Bednar warned: "An increasingly cynical and self-absorbed world sees [the] principle of selflessness [in marriage] as 'old school' and paradoxical. But we know that it is paradisiacal." He promises that "as husbands and wives 'lose' their lives in fulfilling these sacred duties of marriage and family, they find themselves—becoming true servants of God and disciples of Jesus Christ."[7]

As Elder Bednar indicates, we believe that the driving force behind the decline in marriage is a subtle, yet harmful, cultural value shift in society toward self-interest. Such selfishness has been the catalyst leading society to become more casual in its commitments, agreements, and promises as a whole, and marriage in particular. Parties of agreements no longer have high expectations that their contracts will be honored. Such a tendency can be found in business, law, politics, and professional sports, in which breaking promises and contracts is becoming an accepted part of the natural operation of things. Yet perhaps no other aspect of society has been affected as significantly by this trend than has the institution of marriage. What was once a promise of *until death do us part* has now shifted to *until debt do us part*. The once holy binding of husband and wife is now seen as probationary, often entered into with prenuptial agreements, signaling an odd anticipation of divorce even before the marriage begins.

Historically, marriage was largely viewed by both individuals and society with a deep level of commitment. From a social science perspective, this high level of commitment is not misplaced, because the evidence is clear that it provides greater social stability and well-being. In their widely acclaimed book, *The Case for Marriage*, Waite and Gallagher reported that married individuals have, on average, significantly higher levels of happiness, physical and emotional health, and financial well-being when compared to singles, cohabiters, or divorcees. In addition, they found that the large majority (86 percent) of unhappily married people who stayed married had happier marriages five years later.[8] In other words, "permanent marital unhappiness is surprisingly rare among the couples who stick it out."[9]

Further analysis by Waite and colleagues found that "unhappily married adults who divorced or separated were no happier, on average, than unhappily married adults who stayed married." They also reported that "even unhappy spouses who had divorced and remarried were no happier, on average, than unhappy spouses who stayed married." Thus, if people choose divorce because they think it will bring them a sense of greater happiness, existing research shows little if no evidence that their assumption is true.[10]

A second, more recent witness to these findings comes from researchers who analyzed data from 10,000 parents with newborn children. Among couples who initially reported their marriage to be unhappy, ten years later two-thirds of them reported that they were now happy in their marriage, with only 7 percent claiming that they were still unhappy.[11] Again, marital happiness is dynamic and rarely settles into a state of chronic unhappiness. Instead, couples find ways to breathe positive feelings back into their marriage over time.

In spite of these compelling findings, around 40 percent of men and women ages fifteen to forty-four in the US continue to agree that divorce is the best solution for couples with ongoing marital difficulties.[12] According to Waite and Gallagher, much of this divorce-culture attitude can be attributed to the "privatization of marriage," in which marriage has become regarded as a private and individual decision.[13] When struggling with marital difficulty and considering whether to divorce, the central question often considered by individuals today is "What would make me happy?" This question is often promoted by lawyers, educators, counselors, and even clergy, reinforcing "the idea that emotional gratification is the main purpose and benefit of marriage."[14]

Elder D. Todd Christofferson of the Quorum of the Twelve Apostles counters this attitude:

> A family built on the marriage of a man and woman supplies the best setting for God's plan to thrive—the setting for the birth of children, who come in purity and innocence from God, and the environment for the learning and preparation they will need for a successful mortal life and eternal life in the world to come. A critical mass of families built on such marriages is vital for societies to survive and flourish. That is why communities and nations generally have encouraged and protected marriage and the family as privileged institutions. It has never been just about the love and happiness of adults.[15]

Unfortunately, our society doesn't see it this way. Harvard law professor Mary Ann Glendon described the present law and attitude toward marriage and divorce: "The American story about marriage, as told in the law and in much popular literature, goes something like this: marriage is a relationship that exists primarily

for the fulfillment of the individual spouses. If it ceases to perform this function, no one is to blame and either spouse may
terminate it at will."[16]

Self-absorption then has become the preeminent purpose
of marriage in society, and unfortunately it's not very compatible with marriage. Selfishness contributes to society's general
anticommitment attitude, which is driving an unprecedented
increase in marital postponement and cohabitation in the US
and other countries and is eroding the barrier that once protected society against a casual acceptance of divorce.

LDS Marriage Today

How have these social and legal trends affected marriage and
divorce among members of The Church of Jesus Christ of Latter-
day Saints? Certainly LDS couples have their own problems and
struggles, but when looking at the LDS population as a whole,
there is good evidence of what President Dieter F. Uchtdorf said:
"Members of The Church of Jesus Christ of Latter-day Saints
are known throughout the world for having some of the finest
marriages and families you can find."[17]

In his research work in 2000, Richard, working with Bruce
Chadwick, found that most marriages in the Church were relatively strong and vibrant. When compared to the national per-
centages, Latter-day Saints were significantly different from their
national peers, showing lower age at first marriage, lower numbers of single-parent families, and larger family size. Like the
national average, Latter-day Saints also ranked extremely high
in marital happiness.[18] Researchers interviewing LDS couples in
2012 found that they believed marriage is meant to be eternal.
As a result, these study participants indicated that they are more
committed, more willing to sacrifice, and more capable of coping
with difficulties and conflict.[19]

Divorce rates among Latter-day Saints are also an important indicator of how they are doing. Many scholars believe that the current lifetime divorce rate in the United States is between 40 percent and 50 percent. In 2000, Bruce Chadwick and Richard, analyzing both civil and temple marriages combined, found an estimated current lifetime divorce rate for returned-missionary men to be approximately 12 percent and for returned-missionary women a divorce rate around 16 percent. They estimated that the lifetime rate for non-returned-missionary men to be approximately 38 percent and about 22 percent for non-returned-missionary women.[20] Although these data are somewhat dated, they give a baseline perspective. Thus, although divorce rates among Latter-day Saints are lower when compared to the general American public, LDS marriages are not perfect, and divorce has definitively found its way into many Latter-day Saint households.

In a bold warning to members of the Church about marriage and divorce, President Gordon B. Hinckley declared:

> Of course, all in marriage is not bliss.
>
> . . . The remedy for most marriage stress is not in divorce. It is in repentance. It is not in separation. It is in simple integrity that leads a man to square up his shoulders and meet his obligations. It is found in the Golden Rule. . . .
>
> There must be a willingness to overlook small faults, to forgive, and then to forget.
>
> There must be a holding of one's tongue. Temper is a vicious and corrosive thing that destroys affection and casts out love. . . .
>
> There may be now and again a legitimate cause for divorce. I am not one to say that it is never justified. But I say without hesitation that this plague among us, which seems to be growing everywhere, is not of God, but rather is the work of the adversary of righteousness and peace and truth.[21]

This prophetic warning helps us as Latter-day Saints to recognize that we must avoid the selfish trends of the world and make a thorough and complete commitment to the marriage vow and to God, who is at the center of a successful marriage.

The ME, WE, and THEE of Marriage

This book is divided into three general areas, presented as part 1, part 2, and part 3, respectively: the *Me*, *We*, and *Thee* of marriage.

The ME of Marriage

As discussed earlier, many in society today are led to believe that the most important question about whether a marriage is successful is "Does it make me happy?" or "What's in it for me?" Part 1 discusses the *Me* in the covenant of marriage from a strikingly different perspective—the intrapersonal ("intra-" meaning "within") contributions for building marriage. Rather than asking "What's in it for me?" we can ask, "What characteristics do I need in order to be a better spouse?" or "What can I do to build the marriage?" At the individual level, each spouse must contribute to the marriage for it to flourish. This is what we call the *Me* in marriage.

Admittedly, the concept of the *Me* in marriage is a hard doctrine. Many spouses may feel threatened to look at the *Me* in marriage, and so it may feel easier to place responsibility on their spouse or God to make the marriage work. Or they want to place blame when it isn't working. In fact, as we structured this book, we wondered if beginning with the *Me* section might be a turnoff to some readers. Yet we realized the book just could not begin in any other way—for marriage cannot begin in any other way. Marriage starts with *me*. We each must accept personal accountability for how we use our own agency in our marriage—the personal contributions we make (or fail to make) to the relationship. This part of the book will challenge and change you. Therefore, please approach part I with an added dose of openness and humility regarding the offerings therein.

Although there are numerous personal virtues individuals may bring to or develop in their marriage, we have chosen to highlight three principles that we believe are often overlooked or avoided in our current culture yet are foundational in strengthening a marriage: commitment, resilience, and forgiveness.

The commitment chapter, chapter 2, focuses on our personal or individual commitment to the covenant of marriage. Some in our society think commitment in marriage is simply a resolve *not* to divorce. This is certainly important, but we also promote making active, purposeful resolutions for the health of marriage. Our presentation of commitment certainly addresses the resolve to physically stay married, particularly for those in chronically difficult marriages, yet the discussion extends far beyond that. If we are committed to our marriage, we will give our spouse our time, attention, and energy. We will make the relationship with them a priority in our lives above other activities or interests. If we are committed, we are not just enduring, but we are always working to make our marriage thrive.

Chapter 3, the resilience and posttraumatic growth chapter, addresses the concept of building our personal reserves. In large measure, this chapter is about how to handle trials with adaptive coping—trials both within and without the marital relationship that influence the spousal relationship. We speak of the agonies of the soul that we all must encounter—how we can rebuild after we've been knocked down and how we can even propel ourselves forward. We present thorough discussions of these principles both from psychological and gospel perspectives. Those who struggle with principles of resilience, perhaps being caught in deeper mental health issues that prevent the healthy flexibility needed to be resilient, are referred to a mental health question and answer discussion found in the appendix of the book.

The forgiveness chapter, chapter 4, focuses on the universal need to forgive and the freeing power that comes to us and our spouse as we forgive them and let go. Likely, our spouse offends us about as frequently as we offend them (even though most of us probably don't like to think that we have ever done anything wrong or hurtful). Although we strive to be Christlike, we often fail and must figure out how to move past those failings. Forgiveness is a key personal ingredient to any happy marriage. We are to forgive *all* things. Sometimes it may be easier to forgive the "big" offenses because they demand our attention so dramatically. Yet, oftentimes, the "little" offenses get neglected; we fail to give them our attention, and the resentments for those offenses build up and become toxic.

The WE of Marriage

As we strengthen our individual resolve to build our marriage, we may then wonder: "What do spouses in good marriages do between themselves that makes their marriage thrive?" Part 2 discusses the We in the covenant of marriage, the interpersonal ("inter-" meaning "between") contributions for building marriage. It looks at the partnership of marriage. It examines the doing of marriage and offers practical marital-enhancement principles to assist couples in working together in their journey toward perfection. Critical topics in interpersonal relationships are covered in this section, including emotional intimacy, the sexual relationship, conflict, and finances.

Chapter 5, the emotional intimacy chapter, highlights the importance of emotional closeness or mutual dependence for the health of the marriage. We present evidence stemming from a seventy-five-year longitudinal study on the lives of men relative to the importance of this topic for men.[22] We discuss communication skills such as talking and listening, paying attention to love languages, building positive sentiment, continuing courtship, and creating shared meaning.

The sexual relations chapter, chapter 6, discusses the salience of the sexual relationship in the marital relationship. We explain how the sexual relationship helps husbands and wives build genuine and deep bonds of emotional intimacy if the true purposes of sex are kept in balance. We present the spiritual purposes in sex, such as partnering as creators with God, finding unity with our spouse, and learning about unity with God. We also discuss principles of charity relative to the sexual relationship. We conclude the chapter with a brief discussion about sexual dysfunction and the LDS Church's position on sexual matters.

Chapter 7, the conflict chapter, thoroughly examines destructive attitudes and behaviors that can destroy and undermine our marital relationships. This chapter relies heavily on the work of John Gottman, the nation's foremost researcher on marital relationships. We present processes in marriage that rupture marital trust and loyalty, and then discuss how we can protect ourselves from these destructive forces. We also present what we believe is a critical concept: clarifying the difference between principles and preferences. This involves identifying issues relative to eternal principles in contrast to issues of temporal preference when faced with differences between ourselves and our spouse. We also offer some practical considerations about the timing of discussions that may have potential conflict.

When all is said and done, couples often don't do so well during conflict, even when they are trying. They may often offend each other, hurt each other, and create opportunities to work through forgiveness anew. Thus, we end the chapter with a discussion about repair attempts, including the importance of making process commentaries and the power of an apology. There is great power in an apology!

We conclude the *We* section with chapter 8 on finances. We examine financial considerations relative to the partnership between husband and wife. We address the importance of both spouses being fully informed and involved in the decision-making processes associated with managing the family finances. We discuss five principles of money management: pay tithes and offerings, avoid debt, use a budget, build a reserve, and teach family members.[23] We discuss each of these areas at length, providing extensive stories to illustrate these principles.

The THEE *of Marriage*

Finally, although the Me and the We contributions to building marriage are essential and necessary, we cannot access all that marriage has to offer us for our journey toward perfection unless we look to God. Therefore, part 3 turns more fully to the Thee in the covenant of marriage, examining the extrapersonal ("extra" meaning "outside" or "beyond") contributions to building marriage. This involves asking questions such as "How is God using our marriage to perfect us?" or "How can Heavenly Father help us as we invite Him more fully into our relationship?" His contribution elevates us above and beyond what our intra- and interpersonal efforts can provide, perfecting and exalting us together as husband and wife into the eternities. We discuss herein principles of personal and couple worship (scripture study, prayer, pondering, and the recording of impressions); the importance of following the prophets and apostles as living oracles, seers, and revelators; and the necessity to fully engage ourselves in honoring the first principles and sacred ordinances of the gospel.

Chapter 9 focuses on worship activities, called "scripture literacy," that are generally done on a personal basis, but expands the discussion to encourage doing these activities with our spouse as well. This allows us to more fully access the Spirit and receive personal and couple revelation to bless our marriage and our life in general. We share how small and simple things like recording a spiritual impression or spending an evening pondering about a family circumstance have significantly influenced our lives and the lives of those around us (including you, as a reader of this book). There is great security and power in having the Spirit—a member of the Godhead—whisper to us truths we need and then guiding us to accurately discern those promptings for the benefit of ourselves, our marriage, our family, and our community.

Chapter 10, the prophets chapter, promotes the importance of following the prophet. The prophets commune with God and relay to us His will in real time for our day. The prophets are seers—they see clearly what is coming and they counsel us and work to prepare the Church and the body of members in advance for what is coming. There is great safety and peace in following the prophets. Herein we discuss the roles of prophets and apostles as watchtowers or satellites in our day and how we can more fully give heed to the prophets' counsel. The prophets have shown throughout all ages that our Father in Heaven is keenly concerned about our marriages and families, for His plan is a family plan. If we want to strengthen our marriage we must recommit today to adhere to the counsel of His prophets.

We conclude the *Thee* section, and our book, with a chapter examining gospel principles and ordinances and their relevance to our marriage. Chapter 11 examines how the first principles and ordinances of the gospel, as related in the fourth article of faith, are critical to our marital relationships. We admit these concepts are not generally linked in this way in general discourse, but we believe a deeper understanding of their relevance to our marriage is critical to more fully accessing the power of God and bringing with it greater power into our marriage. This chapter also discusses the sacredness of temple ordinances, concluding with the message that a temple sealing is the crowning ordinance of God. Here, as we are sealed to our beloved spouse, we can be crowned as kings and queens in His glorious kingdom, that we may receive all that He has to offer us and ultimately receive our exaltation. With such great doctrinal significance attached to the sealing ordinance, we as spouses must do all we can to honor our marriage and our spouse as the priority in our mortal efforts to enact the gospel plan.

Appendix

In the appendix of this book, you will find a mental health primer written in a question and answer format for those that may struggle to find resilience after trials, are struggling with psychological disorders (such as anxiety, depression, and the like), or feel they need marital therapy. The following questions are discussed:

- What is mental illness?
- How do I know if my spouse or I need professional help?
- How do we get the right treatment for our needs?
- How do we find a therapist?
- Do we need an LDS therapist?
- What do I do if my spouse refuses treatment?
- What do I do if my spouse is in crisis?

Holding to the Ideal

We want to note that throughout the chapters of this book we are discussing doctrines, ideas, and solutions that can aid us in attaining the ideal. We are well aware that in mortality, attaining the ideal is not always possible, but seeking after it is. As we have illustrated at the beginning of this chapter, we, ourselves, would be defined by the current societal standard as a "blended family." We have personal understanding of the loneliness of long-term singlehood, the heartache of divorce, the trauma of chronic problems that seem to have no solution no matter how hard one tries to have faith and behave well, and the sensitivity that is required to raise children whose lives are splintered between two households. This personal perspective has supported and even strengthened our religious and scientific convictions about commitment in marriage and has contributed to our strong position about the responsibility each of us has to hold tenaciously to the ideal. Certainly, the manner in which the ideal is implemented in families will vary based on individual circumstances,[24] but we discuss what we believe are core principles that can help guide and sustain us as we make decisions to be fully committed to our marriage.

Reflections

Marrying my husband is the best decision I have ever made. He is my best friend and is an absolute gem. He is the kindest, gentlest person I know. He loves and cherishes me with his whole soul. He adores and loves our children. Our camaraderie is something that makes me laugh during the good times and helps me not to cry during the bad times. I cherish our relation-ship with my whole heart. I can't imagine life without him.

Conclusion

Marriage is more than just an earthly institution that society can redefine at will. Elder D. Todd Christofferson asserts:

> Our claims for the role of marriage and family rest . . . on the truth that [they] are God's creation. It is He who in the beginning created Adam and Eve in His image, male and female, and joined them as husband and wife to become "one flesh" and to multiply and replenish the earth. Each individual carries the divine image, but it is in the matrimonial union of male and female as one that we attain perhaps the most complete meaning of our having been made in the image of God—male and female. Neither we nor any other mortal can alter this divine order of matrimony. It is not a human invention. Such marriage is indeed "from above, from God" and is as much a part of the plan of happiness as the Fall and the Atonement.[25]

Although the institution of marriage is eternal and God given, for us as mortals, it involves two imperfect people working toward building a relationship of God-like, eternal quality. Marriage requires work and constant effort to build and maintain. It requires the commitment to remain together while the imperfections of each partner are being purged. We need to take a long-term view when things are not as we would hope them to be.

Yet marriage is not simply a task of long-suffering—there is stability, there is purpose, there is love, there is joy, and there is peace as spouses work to become unified in love and purpose. The hopeful thread woven throughout the chapters of this book speaks to these possibilities for each of us. President Spencer W. Kimball said: "Real, lasting happiness is possible, and marriage can be more an exultant ecstasy than the human mind can conceive. This is within the reach of every couple, every person. . . . It is certain that almost any good man and any good woman can have happiness and a successful marriage if both are willing to pay the price."[26] As we pay that price and strive to continue forward along the path of Christian discipleship, holding hands as we walk that path side by side with our spouse, we can flourish personally and interpersonally.

Commitment to the Covenant represents both our personal and professional testimonials about the role of marriage in God's great plan of salvation. We pray you will accept our offering, knowing our well wishes are with you and your spouse as you seek to strengthen your marital relationship along the path toward eternal life.

Notes

1. Dallin H. Oaks, "Divorce," *Ensign*, May 2007, 73.

2. David A. Bednar, "The Divinely Designed Pattern of Marriage" (address, Humanum Colloquium, New York City, 9 March 2017), http://www.mormonnewsroom.org/article/elder-bednar-transcript-the-divinely-designed-pattern-marriage.

3. Sheela Kennedy and Steven Ruggles, "Breaking Up Is Hard to Count: The Rise of Divorce in the United States, 1980–2010," *Demography* 51, no. 2 (2014): 587–98. Bella DePaulo, "What Is the Divorce Rate, Really?," *Psychology Today*, 2 February 2017, https://www.psychologytoday.com/blog/living-single/201702/what-is-the-divorce-rate-really.

4. Jonathan Vespa, *The Changing Economics and Demographics of Young Adulthood: 1975–2016* (US Census Bureau, April 2017), 1, https://www.census.gov/content/dam/Census/library/publications/2017/demo/p20-579.pdf.

5. Vespa, *Changing Economics and Demographics of Young Adulthood*, 6.

6. Linda Waite and Maggie Gallagher, *The Case for Marriage* (New York: Doubleday, 2000), 178.

7. Bednar, "The Divinely Designed Pattern of Marriage."

8. Waite and Gallagher, *The Case for Marriage*, 148–49.

9. Waite and Gallagher, *The Case for Marriage*, 148–49.

10. Linda J. Waite et al., *Does Divorce Make People Happy? Findings from a Study of Unhappy Marriages* (New York: Institute for American Values, 2002), 4, http://www.americanvalues.org/search/item.php?id=13.

11. Harry Benson and Steve McKay, "Couples on the Brink," Marriage Foundation, February 2017, http://www.marriagefoundation.org.uk/wp-content/uploads/2017/02/MF-paper-Couples-on-the-brink-FINAL-1.pdf.

12. Jill Daugherty and Casey Copen, "Trends in Attitudes about Marriage, Childbearing, and Sexual Behavior: United States, 2002,

2006–2010, and 2011–2013," *National Health Statistics Reports*, no. 92 (2016).

13. Waite and Gallagher, *The Case for Marriage*, 178.

14. Waite and Gallagher, *The Case for Marriage*, 178.

15. D. Todd Christofferson, "Why Marriage, Why Family," *Ensign*, May 2015, 50–54.

16. Mary Ann Glendon, *Abortion and Divorce in Western Law: American Failures, European Challenges* (Cambridge, MA: Harvard University Press, 1987), 108. As cited in Dallin H. Oaks, "Protect the Children," *Ensign*, November 2012, 43–46.

17. Dieter F. Uchtdorf, "In Praise of Those Who Serve," *Ensign*, May 2016, 77.

18. Richard J. McClendon and Bruce A. Chadwick, "Latter-day Saint Families at the Dawn of the Twenty-First Century," in *Helping and Healing Families: Principles and Practices Inspired by "The Family: A Proclamation to the World*," ed. Craig H. Hart et al. (Salt Lake City: Deseret Book, 2005), 32–43.

19. Michael Goodman, David Dollahite, and Loren Marks, "Exploring Transformational Processes and Meaning in LDS Marriages," *Marriage & Family Review* 48, no. 6 (2012): 555–82.

20. McClendon and Chadwick, "Latter-day Saint Families," 39.

21. Gordon B. Hinckley, "What God Hath Joined Together," *Ensign*, May 1991, 72–74.

22. George E. Vaillant, *The Triumphs of Experience: The Men of the Harvard Grant Study* (Cambridge, MA: Belknap Press, 2012).

23. "Provident Living," The Church of Jesus Christ of Latter-day Saints, http://www.providentliving.org/.

24. "The Family: A Proclamation to the World," *Ensign*, November 1995, 102.

25. Christofferson, "Why Marriage, Why Family," 52.

26. Spencer W. Kimball, "Marriage and Divorce" (speech, Brigham Young University, Provo, UT, 7 September 1976), https://speeches.byu.edu/talks/spencer-w-kimball_marriage-divorce/.

PART 1

The *Me* in Marriage

THE *ME* IN MARRIAGE

You must take personal responsibility.
You cannot change the circumstances, the seasons,
or the wind, but you can change yourself. That is
something you have charge of. —Jim Rohn[1]

At the individual level, each spouse must contribute independently to the marriage for it to flourish. This is what we call the *Me* in marriage. Part I discusses the *Me* in the covenant of marriage from the intrapersonal (*intra* meaning "within") contributions for building marriage. Rather than asking "What's in it for me?" or focusing on what we believe our spouse is doing wrong, we can ask "What characteristics do I need to be a better spouse," "What do I need to change," or "What is my role in our disagreements?" There are numerous virtues individuals may bring to their marriage, and their pursuit is praiseworthy. In this section, however, we have chosen to highlight three virtues that each spouse either must have or must develop personally in order to strengthen their marriage: commitment, resilience, and forgiveness.

CHAPTER 2

THE POWER OF COMMITMENT

Prioritizing Our Marriage Covenant

RICHARD: *Debra and I struggled getting along during our first couple of years together. Although the content of our arguments varied, it was generally sparked by some self-righteous criticism I made of Debra. I am embarrassed to admit that and am sorry I was so hurtful, but my poor actions added to her defensiveness against it. Her energy was fueled by an underlying fear of rejection, a fear that I would possibly leave her. Such a fear was understandable, given her previous divorce as well as the fact that I had broken up with her twice before our marriage. In addition, there were times when I would leave the house after an argument. She felt very vulnerable, and this insecurity added fuel to the fire when disagreements arose.*

I was raised to minimize, if not to completely avoid, any kind of negative emotion. Being around any kind of conflict would create a lot of anxiety in me, and I am sure it played into why it took me so long to get married in the first place. When I started dating Debra, these anxious feelings grew strong when differences arose, causing me to break up with her on two occasions. But the Spirit restrained me and I returned; I knew Debra was a very special person whom I loved and cared for, so I determined to push through my anxiety and learn how to be better and work with my emotions.

Unfortunately, I didn't learn very quickly in those early years. Instead of empathizing and really listening to Debra when she had a concern or worry, I would often minimize it by dismissively giving her a quick answer to her problem. My emotional laziness, lack of warmth, and cluelessness about her processing style often led us into a cycle of distrust and anger. This didn't make me a very nice husband, and it made our marriage harder than it had to be. The arguments continued, and the intensity was high, which fueled my anxiety. These dynamics led me to want to rethink my decision about our marriage, which, of course, made Debra feel panicked and vulnerable.

As I pondered all of this, I realized that our marriage was not an all-or-nothing relationship that required me to rethink its merit after each particular argument, as I had while dating. I had made my commitment over a sacred altar in the temple of God; I knew I was committed and would not look back. But now I realized Debra needed reassurance of my commitment to the marriage. The Spirit whispered to me, "Richard, you need to tell Debra you are committed no matter what!" So that is what I did.

I don't remember the exact circumstances or place, but I sat down with Debra and said to her in the most determined and heartfelt manner, "Debra, I'm not going anywhere!" I explained that I was wholly committed to the marriage and that regardless of arguments or any other challenges in the marriage, I would be true to her and God.

This experience had a profound healing effect on our relationship. Both of us began to change. I stopped leaving the house after arguments, and, more importantly, I took on a more accepting attitude toward Debra. In the meantime, her fears started to slowly melt away. She began to trust me and trust that I wanted to be with her. As she trusted me, I felt and expressed a greater love and loyalty for her. The frequency of our arguments decreased significantly. Over the years since then, this cycle of loyalty and trust has continued to provide ever-increasing positive sentiment in our relationship; it has improved our relationship in both stability and happiness—much to our delight!

As seen here, commitment in marriage takes a tremendous amount of conscious work, sacrifice, and devotion over long periods of time. During the engagement, there is excitement over the process of creating a new life together; there is laughter, joy, and even silly giggles. Yet once the marriage ceremony and receptions are over, the spouses are left with the reality of now living the day-to-day life they have created; this is when the real work begins. We are taught in Doctrine and Covenants 90:24 that "all things shall work together for [our] good, if [we] walk uprightly and *remember the covenant wherewith [we] have covenanted one with another*" (emphasis added). As we remember our marital covenant and approach our marriages with strong levels of commitment, this scripture promises that we will be able to build strong and satisfying relationships.

In this chapter, we first examine the general concept of commitment. Second, we review some cultural difficulties regarding commitment to marriage and discuss how LDS culture and doctrine impact commitment. Then we look at how commitment increases loyalty and trust in our marriage. We also discuss how our internal commitment to our marriage needs to be shown to our spouses through our outward behaviors. Lastly, we examine the principle of commitment relative to three specific types of marriages: new marriages, chronically difficult marriages, and abusive marriages.

The Principle of Commitment

Commitment is the glue of life. It's an essential ingredient in building and holding things together. Most successful endeavors or accomplishments require high levels of commitment. It has been said about

Reflections

"I'm not going anywhere." The reassurance that whatever else happens you will both be together, married, really does make a difference. I found the same to be true in my own marriage. When I quit entertaining any thoughts of divorce, resolving problems got much easier, and feelings of discontent left. Now I'm left wondering how many people never really commit to their marriage and suffer needlessly, simply because they keep staring at an "exit door."

commitment: "Commitment is what transforms a promise into a reality. It is the words that speak boldly of your intentions and the actions that speak louder than words. It is making time when there is none; it is going through time after time after time, year after year after year. Commitment is the stuff character is made of—the power to change the face of things. It is the daily triumph of integrity over skepticism."[2] Thus, commitment to a worthy pursuit requires a deep level of energy, dedication, and patience, as well as a priority status.

It is important to keep in mind that commitment is not just about an approach to life in which we grit our teeth and hold on for dear life, hoping that if we hold on tightly enough, white-knuckling it, as is commonly said, we will prevail. Certainly, holding on and persistently working over the long term are frequently required in life, especially in marital relationships. However, if enduring becomes the end-all of our commitment, it doesn't allow space for building a positive quality of life, exercising hope, calling down the powers of heaven with faith, and finding pure joy. The type of commitment we advocate invites our Father in Heaven to join with us in partnership to accomplish worthy goals (see part 3). In so doing, we bring His power and His goodness and His abilities in to bless our marital relationships and the myriad of other worthy goals and values we seek to live. The commitment we advocate is to include God in the process and to have faith in the miracles His influence will inevitably bring. It has been said: "The moment one definitely commits oneself, then Providence moves too. All sorts of things occur to help one that would otherwise never have occurred . . . which no man could have dreamed would have come his way."[3]

Commitment and Culture

As we've illustrated in chapter 1, in the general culture of our day we have a serious "lack of commitment to commitment."[4] Instead of fixing things that are broken, as did our grandparents and their parents before them, we throw them away and buy the newest, the latest, and the greatest. And, frankly, sometimes we buy the newest, the latest, and the greatest even when the ones we have are *not* broken. Unfortunately, this has carried over into how we as a culture treat the marital relationship: marriages themselves have become "disposable."[5] Speaking of this trend, President Dieter F. Uchtdorf noted:

> In so many societies around the world, everything seems to be disposable. As soon as something starts to break down or wear out—or even when we simply grow tired of it—we throw it out and replace it with an upgrade, something newer or shinier.
>
> We do this with cell phones, clothes, cars—and, tragically, even with relationships.
>
> While there may be value in decluttering our lives of material things we no longer need, when it comes to things of eternal importance—our marriages, our families, and our values—a mindset of replacing the original in favor of the modern can bring profound remorse.[6]

Indeed, in our culture today, divorce frequently becomes the solution of choice when the costs of marriage begin to rise.

Church leaders are mindful of this trend and of the ever-present attacks that Satan places on the family in general. Elder L. Tom Perry warned: "As we know, [Satan] is attempting to erode and destroy the very foundation of our society—the family. In clever and carefully camouflaged ways, he is attacking commitment to family life throughout the world and undermining the culture and covenants of faithful Latter-day Saints."[7] As Latter-day Saints we must not allow Satan to undermine the commitment we have to gospel living and to our sacred covenants; we must be careful to not let him hijack our attitudes about marital commitment through the subtle and overt attitudes and policies of the culture at large.

So how do we as Latter-day Saints protect ourselves against accepting a casual attitude toward commitments, in general, and toward our marital covenants, in particular? One way is to look to the scriptures, particularly the Book of Mormon, in which we find several stories of commitment. The Nephite culture had a strong emphasis on covenant making, and verbal oaths were considered final vows, never to be broken. The story of Nephi and Zoram (see 1 Nephi 4:32–37) illustrates the interpersonal benefit of this type of strong adherence to our commitments. After Zoram discovered that the man he had accompanied outside the walls of the city was not his master, Laban, as he had presumed, the newly discovered Nephi made an oath promising Zoram safety and freedom if he went with them into the wilderness. "Zoram did take courage" at Nephi's oath (1 Nephi 4:35). To this Zoram responded with his own oath that he would "tarry with them from that time forth" (1 Nephi 4:35). Nephi then stated, "When Zoram had made an oath unto us, our fears did cease concerning him" (1 Nephi 4:37). To us today this level of trust in a simple verbal promise seems shocking and perhaps even foolish and naive. Indeed, our society would have strongly counseled Nephi and Zoram to get the agreement down in writing! Yet we can learn much from Nephi and Zoram about commitment and integrity. Does our spouse feel safe in the promises we have made to them? Do we say or do things that create doubt in our marital promise? Let us follow the examples of the Nephites and commit ourselves to be committed. Let us decide to focus our energy on following through wholeheartedly with covenants and obligations that we accept in our lives and in our marriages.

Commitment and LDS Doctrine

We must never forget that as Latter-day Saints, commitment to marriage must be viewed with more seriousness than it is in broader world culture. The seriousness with which we view marriage is not just about common sense but is doctrinally based. Marriage is an eternal principle, not just a contractual arrangement between two parties to be terminated at will. President Spencer W. Kimball taught: "Marriage is ordained of God. It is not merely a social custom. Without proper and successful marriage, one will never be exalted."[8] Likewise, President Russell M. Nelson explained: "Marriage between a man and a woman is fundamental to the Lord's doctrine and crucial to God's eternal plan. Marriage between a man and a woman is God's pattern for a fullness of life on earth and in heaven."[9]

The doctrines of The Church of Jesus Christ of Latter-day Saints offer us the possibility of exaltation *with* our spouse—one of the greatest promises our Savior offers to us! When the Apostle Parley P. Pratt heard of the doctrine of eternal marriage, he expressed his joy this way:

> From [Joseph Smith] . . . I learned that the wife of my bosom might be secured to me for time and all eternity; and that the refined sympathies and affections which endeared us to each other emanated from the fountain of divine eternal love. . . . I had loved before, but I knew not why. But now I loved—with a pureness—an intensity of elevated, exalted feeling, which would lift my soul from the transitory things of this groveling sphere and expand it as the ocean. . . . In short, I could now love with the spirit and with the understanding also.[10]

The blessing of eternal marriage provided by the sealing covenant is a doctrine no other church offers its patrons. Christ has bestowed keys and authority upon his latter-day prophets to bind us in loving ties for eternity. The doctrine of the sealing was set forth by our Savior, Jesus Christ, as given to the Apostle Peter (see Matthew 16:19). In this dispensation, in 1829, Peter, James, and John conferred the Melchizedek Priesthood upon Joseph Smith and Oliver Cowdery (see D&C 128:20), and the keys to exercise sealing authority were given to Joseph Smith when the prophet Elijah brought the keys of the sealing power in 1836 (see D&C 110). The Church of Jesus Christ of Latter-day Saints recognizes that its current prophet is the only person on earth with the authority to exercise all of these keys. Once we understand this doctrine, then we as members of the Church who are sealed to our spouses through sacred temple ordinances and authorized priesthood keys should be more committed to our marriages than any other couple on earth.

The sealing ordinance constitutes a sacred covenant. Elder Jeffrey R. Holland taught: "A covenant is a binding spiritual contract, a solemn promise to God our Father that we will live and act in a certain way—the way of His Son, the Lord Jesus Christ. In return, the Father, Son, and Holy Ghost promise us the full splendor of eternal life."[11] As we bind ourselves to each other and to Christ by way of covenant, abide in His way, and adopt His Christianity for our own, we are granted His power. As we yoke ourselves with the Savior, we must actively do our part to honor the marital covenant He has lovingly provided us. We do this by making a serious commitment to the covenant. This means that in times of relative tranquility, we focus on building, supporting, and loving our spouse; meeting their needs is important to us, and we strive to do so as best we can. It means that in times of trial, we buoy each other up or rely on our spouse for the support and love that we need, looking to them as a source of friendship, love, and strength when we feel depleted. It means that in times of marital difficulty or conflict, we actively work *within* the covenant of marriage for resolution rather than looking *outside* the covenant for a solution.

Commitment and Trust

Commitment to our marital covenant and to our spouse is highly correlated with trust: the more commitment, the more trust, and vice versa. There is a great sense of stability and peace—a feeling of safety—that comes when we know we can rely on our spouse. Elder Bednar described: "Feeling the security and constancy of love from a spouse . . . is a rich blessing. Such love nurtures and sustains faith in God. Such love is a source of strength and casts out fear (see 1 John 4:18). Such love is the desire of every human soul."[12] That trust promotes loyalty to the marriage and to the shared relationship.

Waite and Gallagher show how the correlation between trust and loyalty in marriage creates a kind of self-fulfilling prophecy: the more commitment, the more trust and loyalty; the more trust and loyalty, the more commitment. In other words, when spouses clearly communicate to each other that they are fully committed to honoring their marital vows, they will then invest in their marriage with greater confidence, which likewise promotes greater loyalty and trust. This cycle repeats itself again and again, elevating the marital relationship and leading to stronger bonds and capital which will protect the marriage during tests and trials.[14]

Commitment and Behavior

When we are fully committed to our marriages, our behavior will back it up. Commitment in marriage is not only about whether we are committed to *stay* married. It is also about a commitment to prioritize our spouse and our marriage—to *be* married in an active and living manner (a verb, not a status marker). Perhaps we have been married for thirty years, and we feel our marriage relationship has grown a bit cold or stale. Commitment to our marriage would mean shifting the current status quo and reinvesting our energy and time into

Reflections

When our children were little and there was a Church activity for my wife one weeknight, I told her to go and that I would babysit the kids. She rightfully reminded me that I was not the babysitter but the children's father. I have always remembered that. My wife reminded me of my very important responsibility of being not only her husband but also the father to my children. I know that often I am oblivious to the many responsibilities around the house that my wife knows need to be done, but I have learned that when I go and do something that needs to be done (or I look for things that need to be done and then do them), my wife really appreciates my efforts.

building anew our marriage relationship. Marriage clinician and researcher William J. Doherty commented: "Even if we have an unbending commitment to our mates, most of us are blind to how we lose our marriages by slow erosion if we do not keep replenishing the soil. . . . Commitment without intentionality leads to stable but stale marriages."[15]

Our level of commitment to our marriage and to our spouse is very clearly revealed in the mundane moments of our daily lives. An "accretion of mundane acts"[16] demonstrates to our spouse, our God, and others where our priorities lie.

DEBRA: *The small and simple, even mundane, acts reveal our greatest priorities when done consistently over time. Richard and I have adopted a small and simple tradition to show our marital commitment to each other: sitting next to each other in sacrament meeting. I have always remembered a particular couple from a family ward I attended in my early twenties as a single adult. This couple had a lot of children, including a new baby. Yet I noticed that this couple always sat together in sacrament meeting, the husband with his arm around his wife's shoulders. This was quite noticeable to me, as it clearly contrasted with all the other couples I observed who were sitting apart, with their children in between them. This symbol of their unity was so powerful to me that when Richard and I married we chose to implement this policy and claim the blessings of it for ourselves (when Richard's callings have allowed us to sit together as a family during the sacrament).*

Sitting together in sacrament meeting (or other meetings) when we were first married and had only two children was simple. Yet, with five children, it has been tempting to put children in between us during sacrament meeting for containment purposes. However, we hold to this ideal as a symbol of our marital commitment and look for activities to occupy the children. At times the younger children attempt to squeeze their way in between us, but we don't let them! We remind them that no one sits between Mom and Dad and invite them to sit on either side of us. Sitting together in sacrament meeting creates opportunities to connect and show tenderness even during a worship service as we hold hands, lean against each other, put our arms around each other, or even whisper an occasional comment to each other. This has been one small and simple way we have chosen to remind ourselves and each other that we place our relationship first in our priorities, second only to our relationship with God.

In a Mormon Tabernacle Choir's *Music and the Spoken Word* message, the tender story of an elderly couple illustrates a husband's commitment to his marriage and to his wife. The wife was losing her sight and could not take care of herself the way she had previously throughout their lengthy marriage. The husband took it upon himself to start painting her nails for her. Although she could not see well, he knew that if she held her hands close to her face at just the right angle, she could see her painted fingernails. "They made her smile. He liked to see her happy, so he kept painting her nails for more than five years before she passed away."[17] As we have shown, we must be conscientious about what we are supposed to be doing—building an eternal quality into our relationship. Conscientiousness is initiated by our own self-will or self-control. Researchers have defined self-control as the "capacity to override and alter one's responses, especially to behave in socially desirable ways."[18] These researchers found that relationships fared best when there was a high level of total self-control in the relationship. In other words, if both partners have higher levels of self-control, thus exerting purposeful effort to show their commitment to marriage, the marriage will do better. In their study, areas in which these couples did well

Practice

Here is a journaling exercise you can do to evaluate the values and goals you have surrounding your marriage relationship:

· Write down the type of marital relationship you want to have. Write about how you want this part of your life to look.
· Write down a description of the person you would like to be in your marriage. Try to focus on your role in that relationship. Describe how you would treat your partner if you were the ideal you in this relationship.
· Rate this value in terms of importance. Scale 1–10. 1 (not at all important), 10 (extremely important) _____.
· Now, ask yourself, "How consistent is my life currently (past week or two) in making this value a realization?" Scale 1–10. 1 (not at all consistent), 10 (completely consistent) _____.
· Subtract consistency number from importance number = _____.
· Look at this number. A high score means you have a large discrepancy between what you value as important and how you are honoring or enacting that value in your day-to-day life. A large discrepancy is not desirable. A small number indicates that you are living your life more closely or consistently with your stated values. This is ideal. How are you doing? What are the obstacles, if any? Make a plan to overcome any obstacles.[19]

included the following: relationship satisfaction, forgiveness, secure attachment, accommodation, healthy and committed styles of loving, smooth daily interactions, absence of conflict, and absence of feeling rejected.[20] Our marriage is an example of this truth. Although we are *very* different from each other and do not naturally satisfy each other in many areas, we still try! And with that trying comes happiness and contentment together.

In a devotional at Brigham Young University (BYU), Bruce Chadwick—BYU professor of sociology—shared the following personal experience, an experience that demonstrated to him that he needed to alter his behavior to show marital and family commitment. He received a painful message during a family game one Christmas Day:

> My wife and three sons independently wrote their estimation of my dominant personality trait on small pieces of paper. I was confident I would be labeled by my family as "kind," "righteous," "loving," or similar positive traits.
>
> Imagine my surprise when my wife's paper said, "Bruce is a workaholic." My three boys confirmed her diagnosis! [They] made it clear that in their eyes my career, profession, or work was the most important aspect of my life.
>
> At this point, even though it was Christmas, I protested a little.
>
> One of my sons replied, "Dad, we never went on a family vacation that did not involve your work."
>
> Again I wanted to reply: "True, but you—ungrateful son that you are—have been to Disneyland as well as to Walt Disney World, traveled to Central America, traveled Europe, visited the Holy Land, and lived two summers in a beach house on an island in the Pacific Northwest." But it was Christmas, and I did not want to be a poor sport, so I remained silent.
>
> In the days that followed I tried to justify how I lived my life to myself. But it did not do any good. No matter how I rationalized things, my dear family felt that my career was more important to me than they were. This is not and was not true. But the fact remained that that was the impression I had given by my actions. Since that time I have tried to make my priorities more visible. I occasionally say to Carolyn on Friday morning, "I will be done teaching at noon. Would you like to go to the temple this afternoon? Or go ride around the Alpine Loop, see a movie, or visit the gardens at

Thanksgiving Point?" Or, if I am really feeling expansive, "Would you like to go shopping?"

I hope during the past 15 years that somehow I have altered the perceptions of my family. They are most important to me.[21]

DEBRA: *In one couple therapy session, my client revealed that she had humbly examined her own contributions to the difficulties in the relationship with her husband and asked herself in prayer what sacrifice she needed to make for her marriage. She got the answer and exercised the courage to implement it. The change meant a lot to her husband, as it was an issue for which he had expressed concern repeatedly over time, yet her inattention led him to feel like she was disregarding his feelings. Now, by altering her behavior, she had created positive sentiment between them and contributed to the healing of some of their marital pain.*

As seen by these examples, it takes self-control to alter our responses and do things purposefully to enhance our marital commitment. A common phrase we like to use is that we have to do our marriage *on purpose*. As we actively and intentionally do this, our marriage will be blessed.

Two very important principles, patience and selflessness, if learned and applied, can be particularly useful as we consider how our behavior toward our spouse demonstrates our commitment to them.

Patience

President Dieter F. Uchtdorf defined patience: "Patience is not passive resignation, nor is it failing to act because of our fears. Patience means active waiting and enduring. It means staying with something and doing all that we can—working, hoping, and exercising faith; bearing hardship with fortitude, even when the desires of our hearts are delayed. Patience is not simply enduring; it is enduring well!"[22]

In the Book of Mormon, Ammon, Aaron, Omner, and Himni served missions among the Lamanites. It was long and difficult work in which they "suffered every privation" (Alma

26:28) and "suffered all manner of afflictions" (Alma 26:30), yet when they were discouraged and "about to turn back" (Alma 26:27), the Lord told them to be patient in their afflictions and He would bless them with success. He did bless them, and they were extremely successful.

Patience is vital in marriage. How patient are you with your spouse? If they make mistakes or have certain quirks, are you willing to show your commitment by loving them anyway, without anger or resentment?

RICHARD: *Debra is a really good driver. But she has an Achilles heel: backing out of a carport or garage. I smile every time I think about it (while she cringes), but during the course of our marriage to date, she has broken off five driver's side mirrors. Yes, five! For some reason, as she backs up, she miscalculates how close the car is to the left side of the wall of the garage door and the mirror gets ripped right off of its mount. The fourth time this happened, to my horror, I was actually there watching. I could see it unfolding right before my eyes, and I was trying to get her attention by yelling at her to stop, but to no avail. The mirror was now dangling off the side of the car! My first reaction was extreme frustration. But then when I saw her get out of the car in complete tears, exasperated at herself for having done it again, I realized that she was more frustrated with herself than I was. I knew, instead of anger and judgment from me, she needed consolation and love. And I needed patience. We had a few minutes of hugs, tears, some excuses about the kids in the back seat noisily distracting her, and a bit of laughter as I chided her. I then reminded her that, like the previous times, I could order a new replacement mirror online and have it fixed shortly. Problem solved! She has demonstrated her commitment to me as she has been patient with me for such things as slurping my cold cereal, burning the chicken wings while barbecuing, or repurchasing tools that I already own because I couldn't find them in my messy garage, so the least I could do was patiently love her myself.*

President Uchtdorf taught that since the Lord is patient with us, we should be patient with ourselves and others. He indicated that we also make mistakes, and just as we want others to be understanding of us, we should be patient with them.[23] This is a developmental process, and most often changes occur in a subtle

Reflections

I am very time oriented, and punctuality is of the utmost importance to me. I am extremely efficient with my time and can accomplish a lot in a short amount of time because I am organized and always in a hurry. My husband is my polar opposite. He doesn't feel the need to rush like I do. He is very detail oriented, and when he does something, he does it very well but takes much longer to do it than I deem necessary. He is much more patient, and being late isn't a big deal to him. This single thing has been a tremendous strain on our marriage. I see him as lacking, whereas he sees me as impatient and high strung. Since I am extreme in one direction, and he is extreme in the other direction, this issue is a major battle for us. I am always upset that he shows up late or can't do something faster, and he feels attacked (and rightly so). For a long time I was so focused on what I thought he was doing wrong and on how clearly I was right that I was bitter and angry, even though he is a truly remarkable person with countless amazing qualities. I could see only what I thought he lacked. A quote from Henry B. Eyring has helped me: "Pray for the love which allows you to see the good in your companion. Pray for the love that makes weaknesses and mistakes seem small. Pray for the love to make your companion's joy your own. Pray for the love to want to lessen the load and soften the sorrows of your companion."[24] This quote has been life altering for me.

manner over lengthy periods of time. Thus, we will have to be patient as we work to develop patience.

Selflessness

Closely connected to impatience is selfishness. If we are struggling with patience, it generally indicates that we are focused on ourselves, on what we want or need, and on how a particular situation is failing to satisfy that self-focus. Selfishness causes us to lose perspective relative to our standing with our fellow men and makes us believe that our own personal fulfillment and happiness is of preeminent priority. President Gordon B. Hinckley taught that selfishness is the root of many of the problems seen in families today and that it is "the antithesis of love."[25] When it comes to marriage, President Spencer W. Kimball said:

> The marriage that is based upon selfishness is almost certain to fail. . . . But the one who marries to give happiness as well as receive it, to give service as well as to receive it, and who looks

after the interests of the two and then the family as it comes will have a good chance that the marriage will be a happy one.[26]

More recently, in his address to the Vatican Summit on Marriage, Henry B. Eyring indicated:

> You have seen enough unhappiness in marriages and families to ask why some marriages produce happiness while others create unhappiness. Many factors make a difference, but one stands out to me.
>
> Where there is selfishness, natural differences of men and women often divide. Where there is unselfishness, differences become complementary and provide opportunities to help and build each other. Spouses and family members can lift each other and ascend together if they care more about the interests of the other than their own interests . . . [and] replace their natural self-interest with deep and lasting feelings of charity and benevolence. With that change, and only then, will people be able to make the hourly unselfish sacrifices necessary for a happy marriage and family life—and to do it with a smile.[27]

So if we are to show our commitment to our spouse, we need to develop a selfless attitude toward life, especially when it comes to marriage.

Commitment in Specific Types of Marriages

We have been talking about principles of commitment that are important for every type of marriage, such as prioritizing the marriage ahead of other aspects of life, including self, children, or work demands. However, we would like now to look at three special types of marriages that require additional consideration when it comes to commitment: new marriages, chronically difficult marriages, and abusive marriages.

New Marriages

The concept of commitment in marriage takes on acute importance in the newlywed phase. You will find research and stories relative to newlyweds throughout this book, yet here we focus on one important piece of counsel relative to commitment: keep the long-term perspective.

When the honeymoon is over and reality sets in, our beloved spouse's faults can suddenly become glaring. In these times, it may become very easy to begin rethinking the whole concept of commitment. We understand how painful some of those early interactions can be; it is a refining process as we learn to adjust to each other and adjust to being married. Hang on. The course of your eternal marriage cannot be fully determined in only the first few months. President Spencer W. Kimball spoke about this adjustment period:

> Two people coming from different backgrounds learn soon after the ceremony is performed that stark reality must be faced. There is no longer a life of fantasy or of make-believe; we must come out of the clouds and put our feet firmly on the earth. Responsibility must be assumed and new duties must be accepted. Some personal freedoms must be relinquished, and many adjustments, unselfish adjustments, must be made. One comes to realize very soon after marriage that the spouse has weaknesses not previously revealed or discovered. The virtues which were constantly magnified during courtship now grow relatively smaller, and the weaknesses which seemed so small and insignificant during courtship now grow to sizable proportions. The hour has come for understanding hearts, for self-appraisal, and for good common sense, reasoning, and planning.[29]

Reflections

My husband and I have been married barely five months. Marriage has been an endless amount of changes, adjustments, and learning phases. Marriage is amazingly hard, but it's also the best thing ever! There's been so many nights where I just cry and my husband just holds me. I like to escape my stresses and problems by running away, and the biggest adjustment for me has been that I can't do that and be married. I can't run away from hard things anymore; this is for eternity. It's been difficult to always be vulnerable and let my husband in on my feelings that I try so hard to bury. I didn't quite understand how hard it would be. I need both my Heavenly Father and my husband to get through my feelings of wanting to run away during fights, of feeling unworthy as a wife or that I'm not good enough when I just see all of my shortcomings. I have to remember that no one is perfect and all I can do is wake up each morning and try my best for that day. I wouldn't change any of these experiences for the world. It's just that it is new, different, and scary—and that's okay!

The hour *has* come. Particularly as newlyweds it is important, when conflict arises, to give your spouse the benefit of the doubt, have an accepting attitude, and keep a long-term perspective. Each of us has to learn how to be married, and this is a developmental process that takes time—it can't be pressured, rushed, or forced. A significant aspect of learning how to be married is learning how to accept another person not only for the things we love about them, but also for the ways in which they are different from us. President Gordon B. Hinckley, quoting from Unitarian minister Jenkin Lloyd Jones, acknowledged this reality when he said, "Most successful marriages require a high degree of mutual toleration."[30] As you work in this manner, you will find your levels of commitment to your new marriage increase as peace comes more consistently into the relationship and bonds of love and affection grow.

Reflecting on their marriage, Sister Marjorie Hinckley, wife of President Gordon B. Hinckley, related:

> I was just sure the first ten years would be bliss. But during our first year together I discovered . . . there were a lot of adjustments. Of course, they weren't the kind of thing you ran home to mother about. But I cried into my pillow now and again. The problems were almost always related

to learning to live on someone else's schedule and to do things someone else's way. We loved each other, there was no doubt about that. But we also had to get used to each other. I think every couple has to get used to each other.[31]

Sister Hinckley illustrates for us here that many of the challenges in marriage as newlyweds are issues of minor adjustment and can be resolved within some weeks or months. At the time, these adjustment issues can be acutely painful, but if you remain committed to work the marriage process according to the principles of Christianity, in time many of these difficulties will be resolved. Elder David B. Haight, at the age of ninety-four, had this to say about his own marriage process:

> When Ruby and I knelt at the Salt Lake Temple at the altar on September the fourth, 1930, holding hands and looking at one another, little did we ever realize what would lie ahead for us. . . .
>
> Now, after we have been married 70 years, I can say to all of you that it gets better, that it gets better year after year, with the preciousness and the tenderness and the realization of some of the eternal blessings that lie ahead for us.[32]

More recently, President Boyd K. Packer echoed this sentiment: "And if you suppose that the full-blown rapture

Reflections

I have been married for almost eleven months. In that time, we have had two deaths, three moves, three different cars, and four different jobs—not to mention that we both had been home from our missions for only about six months when we got married. Marriage sometimes is awful, but there are times when it is the most rewarding thing. From my limited experience, starting a marriage is like starting a very heavy and intense workout program after never working out. Disagreements in marriage are like running laps. Just like you feel sore after a hard run, with that stiffness and achiness carrying on to the next time you try running, in marriage the pain, frustration, and anger carry on to the next disagreements or differences of opinion. So the first bit of marriage is painful and hard, and you want to quit because there are differences that you think you will never overcome. But just like our muscles get stronger as we continue to work out, I have faith we will get stronger in our marriage.

of young romantic love is the sum total of the possibilities which spring from the fountains of life, you have not yet lived to see the devotion and the comfort of longtime married love. Married couples are tried by temptation, misunderstandings, financial problems, family crises, and illness, and all the while love grows stronger. Mature love has a bliss not even imagined by newlyweds."[33]

Chronically Difficult Marriages

We feel a great duty within the pages of this book to speak to the yearning and desperate hearts of those in chronically difficult marital relationships. Here we offer a brief discussion and suggest that more is to be found throughout additional chapters (we would particularly refer you to the latter half of chapter 3 and also chapter 7).

Sometimes marriage is a continual struggle as spouses seek to become unified. In these circumstances, it is frequently the case that the concept of commitment is reevaluated, as one is provoked repeatedly to ponder how much pain one must endure for the sake of their sealing covenants. Elder Timothy Dyches reminds us about the role of opposition in our lives: "As we draw near to Him, we realize that mortality is meant to be difficult and that 'opposition in all things' (2 Nephi 2:11) is not a flaw in the plan of salvation. Opposition, rather, is the indispensable element of mortality and strengthens our will and refines our choices. The vicissitudes of life help us fashion an eternal relationship with God—and engrave His image upon our countenance as we yield our hearts to Him (see Alma 5:19)."[34]

Commitment in difficult marital relationships may be more difficult to procure, but when we partner with our Savior He will show us how we can honor our marital covenants and remain committed to our spouse. Such is found in a story by Elder Spencer Condie:

A few years ago my wife, Dorothea, and I were walking across the grounds of a temple in a foreign land when we met a very radiant, cheerful, silver-haired sister. Her cheerful, Christlike countenance seemed to set her apart from those around her, and I felt inclined to ask her to explain why she looked so happy and content with life.

"Well," she said with a smile, "several years ago I was in a hurry to get married, and quite frankly, after a few months I realized I had married the wrong man." She continued, "He had no interest in the Church as he had initially led me to believe, and he began to treat me very unkindly for several years. One day I reached the point where I felt I could go on no longer in this situation, and so in desperation I knelt down to pray, to ask Heavenly Father if He would approve of my divorcing my husband.

"I had a very remarkable experience," she said. "After I prayed fervently, the Spirit revealed a number of insights to me of which I had been previously unaware. For the first time in my life, I realized that, just like my husband, I am not perfect either. I began to work on my intolerance and my impatience with his lack of spirituality.

"I began to strive to become more compassionate and loving and understanding. And do you know what happened? As I started to change, my husband started to change. Instead of my nagging him about going to church, he gradually decided to come with me on his own initiative.

"Recently we were sealed in the temple, and now we spend one day each week in the temple together. Oh, he's still not perfect, but I am so happy that the Lord loves us enough to help us resolve our problems."[35]

Reflections

My husband and I have been married over twenty years. Being married has been the hardest thing I have ever done in my life. Staying in this relationship continues to be a daily struggle. Each day I try again. There are positives and negatives. I try to be committed to my children and the family we are raising. [She began to cry.] I don't want to be a single parent, and I don't want to be divorced. I don't want to desert my husband, and I don't want to give up.

As Elder Condie illustrates, the Lord can provide us with the personal revelation we need relative to our difficult marital relationships. There is great power in seeking the whisperings of the Spirit through prayer and pondering. We discuss principles of personal revelation relative to our marriages in chapter 9. We also discuss the importance of humility and the willingness to look at our own contributions to our marital difficulties in chapter 7.

Some spouses in chronically difficult marriages are unified in their desire to improve the quality of the relationship and will work together to try to do so but simply continue to struggle in the practical application. These couples will find that the ideas throughout this book speak to them and encourage them in their journey. However, in some marriages spouses are not unified in this desire. It is not uncommon to have one spouse that is willing to work to improve the relationship while the other spouse seems to have "checked out." If this is the painful situation in which you find yourself, please know that a great deal of what we address in this book to improve the quality of marriage can be done *without* your spouse's participation. We can practice or implement of our own accord various strategies to improve the relationship with our spouse, exercising our agency to do good things and behave well in our marital relationship, regardless of whether our spouse is on board. For example, we can choose to increase the positivity-to-negativity ratio in our relationship (see chapter 5) by saying a kind word, leaving a supportive note, or doing an act of service in spite of how they treat us or their overall attitude toward our marriage or the gospel.

Furthermore, if you find yourself in this most painful circumstance, be assured that this difficult marriage can be the very thing to exalt you—through humbly receiving schooling from the Spirit. Regardless of whether your spouse ever makes any efforts to better their relationship with you, the process of showing love, patience, tolerance, or any other Christlike virtue on your part will change you. You will learn more about the Savior in the process of emulating Him; He knows the pain of rejection, and He is "acquainted with grief" (Mosiah 14:3). Ultimately, the marital relationship, although not as you may expect, will have served you well relative to your efforts to seek Christ and to take His "image in your countenance" (Alma 5:14).

Chronically difficult marriage produces a refiner's fire that is white hot. There are tremendous sacrifices and pain required in these circumstances. There is disappointment of not having all we had hoped for interpersonally, spiritually, or even romantically. If you are in this type of marriage, we are sensitive to your plight and plead for your welfare. Yet we have a tenacious testimony of the promise that Christ will compensate us for every loss, as taught by Elder Joseph B. Wirthlin of the Quorum of the Twelve Apostles: "The Lord compensates the faithful for every loss. That which is taken away from those who love the Lord will be added unto them in His own way. While it may not come at the time we desire, the faithful will know that every tear today will eventually be returned a hundredfold with tears of rejoicing and gratitude."[36]

Reflections

Prior to our marriage, I was unaware that my wife had been abused as a child. However, shortly into the relationship the consequences of that abuse became evident. Like many abuse victims, my wife lives in a mode of self-preservation. Because her abuser often controlled her, as an adult she understandably feels the need to control everything and everyone. That control manifests itself in many ways, including an insistence on a life of celibacy. Many of my wife's struggles are of such a nature that were I not a Latter-day Saint and a believer in eternal families, I would have left many years ago. However, the gospel and my temple covenants have given me perspective on relationships, mental health, and human frailties. They have given me the strength to endure a very painful and unfulfilling relationship—and even the motivation to nurture and love her in spite of her inability to emotionally and physically love me. Some will feel my choice to stay, love, and nurture in spite of this is the wrong choice. However, the gospel convinces me that she needs my love and that the selfless taking up of this cross is what Christ would have me do.

Reflections

Before marriage I saw in my husband-to-be all the traits of a fine, upstanding man. Shortly after our marriage he broke temple covenants but remained active in the Church. He personified the wonderful, friendly, loving, helpful man in public, but in the privacy of our home he was difficult and unpredictable. I never gave up on him. I forgave. I tolerated. I counseled with him. I prayed for him and for me. He never overcame his weaknesses— they only got worse. There came a time I contemplated leaving him. As I prayed about it, the answer was that I didn't have a celestial marriage and I could leave, but if I wanted to learn more about the Savior, I could stay. I chose the latter. We have now been married more than fifty years. The Savior has been my partner through these difficult years. Every day is a challenge, and every day I turn to the Lord for help and strength. I try to follow Him. I strive to be the best I can be. I am committed to my temple covenants. My commitment to my temple covenants has brought great peace and joy to me, as well as a more intimate relationship with the Savior.

As our Father in Heaven accomplishes His work in us, we will not only be compensated for our losses, we will be transformed because of them. We firmly believe that the refiner's fire will ultimately be the very thing that helps us to become Christlike and lift us up eternally. Christian author C. S. Lewis wrote about God's ability to make us new creatures, to transform the wretched. We assert God's plan to do this for difficult marriages as well. He implores us:

> Do not despair. He knows all about it. You are one of the poor whom He blessed. He knows what a wretched machine you are trying to drive. Keep on. Do what you can. One day (perhaps in another world, but perhaps far sooner than that) He will fling it on the scrap-heap and give you a new one. And then you may astonish us all—not least yourself: for you have learned you're driving in a hard school. (Some of the last will be first and some of the first will be last).[37]

Abusive Marriages

As we speak with conviction about being committed in marriage, even throughout difficult or chronically painful relationships, let us not be misunderstood. We are not in any way advocating subjecting oneself to abuse. Abuse is not acceptable. Those who abuse others will be held accountable to God and to the Church. President Gordon B. Hinckley said: "No man who abuses his wife or children is worthy to hold the priesthood of God. No man who abuses his wife or children is worthy to be a member in good standing in this Church. The abuse of one's spouse and children is a most serious offense before God, and any who indulge in it may expect to be disciplined by the Church."[38]

Abuse may come in a variety of forms, such as physical abuse, sexual abuse, verbal abuse, emotional abuse, or even financial abuse. We also recognize that abuse can be perpetrated by either spouse, that women can also take on the role of abuser in some marriages.

It is difficult for those in abusive relationships to know the best way to confront and handle the abuse. Particularly, those who are conscientious of their Christianity may struggle as they weigh their efforts to apply various gospel principles, such as commitment, charity, or patience to their circumstances. As second counselor in the Relief Society General Presidency, Sister Aileen H. Clyde declared the following in general conference:

> If charity is not always quick to our understanding, it may occasionally be quick to our misunderstanding. It is not charity or kindness to endure any type of abuse or unrighteousness that may be inflicted on us by others. God's commandment that as we love him we must respect ourselves suggests we must not accept disrespect from others. It is not charity to let another repeatedly deny our divine nature and agency. It is not charity to bow down in despair and helplessness. That kind of suffering should be ended, and that is very difficult to do alone. There are priesthood leaders and other loving servants who will give aid and strength when they know of the need. We must be willing to let others help us.[39]

Sister Clyde clearly teaches us that we are not to tolerate abuse. How might one alter abusive circumstances in their marriage? In the current culture of our day, as divorce is quickly recommended for many minor issues, it is also readily recommended for more severe, abusive circumstances. Although divorce is strongly discouraged within the Church generally, Church leaders have acknowledged that sometimes divorce is appropriate. Elder James E. Faust expressed: "'Just cause' [for divorce] should be nothing less serious than a prolonged and apparently irredeemable relationship which is destructive of a person's dignity as a human being. At the same time, I have strong feelings about what is not provocation for breaking the sacred covenants of marriage. Surely it is not simply 'mental distress,' nor 'personality differences,' nor having 'grown apart,' nor having 'fallen out of love.' This is especially so where there are children."[40]

If the presence of abuse suggests "just cause" for divorce, divorce need not *necessarily* be the choice when abuse becomes a player in marital discord. We will now discuss several short-term/ crisis interventions or longer-term options that we feel seek to honor commitment to the marital covenant and may be helpful while also proving useful in healing and reclaiming health from an abusive relationship.

First and foremost, if your life is in danger, do not hesitate to call 911. When other intense circumstances develop in your relationship, safety planning can be crucial to your welfare in the event of a dangerous exchange. This type of plan may include calling a domestic-abuse hotline or accessing its information online. For example, the National Domestic Violence Hotline[41] is available 24/7 and offers information regarding the following: types of safety planning (including safety planning when pregnant, safety planning with children, or emotional safety planning), advice on how to leave a relationship, and legal procedures (such as restraining and protective orders). It also provides broader information on how to define abuse and how to enact elements of healthy relationships and healthy conflict resolution. Another option for crisis intervention may be going to a shelter or another safe location.

Longer-term options to address abuse may include counseling with priesthood leaders or your Relief Society president. Although most local Church leaders are not trained, licensed mental health professionals, because they have stewardship over you, the Lord will bless them with spiritual insights and counsel that can soften hearts and assist you in navigating this delicate circumstance. A priesthood leader, as a judge in Israel, can also provide Church discipline when necessary and be a valuable sounding board if divorce becomes a serious consideration. If the nature of your abusive circumstance renders working with priesthood leaders unreasonable or additionally threatening for you, counseling with your Relief Society president may be an option that could provide similar supports.

In addition, another longer-term option to address abusive dynamics in a marital relationship may be to attend therapy. Ideally, attending

Reflections

Abuse in my relationship began with the control of sex. As we got further into life, the verbal abuse became terrible. There was also some physical abuse. If I didn't work, I was trash. If I didn't have sex with him, I then wasn't good enough to sleep in the same bed. I realized that this was becoming a normal routine for us, and I could not leave or walk away—I was always too afraid to be alone. I coped by eating and drinking soda. Everything I felt was put into food. I also worked more hours at my job than needed so I didn't have to go home. So many times there were threats of separation or divorce, and I would encourage him to stay, which I thought was better than being alone with four small children. He paid me money to keep me quiet. Eight months ago, after a long eighteen years, we separated. I felt strong and weak at the same time. My teenagers and I quit fighting. I am overcoming my eating disorder. My kids are in counseling at school. They sleep with me for security and rely heavily on the arm of God. I am now teaching them to never give up and that they can do hard things. Moving on from abuse is so difficult. You feel alone and that you would like to give up, but then the next day dawns and the sun shines and your children look to you for all—and you get up and do it. I'm not sure if my husband and I will survive this separation. I love him and pray daily he and I could get counseling and make this marriage eternal, but he has not yet been willing. But I love myself more every day and my children more every second, like a new birth for each of us.

Reflections

My husband and I met and fell in love pretty quickly and married in an LDS temple. Early on, it was clear to me that my husband's expectation of a marriage was far different than mine. When he came under stress, he directed that towards me. The verbal abuse was just getting worse, including an altercation where I feared for my life and called 911 for help. After four years of a rocky marriage, I took our two sons and left. It was extremely liberating to finally be free from his abuse. For six months, I lived as a single mom working two jobs while he was across the country. I wanted things to work out; I wanted him to wake up! But even over the phone, knowing he could lose me forever, his cruel words cut deep. I filled out the divorce papers. The kids and I visited him for Christmas, and we saw a therapist a couple times. At the end of our visit, my husband mentioned moving back from New York to Utah—I was shocked he was willing to do so. I will never forget the day he came home. He was a changed man. He washed dishes, played with the kids, helped cook dinner, and expressed appreciation for me. I completely forgave him based on my faith in our Savior's Atonement healing our wounds. It was as close to a fairytale as you can get! It has been seven years since then. We now have six children and a love that I never knew existed. Change and forgiveness are possible!

counseling as a couple would prove the most beneficial to begin the long process of restructuring the marital and interpersonal relationship dynamics and reducing abusive behaviors. However, one spouse can still make great strides attending therapy alone. A therapist can assist in setting appropriate boundaries, improving communication skills, promoting self-confidence, changing dysfunctional attitudes and behaviors, and working toward forgiveness. Therapy is a process (see the appendix to this book for a more thorough discussion on the therapy process), and it will take time to see the fruits of the process bear out, but it can be life changing for both partners as the marriage moves toward a healthier state. Yet for more severe cases of abuse, "counseling for both spouses may not be effective and may even increase the risk of further abuse. In such cases the most effective treatment may be court-ordered domestic violence counseling for the perpetrator."[42]

Lastly, if abusive patterns continue, temporary separation may be an option that could promote healing. Separation could include financial separation in cases of financial abuse, or a physical separation in the case of physical, sexual, verbal, or emotional abuse. Sometimes a separation encourages healing as the pattern of abuse is interrupted, and spouses are given the space and time to reflect and decide what they really want out of the marital relationship. Seeking counseling during the separation can be very helpful in order to learn how to more effectively interact with each other in a healthy manner.

In some marriages, the circumstances will not improve, and divorce may be entirely appropriate and necessary. How does one know when that time has come? This can be known only to each person individually through the gentle whisperings of the Holy Spirit. In order to be worthy to discern the Spirit's promptings, you will want to rid yourself of anger, malice, resentment, or a desire to retaliate toward the abuser (see chapter 4 on forgiveness). Mighty prayer and reliance on the grace of our loving Savior will help you know the right choices for you in your particular circumstance and to help you know of God's great love for you as His child. In these very stressful yet critical times, we advocate attending therapy as well as visiting with Church leaders to receive the support, comfort, skills, and assistance to guide you through the difficult process of divorce and the critical post-divorce healing process.

Conclusion

We can create a stable and happy marriage by fully committing with our hearts, words, and behaviors to our relationship with our spouse. We must maintain tenacious commitment, even when times get difficult. We must check ourselves relative to how the current culture of our day may be negatively influencing our view of marriage and our willingness to do the work required to build and grow together over time. When we are committed, our spouse knows it, and the trust and security they feel will help us to feel more loyal to them. This will bring the blessings we desire to fruition, one day at a time, with continued and hopeful commitment to our marriage and God's process for the exaltation of His children. We can secure and maintain joy and happiness of an eternal quality, finding fulfillment as we "strive together toward perfection."[43]

Notes

1. Jim Rohn, *The Seasons of Life* (Grapevine, TX: Jim Rohn International, 2011).

2. Commonly attributed to Abraham Lincoln or Shearson Lehman Brothers. See, for example, Teresia LaRocque, "Commitment Transforms a Promise into Reality!," March 7, 2012, http://erickson.edu/blog/commitment-transforms-a-promise-into-reality/.

3. William H. Murray, *The Scottish Himalayan Expedition* (London: J.M. Dent and Co., 1951).

4. Ed Wheat and Gaye Wheat, *Intended for Pleasure: Sex Technique and Sexual Fulfillment in Christian Marriage*, 3rd ed. (Grand Rapids, MI: Revell, 1977), 31.

5. Wheat and Wheat, *Intended for Pleasure*, 32.

6. Dieter F. Uchtdorf, "In Praise of Those Who Save," *Ensign*, May 2016, 77.

7. L. Tom Perry, "Becoming Goodly Parents," *Ensign*, November 2012, 27.

8. Spencer W. Kimball, "Oneness in Marriage," *Ensign*, March 1977, 5.

9. Russell M. Nelson, "Decisions for Eternity," *Ensign*, November 2013, 108.

10. Parley P. Pratt, *Autobiography of Parley P. Pratt*, ed. Parley P. Pratt Jr. (Salt Lake City: Deseret Book, 1938), 297–98.

11. Jeffrey R. Holland, "Keeping Covenants: A Message for Those Who Will Serve a Mission," *New Era*, January 2012, 3.

12. David A. Bednar, "More Diligent and Concerned at Home," *Ensign*, November 2009, 17–18.

13. John Bytheway, *When Times Are Tough* (Salt Lake City: Deseret Book, 2004), 38.

14. Linda Waite and Maggie Gallagher, *The Case for Marriage* (New York: Doubleday, 2000), 180.

15. William J. Doherty, *Take Back Your Marriage: Sticking Together in a World that Pulls Apart*, 2nd ed. (New York: Guilford Press, 2013), 8–9.

16. Angela Duckworth, *Grit: The Power of Passion and Perseverance* (New York: Scribner, 2016), 38.

17. Joseph B. Wirthlin, "The Great Commandment," *Ensign*, November 2007, 28–29.

18. Kathleen Vohs, Catrin Finkenauer, and Roy F. Baumeister, "The Sum of Friends' and Lovers' Self-Control Scores Predicts Relationship Quality," *Social Psychological and Personal Science*, 2, no. 2 (2010): 138.

19. Adapted from Kelly G. Wilson, Emily K. Sandoz, Jennifer Kitchens, and Miguel Roberts, "The Valued Living Questionnaire: Defining and Measuring Valued Action within a Behavioral Framework," *Psychological Record* 60 (2010): 249–72.

20. Vohs, Finkenauer, and Baumeister, "Sum of Self-Control Scores," 138–45.

21. Bruce A. Chadwick, "Hanging Out, Hooking Up, and Celestial Marriage" (devotional address, Brigham Young University, Provo, UT, May 7, 2002), https://speeches.byu.edu/talks/bruce-a-chadwick_hanging-hooking-celestial-marriage/.

22. Dieter F. Uchtdorf, "Continue in Patience," *Ensign*, May 2010, 57.

23. Uchtdorf, "Continue in Patience," 58.

24. Henry B. Eyring, "Our Perfect Example," *Ensign*, November 2009, 70.

25. Gordon B. Hinckley, "What God Hath Joined Together," *Ensign*, May 1991, 73.

26. Spencer W. Kimball, "Marriage and Divorce" (devotional address, Brigham Young University, Provo, UT, September 1976), https://speeches.byu.edu/talks/spencer-w-kimball_marriage-divorce/.

27. Henry B. Eyring, "Transcript: President Eyring Addresses the Vatican Summit on Marriage," November 18, 2014, http://www.mormonnewsroom.org/article/transcript-president-eyring-addresses-vatican-summit-marriage.

28. Jack Kornfield, *The Wise Heart: A Guide to the Universal Teachings of Buddhist Psychology* (New York: Bantam Books, 2008), 76–77.

29. Kimball, "Oneness in Marriage," 3.

30. Gordon B. Hinckley, "A Conversation with Single Adults," *Ensign*, March 1997, 60.

31. Sheri L. Dew, *Go Forward with Faith: The Biography of Gordon B. Hinckley* (Salt Lake City: Deseret Book, 1996), 118.

32. David B. Haight, "Be a Strong Link," *Ensign*, November 2000, 19.

33. Boyd K. Packer, "The Plan of Happiness," *Ensign*, May 2015, 26.

34. Timothy J. Dyches, "Wilt Thou Be Made Whole," *Ensign*, November 2013, 38.

35. Spencer J. Condie, "A Mighty Change of Heart," *Ensign*, November 1993, 15.

36. Joseph B. Wirthlin, "Come What May and Love It," *Ensign*, November 2008, 28.

37. C. S. Lewis, *Mere Christianity* (New York: HarperCollins, 1952), 169.

38. Gordon B. Hinckley, "What Are People Asking about Us?," *Ensign*, November 1998, 72.

39. Aileen H. Clyde, "Charity Suffereth Long," *Ensign*, November 1991, 77.

40. James E. Faust, "Father, Come Home," *Ensign*, May 1993, 35.

41. http://www.thehotline.org/ or call 1-800-799-SAFE (7233) | 1-800-787-3224 (TTY).

42. Anne Horton, John Nelson, and Brent H. Bartholomew, "A Conversation on Spouse Abuse," *Ensign*, October 1999, 26.

43. Dallin H. Oaks, "Divorce," *Ensign*, May 2007, 73.

CHAPTER 3

BOUNCE BACK AND MOVE FORWARD

Resilience and Posttraumatic Growth

DEBRA: *Due to extenuating circumstances, we were compelled to have our last three children very close together in age, with only a year between each of them. As we anticipated the realities of this situation, we knew that we were in for some very intense, stressful baby and toddler years. While caring for two baby boys and pregnant with a third baby, people would praise me for my bravery. I would reply that I was more likely stupid than brave. I would then generally comment that I wasn't too worried about when the baby was young and immobile, but I was apprehensive about the baby beginning to walk—when I would have three kids ages three, two, and one, all of them walking and none of them reliable. I knew that was going to be when the trial amped up its energy something fierce.*

As expected, things were difficult once our baby girl was born. As Richard went to work each day, I was left with three very young children, each of them in different developmental stages yet all of them screaming at the same time for different reasons. As the littlest one grew and began to crawl and get into things, the stress indeed increased monumentally. Then it happened, the very week the baby began to walk—the very time for which I had been the most afraid—Richard was called to be the bishop of our ward. The blow was immense. I felt my husband

had been stolen from me at the time I needed him most, and, in light of the specific
timing, I knew that God had done it to me on purpose. Thus began a very difficult
physical and spiritual journey for me. I will share more about this trial throughout
this chapter to illustrate various principles of resilience.

We all seem to have trials in which we feel our world has been turned upside down; we experience the difficulties of the flesh, the imperfections of the mortal condition, and the struggle of human frailties. What happens when our spouse is diagnosed with cancer, multiple sclerosis, panic attacks, debilitating depression, or dementia? What happens when jobs, investments, or homes are lost? What happens if we can't have our own biological children, our children have special needs, or we lose one of our children to death? What happens if our spouse leaves the Church? Lehi declared, "But behold, all things have been done in the wisdom of him who knoweth all things" (2 Nephi 2:24). We seek to trust in the wisdom of our Father in Heaven; we seek to remind ourselves that all these things are for our eternal benefit. Something that feels devastating to us can be ultimately part of our Father in Heaven's plan for our growth, happiness, and eternal salvation. Elder Quentin L. Cook of the Quorum of the Twelve Apostles encouraged, "Adversity should not be viewed as either disfavor from the Lord or a withdrawal of His blessings. Opposition in all things is part of the refiner's fire to prepare us for an eternal celestial destiny."[1]

Yet, even with our best intentions and efforts to keep this eternal perspective in the forefront of our minds and to remain faithful and fearless, sometimes the burdens of life become overwhelming. Do we bounce back after a brief period? Do we find ourselves some months down the road feeling like ourselves again? Might we even find ourselves feeling stronger for having had the experience? Or do we collapse into depression, despair, and dysfunction?

In the trials that come to us in marriage, ideally we seek a partnered effort to support and strengthen each other. Yet, regardless of what the *We* does or does not do, the *Me* is critical, and as individuals we retain ultimate power regarding our own attitudes and behaviors. How we choose to handle our stresses and trials or to interact with our spouse during difficult moments—even when those moments stretch into years and sometimes decades—is entirely up to us individually. To maximize our own personal power to influence the relationship, we must foster and build resilience within ourselves. With each new day, we must do what we can to help ourselves and help our marriage. Research has found that how one perceives their relationship stress is related with their own external stress—that one's own stresses or trials spill over into the intimate relationship and exacerbates one's own relationship stress.[2] This means that how we personally handle our trials and stresses directly impacts the quality of our marital relationship.

In this chapter we address two major areas: resilience and post-traumatic growth. We discuss how

Reflections

Life hit us with an unexpected challenge the day our son was born. His umbilical cord was wrapped around his neck twice, so labor contractions deprived his brain of oxygen. As he developed, he was diagnosed variously as having ADHD, bipolar disorder, and Asperger's syndrome. In adolescence, our relationship deteriorated as he struggled and acted out in increasingly defiant and disturbed ways. We came to know the adolescent therapeutic community and the juvenile justice system well. Through all of this we struggled to understand and to cope. This had dramatic effects on our marriage. Stress over our son's issues and our differences of opinion about how to approach them exacerbated our own problems and nearly led to divorce. What we learned over these years was simply not to give up—either on each other or on our son. We made many mistakes, but we learned from our failures and kept trying. We tried to listen better, trust each other more, take each other's perspectives a little more often, and prioritize the health of our marriage. Things are still not perfect, but just staying in the game—not giving up, keeping communication open, and keeping our faith—has made a difference.

Reflections

My mother and father were divorced when I was five months old. My father totally deserted us, leaving my mother to raise five young children. That required my mother to go back to school to get a teaching certificate and then work to support our family. That began years of babysitters and daycare centers for me. Needless to say, I had attachment and abandonment issues. I also had no male figures in my life. Not one. I knew my life's mission was to marry in the temple and raise an eternal family, and I also knew that I was inadequately prepared for marriage due to my upbringing. So I sought empowerment by learning all I could about how to have a successful marriage and raise a righteous family. I took college courses and attended conferences aimed at personal development. I read books and studied the scriptures. I sought healing through the Atonement of Jesus Christ, as well as by counseling with a therapist. Today, I have a very happy and successful marriage and a close, strong family.

to endure adversities and difficulties with personal resilience—the ability to maintain or regain positive mental health despite adversity. As we foster resilience within ourselves, we will have a greater capacity to endure the trials of life and bless the quality of our marital relationship. We also go beyond the basic bounce back of resilience and discuss posttraumatic growth in which we can harness power from the adversity for our growth and thriving.

Resilience

Our ability to press forward and carry on in the face of disappointments, discouragements, or trauma—or our inability to do so—speaks to our level of resilience. Resilience is generally understood by researchers to be an adaptive function in which individuals are able to maintain or regain positive mental health in the face of trial and adversity.[3] Resilience is critical to our ability to navigate our lives and our marriages, for as we know, "it must needs be, that there is an opposition in all things" (2 Nephi 2:11). Opposition will come—it does come—and it is with us even now. How are we handling it? We see an example of resilience in the story of Job in the Old Testament. He is tested with severe trial by losing his

Reflections

As an entrepreneur, the money was better than I could have made as an employee, but there was a cost. My business was inconsistent and my income unpredictable. I didn't often see my children. I was often stressed out. Unfortunately, I brought this stress home. My marriage suffered. I was impatient. I was sullen. I either spewed forth all my frustrations on my ever-listening and ever-loving wife or withdrew and retreated into my home office, trying to solve all my own problems. There were periods when I didn't talk with her for days. She began to complain about our lack of relationship. I made a job change and became an employee. I took a 50 percent pay cut. I would love to say that I became the ultimate husband and father. While I enjoyed the consistent income, I still often retreated into my home office when times were challenging at work or when my wife and I had a heated argument. My previous bad habits had followed me, and the ugly truth slowly emerged: the problems that I had getting along with my wife were not just because of my previous job! I later moved and entered real estate. In the recession, I lost a lot of money on bad deals and racked up a huge debt. Our relationship has not been much better. Because of the financial stresses, both my wife and I have felt like we can barely breathe. I am still impatient at times. While I don't yell, I still withdraw into my home office when life is hard. My tendency to avoid problems is magnified. Can I finally turn the corner and apply all the "lessons learned" from twenty-eight years of marriage? Can I breathe? Can I not run away from disagreements and love my wife no matter what? I certainly believe I can improve my marriage as I learn how to handle my own stress better. I committed to be "one" with my spouse, and I believe with the Lord's help we can truly become not just friends but "eternal companions."

Reflections

I grew up in a very troubled alcoholic family that very nearly took me apart emotionally over the years. Somehow I stayed the course and pushed forward. I think there was, in me, a certain level of natural resilience. Knowing who I am helps me to act accordingly, even when I am suffering. My wife and I have been married forty-six years and have children and grandchildren. We have faced some difficult challenges. I have tried to remember that I did it for years as a child and a youth and I can continue to do it if that is my choice. It is my choice and I will do it. When I face hard times, even now, I still cry and sometimes feel doubtful of myself . . . but then I ask myself to remember my journey. I remind my wife and family around me that we can and will be able to go on if each draws upon his or her own strength and faith and then decides to go forth. Hand in hand we do it. That is how it has helped me in marriage and family life as we have faced our challenges. The road is still bumpy but continues forward.

property, his children, and his health. He struggles, yet "in all this Job sinned not, nor charged God foolishly" (i.e., he didn't blame God; Job 1:22). He was then attacked through the shame and blame and bad advice of friends; they accused him of sin. In all of these trials, Job continued to press forward: "Though he slay me, yet will I trust in him: but I will *maintain* mine own ways before him" (Job 13:15; emphasis added). Job did maintain his ways before God, an impressive example of resilience despite a great deal of trauma. In the end, God speaks to Job and rewards his faithfulness.

Joseph Smith, as a prisoner in Liberty Jail, was also instructed of the Lord to maintain his ways: "Hold on thy way" (D&C 122:9). He was told that as he did so, the priesthood would remain with him and that his enemies would not be able to thwart his mission for God. The Lord counseled, "Fear not what man can do, for God shall be with you forever and ever" (D&C 122:9).

DEBRA: *To these examples, I will add more about my personal story. When Richard was made bishop, I was tested with isolation and was overwhelmed. As bishop, Richard had major responsibilities and stewardships for the ward flock, yet he was surrounded by a large supporting cast. I also had major responsibilities, but they were for our personal flock, and I was more isolated than I had ever been now that I spent many additional hours alone with the children each week.*

Getting to church was a monumental endeavor. Emotional meltdowns were a weekly occurrence—for both the children and me. By the time I got to church, I felt emotionally exhausted. During sacrament meeting, even though friends were very generous to sit with me, the three little ones were young enough that they often would not let my friends help because they only wanted Mom. The meeting was all about child management, probably looking more like a wrestling match than a worship service to those sitting around us. I was embarrassed that we were so noisy. I fought back tears through many of those meetings in those early bishop years. In all honesty, sacrament meeting was the worst part of my week.

In spite of these dynamics, I really did do my best to do my duty with a positive attitude. Yet reality was that I was struggling with feeling overwhelmed and abandoned. I felt like I was drowning and expressed this to Richard quite often. This led to moments of conflict some Sunday evenings after Richard returned home from his bishop work as I expressed my feelings of exasperation after a long week with the children. We went to bed those Sunday nights with tension in the air. This negativity made it difficult for Richard; he wondered how he could possibly continue to serve as bishop when it seemed to be exacerbating problems at home. As he began to struggle, I began to see more clearly the importance of my Me *contribution. I knew that when I struggled, Richard struggled, and it compounded his burdens, interfered with his ability to serve with the Spirit as a bishop, and diminished the quality of our marital relationship.*

RICHARD: *Debra is one of the most resilient and gritty[4] people I know, as you might have sensed from her story at the beginning of chapter 1 as she spoke of continuing a PhD after her divorce and while continuing to raise two small daughters. She amazes me at how she always gets back up when life pushes her down, utilizing strong determination to not be beaten and to do what she can to help herself move forward. Even knowing this about her, once I was called as bishop, I knew it was going to be challenging to manage the added ward responsibilities while also trying to find ways to support Debra and the kids during my additional absences. I could feel that Debra was struggling. She was truly trying to be supportive of my call, but deep inside she was having resentful feelings that she had been put on the altar of sacrifice in order for me to serve. I felt trapped between my calling and Debra. It's part of my nature to think about ways to support Debra*

*My entire childhood
I was surrounded by
divorce and devastation
in relationships. My
parents were divorced.
All my mother's friends
were divorced. Both of
my older sisters were
divorced. The only stable
marriage I saw was that
of the parents of my grade
school best friend. My
husband and I married
at age twenty. Looking
back now, I think, in
part, it was to escape such
instability in my home.
When I am asked, with
that history, how we have
survived thirty-six years
of marriage, I don't really
have a good answer. Like
running a marathon, I
think I just put my head
down and kept going.*

and to alleviate her stress and burdens; I did extra things at home during the week, yet, in spite of these and other efforts, it wasn't enough.

One Sunday evening, after coming home to a frustrated and discouraged wife, we started counseling together. We identified some more things I could do to ease her burdens specifically on Sunday: I adjusted my Sunday schedule to allow for a return home immediately after church to visit and eat a meal with the family before going back for afternoon and evening appointments. This allowed Debra and the children to see me in the middle of the day rather than having to endure the whole day without me. Debra's feelings of abandonment were significantly diminished by this one simple change. I also limited my ward business almost exclusively to texting during the week, which eliminated the need for a midweek bishopric meeting. In addition to these changes, we also brought a babysitter into the home a couple of mornings a week for a few months, giving Debra a break for a few hours while I was at work. We felt the Spirit guide us in this. These adjustments helped relieve the pressure of the situation not only for Debra but for me, because now I came home to a wife that was not as severely overwhelmed. These solutions may not have been found if I had not been willing to examine my part in finding a way to support Debra. It allowed both of us to be more resilient in an otherwise difficult circumstance.

DEBRA: *These changes were big improvements, and I was very grateful to Richard for his flexibility, but of course, by virtue of having three children so young and close in age, it continued to be a tremendous and stressful undertaking. After some months of struggling along with my new normal, I had a dream. In my dream, I was on a large ship, like the* Titanic, *and as did the* Titanic, *the*

ship was sinking. I was on a lower level of the ship, sitting in a seat confined by a seat belt (such as if I had been seated on an airplane). The ocean water had risen so that I had to stretch my chin as high up in the air as I could in order to keep my mouth and nose above the water. In one moment, the water would rise again and I would drown. I felt intense panic. Then, in one "aha" moment, I realized that there was an upper deck to the ship and that I didn't need to drown at that very moment. Immediately upon having that thought, I found myself standing on the upper deck of the great ship. As the ship continued sinking, Richard was moving quickly back and forth, assisting others, appearing not to see me. Yet I felt calm and patient, with no resentment of his work to help others now that I was no longer drowning myself. I knew I was still in danger as the ship continued to sink, but somehow it was okay. I knew Richard would eventually get to me, and I felt proud of him for his great service to others.

This dream prompted me to make some changes. I very consciously made the decision to stop saying that I was drowning. Using that word was negatively affecting how I was thinking about my situation. With that, I made some positive shifts. I chose to accept the time of Richard's bishop service each week without resentment. I felt less distress about the calling and recognized that it was actually temporary *and that I had not lost Richard completely. Richard soon began to feel less angst about coming home after serving, particularly if he'd been out late unexpectedly. This helped us feel more connected as partners in his service, instead of me just feeling left behind and abandoned. I still struggled managing the children on my own, but my distress was now focused on the very real difficulty of caring for the children alone rather than being upset about the bishop calling. Our marriage quality, which had significantly decreased in the first few months after Richard received his calling as bishop, began to improve again. Thus, I ultimately was able to bounce back. I realized there was much I could do to influence my own quality of life and the quality of our marriage, in spite of the unchangeable nature of the bishop calling. This change is an illustration of the kind of positive power and resilience that can come into our lives and marriages when we create more flexibility in our thinking and perceptions.*

Strategies of Resilience

Resilience provides psychological protection, as it helps prevent negative outcomes following traumatic experiences.[5] Those with higher levels of resilience are more psychologically adjusted, with fewer symptoms of anxiety, depression, and readjustment difficulties compared to those with lower levels of resilience.[6] Thus, it is desirable that we work to increase our levels of resilience.

Building distress tolerance is a fundamental step to creating emotional reserves and building resilience. It includes self-soothing, distraction, and activities that increase positive sentiment.[7] These can be particularly helpful to those who may be in a severe time of trial or what feels to them like a crisis in which they are struggling to regulate their emotions. Let's take a look at each of these techniques.

First, in a moment of heightened emotion, it is important to learn how to self-soothe. To calm the intensity of emotion, self-soothing strategies need to be able to be done at any time, generally not dependent on others or particular circumstances.

In efforts to self-soothe, we can choose activities that appeal to each of the five senses:

1. What sights soothe you? A beautiful view of the mountains, stargazing, a lovely flower, looking through an art book, watching a candle flame flicker, a favorite movie.

2. What sounds calm you? Peaceful or inspiring music, the rhythm of drums, the sound of running water, little children laughing, humming a gentle tune, a favorite song.

3. What tastes soothe you? A smooth dark chocolate; peppermint tea; warm tapioca pudding; a good meal; sugary, cold cereal (one of Richard's favorite comfort foods). A cautionary note here: This is not about promoting emotional eating or bingeing. The taste is to soothe, not cope. If eating is a problematic area for you, do not use food to soothe but try herbal tea, mints, or gum, or skip this area completely.

4. What smells soothe you? A hot churro with its brown sugar and cinnamon, a favorite flower, a favorite perfume or cologne, standing outside after it has rained.

5. What touches calm you? A self-hug, the texture of your favorite fuzzy blanket, massaging your hand or foot, brushing your hair, taking a hot shower or bubble bath. (Deep breathing engages the body and is an excellent one to try here.)

Second, once the self-soothing has reduced the emotional intensity of the moment, we can choose an activity to distract us for a moment or a longer while from the distressing circumstance. This serves to give us a break from having to think about the issue for a few minutes. Here it is important to do activities that keep us busy or engaged. For example, we can call a friend, exercise, do yard work, or work on a project such as cleaning, organizing, scrapbooking, etc. After a period of distraction, it is often easier to go back to working on the distressing situation with more clarity of thought.

Third, in addition to using distraction to give ourselves a mental break, we should purposefully include into our daily activities things that will create positive sentiment and will offset the intense negative energy of the crisis. What do you enjoy doing? Do it! Examples may include listening to energetic music, playing an instrument, spending time with friends, reading a good book, playing games, learning something new, watching a movie or sports, working on a meaningful project, or going out to dinner with friends. When we are in times of trial, we would be wise to make purposeful efforts to do several activities we enjoy every day. Not only is this great for traumatic moments or stressful periods of time, but it is a general life strategy for optimizing mental health and feeling happiness and joy.

These strategies do not need to be burdensome or take a lot of time. We can do some of these while driving, doing chores, working, or other such activities when we may not have extra time. For example, after a tense situation with our spouse, we can easily take a few deep breaths (self-soothing) and then turn on some uplifting or energetic music (both distraction and positive sentiment).

Beyond examining the benefits of building distress tolerance, researchers have learned a lot about how to help us build resilience so that we, like Job, may maintain our

Reflections

After over twenty-five years of marriage, I have learned to accept my spouse for who he is—his personality, his value system, his way of looking at the world, his unwritten rules for living. I have learned to accept that sometimes he will be unable or unwilling to try to fulfill my dreams. I have had to muster a great deal of selflessness to put aside my own dreams when they have not been fulfilled. I do this better with certain types of problems than with others. Wishing things were different doesn't make it happen. Getting upset just makes the problem worse. I have had to look different directions to have some dreams fulfilled, but other dreams I have had to let go. I have had to work to make this a genuine gift of love, not an act of grudging, eye-rolling surrender.

ways as we struggle through our trials. Factors that influence our level of resilience include

- Our perception of whether social supports are available to us.
- Our perception of personal control and the use of our time and energy in ways that will benefit us.
- Our ability to manage negative emotions and have positive emotions (as in our discussion above about the use of soothing and positive-sentiment activities).
- Our ability to use cognitive flexibility, such as in problem solving and acceptance practices.
- Our ability to engage in activities that are meaningful and fulfilling to us and align with our life values and priorities.
- Our ability to access our own social, emotional, or material supports (such as empathetic or financial supports).
- Our ability to face our difficulties, work through them, and share them with others; this is contrasted to avoidance or denial of pain and negative emotions.[8]

Many of these factors speak to orienting our thoughts toward health. Martin Seligman is known as the father of positive psychology, a branch of psychology dedicated to optimizing mental health and happiness in normal populations (as opposed to abnormal psychology, which studies those with mental illness). He has researched issues such as failure, hopelessness, and optimism for decades. He found that "even in the face of terrible failures . . . men and women [can] flourish rather than flounder" when they are resilient.[9] Seligman found that people who persevere when they are faced with opposition tend to interpret problems as temporary (i.e., "this will be over soon"), local (i.e., "it was only that one time; the other situations worked out"), and changeable (i.e., "I can influence this situation").[10] In the field of psychology, this type of interpretation of life circumstances is addressed within cognitive theory; *cognition* is a formal word to refer to our thinking, and cognitive theory identifies how our thoughts and beliefs affect our emotions. Sometimes we get ourselves stuck into thinking errors, thinking traps, or cognitive distortions. Debra experienced such a trap.

DEBRA: *I felt depleted and thought that I could not handle my circumstance as a bishop's wife with three young toddlers who seemed to be screaming, hitting, destroying things, making messes, and making demands almost continuously. I told myself I was drowning and so I was. As my dream made me aware of this cognitive trap, I was able to liberate myself from it.*

As we become aware of any distortion, it is much easier for us to change those problematic aspects of our thinking. There are many different types of thinking traps. For example, all-or-nothing thinking is when we believe everything is either perfect or is a complete failure.

As you read the list of cognitive distortions in the margin, do you recognize any of these patterns in yourself?

For example, have you ever found yourself overgeneralizing, such as by using the phrase "you always" when upset with your spouse? In examining this, you can acknowledge that imperfect human beings are not consistent enough to always do *anything*. This can help you reframe the "always" to a more accurate "you often" or "you sometimes," which can immediately deflate some of the negative emotional intensity of a difficult moment. We will need to work with ourselves throughout our lives, especially in our marriages, to avoid falling prey to our own pet distortions.

As we consider these aforementioned resilience-building factors, here is a specific

Other Cognitive Distortions

- *Magnification or minimization:* You blow things up or shrink them down, out of proportion to their actual impact. "Our world is over as we know it!" or "No big deal. Don't cry about it. It's fine."

- *Emotional reasoning:* Your feelings dictate your reason: "I feel like a horrible wife, so I must actually be one."

- *Labeling:* Instead of saying, "It wasn't my best moment" or "That didn't go very well," you tell yourself, "I'm a loser" or "I am a failure."[11]

self-help model designed to increase resilience that may be help-ful as you evaluate how you are handling your own personal cir-cumstances. It follows the acronym of THRIVE:

- Taking Stock: make sure you are safe and have what you need, take care of personal needs, face circumstances rather than avoiding them, and the like.
- Harvesting Hope: look to the future (more on hope in our following section).
- Re-authoring: change victim mindset into a survi-vor mindset and then eventually into a thriving mindset through pondering, writing, and other types of exercises.
- Identifying Change: track your growth.
- Valuing Change: work through how the circumstances have influenced your growth and improvement, such as with gratitude and journaling (more on gratitude in our following section).
- Expressing Change in Action: make choices to align your growth into everyday behaviors and attitudes.[12]

Gospel Principles to Strengthen Our Level of Resilience

The gospel of Jesus Christ teaches many principles that will con-tribute to a more resilient life. As seen in the THRIVE model, hope and gratitude are significantly related to resilience in the research literature.

Hope

In large measure, resilience may be synonymous with hope: an overall expectation that goals can be met. Researchers have claimed that hope may be identified as a defining attribute of resilience,[13] that resilience is positively related with hope, and that both have a direct, positive influence on life satisfaction.[14] LDS Topics online defines hope in this way: "Hope is the confident expectation of and longing for the promised blessings of righteousness. . . . In the language of the gospel . . . the word *hope* is sure, unwavering, and active. . . . When we have hope, we trust God's promises."[15] Elder Neal A. Maxwell explained, "Real hope . . . stiffens, not slackens, the spiritual spine. . . . Hope is realistic anticipation which takes the form of a determination—not only to survive adversity but, moreover, to 'endure . . . well' to the end (D&C 121:8)."[16]

The type of hope herein described is centered in our Savior, Jesus Christ. "Ultimate hope is . . . tied to Jesus and the blessings of the great Atonement."[17] Thus, through the Atonement of Jesus Christ, we are able to build a resilient nature that is brought to us through the power of the Holy Ghost. Elder Maxwell outlined the relationship between the Atonement of Jesus Christ, the Holy Ghost, and resilience:

> While so striving daily, we will fall short. Hence the avoidance of discouragement is so vital. So where is the oft and much needed resilience to be found? Once again, in the glorious Atonement! . . .
>
> By applying the Atonement we can continue to access the other nurturing gifts of the Holy Ghost, each with its own rich resilience. The Holy Ghost will often preach sermons to us from the pulpit of memory. He will comfort us and reassure us. The burdens not lifted from us, He will help us to bear, thus enabling, even after we err, to continue with joy the soul-stretching journey of discipleship.[18]

These are wonderful blessings of hope. Indeed, researchers have found that hopeful individuals experience more positive emotions.[19] As such, when adversity and trauma come to us, hope in the great power of the Atonement of Jesus Christ brings confidence and calm into our hearts and minds. Hope in our Savior is stronger than any feelings we may have of desperation or fear—if we will but believe. When our hope wanes, fear thrives, yet "God hath not given us the spirit of fear; but of power, and of love, and of a sound mind" (2 Timothy 1:7).

When it comes to marriage, hope in our Savior Jesus Christ is our anchor in the sometimes stormy seas of adversity (see Ether 12:4). This anchor will tether us to each other as spouses and to our Savior so "that when the devil shall send forth his mighty winds, yea, his shafts in the whirlwind, yea, when all his hail and his mighty storm shall beat upon [us], it shall have no power over [us]" (Helaman 5:12).

Gratitude

Gratitude, the ability to respond with appreciation for perceived benefits or positive aspects of events, contributes to a resiliency of spirit. It is also an important personal virtue that will protect one's marriage. One researcher commented, "Gratitude may be a mindful awareness—specifically, awareness of how one's very life is held together through the benevolent actions of other people. Grateful people, on recalling a positive outcome in their lives, are mindful of the causal agents (namely other people, but also, for some, God or a higher power) who have acted in ways that benefitted them."[20]

In psychological research, the relationship between gratitude and hope is strong. "Grateful and hopeful people may both possess the cognitive habit of savoring their life circumstances, appreciating fully the good circumstances that come their way in the past and the meaningfulness of the goal pursuits they undertake in the present."[21]

This savoring has been shown to be helpful as researchers have examined exercises to increase feelings of gratitude. Seligman and colleagues examined several strategies for increasing positive sentiment, including two gratitude exercises. They asked research participants to record every night for one week three things that went well each day and their causes. They also asked participants to do a *gratitude visit* in which they were given one week to write and hand deliver a letter of gratitude to a person who had been particularly kind to them but who they had never properly thanked. They found that keeping track of the good things that happened each day increased happiness and decreased depressive symptoms for six months. They also found the *gratitude visit* "caused large positive changes for one month."[22]

DEBRA: *I have applied the principles of this research into my personal life and benefitted from it over many years. I modified the activity a bit, using it as a gratitude list I call my "happy list." On an ongoing basis, I list the good things that I experience each day and include anything for which I am grateful—things that give me joy, peace, amusement, pleasure, happiness, contentment, and the like. Some of my more frequent entries include a hot shower, a good workout session, a smile or hug from one of the children, a visit with a friend, seeing deer in the back-yard, a phone call from Richard during the day, a good therapy session with one of my clients, the positive feelings associated with teaching and presenting or receiving and giving service, watching the children play together, enjoying a beautiful view, dark chocolate and mint, holding one of the kids on my lap and reading them a story, and singing silly toddler songs with the kiddos.*

Looking for the positive things in my life each day and writing them down increases their positive influence, even as it increases the amount of time I attend to them. A smile or hug from one of my children can last only a fraction of a moment, but thinking about it and writing it down and then later reading what was written extends that smile well beyond the time it took to actually happen. When I have a particularly difficult day or am going through a trial, I work even harder to find positive things to put on my list. This helps me follow the dictum "always [return] thanks unto God for whatsoever things ye do receive" by gaining awareness of even the small things for which I am grateful (Alma 7:23). Doing this on an ongoing basis over many years has created a great deal of positive sentiment that has fla-vored my life for good—even through my difficult trials.

Church leaders encourage us to look beyond even the things we are grateful for and foster a grateful heart with an overall attitude of gratitude. President Dieter F. Uchtdorf taught that although it is important for us to identify our blessings fre-quently, we should be grateful in all of our life circumstances, regardless of whether things seem to be going well or not. He indicated that this is "a gratitude . . . of the soul."[23] President Uchtorf explained that when we are continuously grateful, we can feel peace even in the middle of our trials. Indeed, researchers have conceptualized gratitude as a protective influence, reducing the negative effects of trauma, in that it encourages positivity and helps create positive outcomes.[24]

Posttraumatic Growth

Every trial can be seen as a growth opportunity—if we choose. Rather than getting back to just where we were prior to a trial, we want to move and expand beyond it, especially in marriage. Seligman teaches people how to foster posttraumatic growth. He emphasizes that our ability to improve and transform comes from a "renewed appreciation of being alive, enhanced personal strength, acting on new possibilities, improved relationships, or spiritual deepening."[25] As part of this training, Seligman encourages people to revise their trauma narrative to include not only the difficulties of their story but more positive elements, such as how they utilized their personal strengths during the trial, things they are grateful for, and what they have gained since the trial began.

DEBRA: *In our bishop scenario, I was able to increase my level of resilience and find more patience and calm, even though the difficulty of parenting five children, three of them toddlers, remained. The revelatory dream, as well as the practical solutions Richard and I implemented to relieve some of the burden, helped me tremendously. In an effort toward growth, I sought to utilize my strengths, such as spending more time teaching the children (rather than just supervising them) and doing service for others. I also sought to be more grateful for the times Richard was home, the health and maturing development of the children, and those people that were part of my life.*

With all of this, even though I had made peace with the calling for Richard, the calling still just made everything more difficult for me. I would comment to those close to me: "I know this calling is good for the ward; Richard is a great bishop. I know the calling is good for Richard; he is more connected to others and seems happier in his service. I do not yet know how this calling is good for me." My limited vision illustrates the nature of our lengthy trials and the types of expectations we may have—we may not be able to see growth midstream but only when the trial is over (posttraumatic growth). I believed in faith that this circumstance would ultimately propel me forward on my eternal journey, yet beyond acknowledging that I was more sensitive to the needs of others because of my own suffering, I could not see my own growth. However, Richard saw growth in me, even when I could not yet see it in myself. He saw me exercise my faith and receive answers to my prayers, he saw my grit propel me to try again the next day no matter what happened the day before, and he saw a major transformation in how I reacted to his time serving as the Lord borrowed him.

The Prison–Temple Experience

Traumatic and painful experiences seem to be common to us all. For example, one mother of a son with schizophrenia indicated that she wouldn't need to die and go to hell in order to know what it was like because she was already experiencing hell in life as she dealt with her son's illness. In some trials it *is* the case that we are standing before the gaping jaws of hell. The anguish and trauma caused by these trials are soul searing at its deepest level. Yet we have been taught that these types of experiences are part of Father in Heaven's plan for our exaltation; there is purpose in the hell we may be enduring, and often that purpose involves our experience and ultimate growth.

Posttraumatic growth is a fundamental doctrine within the gospel. We are familiar with the concept of posttraumatic growth through our study of Church history and the experiences of Joseph Smith while he was a prisoner in the Liberty Jail. The Lord revealed to Joseph Smith in the squalid conditions of prison that "if the very jaws of hell shall gape open the mouth wide after thee, know thou, my son, that all these things shall give thee experience, and shall be for thy good" (D&C 122:7).

And what good do these kinds of experiences do for us? Elder Jeffrey R. Holland explored the idea that we can receive opportunities for growth and revelation, as in the temple, while we remain in the greatest difficulties of our lives. He used this example of Joseph Smith and taught that Liberty Jail can be called a temple because

> you can have sacred, revelatory, profoundly instructive experience with the Lord in any situation you are in. Indeed, . . . you can have sacred, revelatory, profoundly instructive experience with the Lord *in the most miserable experiences of your life*—in the worst settings, while enduring the most painful injustices, when facing the most insurmountable odds and opposition you have ever faced. . . .
>
> Every one of us, in one way or another, great or small, dramatic or incidental, is going to spend a little time in Liberty Jail—spiritually speaking. . . . The lessons of the winter of 1838–39 teach us that *every* experience can become a *redemptive* experience if we remain bonded to our Father in Heaven through that difficulty. These difficult lessons teach us that man's extremity is God's opportunity, and if we will be humble and faithful, if we will be believing and not curse God for our problems, He can turn the unfair and inhumane and debilitating prisons of our lives into temples—or at least into a circumstance that can bring comfort and revelation, divine companionship and peace.[26]

In the midst of difficult circumstances, we know some days are better than others, but when emotions become heightened and the crisis of a moment leads us to despair, we encourage reflection upon the prison-temple concept of Elder Holland. He continued:

> Through it all, *God is with us*. . . .
>
> We are not alone in our little prisons here. When suffering, we may in fact be nearer to God than we've ever been in our entire lives. *That* knowledge can turn every such situation into a would-be temple.[27]

We can choose to reflect upon the trials and challenges we've experienced, even trials relative to a difficult marital relationship or a spouse's addiction or mental illness, and likely find, to our amazement, the realization of spiritual blessings that have come to us. As we do this, we find that the agony of the moment is set aside by the warmth and love of the Savior that is received by the power of the Holy Ghost. We can allow this great and soothing influence to witness to us that even while facing the very jaws of

LIZ LEMON SWINDLE, *Joseph [Smith] in Liberty Jail.*

hell, the Savior's love and His interest in our eternal welfare are ever present.

In trials, we are not simply subject to circumstances or to the agency of another, left without power to influence our circumstances; we are not the victim of our trials even when the refiner's

DEL PARSON, *Joseph Interprets the Prisoners' Dreams.*

fire is so very hot! We have the ability to exercise our agency to do
that which does lie within our power. Viktor Frankl, an interna-
tionally renowned psychiatrist, spent many years as a prisoner in
Nazi death camps during the Holocaust. Writing of his horren-
dous experiences being tortured, starved, and living on the verge
of death, he observed, "Everything can be taken from a man but
one thing: the last of the human freedoms—to choose one's attitude in any given set of circumstances, to choose one's own way."[28]

Joseph Smith, counseling the Saints while he was in Liberty Jail, encouraged, "Therefore . . . let us cheerfully do all things that lie in our power; and then may we stand still, with the utmost assurance, to see the salvation of God, and for his arm to be revealed" (D&C 123:17). We see here the partnership required of us during our trials—we do what is in our power *and* we wait on God and trust in His saving power. We cannot just wait on Him without doing our part. We see this partnership in our Great Exemplar, Jesus Christ, as He revealed His experience of suffering as He enacted the Atonement:

> Which suffering caused myself, even God, the greatest of all, to tremble because of pain, and to bleed at every pore, and to suffer both body and spirit—and would that I might not drink the bitter cup, and shrink—nevertheless, glory be to the Father, and I partook and finished my preparations unto the children of men." (D&C 19:18–19)

In his immense suffering, Christ glorified the Father and waited on Him while also doing His part as "[He] partook and finished [His] preparations." What preparations are ours? What is the part we can play in exercising our agency while seeking to navigate our specific trial?

The story of Joseph of Egypt is a comprehensive story illustrating periods of growth following trial and adversity. Joseph was sold by his own brothers into slavery. In the house of Potiphar, he rose after that setback: "And the Lord was with Joseph, and he was a prosperous man" (Genesis 39:2). This resilience created opportunity for posttraumatic growth: "And his master saw that the Lord was with him, and that the Lord made all that he did to prosper in his hand. And Joseph found grace in his sight, and he served him: and he made him overseer over his house, and all that he had he put into his hand" (Genesis 39:3–4).

A second trauma occurred as Joseph was thrown into prison by Potiphar—who had exalted him within his household—in reaction to a false report from his wife that Joseph had tried to seduce her. Joseph rose again and was made stronger: "But the Lord was with Joseph, and shewed him mercy, and gave him favour in the sight of the keeper of the prison. And the keeper of the prison committed to Joseph's hand all the prisoners that were in the prison. . . . And that which he did, the Lord made it to prosper" (Genesis 39:21–23).

Within the "dungeon" (Genesis 41:14), Joseph continued to extend himself and serve others by interpreting dreams. One of the men for whom he interpreted a dream was released from prison and later referred Pharaoh to Joseph to receive a dream interpretation. Joseph not only interpreted the dream, as God had blessed him to be able to do so, but continued to move forward, proposing to Pharaoh a grain-storage system for managing the dream's predicted famine. And Joseph rose again: "Thou shalt be over my house, and according unto thy word shall all my people be ruled. . . . And Pharaoh said unto Joseph, See, I have set thee over all the land of Egypt" (Genesis 41:40–41). Joseph, who had been both a slave and a prisoner, continued to press forward and, as a result, was blessed with repeated periods of growth and prosperity; ultimately, he was given rings, fine clothing, and gold chains; rode in Pharaoh's second chariot; was married; and served as governor of the land.

These stories and teachings may be summarized with these thoughts by researchers: "A biblical perspective on posttraumatic growth will therefore emphasize the outcomes of brokenness, humility, and deeper Christlikeness, rather than greater strength and self-confidence. It will focus on God's strength or power being made perfect in our weakness (2 Cor. 12:9–10), and how weakness is the way or key in the Christian spiritual life and not self-sufficiency that can lead to pride."[29]

DEBRA: *Let's return now to my story parenting five children—three of them toddlers—while Richard served as the bishop of our ward. I had made much progress in my ability to bounce back and even move forward and was functioning well after those initial months. During this time, I worked hard to do all the*

TED HENNIGER, *Joseph Making Himself Known to his Brothers*. © 1980 INTELLEC-
TUAL RESERVE, INC.

"right" things—I read my scriptures, listened to general conference talks, made extra efforts to be grateful for my blessings, fulfilled my church calling, sought to serve others, and parented our children to the best of my ability. But adding to the difficulty of the circumstance, other circumstances in my life began to unravel. It seemed that my physical health and everything around me was falling apart. A surgery; long-term, painful physical therapy; and a myriad of heart-wrenching and stress-inducing circumstances greatly intensified this period of time. Richard likened my experience to Nephi going on the Lord's errand to get the brass plates but then failing in his first two attempts (see 1 Nephi 3:9–28).

Near the end of this intense first bishop year, bitterness and resentment began to grow. This bishop thing was the Lord's plan, so couldn't He have eased my burdens in some other areas and cut me some slack? I struggled with feeling that God was purposefully making my situation as difficult as possible without concern for my quality of life and personal feelings. I could see blessings from God in my life and cognitively understood that He loved me, but I could not feel it. I felt a numbness of spirit that I had never experienced previously, even during other significant trials. I prayed and prayed that I would be able to feel God's love, but it did not come. I told myself I just had to keep moving forward in spite of this emptiness.

During this time, encounters with our stake president, a very loving and warm man, became excruciating because I felt he could see right through me. I wrote in my journal: "I cannot meet him—I cannot even look his way when he comes to our ward sacrament meeting and he is sitting up on the stand. I can't look at him because I am embarrassed and pained to speak the truth of my experiences and life the last year since he put Richard in as bishop of our ward. It has been the worst year of my life. . . . I cannot speak the truth of my life to him because it will sound faithless and unsupportive."

Perhaps not surprisingly, it wasn't long before our stake president asked to meet with me. I was very nervous about this meeting, concerned about how to share my experiences and feelings from the past year in only a few brief moments without sounding like I was whining. Miraculously, and to my great relief, he spared me from having to attempt the task. When I arrived at his office, he did not ask me how I was doing, as would have been typical for his caring style—he already knew. Instead, he started the interview with a comment to the effect of "let me tell you why you are in here." Wisely recognizing my struggle, he spoke to me about the "doctrine of prison." I began to smile knowingly and remarked to him that we had written about this in our book, feeling somewhat shameful that I needed to be reminded of it.

After the meeting, I pondered our stake president's words and reread what we had written here, realizing that I had failed to liken my own situation to the prison-temple. In this pondering, my feelings were confirmed: yes, on purpose God had called Richard to serve as bishop the very week the third toddler began to walk—he had put me in prison! Through the doctrine of the prison-temple, I realized that although he had put me in prison, He had put a great many people, even prophets, into prison as well—and there must be a reason for it. Surprisingly, this hard doctrine paradoxically brought relief from bitterness and resentment. Instead of feeling unloved or thwarted by God, I began to view my circumstance as more purposeful. I began to feel more faith and more hope.

This begs the question, Why would God put His beloved prophets in prison? And then, why does He put us in prison, too? One answer comes from the story of Alma and Amulek in the Book of Mormon as they went out to preach:

> They were filled with the Holy Ghost.
> And they had power given unto them . . . ; nevertheless they did not exercise their power until they were bound in bands and cast into prison. *Now, this was done that the Lord might show forth his power in them.*
> And it came to pass that they went forth and began to preach and to prophecy unto the people, *according to the spirit and power which the Lord had given them.* (Alma 8:30–32; emphasis added)

In other words, God places us in prison in order to show His power both to us and others. This kind of spiritual power is available to all who seek to grow from their prison-temple experiences. President Russell M. Nelson taught:

> When you reach up for the Lord's power in your life with the same intensity that a drowning person has when grasping and gasping for air, power from Jesus Christ will be yours. When the Savior knows you truly want to reach up to Him—when He can feel that the greatest

desire of your heart is to draw His power into your life—you will be led by the Holy Ghost to know exactly what you should do.

When you spiritually stretch beyond anything you have ever done before, then His power will flow into you.[30]

RICHARD: *This prison-temple concept helped Debra, and it made a big difference in our marriage. I felt that Debra was much more settled even though none of the circumstances of her life had changed. This allowed me to have a more positive outlook on my calling and our marriage. I still came home sometimes Sunday evenings to an exhausted wife, but her demeanor and attitude were different and more positive. That was a big relief, and it increased the level of empathy and love in our marriage. Debra's personal efforts to work through this trial with faith and resilience brought a sense of peace into our relationship that had a palpable and pervasive positive influence. I also sensed the spiritual growth and power that God was bestowing upon both of us. In this, Debra recognized the love of God and His approval of her offering.*

Joy

Our intention herein has not been to give a message of "gloom and doom" or perpetual suffering but to give a message of hope and encouragement. The Apostle Paul counseled the Hebrews: "Now no chastening for the present seemeth to be joyous, but grievous: nevertheless afterward it yieldeth the peaceable fruit of righteousness unto them which are exercised thereby" (Hebrews 12:11). There is great joy available to us when we are "exercised thereby" as we seek purpose, focus on the Savior and His Atonement, and live according to our commitments. President Russell M. Nelson gave a discourse about the ability to find joy even in difficult circumstances:

> Saints can be happy under every circumstance. We can feel joy even while having a bad day, a bad week, or even a bad year!
>
> My dear brothers and sisters, the joy we feel has little to do with the circumstances of our lives and everything to do with the focus of our lives.

When the focus of our lives is on God's plan of salvation . . . and Jesus Christ and His gospel, we can feel joy regardless of what is happening—or not happening—in our lives. Joy comes from and because of Him. He is the source of all joy.[31]

President Nelson later continued:

When we choose Heavenly Father to be our God and when we can feel the Savior's Atonement working in our lives, we will be filled with joy. Every time we nurture our spouse and guide our children, every time we forgive someone or ask for forgiveness, we can feel joy.

Every day that you and I choose to live celestial laws, every day that we keep our covenants and help others to do the same, joy will be ours.

. . . As this principle is embedded in our hearts, each and every day can be a day of joy and gladness.[32]

DEBRA: *Several years into Richard's calling as bishop, I began to learn this very complex—even graduate-level—concept of having joy even while in our trials. As I dug deep, purposely working and grasping to access the real power that faith brings into our lives, I was testing the Lord at His word. It took some years, but, in time, that power became manifest. I received powerful, even miraculous, answers to help address some significant life concerns and health issues, as well as heavenly assistance in attaining some of the goals that were personally meaningful to me. The promises of God that I had read over and over again in the scriptures were coming alive in my life in a very real, life-breathing sense.*

A quiet sense of excitement grew deep within me. I knew God was doing His work in my life. Of course, I had known this cognitively throughout the trials, and I knew it from exercising faith in my full-time missionary work, callings, and other personal circumstances throughout my life. But through the severe intensity of the trials of these years, it manifested in such a distinct and powerful way that my testimony became secure at a level much deeper than what I had ever previously known. When the crises came and I held on tenaciously in faith, believing God's promises, He showed me that He would keep those promises for me personally. I felt a quiet joy and confidence rising up within me, knowing I had a very real, very personal relationship with my Father and that He knew me, heard me, loved me, and was actively working in my life to promote my growth and ultimate happiness.

Mental Health and Resilience

Sometimes, even with our best efforts, we can't seem to move beyond the devastating effects of life's trials or challenges. There may be extenuating circumstances beyond our control. There may be a particular knowledge deficit. There may also be complications caused by mental health issues. If you or your spouse continues to struggle to build resilience and move beyond trauma or other difficulties, we refer you to our appendix on mental health, presented in a question and answer format. This appendix discusses a variety of principles, such as how to identify mental illness, how the psychotherapy-treatment process works, and whether it is important to secure the services of an LDS therapist. Most importantly, it offers hope to those struggling— hope that there is help available and that healing and vitality can come with appropriate treatment. Included therein are several stories written by those who have attended psychotherapy. These stories illustrate the wonderful, liberating changes that came into their lives as they made the courageous decision to seek treatment for their difficulties.

Conclusion

Psalm 37:23–25 offers this comforting counsel: "The steps of a good man are ordered by the Lord. . . . Though he fall, he shall not be utterly cast down: for the Lord upholdeth him with his hand. I have been young, and now am old; yet have I not seen the righteous forsaken."

The doctrines of this chapter speak to our ability to do hard things, stay healthy while doing them, and grow and gain spiritual power because of the challenge. The principles of resilience and posttraumatic growth are critical as struggle comes to each of us. When these principles are applied, they will provide a well of strength that will influence not only our personal lives but also our marital relationship. Our personal illustration woven throughout this chapter has sought to teach the critical relationship between our own personal trials and our marital relationship. Simply put—if we fall apart, so will our marriage. Yet as we foster resilience, our relationship can be blessed with a sense of security, peace, and joy, even if the trial is ongoing.

We have discussed a number of ways to help build resilience. Resilience will foster our ability to continue forward when the trials of life and the trials of our marriage test us. Keep moving forward, one step at a time. As we have seen with the examples of Job, Joseph Smith, and Joseph of Egypt, we too will be blessed by the Lord as we *maintain our ways*.

We can not only bounce back from trials with resilience but move forward by accessing the power of Christ's Atonement, fostering posttraumatic growth, and finding joy in the process. Elder Jeffrey R. Holland summarized the concepts of this chapter when he taught:

> On this upward and sometimes hazardous journey, each of us meets our share of daily challenges. . . .
>
> . . . The tests of life are tailored for our own best interests, and all will face the burdens best suited to their own mortal experience. In the end we will realize that God is merciful as well as just and that all the rules are fair. We can be reassured that our challenges will be the ones *we* needed, and conquering them will bring blessings we could have received in no other way.[33]

The Lord, in His great love and mercy, will give us "beauty for ashes, the oil of joy for mourning, the garment of praise for the spirit of heaviness" (Isaiah 61:3).

Notes

1. Quentin L. Cook, "Foundations of Faith," *Ensign*, May 2017, 130.

2. Thomas Ledermann et al., "Stress, Communication, and Marital Quality in Couples," *Family Relations* 59 (April 2010): 195–206.

3. Helen Herrman et al., "What Is Resilience?," *Canadian Journal of Psychiatry* 56, no. 5 (2011): 258–65.

4. According to researcher Angela Duckworth, those with grit have passion and perseverance. Angela Duckworth, *Grit: The Power of Passion and Perseverance* (New York: Scribner, 2016), 38.

5. Julie Vieselmeyer, Jeff Holguin, and Amy Mezulis, "The Role of Resilience and Gratitude in Posttraumatic Stress and Growth Following a Campus Shooting," *Psychological Trauma: Theory, Research, Practice, and Policy* 9, no. 1 (2017): 62–69.

6. Don Meichenbaum, *Roadmap to Resilience: A Guide for Military, Trauma Victims and Their Families* (Clearwater, FL: Institute Press, 2012). Siang-Yang Tan, "Resilience and Posttraumatic Growth: Empirical Evidence and Clinical Applications from a Christian Perspective," *Journal of Psychology and Christianity* 32 (2013): 358–64.

7. Marsha M. Linehan, *Skills Training Manual for Treating Borderline Personality Disorder* (New York: Guilford Press, 1993), 167.

8. Meichenbaum, *Roadmap to Resilience*, 6.

9. Martin E. Seligman, "Building Resilience," *Harvard Business Review* 89, no. 4 (April 2011): 106.

10. Adapted from Seligman, "Building Resilience," 102.

11. David D. Burns, *Feeling Good: The New Mood Therapy* (New York: William Morrow, 1980), 18.

12. Stephen Joseph, *What Doesn't Kill Us: The New Psychology of Posttraumatic Growth* (New York: Basic Books, 2011), 175–76.

13. Brigid M. Gillespie, Wendy Chaboyer, and Marianne Wallis, "Development of a Theoretically Derived Model of Resilience through Concept Analysis," *Contemporary Nurse* 25, nos. 1–2 (2007): 124–35.

14. Hui-Ching Wu, "The Protective Effects of Resilience and Hope on Quality of Life of the Families Coping with the Criminal Traumatization of One of Its Members," *Journal of Clinical Nursing* 20, nos. 13–14 (2011): 1906–15.

15. "Hope," The Church of Jesus Christ of Latter-day Saints, 2014, https://www.lds.org/topics/hope?lang=eng.

16. Neal A. Maxwell, "Hope through the Atonement of Jesus Christ," *Ensign*, November 1998, 62.

17. Maxwell, "Hope through the Atonement," 61.

18. Neal A. Maxwell, "Apply the Atoning Blood of Christ," *Ensign*, November 1997, 23–24.

19. Michael E. McCullough, "Savoring Life, Past and Present: Explaining What Hope and Gratitude Share in Common," *Psychological Inquiry* 13, no. 4 (2002): 302–4.

20. McCullough, "Savoring Life," 303.

21. McCullough, "Savoring Life," 303.

22. Martin E. P. Seligman et al., "Positive Psychology Progress: Empirical Validation of Interventions July–August 2005," *American Psychologist* 60, no. 5 (2005): 410–21.

23. Dieter F. Uchtdorf, "Grateful in Any Circumstances," *Ensign*, May 2014, 76.

24. Vieselmeyer, Holguin, and Mezulis, "The Role of Resilience," 62–69.

25. Seligman, "Building Resilience," 104.

26. Jeffrey R. Holland, "Lessons from Liberty Jail" (devotional address, Brigham Young University, Provo, UT, 7 September 2008), https://speeches.byu.edu/talks/jeffrey-r-holland_lessons-liberty-jail/.

27. Holland, "Lessons from Liberty Jail."

28. Viktor E. Frankl, *Man's Search for Meaning* (1984; repr., New York: Washington Square Press, 1959), 86.

29. Tan, "Resilience and Posttraumatic Growth."

30. Russell M. Nelson, "Drawing the Power of Jesus Christ into Our Lives," *Ensign*, May 2017, 42.

31. Russell M. Nelson, "Joy and Spiritual Survival," *Ensign*, November 2016, 82.

32. Nelson, "Joy and Spiritual Survival," 84.

33. Jeffrey R. Holland, "What I Wish Every New Member Knew—and Every Longtime Member Remembered," *Ensign*, October 2006, 14–15.

CHAPTER 4

"I Forgive You"

The Freedom of Forgiveness

*R*uth Bell Graham, wife to evangelist Billy Graham, is cred-ited with having said, "A happy marriage is the union of two good forgivers."[1] With wry smiles, we certainly agree, as we have so generously created for ourselves many opportunities to practice becoming good forgivers! Forgiveness is another *Me* characteristic in marriage. Each of us can develop and apply the principle of forgiveness to bless ourselves and our marriages.

Most couples will experience disagreements, misunder-standings, and a few arguments in their marriage. These dif-ficulties may be particularly frequent in the early transitional years, as newly married couples are trying to navigate the merg-ing of their old single selves with their new shared selves. In a speech given to students at BYU, Elder Marlin K. Jensen of the Seventy provided a humorous example of one of these instances from early in his own marriage:

> We were living in Salt Lake City, where I was attending law school and Kathy was teaching first grade. The stress of both of us being new to the city, to our schools, and to each other became a little heavy and our relationship a bit testy. One night about dinnertime we had a quarrel that convinced me

there was no hope for nourishment at home. So I left our modest apartment and walked to the nearest fast food restaurant a block away. As I entered the north door of this establishment, I looked to my right and, much to my surprise, saw Kathy entering through the south door! We exchanged angry glances and advanced to opposing cash registers to place our orders. We continued to ignore each other as we sat alone on opposite ends of the restaurant sullenly eating our evening meal. We then left as we had entered, taking separate routes home, finally ending this utterly ridiculous episode by reconciling and laughing together about how infantile we had both been. I realize now that such little tiffs are not uncommon in the early stages of most marriages.[2]

Like Elder Jensen, we have had a few of those tiffs in our marriage over the years; we, too, have hurt and offended each other. In spite of our genuine intentions and efforts to follow Christ, we have our lapses; sometimes we are impatient, sometimes we are selfish, sometimes we are thoughtless, and sometimes we are abrupt in our communications. In these offending moments, we create the necessity to forgive. Dedicated practice in both asking for and giving forgiveness has made the process easier for us as the years have passed. When we were newlyweds, we had to thoroughly discuss and work through each small offense that occurred between us; the process was tedious and our efforts, in some ways, served to only prolong the strife. It seemed that in essence we were trying to get to the point where we felt the other *deserved* our forgiveness. In time, we came to understand each other's motives and intentions. This helped increase our ability to forgive each other quickly because we knew that any offense was not maliciously intended. With each successive year of marriage, our ability to quickly forgive improved. Now, we often forgive each other, let go, and move on *without* discussing the conflict or working through it with the other when the issue is of a minor nature. In other words, as we have practiced forgiveness in our marriage, we have *gained a willingness in our hearts to simply choose to forgive* without trying to decide if that forgiveness is deserved.

In this chapter, we define forgiveness—both what it is and what it is not. We discuss forgiveness in marriage as a gift of the Spirit that requires a great deal of personal effort as well as emotional and spiritual maturity. We explain that to both seek forgiveness and offer forgiveness is a choice made by each spouse individually that is foundational for the success of couples as they navigate their life together. Finally, we discuss the fruits of forgiveness and how the decision to forgive is marriage saving.

What Is Forgiveness?

Forgiveness is a ubiquitous term, yet as a concept it is infrequently defined because we tend to assume everyone else thinks about it the same way we do. This assumption can limit our understanding of how to truly forgive others in our own lives. Researchers have defined forgiveness as "replacing the bitter, angry feelings of vengefulness often resulting from a hurt, with positive feelings of goodwill toward the offender."[3] The LDS Church website defines forgiveness in this way: "To forgive is a divine attribute. It is to pardon or excuse someone from blame for an offense or misdeed."[4] These definitions indicated that

Reflections

The past thirty-four-plus years have taught me that marriage is impossible without forgiveness. I remember being a young twenty-year-old. . . . I was so mature, prepared, in love, and ready to share everything for the rest of my life and beyond with this handsome twenty-year-old I declared to be the perfect match for me. I knew that the counsel and advice offered by everyone around me was of no use, because we were the perfect match. . . . Oh, what little I actually knew! I have had to understand a negotiation process that would become more about forgiveness than compromise. We are both children of our Heavenly Father and are committed to understanding what that means in our hourly, daily, yearly, lifetime acts; we have never had to reevaluate these commitments. What we have had to address almost continually is how to negotiate all of the little issues, the accidental words, the misunderstood glances, the tiredness, the fatigue, and the insecurities that are natural to us as human beings in this mortal state. Forgiving each other, as well as forgiving ourselves, is critical to creating and maintaining a good working relationship as well as our love connection, both of which are vital for inviting the Holy Spirit into our family.

Reflections

Even though I knew that bad things happen to good people, I was never prepared to be the protagonist in a case of infidelity. I will never forget the day my husband called me at work, crying, to tell me we needed to talk. As he revealed to me that he had recently been unfaithful, following years of consuming soft pornography, my heart sunk. Why me? How could I not have seen this coming? However, as he sobbed and apologized for the mistakes he had made, the spiritual guidance I received was that I needed to stand strong with him as he went through the process of repentance and that my children needed me to work on forgiving him. The next few months were filled with humbling spiritual experiences; absolute honest communication; rereading of our journals, reminding us why we fell in love in the first place; and a beautiful understanding of how repentance and forgiveness work. As hurt as I was, I knew he was also hurting, and we both needed each other to heal. Throughout the process, I was also reminded of how strong I really am and that our Heavenly Father knows how much each person can withstand. A couple of years have now passed, and time has helped diminish the pain as we work on making our marriage stronger by practicing daily acts of forgiveness.

in forgiveness we pardon or excuse someone for a misdeed against us. It is important to note that they don't suggest that one should approve of bad behavior or that bad behavior in and of itself should be considered okay. Forgiveness is absolving the offender from any further responsibility—or future grudges or retaliation—for the hurt they have caused us.

Researchers have identified various levels of forgiveness specificity. For example, trait forgiveness is a generally consistent attitude of forgiveness or a tendency to forgive that occurs across relationships, offenses, and situations. Dyadic forgiveness is focused on forgiveness of your spouse across multiple offenses. And offense-specific, or episodic, forgiveness is a single act of forgiveness for a specific offense within a particular interpersonal context.[5] Each of these types of forgiveness becomes relevant in the marital relationship as we seek to have a general Christlike attitude of forgiveness, to be willing to daily forgive the mundane, and to forgive the more difficult, significant grievances. To further explore forgiveness, it can be helpful to consider what forgiveness is *not*. Forgiveness is not just reducing hostile feelings toward the offender, or "reducing unforgiveness,"[6] so that one is *less* hurt or *less* angry. Forgiveness is not just forgetting about the offense; condoning the offense; or reconciling without addressing the offense in some way, either working through it intrapersonally or working through it interpersonally. Forgiveness is not just ignoring the offense. Nor is it offering *counterfeit* forgiveness to absolve our spouse of the offense by verbally offering forgiveness to them quickly without actually working forgiveness in our heart—in that, we have not truly forgiven them.[7] Forgiveness is not acceptance; one can accept the realities of the hurtful circumstance without "a more encompassing softening of feelings on the part of the offended spouse toward the offender, including an increase in positive feelings and behaviors toward the offender."[8]

Lastly, forgiveness is not *conditional* forgiveness. Conditional forgiveness is illustrated by ideas such as "Before I can forgive others, they must apologize to me for the things they have done" and "Before I can forgive others, they must promise not to do the same thing again." Forgiveness researchers explain that although apologies and the like can ease the forgiveness process,

> if these acts of contrition are viewed as necessary conditions

Reflections

After having been morally unfaithful to my wife, there had to be a time of cleansing and healing. The hurt to my wife was hard to soothe. A hand-written letter beginning with the four important words "I am so sorry" was the beginning. Pride and selfishness caused the sin, and having to write the words took a great deal of humility on my part. She responded of course with tears; many tears had been shed before, but this apology seemed to be the beginning of fewer tears on my wife's part. I felt like a terrible and worthless person. She then actually started to buoy me up. Her feelings of value as a woman had been badly hurt, and her actions to help strengthen me seemed to help her with her own feelings of self-worth. The apology was just the beginning to start to release the pain; sadness still continued but diminished over time. We had more talks about how each of us felt on a deeper level, rather than just skirting those issues. It was hard for me to do that, as it can be a "digging down" experience, and I don't like that. She realized that it was hard for her also. Praying together for strength for each other was so helpful, partly because of the words uttered and also because of the heavenly help given. We realized that the Atonement was to help the sinner (me) but also to relieve pain for those sinned against (her).

or prerequisites required before forgiveness can be offered, then there will likely be fewer instances of forthcoming forgiveness for that individual. This is due simply to the fact that those who cause an offense will not always fulfill such conditions, regardless of their appropriateness, and the offended party does not have the power to make them occur. Conceptualizing these responses as requirements for forgiveness also prevents access to forgiveness for those who are unable to identify whether acts of contrition are occurring, for instance, in cases where the wrongdoer is deceased or no longer present for other reasons.[9]

We have sought to teach true forgiveness in our own home. When our three youngest children were all toddlers trying to learn to navigate their world and their interactions with others, there was a lot of screaming and hitting among them. When one toddler hit another, we required them to serve a time-out to help them calm down, and then they had to give the offended child a hug and a kiss and say they were sorry. The injured party then had the responsibility to say to the offending sibling, "I forgive you." This was so frequent an occurrence that our children got very good at this exchange so that even while they were still young, they were able to bestow forgiveness upon their siblings without any prompting from us. It is a heartwarming sound to hear a child say in their sweet little voice: "I forgive you." How much more heartwarming to hear spouses say it to each other in a genuine effort to reconcile and reconnect.

In contrast to this, in our current culture, when there has been an offense the interchange often goes differently—the offending party quickly says something to the effect of "I'm sorry," while the offended party quickly replies, with a downward glance and shrug of the shoulders, "It's okay." Although we all generally recognize that this exchange is made in an effort to move past a grievance, we assert that the words we use are vital and this exchange doesn't cut it. It is not just a matter of semantics. The response "It's okay" implies there was no problem with the person's behavior. Yet, really, it is *not* okay. It is not okay to slight, offend, reject, deceive, or do any of the myriad of other things we do to hurt each other. It is not okay and it is certainly not Christian. But, nevertheless, as mortals suffering the weakness of the flesh, it does happen, and, unfortunately for all of us, it happens quite frequently. We have all given offense and taken offense.

So what is the answer? The answer is that *although it is not okay, it can be forgiven.* The response "I forgive you" makes explicit the reality of the situation: "There was a problem with what you did, and it hurt me, but I choose not to let it hinder my regard for you or damage our relationship." So offering forgiveness to another is an advanced spiritual principle in that it requires the offended party to do more than just shrug it off, perhaps attempting to make light of something that was indeed quite painful. Instead, forgiveness requires disciplined effort of the offended party to pardon the negative effects that a fault had on them personally without excusing the fault itself.

Nephi illustrates for us the concept of true forgiveness. His brothers were extremely angry with him; they had put their hands on him to beat him, they had tied him up, and they had sought to kill him. Yet Nephi stated in his record, "And it came to pass that I did frankly forgive them all that they had done" (1 Nephi 7:21). Nephi chose to "frankly," or openly and freely, forgive his brothers of grievous offenses. They had abused him and sought to kill him, yet he did not wallow, nor did he justify and rationalize his own desire to be offended because of the grievousness of his brothers' crimes against him. Instead, he chose the better part and gave himself the gift of forgiveness. That forgiveness also became a motivator for his brothers that prompted them to then pray to God to ask Him for forgiveness. We, too, can choose to "frankly" forgive our spouse of both the small and grievous offenses.

Forgiveness in the Marital Relationship

Forgiving our spouse is required by our Savior, Jesus Christ. In exchange for offering us His great mercy, the Lord imposes upon us a requirement that we in turn extend forgiveness to our fellow human beings: "I, the Lord, will forgive whom I will forgive, but of you it is required to forgive all men" (D&C 64:10). As often as our spouse sins against us, we are obligated to forgive. Our Savior taught in Matthew 18:21–22: "Then came Peter to him, and said, Lord, how oft shall my brother sin against me, and I forgive him? till seven times? Jesus saith unto him, I say not unto thee, Until seven times: but, Until seventy times seven."

In a BYU devotional, Elder Lynn G. Robbins of the Seventy shared a story of how both repentance and forgiveness are required of us. He used the example of an abusive marriage.

> In this scenario of the abused wife, we have two parties—the abusive husband and the victim-wife, both of whom need divine help. Alma teaches that the Savior suffered for both: for the sins of the man and for the anguish, the heartache, and pain of the woman (see Alma 7:11–12; Luke 4:18).
>
> To access the Savior's grace and the healing power of His Atonement, the Savior requires something from both of them.
>
> The husband's key to access the Lord's grace is *repentance*. If he doesn't repent, he cannot be forgiven by the Lord (see D&C 19:15–17).
>
> The wife's key to access the Lord's grace and to allow Him to help her is *forgiveness*. Until the wife is able to forgive, she is choosing to suffer the anguish and pain that He has already suffered on her behalf. By not forgiving, she unwittingly denies His mercy and healing.[10]

We read in Doctrine and Covenants 64:8–10 that in His day, the Lord chastened those that did not forgive. President Spencer W. Kimball, in his seminal volume *The Miracle of Forgiveness*, commented on these verses:

> The lesson stands for us today. Many people, when brought to a reconciliation with others, say that they forgive, but they continue to hold malice, continue to suspect the other party, continue to dis-

Reflections

Growing up, my family life was filled with much strife, contention, and unforgiveness, culminating in my parents' divorce when I was about twelve years old. I decided at a young age that I would choose differently because that culture invited misery rather than happiness into our lives. In my own married life today, I am often frustrated with my wife and often frustrated with myself as I sometimes emulate that early negative training of my childhood, despite my conscious choice to follow the better path. Yet I am grateful to be able to rediscover on a daily basis that only through the sweet gifts of forgiveness and mercy can peace and abundant love fill our home with the inspiration and tremendous joy that we need in our precious family! As I learn to forgive my wife daily, even "seventy times seven," I always find the sweet "peace that passeth all understanding" and joy to overflowing in my sacred relationship with her! Besides, doesn't she have to live with and forgive me of my myriad of weaknesses daily? And am I not freely forgiven hourly by a merciful Savior who gave everything for me so I could repent and learn to be like Him? This is why I choose forgiveness in my marriage, and I learn to love my wife more eternally every day!

believe the other's sincerity. This is sin, for when a reconciliation has been effected and when repentance is claimed, each should forgive and forget, build immediately the fences which have been breached, and restore the former compatibility.[11]

Over the course of a lifetime together, each of us, being imperfect, will quite assuredly say or do things that will hurt our spouse. When forgiveness is applied, openness and love flow freely. In the Church, we often talk about the importance of having the Spirit. The gift of the Holy Ghost is closely linked to the marital relationship. When the relationship is going well, there is a freeing feeling about life and a closeness to the Spirit that is natural. However, when contention enters into a marriage, the Holy Ghost will often leave and, until there is forgiveness and reconciliation, the Spirit remains withdrawn.

We have experienced this many times over the years. When there is conflict between us, our spirits are uneasy, and we have little positive energy for the other things in our lives, such as caring for our children or serving in the Church. Forgiveness frees us up from bitter feelings and negativity that sap our energies. It allows us to get back to building a life consistent with our values and allows us to reconnect with the Holy Spirit and with each other.

How do we forgive our spouse when there has been conflict or when they have hurt us? As Joseph Smith illustrated for us, he spent a long time in prayer seeking a humble heart. Once he was able to feel his heart soften, he then went to his wife to ask her forgiveness—he talked to her and sought reconciliation. This is the greatest secret to learning how to forgive: our own efforts to forgive need to work in concert with the power of our Savior. Forgiveness is a gift of the Spirit. When the synergistic partnership of our humble heart and willingness to follow God is added to His all-powerful, yet merciful, grace, it will bring about true forgiveness. Indeed, in large measure, forgiveness requires purposeful efforts such as scripture study, fasting, pondering, and prayer to access the healing that the Spirit can offer us by virtue of the Atonement of Jesus Christ. Through Christ, we can forgive even the most grievous offenses we endure.

Corrie ten Boom had suffered in concentration camps during World War II. After the war, she gave lectures of her experiences, speaking of healing and forgiveness possible only through Jesus Christ. On one occa-

Reflections

After ten years of marriage, it still amazes me how relatively small disagreements can make me feel like I have made no progress in my marriage, like my marriage is hanging by a thread only kept from snapping and shattering on the floor by some strange stroke of luck. I often find myself in justification mode shortly after one of these encounters, recounting the many supposed grievances against me. "I didn't get what I put in! What have I worked so hard for? How many times have I been the one to give in? My 'score' is so much higher!" After some time has passed, often after my wife has already moved on, I realize my shortsightedness. Did I ever really forgive anything? How could I have forgiven if I keep reliving incident after incident, feeling the anger, frustration, and hopelessness rise within me? It is in that moment that I remember my faith in the Atonement of Christ. If I can't forgive my wife for petty infractions, can I really forgive myself? Do I really believe that there is a power that can heal and unite us in a celestial manner? I repent, try my best, and move on.

sion she spoke at a church service in Munich, Germany. Here she
encountered for the first time one of her own jailers; this man
had stood guard at the shower-room door in the processing center at Ravensbrück, Germany. He approached her as the service
ended:

> "How grateful I am for your message, *Fraulein*[,]" he said. "To think
> that, as you say, He has washed my sins away!"
>
> His hand was thrust out to shake mine. And I, who had
> preached so often . . . the need to forgive, kept my hand at my side.
>
> Even as the angry, vengeful thoughts boiled through me, I saw
> the sin of them. Jesus Christ had died for this man; was I going
> to ask for more? Lord Jesus, I prayed, forgive me and help me to
> forgive him.
>
> I tried to smile, I struggled to raise my hand. I could not. I
> felt nothing, not the slightest spark of warmth or charity. And so
> again I breathed a silent prayer. Jesus, I cannot forgive him. Give
> me Your forgiveness.
>
> As I took his hand the most incredible thing happened. From
> my shoulder along my arm and through my hand a current seemed
> to pass from me to him, while into my heart sprang a love for this
> stranger that almost overwhelmed me.
>
> And so I discovered that it is not on our forgiveness any more
> than on our goodness that the world's healing hinges, but on His.
> When He tells us to love our enemies, He gives, along with the
> command, the love itself.[12]

This deeply felt exchange beautifully illustrates the very real
challenge that lies before us. Through Jesus Christ it is possible to forgive those who have abused us, lied to us, cheated on
us, disrespected us, and the like. Yet, admittedly, as we saw with
Corrie ten Boom, with deep pains such as these, forgiveness may
be impossible if we try to rely alone upon on our own efforts.
We must take our Savior's forgiveness as our own. The power of
Christ and His graceful Atonement makes obtaining this type
of love—this charity—possible, even for those who have severely
wounded us. President Dieter F. Uchtdorf observed that when we
choose to fill our hearts with the love of God, it becomes easier to
love others, and feelings of anger or hatred dissipate.[13]

Avoiding Offense

As we focus on how the Savior can help us forgive, we can help ourselves by learning to avoid offense in the first place. For example, keeping things in proper perspective can do wonders for not feeling offense in the first place or for forgiving a felt offense: "Did my spouse intend to hurt my feelings?" or "What was the motive behind this behavior?" Oftentimes through this simple evaluation we come to see that our spouse did not intend malice or try to hurt us but was simply thoughtless or careless and in the process caused us pain. It is often not difficult to forgive these types of minor, unintentional offenses. The following personal story provides an illustration.

DEBRA: *When Richard was called to be a bishop, we worked to set some boundaries around his service so he could serve ward members while also respecting the needs of the family. One of those boundaries was that he would not text or take phone calls at dinner time. One evening, Richard was supposed to take a babysitter home so we could sit down and eat dinner together as a family, but all of a sudden, I found him absorbed in a private phone call. As I tried to encourage him to take the babysitter home while I finished up food preparations, he waved me off and disappeared into the bedroom. This left me to take the babysitter home and eat dinner alone*

Reflections

My father sexually abused me from the age of twelve to seventeen. During and after the abuse, I never blamed God, but I blamed the closest person to me: my husband. I had a brattiness to me which helped me get through the abuse, but it did not help me in my marriage. If my husband hurt me, I wanted to get back at him; I wanted to hurt him more. I knew I was hurting him, and I didn't know how to stop because I had so much built-up emotion. Doing forgiveness work, I was able to see how truly sick my father was and came to have true empathy for him. My husband said that as I went through the forgiveness process my countenance changed. The Holy Ghost let me know I truly forgave my dad. As a result, I was able to be a kinder, nicer, softer person. I was no longer having to blame anyone or hurt anyone because of my abuse. As much as I changed and was happier, my husband was even happier! Things that would bug me or make me upset didn't make me upset anymore; he didn't have to walk on pins and needles around me. I was serving him in ways I had never done before. I was not afraid to be vulnerable, and the trust between us grew.

with the children—and then the cabbage was soggy. I felt angry about this but then chose to do my own work on the issue. I told myself that since Richard was pretty good about respecting the boundaries that were set around his ecclesiastical service, I would not begrudge him for choosing to follow the Spirit if he felt prompted to answer this particular call. As I worked through this, my initial instinct to give him a piece of my mind faded. I determined to give him the benefit of the doubt, let it go, and not let it ruin the evening. I decided not to say a word about it.

Once Richard rejoined the family, we went on as if nothing out of the ordinary had occurred. Feeling bad about the situation, he felt a need to address it. He told me that he fully intended to honor family time and planned to call the person back later, but by mistake, he accidently pushed the "answer" button. Realizing his mistake, he immediately hung up. However, since the call had initially connected, the caller thought he was available to talk, so they called right back. Richard felt obligated to answer it due to his mistake. When he did, immediately there was distress on the other end, and he felt, of course, the need to soothe an upset ward member. I told him that I had been initially upset about it but figured something must have happened—period. I didn't do any more explaining. The situation was closed, having had no drama or escalation of conflict; I had forgiven the issue.

So what do we do when our spouse does something on purpose? Forgiveness is also necessary when the offense is known to have been purposeful or is very severe. In marriage, sometimes out of their own hurt, pride, or anger, or from their own self-deception or addiction, our spouse does things that knowingly hurt us—and we must in all honesty and humility acknowledge that sometimes we may do the same to them. First, we must remember that a purposeful offense does not always mean the offense was done with malicious intent. It may be helpful to check ourselves on assuming the motive we attribute to the offense to be correct. The malicious motive or intention that we often feel is fact (for example, "They did this because . . .") is frequently discovered not to be fact at all. Although the person admits to having done something purposefully, they often report that the reason they did it was for some other purpose than for the purpose we attributed to them (e.g., "I didn't think through the behavior and realize it would hurt you. In that moment, I didn't even think about how it would make you feel. I just acted out of my own focus on . . ." or "I knew it would hurt you, but I just didn't care in that moment because I was so . . ."). So we need to be very careful not to jump to conclusions.

Other strategies can also be helpful in trying to avoid being offended or in putting an offense into proper perspective to allow greater ease in forgiving and letting go. For example, reading scriptures and studying or listening to general conference talks on the topic of forgiveness can be very helpful in facilitating forgiveness. In addition, bringing our thoughts and motives into awareness through prayer, pondering, journaling, or talking with a trusted family member, friend, mentor, or therapist to work through any long-held resentments can be purging and healing. As we come to more fully understand our feelings, we can write a letter expressing those feelings (which may or may not be given to our spouse, but just writing it proves therapeutic), paint or do another artistic project to express our feelings, write down the resentments and then burn them or flush them down the toilet as a representation of the letting-go process, and so on.

These strategies generally utilize our own *Me* efforts. However, we can also work toward forgiveness as a couple (accessing the power of the *We*). There are a variety of research studies that address this issue, each with its own advocated steps toward forgiveness. One very detailed report is from a study in which researchers examined forgiveness in Christian couples. They found that one decision-based therapeutic forgiveness session with a counselor (about three hours long) was successful in promoting forgiveness, increasing marital satisfaction and decreasing depression.[14] This lengthy session involved thirteen steps divided into three sections: defining and preparing (Steps 1–3); seeking and granting forgiveness (Steps 4–12); and designing the ceremonial act (Step 13). To provide some specific structure about how we can work together toward forgiveness in our own

marriages, the thirteen steps are detailed below (please see original reference for thorough descriptors of each step, if desired).

Step 1: Definitions of forgiveness are discussed.

Step 2: The focus on each person having the opportunity to
seek forgiveness for his or her wrongful actions is established.

Step 3: Introduction to the forgiveness treatment and decision whether or not to participate.

Step 4: Statement of the offense.

Step 5: Offender provides explanation.

Step 6: Questions and answers about the offense.

Step 7: Offended person gives emotional reactions.

Step 8: Offender shows empathy and remorse for the hurt he
or she caused the other.

Step 9: Offender develops plan to stop and prevent behavior.

Step 10: Offended spouse shows empathy for the offender's
hurt.

Step 11: Emphasis on choice and commitment involved in letting go.

Step 12: Formal request for forgiveness.

Step 13: Ceremonial act.

The ceremonial act is a symbolic expression that the offense
has been formally and permanently forgiven (for example, writing down your grievances and burning them).[15]

The requirement to forgive is upon us. Therefore, we must
remember that these and other intrapersonal and interpersonal
efforts should be joined with the grace and mercy of our Savior,
Jesus Christ, by inviting Him into our forgiveness process.

The Challenge to Forgive

Most of us know that the need to forgive is an eternal truth, and
we theoretically believe we *should* forgive, but sometimes we may
still refuse to forgive our spouse for their offenses against us. Why
do we do this when it is contrary to not only God's command but

to our own personal beliefs and values? Some in Church circles may couch the answer in terms of pride, but we believe that the more general motivation in struggling to forgive is not that oppositional in nature. We believe that this defiance is motivated by deep hurt and excruciating pain. Simply put, we hurt and we don't want to hurt anymore—and doing the *work* of forgiveness means we must face and interact with the pain which we believe will hurt us more. In other words, refusing to forgive may really be borne from a self-protective instinct.

DEBRA: *One client came to me for psychotherapy having suffered for fifteen years relative to someone's abusive behavior toward her. The trauma bled into every aspect of her life, and she suffered in misery and depression. In the latter part of our therapy work together, I indicated that to fully move on in her life she would ultimately have to forgive. This client became very resistant and openly declared she did not want to forgive this person. She wanted to stay angry and hold on—in spite of the years of agony she had felt. Forgiveness felt very threatening to her— she believed that if she forgave she would be condoning or approving the abusive behavior, thus validating the abusive behavior and condemning her own sense of worth. She wanted justice and felt holding him accountable in her mind by failing to forgive was the only way she could assert personal power and reclaim her own sense of worth. Yet, paradoxically, she also knew that by failing to do so she was going to continue to be miserable.*

In examining forgiveness with me more closely, she realized she misunderstood the nature of forgiveness. She came to realize that by not forgiving this man and holding onto feelings of hatred, she was colluding with his evil rather than living consistent with the love she had sought to build into her life. She came to believe that forgiveness actually represented the condemnation of the behavior, not the approval of it—for if there had been nothing wrong with the behavior, then there would have been nothing to forgive. Forgiving this man, instead, represented her assertion that the behavior was wrong and that she was going to choose to rise above his darkness and bring love into her heart. Light came into her heart as she pondered, journaled, and discussed these ideas over some weeks. Forgiveness for this person soon followed, and more importantly, peace entered her heart at a

Gems

"Two traveling monks reached a town where there was a young woman waiting to step out of her sedan chair. The rains had made deep puddles and she couldn't step across without spoiling her silken robes. She stood there, looking very cross and impatient. She was scolding her attendants. They had nowhere to place the packages they held for her, so they couldn't help her across the puddle.

The younger monk noticed the woman, said nothing, and walked by. The older monk quickly picked her up and put her on his back, transported her across the water, and put her down on the other side. She didn't thank the older monk, she just shoved him out of the way and departed.

As they continued on their way, the young monk was brooding and preoccupied. After several hours, unable to hold his silence, he spoke out. 'That woman back there was very selfish and rude, but you picked her up on your back and carried her! Then she didn't even thank you!'

'I set the woman down hours ago,' the older monk responded. 'Why are you still carrying her?'"[17]

deep soul-touching level for the first time in fifteen years. The light that came into her eyes was beautiful.

As seen with this client, true forgiveness allows us to release any desire for justice and vengeance. In marriage, complete forgiveness also includes resisting the impulse to throw out an "'I told you so!" or "Remember when you did . . ." in a strategic moment; these kinds of comments may seem innocuous but truly betray deep bitterness and resentment. Elder Neil L. Andersen related this experience: "When Parley P. Pratt, in 1835, was judged unfairly, bringing embarrassment and shame to him and his family, the Prophet Joseph Smith counseled, 'Parley, . . . walk such things under your feet . . . [and] God Almighty shall be with you.'"[16] If we find that we cannot "walk such things under [our] feet" and find that we continue to think about a former misdeed of our spouse or we bring up a former hurt to our spouse during a new conflict, then we would be wise to soberly accept that our forgiveness is not yet complete—that we have more work to do. In an energetic discourse given to students at BYU, Jeffrey R. Holland described the dysfunctional relationship processes that often occur when spouses fail to truly forgive each other:

> I can't tell you the number of couples I have counseled who, when they are deeply hurt or even just deeply stressed, reach farther and farther into the past to find yet a bigger brick to throw through the window "pain" of their marriage. When something is over and done with, when it has been repented of as fully as it can be repented of, when life has moved on as it should and a lot of other wonderfully good things have happened since then, it is *not* right to go back and open up some ancient wound that the Son of God Himself died trying to heal.
>
> *Let people repent. Let people grow. Believe that people can change and improve.* Is that faith? Yes! Is that hope? Yes! Is it charity? Yes! Above all, it is charity, the pure love of Christ. If something is buried in the past, leave it buried. Don't keep going back with your little sand pail and beach shovel to dig it up, wave it around, and then throw it at someone, saying, "Hey! Do you remember *this*?" Splat!
>
> Well, guess what? That is probably going to result in some ugly morsel being dug up out of *your* landfill with the reply, "Yeah, I remember it. Do *you* remember *this*?" Splat.
>
> And soon enough everyone comes out of that exchange dirty and muddy and unhappy and hurt, when what God, our Father in Heaven, pleads for is cleanliness and kindness and happiness and healing.
>
> Such dwelling on past lives, including past mistakes, is just not right! It is not the gospel of Jesus Christ.[18]

One such type of *dwelling on past lives* often occurs in couples in which one or both spouses have struggled with pornography use. Pornography is very damaging to the marital relationship and creates high levels of distress and pain for the betrayed spouse. Spouses may struggle to forgive because the sexual nature of the discretion contrasts starkly with the high value we, as members of the Church, place on purity and sexual fidelity before and during marriage.

DEBRA: *One of my therapy clients shares her powerful story of working to forgive her husband for his pornography use:*

> I am a mental health therapist working with spouses of individuals who struggle with pornography addiction. The main focus

of therapy is to work through the spouse's betrayal trauma. Interestingly, I, too, am a spouse of someone who is recovering from a pornography addiction. Though our stories and experiences differ, my clients and I share feelings of hurt, pain, and betrayal. For me, a majority of my negative emotions stemmed from feeling like I deserved better. I lived a chaste, pure, moral life and hated that my spouse did not do the same.

I knew about my husband's addiction prior to our marriage but did not fully understand how it would impact our relationship. Years into marriage, I recognized growing anger, contempt, and disconnection . . . coming from me! I was angry and wanted to somehow teach him a lesson or punish him. I developed walls that prevented me from connecting with him. My husband rarely relapsed (with several months to a year of sobriety at a time), yet I was actively punishing him for the choices he made one to two decades earlier. Sadly, he had no idea why I was acting in this manner.

Years later, I began my own therapy to address this anger and inability to forgive. I wanted so badly to forgive my husband of his past, but I was hesitant because I still wanted my husband to "pay." Over several months of therapy, I explored my past and how multiple dimensions of my life led me to the decisions I did or did not make. I also examined my husband's life and recognized the lack of safety, support, and healthy connections or examples. I recognized his pain. I began to see him differently. I saw how his choices growing up were a symptom of a much bigger problem in his life.

Through this process my heart changed and I began to forgive. Though occasional feelings of pain and hurt pop up, my anger is gone! My resentment towards him has faded. My walls are breaking down and we are connecting in new, deeper, ways. Our marriage is far from perfect, but forgiveness has allowed me to give myself to the marriage and allow the relationship to progress. I am no longer actively halting our growth.

My client's story clearly illustrates for us all the negative consequences that come to us, and into our marital relationships, when we fail to forgive. These negative consequences became vital clues to her; they communicated to her a need to take seriously her own pain, as it had taken on a destructive power of its own. This prompted her to seek out assistance in order to work on the issues in a productive and healing way so she could learn to forgive her spouse, since she had been unable to do so on her own.

As seen here, when clues emerge in our own marriages that tell us our forgiveness work is not yet complete, it takes deep humility to accept the opportunity to work through the issue to complete the forgiveness process. This can be difficult, and it may take some time to humble ourselves enough to be willing to engage in the forgiveness process.

Such was my experience. While writing this chapter, I was prompted to recognize one lingering issue in our relationship that indicated a failure to completely forgive Richard. Shortly after becoming engaged, we attended a stake Valentine's dance. It was at this activity that Richard, then forty-four years old, announced his long-awaited engagement to his ward and stake members, who had been praying for many years on his behalf. I never really liked dancing, but that night I was feeling free and happy with the excitement of the engagement and danced without a care in the world.

Unbeknownst to me, after the dance Richard's anxiety about getting married escalated intensely; he didn't sleep and struggled with his anxiety all night. In the morning, he ended our engagement and even took back the wedding ring. Fortunately, in spite of this and other dramas, things eventually worked out and we were married. However, after many years of marriage, I noticed that I had not danced with Richard since that Valentine's activity. Since I don't like dancing anyway, my failure to fully recognize my resentment toward Richard had remained hidden; it was easy to turn down opportunities to dance without a second thought. However, as we wrote this chapter, I recognized the truth in my heart—I did not want to dance with Richard. The negativity was more toward Richard than it was toward the dislike of dancing, a significant clue to me that I needed to do some forgiveness work. Yet, in all honesty, I wasn't very humble; I didn't really want to forgive him because I was still so hurt, and I let the issue sit for many months.

As work on this book continued, I began to humble myself and accepted that I needed to do some purposeful forgiveness work to cleanse my heart. In an effort to work the forgiveness process, I prayed that Heavenly Father would help me to forgive Richard for hurting me so deeply years earlier. I also initiated several discussions with Richard about this experience and about dancing in general in which I expressed the sense of vulnerability and rejection I had felt. Those discussions provided an opportunity for Richard to be able to more fully explain his motivations; he assured me that the hurtful rejection had been about his own anxiety and had nothing to do with my own value and acceptability as a person, or anything to do with some negative evaluation of my carefree dancing that evening. I was able to ponder on these discussions over time.

As the forgiveness process unfolded, I felt some concern that I still had no desire to go dancing, in spite of my purposeful work to forgive. As we counseled together, Richard suggested that my continued indifference to dancing was because I didn't like dancing in the first place and that he believed, from all we had worked through in those months, that I had, by that time, forgiven him. The Spirit confirmed that in my heart, and I felt much lighter inside.

Before I engaged in the forgiveness work, I knew in my heart that I did not want to dance with Richard, but now I knew I just didn't want to dance. All resentment toward Richard surrounding the Valentine's rejection was gone, and I could say I had fully forgiven him and felt blessed for my efforts to do so.

Did you think of any unresolved issues from your own marriage as you read our struggle with forgiveness? What must you work through to allow the metaphorical air in your marriage to clear?

Self-Forgiveness

Self-forgiveness is also an important concept as we talk about the need to forgive. Researchers have examined the concept of self-forgiveness and have found that it is not only important intrapersonally, for ourselves, but important interpersonally in our marital relationship. It helps both parties to resolve an issue that has a potential for ongoing negative consequences.[19]

Yet some people are hard on themselves and have a difficult time letting go of things they have done to offend others, particularly their spouse. Sometimes it may be easier for us to forgive a spouse who may have wronged us and caused us pain than it is to extend that same forgiveness to ourselves when we have hurt our spouse, done wrong, or contributed to our own difficulties in some way. Some of us may be particularly condemning of ourselves. President Russell M. Nelson taught:

The reality of imperfection can at times be depressing. My heart goes out to conscientious Saints who, because of their shortcomings, allow feelings of depression to rob them of happiness in life.

We all need to remember: men are that they might have joy—not guilt trips![20]

We need to be mindful that using self-condemnation as a motivator to try to do better next time is not helpful and is promoted by the adversary. It will never motivate us to do better but rather will only tear us down. Elder Cecil O. Samuelson of the Seventy extended this idea, indicating "that being too hard on yourself when you make a mistake can be as negative as being too casual when real repentance is needed."[21] Upon recognizing these types of negative feelings, we can turn toward our Savior, seeking healing by way of His glorious Atonement. Rather than condemning ourselves, we would do well to "seek this Jesus" (Ether 12:41) and allow "our eyes [to] wait upon the Lord our God, until that he have mercy upon us" (Psalm 123:2). His healing power will enable us to forgive as He forgives.

The Cost of Unforgiveness

As we consider what we might do to forgive, it can be helpful to consider how to increase our motivation, desire, or willingness to do the work of forgiveness. One method is to consider the cost of not fully forgiving. We will discuss three costs of unforgiveness: damage to our physical health, internal or emotional suffering, and damage to our marriage relationship.

First, a significant cost of unforgiveness is damage to our physical health. Using a nationally representative data set of adults sixty-six years of age and older, researchers found that a failure to forgive can predict mortality. Specifically, these researchers found that conditional forgiveness was predictive of higher mortality. These researchers indicated that "physical health was identified as the sole unique mechanism bridging the connection between forgiveness and mortality."[22] In addition, researchers have found that our cardiac health is particularly impacted by failing to forgive.[23]

Second, another cost of unforgiveness is the acute mental or internal suffering it causes us. Lack of forgiveness is associated with poorer mental health outcomes, such as higher levels of anger, depression, anxiety, and vulnerability to substance use.[24]

Jack Kornfield, a writer on Buddhist psychology, related a story about students who were taught by a great teacher that if they were suffering during meditation they were holding on too tightly. He then made this commentary: "Suffering is like rope burn. We need to let go."[25]

When we hold on too tightly to our bitterness and resentment, failing to do the necessary work of forgiveness, we suffer and hurt. Unforgiveness traumatizes us, never allowing ourselves or our spouse the chance to move forward. In this unforgiveness, we create many additional problems that cause greater pain and even bring trauma into our lives. In other words, failing to forgive hurts a lot more and a lot longer than the pain of the original offense!

This cost of being unforgiving is illustrated using the psychological concepts of clean and dirty pain. Pain in life is inevitable and cannot be avoided; this is often called *clean pain*. Clean pain is the hurt of rejection, job loss, serious medical problems, difficulties with children, relationship difficulties, financial worries, and other such painful life events. *Dirty pain* constitutes dysfunctional attitudes (such as unwillingness, resistance, anger, bitterness, etc.) or behaviors (such as drinking, working long hours, picking an argument, binge eating, pornography use, etc.) that we layer on top of the clean pain because we don't want to deal with it. This extra junk causes more pain and more problems, above and beyond the pain and problems of the original issue. Here now we have taken a difficult clean-pain circumstance and, rather than dealing with it appropriately, created for ourselves a much more agonizing trauma with the addition of all the dirty pain.

We tend to do this to ourselves in a misguided effort to defend against the clean pain of life. We want to minimize, numb, ignore, or avoid the pain because, of course, it hurts and we do not want to hurt. Yet it is usually through those efforts of defense or avoidance that we get into the realm of dirty pain and the subsequent feelings of trauma. Steven Hayes, developer of acceptance and commitment therapy, and his colleagues have taught, "Psychological trauma is pain compounded by an unwillingness to experience the pain."[26] As we build things up in ourselves, they take on a presence in our lives that in no way resembles reality. These additional difficulties bleed into every aspect of our lives and onto the other people around us.

Yet, when we courageously choose to face clean pain and deal with it appropriately, with great relief we discover that the angst of dealing with the clean pain of forgiveness (or any other issue) usually proves to be much less than we had fantasized. Additionally, the clean pain is usually of shorter duration than we anticipated. If we are willing to push through the initial discomfort, we are always happier and healthier for having done the work. Our marriages will also be happier and healthier as we choose to address the necessary clean pain of the work of forgiveness.

Finally, when it comes to marriage, unforgiveness has a negative effect on marital well-being. In many ways, we put the quality of our marital relationship on the altar of sacrifice in order to indulge our pride and ego. Researchers studied couples who were in relatively new marriages as well as long-marrieds and found that wives' lower levels of benevolence and husbands' higher scores on avoidance created difficulty resolving conflicts.[27] One researcher commented that a "relationship may endure in the absence of forgiveness but it will not be completely restored to health."[28]

The Fruits of Forgiveness

To contrast our discussion on the costs of unforgiveness, let us now consider the marvelous physical, emotional, marital, and spiritual fruits that come into our lives and the lives of our spouses as we do the work to exercise genuine forgiveness.

The physical blessings of forgiveness have been well documented. Those that forgive report fewer health problems in general than those that do not forgive. As we discussed in the previous section, as unforgiveness puts our cardiac health at risk, forgiveness improves our heart health. Researchers have found that forgiveness impacts cardiovascular health by lowering heart rates and mean arterial pressure, particularly diastolic blood pressure.[29]

Forgiveness has also been found to predict a variety of positive mental health outcomes, such as reduced levels of anger, depression, anxiety, and vulnerability to substance use.[30]

There are many blessings of forgiveness for the marital relationship. Researchers have found that greater tendency for forgiveness predicted higher relationship satisfaction over time.[31] Studies have identified a variety of related positive outcomes of forgiveness in marriage, including the following: investment in marriage, marital commitment, marital longevity, dyadic adjustment, generally positive marital adjustment, positive interpersonal interactions, positive assumptions toward self and partner, psychological closeness with partner, empathy, and shared power in marriage.[32]

The spiritual fruits of forgiveness refine our hearts as we seek to emulate our Savior. Forgiveness is a purifying process. As we become purer, as we transform and become more like Him, it empowers us and enables us to be able to someday walk through heaven's gate. President Dieter F. Uchtdorf said, "Remember, heaven is filled with those who have this in common: They are forgiven. And they forgive."[33]

In this process of being ultimately purified and exalted, there are also very practical fruits that come to us right now as we exercise forgiveness in our marriage. These fruits of forgiveness are available first to the one extending forgiveness and then to the one receiving forgiveness.

First, when we have been injured and we extend loving forgiveness to our spouse for their misdeed against us, we ourselves become liberated. Elder David E. Sorenson of the Seventy taught:

> It can be very difficult to forgive someone the harm they've done us, but when we do, we open ourselves up to a better future. No longer does someone else's wrongdoing control our course. When we forgive others, it frees us to choose how we will live our own lives. Forgiveness means that problems of the past no longer dictate our destinies, and we can focus on the future with God's love in our hearts.[34]

Forgiveness eradicates the darkness of resentment, anger, and unforgiveness, and opens a space within our souls to receive a greater portion of the Spirit of God. Peace comes, sometimes for the first time in many decades. Love, within what has perhaps been a strained marital relationship, can begin to bloom again. "But the fruit of the Spirit is love, joy, peace, longsuffering, gentleness, goodness, faith, meekness, [and] temperance" (Galatians 5:22–23).

Second, when, as the guilty party, we receive forgiveness from our spouse, it frees us up to better ourselves and move forward in becoming more like our Savior, Jesus Christ. We are not held captive to past errors or even past sins and are allowed to flourish, if we so choose. The story of the Apostle Paul, formerly Saul, is a good example of this principle. Saul of Tarsus severely "persecuted the church of God" (Galatians 1:13), including being present at the stoning of Stephen (Acts 7:58). Yet he was forgiven for his grievous offenses; a name change to Paul represented the new life he began with his forgiveness and conversion to Jesus Christ. He became one of the greatest missionaries of all time, and his great testimony of Christ fills the pages of our New Testament.

The story of Paul is evidence of the power of forgiveness to propel the forgiven. It is also evidence of God's great power, mercy, and grace in forgiving, and that, in the words of Presbyterian publisher Charles Scribner, there is "no fall so deep that grace cannot descend to it."[35]

DEBRA: *Perhaps the best way to summarize these various fruits of forgiveness is with one word: freedom. Freedom for ourselves; freedom for our spouses. I felt tremendous freedom as I wrote to Richard on one of our wedding anniversaries: "The honest description is not that you and I have a perfect marriage; rather, it is that . . . we both try, we both forgive, and we both seek Christ's atoning power when we do share grievances. Thank you for your 'commitment to the covenant!' At this stage in our marriage I have a sense of stability I've never felt before in my life and it feels wonderful!"*

Conclusion

The Savior, Jesus Christ, while walking the dusty roads of Judea, taught the principle of forgiveness on numerous occasions. During one instance, He reminded several accusers of an adulterous woman, "He that is without sin among you, let him first cast a stone at her." One by one, the accusers walked away, leaving the woman and Jesus alone. With compassion, He spoke to her, saying, "Woman, where are those thine accusers? hath no man condemned thee? She said, No man, Lord. And Jesus said unto her, Neither do I condemn thee: go, and sin no more" (John 8:7–11).

The Prophet Joseph Smith understood this type of compassion and forgiveness when he said, "The nearer we get to our Heavenly Father, the more we are disposed to look with compassion on [others]—we feel that we want to take them upon our shoulders, and cast their sins behind our backs."[36]

As we choose to forgive, we make a choice *for* the life and health of our marriage. In doing so, the influence of the Spirit is allowed into our hearts and our relationship. The loyalty and trust cycle we discussed in chapter 2 is strengthened, and the security we experience promotes both intrapersonal and interpersonal peace, happiness, and freedom. Ultimately, it will promote our transformation into a more Christlike and charitable individual, which will make all the difference as we seek to strengthen and nurture our marital relationship.

Notes

1. Ruth Bell Graham, quoted in K. Q. Duane, "The Sacrament of Marriage—Ruth Bell Graham," *It's the Women, Not the Men! Surviving Feminism* (blog), 7 March 2015, kqduane.com/2015/03/07/the-sacrament-of-marriage-ruth-bell-graham/.

2. Marlin K. Jensen, "Loving with the Spirit and the Understanding" (devotional address, Brigham Young University, Provo, UT, 28 March 1993), http://speeches.byu.edu/talks/marlin-k-jensen_loving-spirit-understanding/.

3. Nathaniel G. Wade, Donna C. Bailey, and Philip Shaffer, "Helping Clients Heal: Does Forgiveness Make a Difference?," *Professional Psychology: Research and Practice* 36, no. 6 (2005): 634–41.

4. "Forgiveness," The Church of Jesus Christ of Latter-day Saints, 2015, https://www.lds.org/topics/forgiveness?lang=eng.

5. Michael E. McCullough, William T. Hoyt, and K. Chris Rachal, "What We Know (And Need to Know) About Assessing Forgiveness Constructs," in *Forgiveness: Theory, Research, and Practice*, ed. Michael E. McCullough, Kenneth I. Pargament, and Carl E. Thoresen (New York: Guilford Press, 2000), 65–90.

6. Nathaniel G. Wade and Everett L. Worthington Jr., "Overcoming Unforgiveness: Is Forgiveness the Only Way to Deal With Unforgiveness?," *Journal of Counseling and Development* 81 (2003): 343–53.

7. Rory C. Reid and Dan Gray, *Confronting Your Spouse's Pornography Problem* (Sandy, UT: Silverleaf Press, 2006), 147–48.

8. Jana Anderson and Rajeswari Natrajan-Tyagi, "Understanding the Process of Forgiveness after a Relational Hurt in Christian Marriages," *Journal of Couple & Relationship Therapy* 15, no. 4 (2016): 317.

9. Loren L. Toussaint, Amy D. Owen, and Alyssa Cheadle, "Forgive to Live: Forgiveness, Health, and Longevity," *Journal of Behavioral Medicine* 35, no. 4 (2012): 383.

10. Lynn G. Robbins, "Be 100 Percent Responsible" (BYU Education Week devotional, Brigham Young University, Provo, UT, 22 August

2017), https://speeches.byu.edu/talks/lynn-g-robbins_be-100-percent
-responsible/.

11. Spencer W. Kimball, *The Miracle of Forgiveness* (Salt Lake City: Bookcraft, 1969), 262–63.

12. Corrie ten Boom, *The Hiding Place* (New York: Bantam Books, 1971), 238.

13. Dieter F. Uchtdorf, "The Merciful Obtain Mercy," *Ensign*, May 2012, 70–77.

14. Frederick A. DiBlasio and Brent B. Benda, "Forgiveness Intervention with Married Couples: Two Empirical Analyses," *Journal of Psychology and Christianity* 27, no. 2 (2008): 150–58.

15. Frederick A. DiBlasio, "Christ-Like Forgiveness in Marital Counseling: A Clinical Follow-Up of Two Empirical Studies," *Journal of Psychology and Christianity* 29, no. 4 (2010): 291–300.

16. Neil L. Andersen, "Never Leave Him," *Ensign*, November 2010, 40.

17. Jon J. Muth, "A Heavy Load," in *Zen Shorts* (New York: Scholastic Press, 2005), 30–33.

18. Jeffrey R. Holland, "Remember Lot's Wife: Faith Is for the Future" (devotional address, Brigham Young University, Provo, UT, 13 January 2009), http://speeches.byu.edu/talks/jeffrey-r-holland_remember-lots
-wife/.

19. Sara Pelluchi et al., "Self-Forgiveness in Romantic Relationships: It Matters to Both of Us," *Journal of Family Psychology* 27, no. 4 (2013): 541–49.

20. Russell M. Nelson, "Perfection Pending," *Ensign*, November 1995, 86.

21. Cecil O. Samuelson Jr., "Testimony," *Ensign*, May 2011, 41.

22. Toussaint, Owen, and Cheadle, "Forgive to Live," 383.

23. Loren L. Toussaint and Alyssa C. D. Cheadle, "Unforgiveness and the Broken Heart: Unforgiving Tendencies, Problems Due to Unforgiveness, and 12-Month Prevalence of Cardiovascular Health Conditions," in *Religion and Psychology*, ed. Michael T. Evans and Emma D. Walker (New York: Nova Publishers, 2009).

24. See for review: Jonathan R. Olson et al., "Shared Religious Beliefs, Prayer, and Forgiveness as Predictors of Marital Satisfaction," *Family Relations* 64, no. 4 (October 2015): 519–33.

25. Jack Kornfield, *The Wise Heart: A Guide to the Universal Teachings of Buddhist Psychology* (New York: Bantam Books, 2009), 247.

26. Steven C. Hayes, Kirk D. Strosahl, and Kelly G. Wilson, *Acceptance and Commitment Therapy: An Experiential Approach to Behavior Change* (New York: Guilford Press, 1999), 251.

27. Frank D. Fincham, Steven R. H. Beach, and Joanne Davila, "Forgiveness and Conflict Resolution in Marriage," *Journal of Family Psychology* 18, no. 1 (2004): 72–81.

28. Stephen T. Fife, Gerald R. Weeks, and Jessica Stellberg-Filbert, "Facilitating Forgiveness in the Treatment of Infidelity: An Interpersonal Model," *Journal of Family Therapy* 35 (2013): 343–67.

29. See for review: Frank D. Fincham, Ross W. May, and Marcos A. Sanchez-Gonzalez, "Forgiveness and Cardiovascular Functioning in Married Couples," *Couple and Family Psychology: Research and Practice* 4, no. 1 (2015): 39–48.

30. See for review: Olson et al., "Shared Religious Beliefs, Prayer, and Forgiveness," 519–33.

31. Scott Braithwaite et al., "Trait Forgiveness and Enduring Vulnerabilities: Neuroticism and Enduring Vulnerabilites: Neuroticism and Catastrophizing Influence Relationship Satisfaction via Less Forgiveness," *Personality and Individual Differences* 94 (2016): 237–46.

32. See for review: Olson et al., "Shared Religious Beliefs, Prayer, and Forgiveness," 519–33.

33. Uchtdorf, "Merciful Obtain Mercy," 77.

34. David E. Sorenson, "Forgiveness Will Change Bitterness to Love," *Ensign*, May 2003, 12.

35. Johann Peter Lange, ed., *Lange's Commentary on the Holy Scriptures*, vol. 8 (Grand Rapids, MI: Zondervan, 1960), 24.

36. Joseph Smith, "History, 1838–1856, volume C-1 Addenda," 74, The Joseph Smith Papers, http://www.josephsmithpapers.org/paper -summary/history-1838-1856-volume-c-1-addenda/74.

PART 2

The *We* in Marriage

THE *WE* IN MARRIAGE

*Almost all marriages could be beautiful, harmonious, happy,
and eternal ones, if the two people primarily involved would
determine that it should be, that it must be, that it will be.*
—*Spencer W. Kimball*[1]

As we strengthen our individual resolve to build our marriage, as discussed in part 1, we may wonder, What do people in good marriages do between themselves that makes their marriage good? Part 2 discusses the *We* in the covenant of marriage, the interpersonal ("inter-" meaning "between") contributions for building marriage. It examines the doing of marriage and offers practical marital enhancement principles to assist couples in their journey toward perfection. We discuss the salient issues of emotional intimacy, sexual relations, conflict, and finances in the partnership of marriage.

CHAPTER 5

CLOSE TO YOU

Fostering Emotional Intimacy

One of the *We* aspects of marriage is emotional intimacy; couples must work together to build emotional intimacy to achieve an eternal-quality type marriage. Although there are many different definitions of intimacy, they all have one aspect in common: connecting and experiencing deep bonds of closeness with your spouse through interpersonal communication.[2] Couples vary in their levels of emotional intimacy: some are like hostile enemies; some are indifferent associates; others are like college roommates, good friends, or even best friends; and some are lovers in every sense of the word, both emotionally and physically. Couples in thriving marriages have high expectations regarding emotional intimacy, in which they aim for the ideal: to love their spouse as God loves, wholly and with every possible facet of their being.

Sadly, some couples are in real trouble when it comes to having any type of genuine emotional intimacy; we have observed couples that just plod along and coexist without any effort to make any deep connections. Elder Neal A. Maxwell observed that "co-existence is not real brotherhood" and if a couple is only coexisting in the same living space—living, in essence, parallel lives—it does not a marriage make.[3] Judith Wallerstein and Sandra Blakeslee have written that marriages that do "not provide nurturance and restorative comfort can die of emotional malnutrition."[4]

By contrast, the path of marriage is God's plan to ultimately exalt us, and therefore it is expected that we will do more than just coexist or live parallel lives in our marriage. Building emotional intimacy is necessary to achieve a thriving eternal marriage. This chapter will discuss the reasons why emotional intimacy is vital in marriage and will present ways in which couples can grow emotionally together, including building communication skills, learning each other's love languages, increasing positive feelings, continuing courtship, and establishing shared meaning or purpose.

Equal Partners to Support Each Other

The principle of emotional intimacy was taught first to Adam and Eve. Eve was given to Adam as his "help meet." As husband and wife, we are the help *meet* for each other. Often we have seen people combine those words talking about Eve as a helpmeet or helpmate to Adam. In the scriptures, they are found as two distinct words: "help meet" (See Genesis 2:18, 20; Abraham 5:14, 21; Moses 3:18, 20). The word *meet* means appropriate or equal to the task. President Russell M. Nelson provided a clear understanding of this term, "From the rib of Adam, Eve was formed (see Genesis 2:22; Moses 3:22; Abraham 5:16). . . . The rib signifies neither dominion nor subservience, but a lateral relationship as partners, to work and to live, side by side."[5] Thus, as husband and wife, we are perfectly suited to partner with each other in working, or striving, toward perfection.

In life's tremendous undertakings, we need a partner in whom we are emotionally connected and in whom we can trust and feel comfortable leaning on when the fatigue of the journey

sets in. Ecclesiastes 4:9–11 teaches, "Two are better than one; because they have a good reward for their labour. For if they fall, the one will lift up his fellow: but woe to him that is alone when he falleth; for he hath not another to help him up. Again, if two lie together, then they have heat: but how can one be warm alone?"

This type of partner is not found in our business relationships, in which we are meeting each other fifty-fifty in contractual obligations; it will only be found in a covenant relationship in which we each give 100 percent. The *only* covenant relationship we have with another person is the marital relationship we have with our spouse.[6] We are to make our marriage a living, eternal relationship. As such, our Father in Heaven expects husbands and wives to be emotionally tied and interdependent in supporting each other through life's joys and life's refining fires.

Missionary companionships can be seen as a type and shadow for the marriage relationship. Book of Mormon missionary companions Alma and Amulek illustrate for us the concept of supporting each other in our respective needs and trials. In Alma 8, Alma returns to the land of Ammonihah to preach, and

Reflections

Strains in a marriage can happen even after more than two decades together. I have a demanding job and have served in busy priesthood leadership callings for most of our marriage. The intensity of those combined demands kicked into high gear for a prolonged period; I was having a difficult time managing the stress and was very unhappy and felt trapped by my obligations. Rather than open up to my wife, I kept it all bottled up so that she wouldn't worry. I became aloof. My wife and family got the short end of the stick and were the easy outlet for my frustration. Pride kept me from sharing my struggles with my wife because I was always the person that "kept it all together." It created a wedge in our marriage. After struggling for a significant period of time, I humbled myself and opened up to my wife. It was only after I was willing to be emotionally vulnerable that our relationship began to heal. The problems haven't completely gone away, but my eternal companion is now at my side, where she should be, supporting me. It is like a light being switched on in a darkened room—hope and happiness have returned.

approaches Amulek to ask, "Will ye give to an humble servant of God something to eat?" (verse 19). Amulek receives him into his house and gives him bread and meat (verse 21). Alma ate "and was filled" (verse 22). Amulek, knowing that Alma had fasted for many days, was sensitive to his needs and allowed Alma to stay with him for many days (verse 27).

As we know, Amulek then became Alma's missionary companion. In doing this, Amulek, "for the word of God," gave up his riches and was "rejected by those who were once his friends and also by his father and kindred" (Alma 15:16). Amulek had lost everything. "Alma having seen all these things" (verse 18) was sensitive to Amulek's plight and lovingly reciprocates the care that Amulek had given to him previously: "Therefore he took Amulek and came over to the land of Zarahemla, and took him into his own house, and did administer unto him in his tribulations, and strengthened him in the Lord" (verse 18).

In our marital relationships, we will need to be aware of and sensitive to the needs of our spouse. We will need to work to create a trust and intimacy upon which we can each rely. If our spouse does not feel close to us, does not feel like we care about them on an intimate level, or doesn't trust us to be able to handle the sensitive material of their lives, then they will likely not choose to share their deepest feelings and involve us in their significant life decisions. The quality of the marital relationship deteriorates when spouses fail to connect to each other in deeply meaningful ways.

Intimacy Is Important for Both Sexes

Culturally and historically, there is a common stigma that women need emotional intimacy more than men. However, men also need warm and intimate relationships in order to flourish in their lives. Some may not necessarily realize or even accept this, but there is research that bears this out.

The Grant study, coordinated by George Vaillant, has become the longest longitudinal study ever done on the lives of men. For more than seventy-five years it has studied Harvard men recruited from the classes of 1939–44. Its purpose was to find what lead to an "optimum life."[7] Ten life accomplishments were identified as factors predicting a man's ability to be a well-adjusted, successful adult. One of these was having a good marriage. They also identified the importance of other emotionally intimate relationships, such as those with mothers, fathers, siblings, and close friends.

The power of these intimate relationships influenced very real aspects of the men's lives, such as income and personal happiness. Relative to income, although all of the study participants entered the workforce with an education from Harvard University, the fifty-eight men who had the highest scores regarding warm relationships made about $150,000 more per year than did the thirty-one men in the study with the worst scores on relationships.[8] Relative to personal happiness, the most successful marriage in the Grant study also produced the happiest man in the study.[9] "In short, it was the capacity for intimate relationships that predicted flourishing in all aspects of these men's lives."[10]

Continuing with the findings from the Grant study, it was shown that the happiest couple in their study, Mr. and Mrs. Chipp (a pseudonym), enjoyed doing a variety of activities together, such as reading, sailing, taking yearly canoeing trips, and walking together. They talked openly about life issues. They kept a sense of humor with each other, even at times of conflict. They depended on each other "just by being there."[11] They rated the quality of their marriage highly for decades, and at age eighty Mr. Chipp proudly told interviewers, "I've lived happily ever after."[12] Vaillant concluded, "The more the men became able to appreciate shared dependence as an opportunity rather than a threat, the more positive feelings they expressed about their marriages."[13]

These opportunities are available to both men and women within the marital relationship. Happiness and joy come when we allow ourselves to be open to our spouse and truly connect in a genuine, validating, and intimate way. What follows is a discussion of some basic practices needed to foster and build emotional intimacy with our spouse.

Talking

Verbal connections are important to emotional intimacy. Yet men and women are generally so diverse in their needs in this area that the discrepancy has become an easy target for jokes and comic strips alike. The gender differences commonly seen in this area have become stereotyped—and for many couples, including ourselves, the stereotype is indicative of their true experience. A story from early in our marriage illustrates these discrepancies; we laugh at ourselves as we reflect back on this story, but we certainly weren't laughing when it happened.

RICHARD: *One evening early in our marriage while we were in our bedroom, Debra was sharing something with me that was a personal concern to her. I was actively listening for the first few minutes but began to grow impatient and to withdraw from the conversation because I had offered her my answer about the problem several times and thought we should be done. Yet Debra continued to talk about the issue from several different angles in order to process and wrap her head around it. Essentially, she shifted into a monologue to which I felt captive.*

After forty minutes, I metaphorically hit the wall, feeling like Debra was recycling the same thing over and over again, and I just couldn't handle it anymore. I made some impatient comment as I went into the bathroom. Debra was surprised and frustrated at my reaction and told me that she wasn't done yet and that I needed to continue to listen. I retorted back in irritation, "I've listened for forty minutes!" To this, Debra yelled back, "Well, this one just might take forty-five!"

We smile as we look back at that experience, because after years of marriage we have come a long way in moving toward a middle ground regarding verbal communication. I now do a much better job at listening and participating in the conversation when Debra wants to talk, knowing that she is using our conversation to help process her concerns rather than just wanting me to answer her problem. I also make a greater effort to share my thoughts or details about my life with Debra. In the meantime, Debra has shifted her approach as well, taking less time to talk through issues than she used to previously. Although we do not always satisfy each other's preferences completely, we have reached a healthy balance that accommodates both of us.

Talking and listening allow words and feelings to be communicated, which then helps spouses feel connected to each other. This has a great power in soothing, comforting, and lifting. Elder Richard G. Scott said:

> Do you tell your wife often how very much you love her? It will bring her great happiness. I've heard men tell me when I say that, "Oh, she knows." You need to tell her. A woman grows and is greatly blessed by that reassurance. Express gratitude for what your spouse does for you. Express that love and gratitude often. That will make life far richer and more pleasant and purposeful. Don't withhold those natural expressions of love. And it works a lot better if you are holding her close while you tell her.
>
> I learned from my wife the importance of expressions of love. Early in our marriage, often I would open my scriptures to give a message in a meeting, and I would find an affectionate, supportive note Jeanene had slipped into the pages. Sometimes they were so tender that I could hardly talk. Those precious notes from a loving wife were and continue to be a priceless treasure of comfort and inspiration.
>
> I began to do the same thing with her, not realizing how much it truly meant to her.[14]

Remembering the importance of words, we must each keep in mind that there is a difference between talking *to* our spouse and talking *with* our spouse. In Richard's story, we can see that Debra had gotten into a cycle of talking *to* Richard, and it was not useful in fostering intimacy. Psalm 55:14 tells us, "We took sweet counsel together, and walked unto the house of God in company." In this verse, the footnote on company says "or fellowship." As we talk with each other, bonds of connection grow and the feelings of fellowship deepen. Nephi illustrates this principle relative to how he managed his intimate relationship with the Lord: "And it came to pass that I, Nephi, returned from speaking *with* the Lord" (1 Nephi 3:1; emphasis added).

Martin Seligman delineates four choices we have in responding to the communications of others:

1. Active constructive communication is to respond authentically, enthusiastically, or supportively.

2. Passive constructive communication is to offer brief, unspecific support.

3. Passive destructive communication is to ignore the stimulus rather than addressing it.

4. Active destructive communication is to point out the negative aspects of the stimulus.[15]

Only the first of these options represents healthy, intimate discourse.

Thus, to build our relationship with our spouse, we want to seek to respond to them in an active constructive manner. For example, if our spouse says, "I got a new calling today!" we can respond with interest and caring: "Great! What are you going to be doing? What are your new responsibilities? How do you feel about it?" This type of communication will stimulate a conversation that creates opportunity to build intimacy and bonds of trust. If we fail to turn toward our spouse with this type of supporting interaction, we may unwisely respond with one of the other unhelpful and even destructive communications. In this example of the new calling, a passive constructive statement may be a simple "That's nice." That type of flat comment cuts the conversation to a very abrupt close. A passive destructive statement may work to change the conversation entirely: "You know, the fire alarm is beeping in the hallway again. I need you to replace the batteries." An active destructive comment may be intended to undermine and discourage your spouse as they begin a new phase of Church service: "I tell you, this new calling is going to take a lot of extra hours every week! And dealing with all those people is going to be nothing but drama!"[16]

As we work to respond and communicate with our spouse in an active constructive manner—thus improving the *process* of our communications—we need to be aware of the quality of the *content* we communicate. Talk can sometimes be cheap, and we want to avoid that pitfall as well. We want to be vulnerable and communicate about things of real importance to us, even things that make us feel vulnerable. For example, Douglas Brinley and Mark Ogletree, LDS marriage and family therapists and BYU religion professors, have taught that there are three levels of communication in marriage.[17] These include the superficial level that is informative and low risk; the personal level that shares deeper parts of ourselves, such as our goals and dreams; and the validating level in which we praise and compliment the other.[18] For a sense of intimacy to be present in the

Reflections

I realized some years ago that when my wife offered me counsel, I often fought against her suggestions because I felt inadequate or incompetent. As a result, my wife felt she could never offer any suggestions to improve our marriage or our family. Soon, we quit talking about the things that mattered most. My wife later revealed to me that she wanted to keep our conversations "safe," so we only discussed things like who would pick up the kids from soccer practice or take the dog to the vet. Deep down, I wanted my wife to be impressed with me. Therefore, every time she challenged an idea or had a better suggestion, I took it personally. I guess it was a blow to my ego.

marital relationship, husband and wife need to make sure their talking includes a balance between all three.[19]

Unfortunately, many couples keep their communication on the superficial level. Ogletree commented: "Superficial communication can supplant deep and meaningful conversations. If couples tiptoe around deeper issues that should be discussed, they will never learn to resolve conflict or connect with each other. Couples bond as they discuss things that matter—not things that don't. I have seen many couples in my practice who have tried to preserve their relationship by keeping their communication at the superficial level. By avoiding the "weightier matters" (Matthew 23:23), they have actually destroyed their marriage.[20]

Instead, we need to be willing to extend ourselves, opening ourselves up to communicating on the personal and validating levels as well. This requires some vulnerability on our part, and for some couples being vulnerable may feel risky or even threatening. Yet, for true intimacy to grow within our relationship, we must share ourselves and allow our spouse access to those parts of us that perhaps others in the world do not see. Those are the types of conversations that can assist in building greater emotional intimacy or even rekindling a sense of closeness that may be lost.

Listening

Talking is only one side of the verbal communication process that fosters an emotionally intimate relationship; we must also be responsive, compassionate listeners. If we remember that we have two ears but only one mouth, perhaps we will remember to use our ears more! Luke reminds us, "He that hath ears to hear, let him hear" (Luke 14:35).

One social science model called the interpersonal process model of intimacy explains that intimacy reflects two primary components: self-disclosure and partner responsiveness. The intimacy process is initiated when the speaker communicates personally relevant and revealing information to the listener, as discussed in the previous section. In return, the listener must respond to the specific content of the initial disclosure and offer understanding, validation, and caring for the speaker. For the interaction to feel intimate to the speaker, the speaker must be able to perceive or interpret the listener's responsiveness.[21] One writer commented on the significance of the speaker being "heard" by their spouse: "Being heard is akin to being loved; in fact, being listened to is one of the highest forms of respect and validation. By listening, we are saying to our spouse, 'You matter to me, I love you, and what you have to say is important.'"[22]

In order to successfully navigate the listening portion of our verbal communication, we must "be swift to hear, slow to speak" (James 1:19) and not listen with the intent to respond but with the intent to truly understand. Elder Neal A. Maxwell counseled, "Let us, therefore, define service to others as including genuine listening—a listening that is more than just being patient until it is our turn to speak; rather, a listening that includes real response, not simply nodding absorption."[23] This requires stillness or calmness in our demeanor.

As we are patient and work to stay present with our spouse during conversation, we must additionally lessen impulsivity, nervousness, or anxiety that makes us want to get our spouse to behave as we'd like in order to get them to conform to our needs. We must allow space for our spouse to communicate fully what they need to communicate without pressuring them to hurry up for *our* sake. Elder Maxwell continued:

> Let our service, at times, include a willingness to hold back in conversation when what we would have said has already been said—and perhaps better. To contribute . . . time and space, so that another can expand is to reflect quiet nobility. There are so many times when to forgo is to make way for another.[24]

It is important that we listen and ask clarifying questions about what our spouse is communicating. To do this requires that we learn to listen with a soft heart. "How vital is a 'listening heart'! The heart hears feelings while the mind attends to words. Often, what we are feeling needs to be heard even more than what we say."[25]

Listening with our heart requires discernment and sensitivity to the underlying messages or issues our spouse is seeking to convey; this may require careful attention to nonverbal communication from our spouse as well. This type of listening does not happen by accident. Listening with our heart requires humility to ask, What is my spouse really communicating? Perhaps a story about a difficulty at work is not really about work but about feeling vulnerable or incompetent. Maybe a diatribe about how hard it is to stay home with the kids is not about diapers or messy houses but a request for help or about feeling undervalued or personally stagnant. It would be excellent if our spouse could always explicitly communicate what they need from us during a particular exchange, but that is not always the case—sometimes they themselves may not know exactly what it is they need. So, as we listen with our hearts, the Spirit will guide us to know the true message our spouse is seeking to convey.

As we talk about using our hearts to listen, there is another aspect we must also consider: "To day if ye will hear his voice, harden not your hearts" (Hebrews 3:15). Sometimes, what we hear is difficult to hear. It may be difficult to hear our spouse talk about what we have done that has hurt them or to have them offer us correction in some way. Yet, if we listen with a soft heart, we will not take offense. We will not become defensive and then hijack the moment and launch into a rant that turns the tables and makes *them* listen to *us*. As we have done our part to listen, in time the natural rhythm of the discussion will allow us to then share our feelings about what we have heard. So we can trust that process and not jump in too quickly in order to react, rebut, retort, or retreat.

Love Languages

Talking and listening are just the start of building intimacy in marriage. The scriptures admonish us to "be ye doers of the word, and not hearers only" (James 1:22). Elder David A. Bednar counseled, "We should remember that saying 'I love you' is only a beginning. We need to say it, we need to mean it, and most importantly we need consistently to show it. We need to both express and demonstrate love."[26]

We can be most successful in demonstrating our love to our spouse when we do for them what *they* value rather than what we value. For example, when we extend love to our spouse in a manner that they value, the message is generally received as such: "I am reaching out to you because I want you to know that I love you." But, if we make an effort to connect in a manner our spouse does not highly value, the sincerity of our meaning may likely be lost. Since 1995, Gary Chapman's book *The Five Love Languages* has resonated with millions of people and has been clinically useful for therapists.[27]

DEBRA: *Indeed, the love language paradigm has been helpful to us in our own marriage and to many of my therapy clients. While Chapman's book*

Practice

If your spouse's love language is words of affirmation and yours is not, you may need to remind yourself. Gary Chapman suggests you remember the mantra "Words are important!" He also suggests activities such as writing a love letter (or love paragraph or even a love sentence) and giving it to your spouse, or complimenting your spouse in the presence of their family or friends.[30]

Reflections

My husband and I have been married over twenty years, and we still struggle with gift giving on Christmas and birthdays. I feel like I can buy "stuff" for myself anytime and would like my husband to think of something thoughtful to give me on these occasions. I'd be happy with a homemade gift as long as there was some kind of thought behind it. In return, I enjoy coming up with thoughtful gifts for my husband, things that show him how much I love and appreciate him. My husband is frustrated with this need I have because he feels like he has to come up with the perfect thoughtful gift or my holiday will be ruined. After an argument we had on Christmas Eve about seven years ago, we started buying our own gifts in order to avoid future Christmas Eve arguments and postbirthday disappointments. Yes, it's a little strange to buy, wrap, and then unwrap our own gifts, but it has made holidays and birthdays much easier—my husband doesn't have to stress about getting me the perfect gift, we get what we want and don't have to return or exchange items, and there are no expectations of one person doing something for the other that would be unfulfilled.

has been a success, we want to note here that there has been very little scientific testing of its claims. However, one study examining the five love languages did show a significant relationship with a commonly accepted relational maintenance scale.[28]

In his work, Chapman identified five ways that people communicate and receive communication of loving feelings: words of affirmation, quality time, receiving gifts, acts of service, and physical touch.[29] What is your love language? Consider how you would fill in the following blanks: "I find it most meaningful when my spouse does _____ for me"; "I find myself asking for _____."

What if our spouse's love language is words of affirmation, but for us talk really *is* cheap? What if our language is receiving gifts, so we spend a lot of time and energy planning and making a gift for our spouse, only to have them unenthusiastically say, "Oh, thanks," and set it aside? As discussed by Chapman, metaphorically speaking, if we speak Chinese and our spouse speaks French, then no matter how genuine and warm our efforts to communicate our sentiments are, if we don't learn some French and our spouse doesn't learn some Chinese, some subtle and nuanced communication is going to be missed. The missed communication is not necessarily because our spouse isn't trying to be loving, give us the benefit of the doubt, or understand us, but without some training in our language, our spouse perhaps *can't* understand us. Chapman addressed the confusion we experience when we find ourselves in this situation: "We are expressing our love, but the message does not come through because we are speaking what, to them, is a foreign language."[31]

If we have different love languages, we will want to learn each other's language "if we are to be effective communicators of love."[32] Once we learn and understand, we can then work throughout our marriage to practice speaking our spouse's language—purposefully using that knowledge by translating our messages of affection into our spouse's language.

DEBRA: *When we first married, I expressed to Richard that it was important to me to hear words of love; I needed to be told I was loved and that the things I did throughout my day to serve Richard and the family were noticed and appreciated. We established traditions of writing love letters to each other for particular special days in the year. Richard has had to work at these letters over the years, but in time they have become easier for him to write. Also, he has improved in his ability to express deeper feelings to me in my love language as he has practiced doing so. In addition, he has made efforts to leave me supportive notes or send me kind emails or texts at random times while he is away at work. I appreciate his efforts to communicate to me in a way that feels meaningful to me.*

RICHARD: *My love language is giving acts of service. I love serving others, especially Debra. It has taken Debra many years to realize that when I am doing an act of service, such as laboring on a house project she wants done, the reason I prioritized the project over doing other things I might prefer to do for myself is that I get a lift by seeing her excited about something I did for her. She always feels grateful for the time and energy I spend working on house projects, but even though she enjoys the practical consequences of the completed project, having the project done doesn't necessarily make her feel "warm fuzzies" of love and intimacy. In fact, sometimes the time it takes for me to do the project means I have less time to spend connecting directly with her, as she would prefer. Once Debra identified that my service was a love offering that satisfied my love language, she began to work harder to not only express gratitude but be warm and affectionate in return.*

Likewise, even though Debra's love language is words of affirmation, in addition to verbal and physical expressions of caring, Debra has made greater efforts to do service for me so that I can feel her love for me in my language. She makes me delicious dinners or makes my favorite Tollhouse chocolate chip cookies. She keeps my laundry clean and folded. She offers foot rubs or back rubs when I've had a particularly tiresome day. These are deliberate efforts; the message she wants me to hear is "I am making a love offering in your language. Please accept my love."

In more recent years, I have tried to make more of an effort to reach out to Debra in her love languages of words of affirmation and quality time. I can often tell when she needs a listening ear and needs to hear empathetic words of comfort and understanding about the challenges she faced that day. I have reached out to cuddle with her. I have also sought to be more open about how my day has been by explaining some of my own frustration, hurts, or challenges. She really loves it when I open up and share these things with her because it helps validate how important she is to me as an equal partner and spouse. I truly respect her insights and opinions, and so making quality time together is a blessing for both of us.

DEBRA: *Quality time is one love language we are continually working on negotiating in our relationship. After a long day of working for our professions, Church callings, children, and home, I want to connect with Richard by spending time alone together and talking. We have sought to prioritize alone time by enforcing bedtimes for the older children, but sometimes this does not always work since our older girls often want time and attention from us in the evenings.*

In addition, once alone, I want to connect in a meaningful way, which to me means more than a five- or ten-minute interaction. This connection time energizes me and sometimes I can talk for quite a while. Richard is often tired in the evenings and wants to wind down, not get into a lengthy or deep discussion. Sometimes he will end the discussion abruptly or fall asleep, and then I feel jilted and unsatisfied emotionally. This is an important time of connection for me, but I have over time come to realize that Richard just isn't as much of a night owl as I am, and his sleep needs are as important as my talking needs. So I have made a more conscious effort to limit my talking in the late evening when Richard has tired out.

Identifying the love language of our spouse can streamline sentimental communication. When we speak in our spouse's language, they likely will receive our love message more clearly and easily than if we communicate in our own love language only and expect them to accurately translate. In addition, recognizing our own love language can assist our spouse in more fully showing love for us. It is requisite that we educate them about what feels meaningful to us so that they can make more efforts to communicate through those means.

Building Positive Sentiment

Building positive sentiment, or creating warm feelings of caring and love within our marriage, is another way we improve emotional intimacy. It's generally not difficult to go out of our way to be nice to our spouse when we already have positive feelings for them. However, even if positive feelings are not present, we can purposefully and intentionally do things to *create* those types of feelings. In this section, we will discuss how to create positive sentiment, more carefully notice positive acts that our spouse is already doing, strengthen foundations of friendship, and continue postwedding courtship.

How do we build positive sentiment so that we can feel more connected and emotionally intimate with our spouse? John Gottman and Nan Silver teach about the process of building positivity in the relationship with a metaphor—the emotional bank account. We can put deposits into our bank account and we can make withdrawals. We can build up a large balance by making many deposits. If we withdraw too much, we can bankrupt the account.[33]

As a couple, making deposits in our emotional bank account helps to build feelings of closeness and intimacy. Deposits include any behaviors that increase positivity in the relationship. Examples include offering a compliment to our spouse, holding

Reflections

My husband passed away eleven years ago, after almost fifty-two years of marriage. Our parents did not show affection to each other. Yet I learned early in our marriage that my husband liked to show affection for me in public. I liked that a lot. It brought us together. He would sit down by me; he would grab my hand and hold it; he would put his arm around me. Whenever we would go for a walk, we would hold hands. We would hold hands in the car. He would always kiss me goodbye when he would go somewhere. These behaviors bonded us—it was a way of bonding us and staying in communication with each other. As his health began to decline, he remarked, "Well, we've had a good run of it, haven't we, my love?" The separation since he passed away has been heart-wrenching. I still feel him close to me during different things, such as baby blessings— like he's watching me. I know I will see him again, that he will come and get me when it is my time to pass. I can't wait to hold his hand again.

hands, kissing our spouse goodbye, and calling or texting our spouse during the workday to touch base and let them know that we are thinking of them. Withdrawals from the account include any behavior that undermines trust or closeness, creating negative sentiment. Examples may include reacting impatiently, thoughtlessly making a rude comment, failing to offer support, failing to follow through with commitments, or any other destructive attitude or behavior (see chapter 7 on conflict). So to begin building intimacy, we can work to increase positive sentiment by making as many deposits as possible into the emotional bank account.

Another way of assessing and increasing the amount of positive sentiment in our marriage can be done through awareness of some research from an area of psychology known as positive psychology. It teaches that people tend to flourish when their ratio for positive and negative affect is 3:1.[34] When the positive outweighs the negative, we feel happy and productive. This 3:1 ratio works for individuals; however, in marital relationships the standard is higher. Gottman found that couples who rated themselves as happily married have a positivity to negativity ratio of 5:1.[35]

Does our relationship with our spouse fall below the 5:1 threshold? The good news is that if we find we are coming up short in reaching the 5:1 positivity to negativity ratio, we can easily increase the positive sentiment in our marriage. We read in Alma 37:7, "And the Lord God doth work by means to bring about his great and eternal purposes; and by *very small means* the Lord doth confound the wise and bringeth about the salvation of many souls" (emphasis added). We don't have to make grand gestures that take a lot of planning or money; we can increase positive sentiment by small and simple means—very small means done on a consistent basis.

EVEN A SHORT, QUICK NOTE CAN CONVEY LOVE AND STRENGTHEN EMOTIONAL INTIMACY. RICHARD PUT THIS NOTE IN THE REFRIGER-ATOR FOR DEBRA TO FIND. COUR-TESY OF RICHARD McCLENDON.

RICHARD: *Things I try do for Debra from time to time include leaving an encouraging note taped inside the refrigerator or on her pillow, sending her a supportive text, bringing a treat home from work to share with her, or praying specifically for her during our evening prayer together. Debra frequently expresses gratitude for my hard work in behalf of the family, praises my handyman skills (excepting those projects completed with duct tape), gives me hugs or kisses, makes me my favorite cookies, or reaches out to hold my hand. Over time, small deposits such as these have created a large balance in our emotional bank account; when trouble comes and withdrawals are made, they do not bankrupt the account—they don't even get close.*

Thus, small things can be very powerful to not only inoculate the emotional relationship but promote flourishing. President Joseph Fielding Smith and his wife, Jessie Evans Smith, illustrated this concept in their own marriage: "During their 33 years of life together she accompanied him most everywhere, near and far. He in turn helped her do the grocery shopping, dry the supper dishes, and bottle fruit in the fall. He had no qualms about being an apostle with an apron on."[36]

Perhaps you may not feel confident that investing the energy to make these types of small efforts will significantly help your marital relationship. Maybe you think it seems superficial or fake. Or perhaps you feel your marriage relationship has too many substantial, even insurmountable, problems. Not so. Don't ignore this easy but powerful opportunity to strengthen and improve your relationship because it seems too simple.

Remember the story of Naaman in 2 Kings 5:1–14. He was angry because the prophet had told him to do something small and simple in order to cure his leprosy. His servants counseled him, "If the prophet had bid thee do some great thing, wouldest thou not have done it? how much rather then, when he said to thee, Wash, and be clean?" (verse 13). Naaman humbled himself and went and did according as directed, and he was made clean.

Elder L. Whitney Clayton of the Seventy shared this testimony about the power of small and simple acts of faith and obedience to bless our lives and help us with our daily concerns. His words are applicable, as well, to small and simple acts of caring in our marital relationship:

> Those who are deliberate about doing the "small and simple things"—obeying in seemingly little ways—are blessed with faith and strength that go far beyond the actual acts of obedience themselves and, in fact, may seem totally unrelated to them. It may seem hard to draw a connection between the basic daily acts of obedience and solutions to the big, complicated problems we face. But they are related. In my experience, getting the little daily habits of faith right is the single best way to fortify ourselves against the troubles of life, whatever they may be. Small acts of faith, even when they seem insignificant or entirely disconnected from the specific problems that vex us, bless us in all we do.[37]

We also testify to the truthfulness of this principle in marriage. Small and simple acts designed to increase positive sentiment in our relationship make small deposits into our emotional bank accounts. With those deposits we can, in time, create a massive positive balance large enough to offset even the most chronically difficult and painful marital dynamics (see the Richard Paul Evans story of saving his marriage in chapter 7).

Notice the Good Already Happening

Another way couples can increase positivity in their marital relationship is by simply noticing the positive efforts that are already present but are currently overlooked. Gottman and Silver reported that those in happy marriages noticed almost all of the positive things their partners did for them, while those in unhappy marriages failed to recognize 50 percent of their spouse's positive acts toward them.[38]

Our earlier discussion on love language becomes salient here. Perhaps our spouse is reaching out positively, but due to differences in our love languages, we're not registering their efforts. Being mindful and aware will help us to give purposeful attention to

Reflections

My husband and I came from different backgrounds and have different personalities. I grew up in between small towns. If we "went to town," we needed to have a list; there was not much spontaneity. We were a very close family; we all worked together in our family business. Our religion was very important. I am conservative, like to plan, and err on the safe side of things. I also tend to worry and sometimes end up being pessimistic. My husband grew up in the city, making it easier to be more involved with his friends. He lived kind of rowdy during his teenage years and was very independent. Religion was definitely not at the forefront of his life during that time. He is very spontaneous, adventurous, and fun. Meshing the two of us together hasn't always been easy. We don't always see eye to eye. Parenting has been a challenge. I get frustrated when he cannot understand or agree with my perspective, but I try to remember that he would never do anything intentionally to upset me or to be hurtful. Also, we have learned that instead of leaving a confrontational situation, if we talk through our problems they can be solved. We have different backgrounds that bring us together and make us a more rounded couple—two lifetimes' worth of different knowledge into one unified companionship. I wouldn't want it any other way.

the behaviors and efforts they are making on behalf of our marital relationship.

Build or Enhance Friendship, Fondness, and Admiration

In addition to trying new things to build positive feelings as well as more consistently recognizing those positive things that are already present, couples can also build emotional intimacy by focusing on just being friends. It is not uncommon to find couples that love each other but don't necessarily *like* each other. This often occurs when couples have not continually fostered positive marital behaviors to build the type of intimacy that maintains friendship. Gottman and Silver advocate building friendship and affection.[39]

In essence, after years of marriage, we can sometimes forget why we got together in the first place. We can ask ourselves these questions: When we were dating previous to our marriage, what kind of conversations did we have together? Have we had a conversation like that *lately*? In marriage, we may need to reacquaint ourselves with our spouse's current life goals, dreams, likes and dislikes, friends, and so on. Spend time getting to know each other again and reconnecting. Gottman and Silver explain: "This may all seem obvious to the point of being ridiculous. People who are happily married like each other. If they didn't they wouldn't be happily married. But fondness and admiration can be fragile unless you remain aware of how crucial they are to the friendship that is at the core of any good marriage."[40]

Sometimes couples are completely different in preferences, styles, and interests. For these *opposites attract* couples, this concept of building and maintaining a friendship may be particularly important, since the differences that seemed exciting when dating can end up creating ongoing friction during marriage. If you and your spouse are one of these couples, you can ask yourself these questions: Even though you knew your spouse was a different *flavor*,

what drew you to marry them anyway? What excited you? How did you think the differences would benefit you?

Be Purposeful in Building Your Relationship

Again, we can build warm feelings for our spouse even when they may not currently be there. We must be intentional and act with deliberate purpose in order to build and create the type of intimacy we desire. If we go on autopilot and mindlessly float along without much effort to dedicate positive energy to improving our marital relationship, then we will never attain the wonderfully strengthening and fulfilling intimacy we desire from our marriage.

Reflections

In premarriage dating I would play and have fun on dates, but much of my life was not playing or having fun. It was mundane. I wanted to see how my prospective spouse behaved while in the midst of mundane tasks. It worked great. By the time my wife and I were married, we had spent hours upon hours in a study lab, had done many loads of laundry together, and may have even filed a tax return or two. We learned that we wanted to be together regardless of what we were doing and that each other's company made any situation more pleasant. After marriage, however, there are no extra points for mundane dates. It is good to know that we can spend time enhancing our relationship in the blandest of circumstances, but such situations are already abundant. Now it is time to go have some fun. This is the woman I am spending my life with! We have now done some of the most exciting things of our lives together and hope to do many more. Some of them have and will account for our most lavish expenditures. Dating plays a critical role in our relationship for the simple fact that with children at home it is a challenge to communicate in a way that is relationship enhancing. A date gives us the precious time we need to talk. A date is also ideal for escaping the mental context in which daily responsibilities become a distraction from reconnecting with each other.

We encourage specificity as we make commitments to more fully build positivity and friendship in our marital relationship. It is hard to achieve a vague goal. What does it mean to be "more loving" to each other? It is hard to do and it is even harder to know whether or not we are being successful. So we can make an *operational definition* (clear, concise, detailed definition) of our goal, if necessary.

For example, we may individually define "more loving" as "one time each day I will go out of my way to do something nice" or "I will text or call my spouse each day with a warm or supportive message" or "I will give my spouse a foot massage when they have had a long day." We may also choose to define a couple's being "more loving" as "we will take time to talk with each other each night after the children have gone to bed" or "we will spend time cuddling on the couch while watching TV." Operational definitions, such as these, make it much more likely that our newfound goal will be easier to accomplish successfully because we will better know what we are trying to do and what we will need to prioritize.

Continued Dating

Relative to building positive sentiment, we must not underestimate the power that dating will have in our marital relationship—it is critical to fostering intimacy. Dating can revitalize us when we are tired and feel disconnected or can keep us from becoming tired and disconnected in the first place. President Spencer W. Kimball taught, "Many couples permit their marriages to become stale and their love to grow cold like old bread or worn-out jokes or cold gravy."[41] He also taught that to prevent this "there must be continued courting and expressions of affection, kindness, and consideration to keep love alive and growing."[42]

When we take the time for dating, increasing positive sentiment becomes easy. A simple activity, such as going out to dinner or an event, provides opportunity for the husband to open the wife's car door, for the wife to reach out and hold her husband's hand during dinner, for each spouse to share thoughts and feelings and to focus our complete attention on no one but each other. A date says to our spouse, "I value our marriage enough to make it a priority."

For those with small children this often takes extra planning and expense, such as the need to secure and pay for a babysitter. Sometimes, as it was for us

Reflections

In the last three years of my twenty-five-year marriage, I have finally allowed myself to not fret over spending the extra money for the occasional nice dinner date. It all came together at one of our favorite Mexican restaurants. Certainly, it takes less than sixty seconds in any grocery store to be forced to wince at the price of food, but we talked that night about the cost of a typical complete home-cooked meal. It was much higher than I had previously thought! Even though we don't eat a lot of meat, we don't eat just rice and beans at every meal either. After subtracting the normal cost of a meal at home from the prices on the menu in front of me, I determined the cost differential, and it was readily apparent that the true cost of the date was significantly less than I had conjured up in my mind. And once you add in the ideas that my wife is not slaving over the stove, that someone else is doing the dishes, and that we are able to be together without needy children for a few minutes, it all seems worth it.

during busy baby and toddler years, physically going out of the house for a date was difficult, so dates were held after the children had gone to bed: we talked with each other while sitting on the back deck, enjoying the view from our home. In dating, the point is to spend time to, in a more formal or personal setting, connect with each other and build positive sentiment. Debra was once taught, "The purpose of the task is to strengthen the relationship." Thus, we advocate creating dating experiences that help us to make more emotionally intimate connections.

In order to accomplish the task of strengthening the marriage, we echo counsel Debra received from a professor during her undergraduate training: "On dates, do not talk about jobs, money, or kids. Dating is for talking about hopes, dreams, future plans, and the like." This counsel challenges us to extend our-selves in a way that can build emotional intimacy. It forces us to get outside of the day-to-day mindset of superficial communica-tion and find meaningful, more lasting ways to connect. Popular social work researcher and TED talker Brené Brown has written, "Connection is the energy that is created between people when they feel seen, heard, and valued; when they can give and receive without judgment."[43] This type of intimate and validating con-nection can be a challenge when we may be more accustomed to connecting around job stresses, bills, or the kids. We will need to be thoughtful and particular about our conversations.

DEBRA: *Richard and I are not perfect at following this counsel, but when we go on dates, we do our best. We like to talk about Richard's travel and work trips to new locations, my professional interests or activities that give me a much-needed break from full-time mommying, and dreams of future travel, such as serving a mission together when the children are grown. We fantasize about life without toddlers and talk about the things we'll do when we have more freedom. We reflect on how far we've come, such as how things have changed in our lives in the last year (or some other designated time frame). We marvel at what we've accomplished and offer compliments to each other for the hard work we have put in to building our marriage and family. We joke with each other that we need to slow down—but we never do. We discuss a gospel principle or something we learned from our daily scripture study. If we attend a cultural event or artistic performance, we discuss our time there, critique the event, or have a discussion of some topic sparked by the content of the activity.*

Again, as we focus on connecting with our spouse in an intimate way that draws us together and makes them feel valued and validated, the possible date opportunities are endless. Our efforts to connect in this way will pay handsome dividends into our emotional bank account.

Creating Shared Meaning

Another principle in building greater intimacy is to create shared meaning in our marital relationship. Gottman and Silver explain, "Marriage isn't just about raising kids, splitting chores, and making love. It can also have a spiritual dimension that has to do with creating an inner life together—a culture rich with symbols and rituals, and an appreciation for your roles and goals that link you, that lead you to understand what it means to be a part of the family you have become."[44]

We learn in Doctrine and Covenants section 25 about how husbands and wives can support and sustain each other in a shared meaningful pursuit. Joseph Smith and Emma Smith were unified in their dedication to the Lord and to their service in His church. The Lord indicated to Emma that her "calling shall be for a comfort unto [His] servant, Joseph Smith, Jun., thy husband, in his afflictions, with consoling words, in the spirit of meekness" (verse 5). What may be less commonly recognized in the section is that the Lord also tells Emma about Joseph's role in supporting her: "And thou needest not fear, for thy husband shall support thee in the church" (verse 9). Joseph and Emma had found a common purpose and they worked together to support each other. What great power came from their relationship to the benefit of all mankind!

Joseph and Emma Smith were also joined together by great love. On several occasions Joseph wrote letters to Emma expressing his heartfelt feelings of affection and concern. It was recorded that a few days prior to her death, Emma told her nurse, Sister Elizabeth Revel, that Joseph had come to her in a vision and told her: "Emma, come with me, it is time for you to come with me." As Emma passed from this life to the next on 30 April 1879, she called out, "Joseph! Joseph!" Thirty-five years after his martyrdom, it was believed that Joseph, her beloved husband, had come from the other side of the veil to escort her home to Father.[45]

We, also, have found a great deal of shared meaning within our marriage relative to our activity in the Church. Activities such as reading to each other from the scriptures or the words of the modern prophets; having discussions about our callings, gospel doctrines, political and moral issues that are encroaching on the teachings of Christ; attending meetings together; and the like all help us feel close to each other.

Another shared purpose that has become quite meaningful, and even joyful, for us is sharing with others what we've learned about marriage through our gospel and professional training. When we first dated and married, we enjoyed having discussions laced with reference to social science principles, and we enjoyed that our professional areas were similar enough that we could talk intelligently with each other. Yet, beyond that, we never expected that there would be a time, not too long after marrying, when we would be marrying our professional interests as well.

We had a good marriage when we began formally writing about the topic of commitment in marriage from a three-fold perspective of sociology, psychology, and religion.[46] Yet, after spending several years writing, giving presentations together, and working on this book together, we realized a fundamental shift for the better had occurred in our relationship. We went from having a good marriage to having a great

Reflections

I introduced my husband to mountain biking when we were first dating, and it was something we could enjoy together. We now bike almost every week during the summer and fall months. We plan out our adventures and look forward to our ride every week. We both feel so grateful to be able to enjoy a sport we are passionate about together. We sometimes bike with a few of my husband's friends whose wives get impatient with them because of the time they take mountain biking. This causes stress in their relationships, and my husband and I feel fortunate that this is not an issue in our marriage. There is nothing we love more than to enjoy breathtaking scenery and feel the excitement and thrill of mountain biking with the person we love most. Biking has definitely brought us closer as a couple, and our children have enjoyed seeing us have a good time together. They feel secure knowing our relationship is strong, active, and healthy.

marriage! Our work constantly reminds us of the things we are supposed to be doing to make our marriage flourish, and so we try to do them often.

RICHARD: *The work Debra and I do together creates a sense of shared meaning for us, in which we experience a great sense of joy and fulfillment. I wrote this to Debra in one of her Valentine's letters:*

> *The writing of our book together has been another highlight of our growth and trust in each other this year. Reading and editing each other's work has brought me closer to you. It has built trust because I have gotten to know your thoughts and beliefs in a way that perhaps I never would have otherwise. I love your testimony of and faithfulness in marriage and the gospel and in every principle we have written about. It brings me a lot of satisfaction to see you light up when you get an idea that you want to write about and then see you go grab your computer and start your fingers buzzing.*

Gottman and Silver state, and from our own experience we agree, that "the more shared meaning you can find, the deeper, richer, and more rewarding your relationship will be."[47]

Creating shared meaning in our marital relationships does not mean that we must always find connection through activities or pursuits which we both *already* enjoy. We have the power to create a new common bond. As a couple seeking to build an eternal-quality marriage, we can share the things we love with our spouse, and they can choose to learn about them, participate with us in doing them, and even learn to love and feel passionate for the things we love. This will often take an active effort on our part, and even if we don't learn to love our spouse's interests, just participating with them can make a positive difference in the building of intimacy. Elder Henry B. Eyring shared this amusing story about his parents' efforts to connect with each other: "My father and my mother were very different from each other. My mother was a singer and an artist. My father loved chemistry. Once at a symphony concert, my mother was surprised when my father stood up and began to leave before the applause began. My mother asked him where he was going. His response was, in all innocence: 'Well, it's over, isn't it?' Only the gentle influence of the Holy Ghost got him there with her in the first place and brought him back to concerts time and time again."[48]

We need to take time to share ourselves with our spouse. We can teach them about our interests, explain why they are exciting to us, and give them experience with our interests so they can more fully understand the role they play in our life (and the role they might play in their life). Ideally, our spouse will grow to be excited about our interests too and want to participate with us. But, if not, through this knowledge they can at least support us in an effort to build and strengthen our relationship rather than feel resentment or jealousy when we spend our own time engaged in that activity.

RICHARD: *I enjoy watching BYU football and the Utah Jazz playoffs on TV. That's about the extent of my TV time. Debra grew up playing soccer, but she never found any interest in watching sports. In our first few years of marriage, I noticed that Debra felt jealous of the time I spent watching football or basketball and felt judgmental that I was just wasting time. I felt that my sports watching was reasonable, but it was hard because I wasn't getting much support from Debra.*

At one point, Debra realized she spent her own downtime on her own interests, yet I never complained. So she decided to be supportive and even, to my surprise, went a step further and took the approach: "If I can't beat him, join him." She intentionally began to show some interest when I was watching a game by stopping in front of the television for a few minutes and asking questions about what was happening, including questions about the rules or a player. Eventually, she began to sit down and watch larger portions of the games and actually began to feel her own interest in what was happening, particularly in the basketball games as she got to know some of the players. Although she's never come to appreciate the football games for herself, she found that she enjoys basketball and was disappointed when the Utah Jazz traded some of her favorite players.

Now, when I want to watch a game on television, I don't feel nervous about Debra feeling jealous of my time, but instead I feel she genuinely wants me to be able to relax and have some entertainment after working so hard for the family throughout the week. Because of that support, I feel much closer to her and have in turn wanted to more fully support her and go out of my way to learn more about her own interests.

As a final note, as we seek to build shared meaning within the marital relationship, it does not necessarily mean we must *do something* together. Building shared meaning may relate more to having a common vision, which then leads to supporting our spouse in their general life pursuits. If we support our spouse in their jobs, education, and callings because we are on board with their goals and efforts, they will be happier and more successful and our marital relationship will be strengthened, as their gratitude for our support will infuse positivity in the relationship. Elder Carlos Godoy, speaking in general conference in his native language of Portuguese, shared an experience he had with his wife in seeking additional educational opportunities: "I undoubtedly needed the support of my wife. . . . [Her] support was essential. I remember that, at first, Mônica and I needed to carefully discuss the change in plans until she felt comfortable and also became committed. This shared vision caused her not only to support the change but also to become an essential part in its success."[49]

Conclusion

Emotional intimacy is an essential building block of successful marriages. An overall tone of mutual interdependence within the relationship creates bonds that strengthen and support each other individually, and creates a thriving and loving relationship. Openly and constructively communicating, becoming proficient at speaking each other's love languages, creating higher ratios of positive sentiment, continued dating, and creating a sense of shared meaning are all necessary to create connection points and improve bonds of affection and trust. As we pursue these qualities in our relationship, we will be able to create and maintain marital friendship so we can say that we not only love our spouse

but like them as well. This creates a vital sense of unity and intimacy which greatly contributes to our ability to find happiness
and joy.

Notes

1. Spencer W. Kimball, "Marriage Is Honorable" (address, Brigham
Young University, Provo, UT, 30 September 1973), https://speeches
.byu.edu/talks/spencer-w-kimball_marriage-honorable/.

2. Jean-Philippe Laurenceau, Lisa Feldman Barrett, and Michael J.
Rovine, "The Interpersonal Process Model of Intimacy in Marriage:
A Daily-Diary and Multilevel Modeling Approach," *Journal of Family
Psychology* 19, no. 2 (2005): 314–23.

3. Neal A. Maxwell, *All These Things Shall Give Thee Experience* (Salt Lake
City: Deseret Book, 1980), 68.

4. Judith S. Wallerstein and Sandra Blakeslee, *The Good Marriage: How
and Why Love Lasts* (New York: Grand Central Publishing, 1995), 240.

5. Russell M. Nelson, "Lessons from Eve," *Ensign*, November 1987, 87.

6. Bruce C. Hafen, "Covenant Marriage," *Ensign*, November 1996,
26; and John Bytheway, *When Times are Tough: 5 Scriptures That Will Help You Get
through Almost Anything* (Salt Lake City: Deseret Book, 2004), 37–38.

7. George E. Vaillant, *Triumphs of Experience: The Men of the Harvard Grant
Study* (Cambridge, MA: Belknap Press, 2012).

8. Vaillant, *Triumphs*, 42.

9. Vaillant, *Triumphs*, 205.

10. Vaillant, *Triumphs*, 40.

11. Vaillant, *Triumphs*, 205.

12. Vaillant, *Triumphs*, 201–2.

13. Vaillant, *Triumphs*, 222.

14. Richard G. Scott, "The Eternal Blessings of Marriage," *Ensign*, May
2011, 95–96.

15. Martin E. Seligman, "Building Resilience," *Harvard Business Review* 89,
no. 4 (April 2011): 100–106, 138.

16. Adapted from Seligman, "Building Resilience," 106.

17. Douglas E. Brinley and Mark D. Ogletree, *First Comes Love* (American
Fork, UT: Covenant Communications, 2002), 123–26.

18. Brinley and Ogletree, *First Comes Love*, 123–26; and Mark D.
Ogletree, "Speak, Listen, and Love," *Ensign*, February 2014, 15–17.

19. Brinley and Ogletree, *First Comes Love*, 123–26.

20. Ogletree, "Speak, Listen, and Love," 15.

21. Harry T. Reis and Phillip Shaver, "Intimacy as an Interpersonal Process," in *Handbook of Personal Relationships*, ed. Steve Duck (Chichester, England: Wiley & Sons, 1988), 367–89.

22. Ogletree, "Speak, Listen, and Love," 16.

23. Maxwell, *All These Things*, 62.

24. Maxwell, *All These Things*, 62.

25. Neal A. Maxwell, *Whom the Lord Loveth: The Journey of Discipleship* (Salt Lake City: Deseret Book, 2003), 143.

26. David A. Bednar, "More Diligent and Concerned at Home," *Ensign*, November 2009, 18.

27. Gary Chapman, *The Five Love Languages: How to Express Heartfelt Commitment to Your Mate* (Chicago: Northfield Publishing, 1995), 14–16.

28. Nichole Egbert and Denise Polk, "Speaking the Language of Relational Maintenance: A Validity Test of Chapman's (1992) Five Love Languages," *Communication Research Reports* 23, no 1. (2006): 19–26.

29. Chapman, *Five Love Languages*, 14–16.

30. Chapman, *Five Love Languages*, 54–55.

31. Chapman, *Five Love Languages*, 14–16.

32. Chapman, *Five Love Languages*, 14–16.

33. John M. Gottman and Nan Silver, *The Seven Principles for Making Marriage Work* (New York: Three Rivers Press, 1999), 83.

34. Barbara L. Frederickson and Marcial F. Losada, "Positive Affect and the Complex Dynamics of Human Flourishing," *American Psychologist* 60, no. 7 (2005): 678–86.

35. John Mordechai Gottman, *What Predicts Divorce: The Relationship Between Marital Processes and Marital Outcomes* (New York: Lawrence Erlbaum, 1994).

36. Joseph Fielding Smith Jr. and John J. Stewart, *The Life of Joseph Fielding Smith* (Salt Lake City: Deseret Book, 1972), 12–13.

37. L. Whitney Clayton, "Whatever He Sayeth unto You, Do It," *Ensign*, May 2017, 98.

38. Gottman and Silver, *Seven Principles*, 83–84.

39. Gottman and Silver, *Seven Principles*, 83.

40. Gottman and Silver, *Seven Principles*, 65.

41. Spencer W. Kimball, "Oneness in Marriage," *Ensign*, March 1977, 5.

42. Kimball, "Oneness in Marriage," 4.

43. Brené Brown, *Daring Greatly* (New York: Gotham Books, 2012), 145.

44. Gottman and Silver, *Seven Principles*, 243–44.

45. Gracia N. Jones, "My Great-Great-Grandmother, Emma Hale Smith," *Ensign*, August 1992, 37–38.

46. Richard J. McClendon and Debra Theobald McClendon, "Commitment to the Covenant: LDS Marriage and Divorce," in *By Divine Design: Best Practices for Family Success and Happiness*, ed. Brent L. Top and Michael A. Goodman (Salt Lake City: Deseret Book, 2014), 93–116.

47. Gottman and Silver, *Seven Principles*, 246.

48. Henry B. Eyring, "To My Grandchildren," *Ensign*, October 2013, 70.

49. Carlos A. Godoy, "The Lord Has a Plan for Us!," *Ensign*, November 2014, 98.

CHAPTER 6

"They Twain Shall Be One Flesh"

Marital Unity in the Sexual Relationship

Sexuality is a human condition; each of us is a divine son or daughter of God *and* as such we are sexual beings. The word *and* here is important because our sexuality does not separate us from nor stand in opposition to our divine nature. Our sexuality is embraced in our divine nature; it is fully a godlike attribute our Father has bestowed upon us so that we may be like Him. We glory in this wonderful gift He has given us.

Unfortunately, the role of sexuality has become skewed in our current culture. The world has become hyperobsessed with sex, which has degraded this special, heaven-sent gift. Elder Bednar has commented: "Never has a global society placed so much emphasis on the fulfillment of romantic and sexual desires as the highest form of personal autonomy, freedom, and self-actualization. Society has elevated sexual fulfillment to an end in itself rather than as a means to a higher end. In this confusion, millions have lost the truth that God intended sexual desire to be a *means* to the divine ends of marital unity, the procreation of children and strong families, not a selfish *end* in itself."[1]

Reflections

When I look at my husband, I wish I were more physically attracted to him. But when I take a step back and see him as more than just his specific physical features, I remember why I love him. His character, loyalty, kindness, ambition, perseverance, and so on bring out an attractiveness that cannot be faked. Those qualities will remain steady over the years, unlike physicality, which changes with time. Don't get me wrong; choosing to focus on his strengths and looking past his weaknesses is not easy. I continue to struggle at times. But it has improved as I choose to focus on his strengths and expand my definition of attraction. As I remember his positive traits and contributions to our family, I feel more attracted to him. Recently, I've caught myself looking at him—really looking at him—and thinking "I love him," rather than pinpointing to myself the little physical features that are less than ideal. My attraction to him is growing and it is strengthening our physical relationship. Our physical intimacy deepens, and sex becomes more about connection rather than strictly physical pleasure. It is our opportunity to be completely vulnerable and have that vulnerability appreciated and returned. With selflessness and validation, unity is present. This unity restores hope and magnifies the joy in our marriage.

We underscore this message as we begin our discussion. As a contrast to the trends of the world, the purpose of this chapter is to emphasize the divine roles of sexuality in a celestial-quality eternal relationship. Sexuality is not primarily about being passionately and physically attracted to one's spouse, receiving or giving pleasure, or satisfying a strong sexual drive. We will discuss three spiritual purposes of sexual relations (going from the more concrete to the more abstract) and will explore some of the emotional and therapeutic issues that surround the role of sexuality in marriage. Research has shown that the sexual relationship is good for our physical and mental health. A wide range of physical benefits are produced from the sexual relationship, such as reduced stress and lower rates of heart disease, breast cancer, prostate cancer, and endometriosis.[2]

Our purpose in this chapter is to provide a how-to relative to deepening intimacy with our spouse and God through the sexual relationship rather than a how-to manual with biology lessons and information regarding various sexual positions or genital stimulation techniques.

Spiritual Purposes of Sexual Relations

Our discussion on the spiritual purposes of our sexual relationships will focus on learning about our role as creators, building unity with our spouse, and understanding more about our unity with God. We use the term *sexual relations* as a descriptor of a whole relationship of attitudes, emotions, touch, and behaviors, rather than simply the singular act of intercourse. Sexual relations have a great purpose in marriage and for marriage. They serve to unify and strengthen the marital relationship through "expressing love and strengthening emotional and spiritual ties."[3] Our discussion herein focuses on this broader understanding of the sexual relationship.

Role of Creators

The first purpose of sexual relations is to learn more about God as our Creator and to foster our role as creators. God our Father has endowed us with the power to provide a mortal body for His spirit children. Sexual intercourse is the means by which a husband and wife are able to join with God in His creative abilities and become partners with Him in His work "to bring to pass the immortality and eternal life" of his children (Moses 1:39). When we understand this partnership and recognize the sober responsibility we bring upon ourselves when we take on parenthood, the decision to have children is a grand undertaking. Pregnancy and delivery are only the beginning—you then have to raise them!

The decision of how many children to have is solely left to couples as they seek God's direction. Elder Neil L. Andersen said, "When to have a child and how many children to have are private decisions to be made between a husband and wife and the Lord. These are sacred decisions—decisions that should be made with sincere prayer and acted on with great faith."[4]

Unity between Husband and Wife

The second purpose of sexual relations is to foster unity between husband and wife. Spiritual purposes of sexual relations require that sex be important in marriage beyond the procreative realm. Indeed, engaging in sexual intercourse for the purpose of reproduction will constitute a fairly small portion of the couple's sexual time together. We read in Mark 10:6–9:

> But from the beginning of the creation God made them male and female.
>
> For this cause shall a man leave his father and mother, and cleave to his wife;
>
> And they twain shall be one flesh: so then they are no more twain, but one flesh.

What therefore God hath joined together, let not man put asunder.

Our Father in Heaven intends for sexual relations to teach us about unity: unity with each other and unity with Him. As president of Brigham Young University, Jeffrey R. Holland spoke of sexual intimacy as a symbol for the type of unity God desires of husband and wife:

> Human intimacy, that sacred, physical union ordained of God for a married couple, deals with a *symbol* that demands special sanctity. Such an act of love between a man and a woman is—or certainly was ordained to be—a symbol of total union: union of their hearts, their hopes, their lives, their love, their family, their future, their everything. . . .
>
> Physiologically we are created as men and women to fit together in such a union. In this ultimate physical expression of one man and one woman they are as nearly and as literally "one" as two separate physical bodies can ever be. It is in that act of ultimate physical intimacy we most nearly fulfill the commandment of the Lord given to Adam and Eve, living symbols for all married couples, when he invited them to cleave unto one another only, and thus become "one flesh." (Genesis 2:24)[5]

This type of physical contact is meant to create a great sense of unity and bonding in the marital relationship. Indeed, it provides a reinforcing quality to the relationship; research has shown that, across all ages, couples that reported higher frequencies of sexual relations also reported

Reflections

Our marriage has been full of difficulty and struggle, but our sexual relationship has been a source of healing and strengthening, making up for some of the deficits we have in other areas. I have often lain in bed, listening to the sound of my husband's breathing as it deepens into sleep, saying a silent prayer of thanksgiving for the immeasurably beautiful gift that God has given to husbands and wives. Such a gift seems to be greater than we could possibly deserve, more full of joy and wonder than two struggling, imperfect people could find in one another. True sexual joy springs from something much deeper than physical pleasure alone. These moments teach me about the unsurpassed love that our Father has for us and in some small way not only represent his desire for us to experience joy but also provide a window into his ability to have joy. On more than one occasion, the Spirit has borne witness to the goodness and rightness of this physical union, always when our spiritual union is strong and deepening.

higher levels of marital satisfaction.[6] There is great power in true sexual intimacy, which expresses itself with tenderness, caring, and closeness. Christian authors Ed Wheat and Gaye Wheat described genuine sexual intimacy as a "security of belonging"[7] with "remarkable power to heal, renew, refresh, and sustain the marriage relationship."[8] A truly intimate sexual relationship will be one in which the couple is enjoying quality sex together. One researcher explains, "Quality sex means orgasm equality." This means that "both parties get the gender-specific stimulation (penis for him, clitoris for her) that most reliably results in orgasm."[9] Orgasm equality will strengthen bonds of unity as we lovingly care for each other while respecting our gender-specific sexual needs. These bonds of caring will increase connectivity and prove to be a strength to the marital relationship not only sexually but in all areas of our life. Ed and Gaye Wheat commented that when true sexual intimacy is achieved, even mundane and nonsexual acts, such as working together in the home or kneeling together in prayer, become acts of *lovemaking* because love is the hallmark of the relationship.[10]

The inverse is also true; failing to nurture the sexual relationship in marriage weakens unity. Research has found that sexual inactivity has been associated with marital unhappiness.[11] Research has also shown that sexual dissatisfaction is associated with increased risk of divorce.[12] Likewise, impersonal sexual relations that fail to honor the higher spiritual purposes of sexual relations will also weaken associations, for "we cannot be truly satisfied with mere physical and physiological relief in sex."[13]

Unity with God Our Father

The third purpose of sexual relations, the most abstract, is unity with our Father in Heaven. The mandate to become one flesh within the marriage covenant is not only discussed in Genesis,

Practice

Intimacy challenge: A basic strategy in the treatment of insomnia is to restrict the use of one's bed to only two activities—sleeping and sex. Just as these restrictions serve to improve one's sleep, they will also improve emotional and physical intimacy in your marriage. Keep all electronics, work projects, or other activities out of bed. Sit in a comfortable chair in your bedroom or do the activities in another room altogether. Take the TV out of the bedroom completely. Preserve the bed only for sleep and building emotional and physical intimacy with your spouse, and allow the bedroom to be sacred space for you as a couple.

in reference to Adam and Eve, but is found throughout the scriptures. Ed and Gaye Wheat state:

> As a matter of fact, the sex relationship in marriage receives such emphasis in the Scriptures that we begin to see it was meant not only to be a wonderful, continuing experience for the husband and wife, but it was also intended to show us something even more wonderful about God and His relationship with us. Ephesians 5:31–32 spells it out: "For this cause shall a man leave his father and mother, and shall be joined unto his wife, and they two shall be one flesh. This is a great mystery: but I speak concerning Christ and the church." *Thus the properly and lovingly executed and mutually satisfying sexual union is God's way of demonstrating to us a great spiritual truth.* It speaks to us of the greatest love story ever told—of how Jesus Christ gave Himself for us and is intimately involved with and loves the Church (those who believe in Him). In this framework, the sexual relationship between two growing Christians can be intimate fellowship as well as delight.[14]

As BYU president, Elder Jeffrey R. Holland discussed sexual relations as symbolic of unity with God our Father, and likened sexual relations to a sacrament, which he defined as "any one of a number of gestures or acts or ordinances that unite us with God and his limitless powers." He taught that the "sexual union is also, in its own profound way, a very real sacrament of the highest order, a union not only of a man and a woman but very much the union of that man and woman with God." In viewing sexual relations in this symbolic fashion, we gain a greater insight into the nature of God, which can strengthen us throughout our lives. Elder Holland further indicated, "And I submit to you that *you will never be more like God at any other time in this life than when you are expressing that particular power.* Of all the titles he has chosen for himself, Father is the one he declares, and Creation is his watchword."[15]

Charity in the Bedroom

In light of these spiritual purposes of sex, we can understand the need for complete soberness and respect for our spouses in our sexual relationship. Moroni defines charity as "the pure love of Christ" (Moroni 7:47). This type of charity is a transformation of our very natures to the core, a process that ultimately allows us to receive His image in our countenance (see Alma 5:14). When we have adopted Christ's charity for our own, it will be manifest in a variety of ways in our daily lives and especially visible in our sexual relationship with our spouse. Charity is critical to the process of becoming unified and creating a fulfilling sexual relationship.

Reflections

After about six months of being married, I finally mustered the courage to tell my wife about that part of me that no one knew about. I had hoped that my sexual attraction to men would go away by virtue of acting on faith to get married and becoming sexually active with my wife, but this was not the case. . . . Our marriage hasn't always been easy, although in many ways it's easier than we expected. Of course, there are things that we continue to work on. In any successful marriage, there needs to be a balance of romance, intimacy (all kinds— physical, emotional, and spiritual for example), and a committed attitude. Most heterosexual men with whom I have spoken find physical intimacy pretty automatic but may struggle with truly being friends with their spouses. Toward my wife, the friendship, commitment, and nearly all types of intimacy came naturally to me. While our sexual relationship was not natural for me at first, I have felt safe to figure it out, and over the first few months of marriage it became easier and more natural. Our sexuality grew as an off- shoot of our friendship, an expression of a deep emotional love. As we grow older, our ongoing efforts to find time for romance and shared positive experiences has led to a stronger friendship and marriage. I truly get to come home to my best friend every day.

Reflections

My husband and I were headed for a very unhappy marriage. I grew up in a women's liberation home where I was taught that men only wanted one thing and that the best thing to do was to bring your man into submission. To make my marriage wonderful, I had to change. . . . Stepping outside of my selfish world changed everything. Sex is now no longer about me—I changed. When I don't desire sex, I desire his happiness, which means I will give myself to him. I end up with a double win because I have fulfilled his need and I feel great. Sex is no longer just about sex. It is a union between us that strengthens us. I try to give him all the physical affection that he personally needs. . . . I do not withhold myself from him. And, yes, sadly, I used to. Since I have changed myself, our marriage is a beautiful thing. My husband gives more and more to me. I then show appreciation and physical affection. Then he gives more, and it continues on and on. I cherish my marriage to him more than anything.

Gina Ogden, a sex-therapy educator and researcher, encourages an exercise in which she asks clients to evaluate how they exhibit true love in their sexual relationship. She has clients write an advertisement seeking "the perfect lover—for *you*—a lover who will fill your desires of body, mind, heart, and spirit."[16] She then encourages clients to take the ad they have generated and apply it to themselves to become the lover they have just written about. For example, if they have written about finding someone who is sensitive and generous, they may then recognize at times their tendency to be insensitive, withholding, or even cruel in their sexual relationship with their spouse. This can be a powerful way to reappraise our approach to our sexual relationship. As a counselor in the Relief Society General Presidency, Linda Reeves taught, "The intimate marriage relationship between a man and a woman that brings children into mortality is also meant to be a beautiful, loving experience that binds together two devoted hearts, unites both spirit and body, and brings a fullness of joy and *happiness as we learn to put each other first.*"[17]

As genuine charity reigns in the bedroom, couples may find that sexual encounters become more enjoyable and more emotionally and physically fulfilling. One of the major findings from a study conducted by Ogden was that sexual satisfaction increases with age; respondents over fifty reported "more sexual pleasure, vitality, eye-contact, sharing, and ecstasy" than did the respondents in their twenties and thirties.[18] The author described this relative to the sharing that occurs over the years of a couple's sexual relationship: "Those in long-term relationships were able to revel in the years of emotional and physical sharing that deepened their sense of erotic connection."[19]

So it may be said that by being serviceable and charitable in the sexual relationship, one actually becomes most likely to be successful at securing for themselves their greatest *selfish* desires as well as their most charitable ones. Waite and Gallagher commented, "This selfless approach to sex, paradoxically, is far more likely to bring sexual satisfaction to both men and women."[20]

Yet service in the bedroom can be a conundrum. To feel sexual pleasure a person largely focuses on themselves—their own thoughts, their own physical sensations, and their own desires. By nature this may become a selfish process, and indeed in many marriages it is so, as the purposes of sex, the needs and desires of one's spouse, and the general principles of Christianity may be overlooked

Reflections

My husband and I have always had a passionate, healthy sex life. A year or so after our last child was born, I started to experience intense pain during and after sex. I went to my gynecologist and he referred me to a specialist; I had blisters in my vagina. The specialist gave me some hormone creams and sent me home. I tried the creams, but they didn't seem to work for me. I became very discouraged. I felt like I was broken and that I was impacting our marriage so that my husband wasn't getting everything he needed. However, my husband was a tremendous support during this difficult time. We continued to have a very passionate and loving sex life that focused on a variety of things that were enjoyable and satisfying but also kept me from feeling pain. I started to feel like we would never have a "typical" sex life again because my condition never seemed to improve over a number of years. My husband was the key to resolving this issue. He didn't just feel like this was "my" problem, but he approached it as "our" problem. He learned about my disorder, found out about a new treatment, and helped me with it. Over the course of a few weeks, I began to see progress. We were finally able to work through this physical challenge and have grown closer because of my husband's patience and deep love for me.

Reflections

My wife and I have been married for almost fifteen years. We were not too far into our marriage when we discovered that our sex drives were not the same. There were a few years when things were a little frustrating for me; she didn't feel a desire to have sex very often and I did. But I didn't want to have sex if she didn't want to have sex. It left me feeling rejected at times and anxious. Those feelings sometimes led to tensions in our home outside of the bedroom. About five years ago, we had a very open conversation about sex. I expressed that I would like to have sex more than we do. She explained that she really enjoys sex about once a week but has a hard time being in the right mental and emotional place more than once a week to really enjoy it. She then proposed that when I wanted to have sex and she wasn't feeling up to a full-scale interaction that she was completely okay with a shorter sexual exchange that was focused on me. In a perfect world, we would both want to have sex the same amount, and it would be a mutual experience every time. But things are definitely better than they were, and I'm much happier and less frustrated than I used to be.

or forgotten. Yet both spouses are faced with the challenge to discipline this natural, selfish tendency within themselves and set aside their focus on their own pleasures to focus on the pleasures of their spouse. In the Book of Mormon, Alma's counsel to his son Shiblon includes "See that ye bridle all your passions, that ye may be filled with love" (Alma 38:12). Indeed, "charity serves as the ruling virtue in our effort to bless one another."[21]

Due to biological differences relative to the sexual response cycle, it is incumbent upon men to be particularly sensitive to this issue of sexual charity. Generally speaking, women take longer than do men to reach adequate levels of arousal and climax to experience orgasm. Before their marriage, John Bytheway and his wife, Kimberly, were given counsel relative to what they should expect from this sexual dynamic, including this one-liner: "Men are like microwaves, and women are like crock-pots."[22] Issues that affect hormones, such as menopause, taking birth control pills, or physical difficulties with reproductive organs, can also cause sex-drive difficulties in women. Thus, the husband may need to patiently serve until his wife has her opportunity for sexual fulfillment. The scripture 1 Corinthians 7:3–4 states, "Let the husband render unto the wife due benevolence: and likewise also the wife unto the husband. The wife hath not power of her own body, but the husband: and likewise also the husband hath not power of his own body, but the wife." Ed and Gaye Wheat have counseled, *"Every wife should be given the opportunity to experience orgasm in every intercourse.* The relationship may be very loving and warm, but this is not enough."[23]

Timing and Frequency of Sexual Relations

The sexual relationship is fully for both husband and wife. Yet it is frequently the case that men and women have varying levels of sexual interest. For example, research on sexual activity has shown that, overall, men are more likely to be interested in sex, more likely to be sexually active, and more likely to be satisfied with their sexual experiences.[24] Thus, just negotiating how often or when to have sexual relations may become a very complex marital issue relative to seeking unity. Couples must be willing to talk together about these issues frequently, openly sharing their honest thoughts and feelings. Each individual and couple is different, so no general standards should be imposed from external sources regarding how frequently couples should have sexual relations. Even within the course of marriage, life circumstances change; and with those changes, the frequency of sexual encounters will likely change too. For example, during pregnancy many women report satisfactory levels of interest and sexual response in the second trimester but poor levels of interest and sexual response in the first and third trimesters.[25] After delivering the baby, physical complaints due to the recovery process and simple fatigue also create difficulties.

Age and health are also factors that affect the frequency of sexual relations. Researchers studying those in their elder years found that men and women reporting very good or excellent health were more likely to be sexually active compared with their peers in poor or fair health.[26] However, those with health concerns generally have sexual relations less frequently. Poor health such as reduced mobility, disease processes, effects of medications, and vasocongestive processes (blood flow) that are important for sexual response contributed to decreased sexual activity in these elder years.[27]

As we are considerate of our life circumstances and sensitive to the context around our spouse's ability to participate in sexual activity (as well as being mindful of the spiritual purposes of sex), we should never feel used, cheated, or left out. Alma's counsel to his son Corianton in Alma 39:9 states, "Go no more after the lusts of your eyes, but cross yourself in all these things; for except ye do this ye can in nowise inherit the kingdom of God." If a spouse *is* feeling used, cheated, or disregarded in your sexual relationship together, then that is a clue that the role of sexuality in the relationship has become skewed.

Unfortunately, some spouses use sexual relations as a bartering tool in marriage. For example, a wife may control the sexual relationship with her husband and only engage in sex if her husband has satisfied her prerequisites, such as first washing the dishes, folding the laundry, helping with the children, or performing some emotional task. On the other hand, a husband may withhold these or other types of services or other needs his wife may have in order to control the sexual relationship. Regardless of the prerequisite established, the overall tone communicates, "You're not doing the things to please me, so I am not going to please you." This type of arrangement is not of an eternal quality and reduces the marital sexual relationship to exploitation.

Scheduling as an Option to Enhance Unity

If the sexual relationship between you and your spouse is a source of interpersonal pain because you continue to struggle relative to finding balance to meet both of your needs or because you struggle in a chronically difficult interpersonal relationship, working toward unity may require additional care and patience. In a study of sexual desire of LDS women by psychologist Jennifer Finlayson-Fife, participants shared ways they found balance in their sexual relationships when there was a discrepancy in sexual desire. One participant indicated:

> Again, it is the timing issue. I mean for a while we would alternate. You know, he wanted sex in the morning and I wanted sex at night, so we would alternate that way. . . . Though, what we would find, even though he is more desiring in the mornings, we clearly do not have as much time as we do at night. So, not only do I not look forward to that because it is in the morning and I am not a morning person, but also because I know it probably won't be as pleasurable for me because it takes me awhile to get excited and always has. . . . So, I mean, we have said, you know, the morning is your time and the night is my time and that has seemed to work pretty well.[28]

This person's experience illustrates the types of arrangements some couples make in order to try to

Reflections

When my wife and I have consistent intimate time together, we get along so much better. When we had these times together, we would always say to each other, "We need to do this more often; it's fun and we get along better." Then life would set in, we would get busy, time would go by, we'd have disagreements, and then we'd finally find ourselves being intimate again. Sometimes the disagreements became pretty big blowups, likely from the strain of neglecting our intimate relationship. It was a horrible cycle and really made no sense. Finally, we decided to schedule our intimate time together. It seemed so contrived and unromantic to set a time to have sex, but we did it anyway. As it turned out, we loved it! Rather than being contrived and unromantic, planned intimacy gave us something to look forward to and a time to hold each other accountable . . . and seriously, who doesn't want to be held accountable to having intimate times with the one they love?! We aren't perfect in our consistency, but we do make sure we're together at least twice a week. It should come as no surprise that our disagreements and blowups are now very few and very far between, and I'm more in love with my sweetheart than ever.

meet the needs of both parties. These negotiations can be helpful in finding balance.

For those not satisfied by this type of arrangement, a temporary arrangement may include creating a monthly or weekly schedule for sexual encounters. Scheduling sexual relations can allow one to feel less anxiety on non-sex days and frees spouses to be affectionate or cuddle without any pressure or expectation of sexual activity. This strategy allows both of you to look forward to sexual activity and plan, and will help you avoid stress and anxiety that may occur on non-sex days due to apprehensions or anxieties about possible misunderstandings or unmet expectations.

Thus, this simple strategy can prevent resentment or even arguments and can actually allow a more relaxed and even romantic experience when you do come together for sexual activity. In that spirit of cooperative caring, arrangements can be reevaluated and adjustments can be made more easily in an effort to more closely meet the needs of each partner.

Scheduling sexual activity can also be a great solution for couples who do not struggle with differing sexual needs or other issues but whose sexual relationship gets neglected because of busy schedules with family, professions, or Church callings. Scheduling the day or days of the week or month that you will have sexual relations may, on the surface, sound unappealing, unromantic, or lacking in spontaneity. Yet scheduling tends to have a paradoxical effect by enhancing the positive experiences of the sexual relationship as partners can look forward to and plan to spend intimate time together. The consistent time together, as opposed to inconsistent encounters, can greatly enhance marital unity.

Working Together to Find Solutions

For some couples, scheduling arrangements such as these may be woefully inadequate in finding and building unity in their sexual relationship. If you and your spouse are in this type of painful situation, unable to find a workable sexual balance, it may be helpful to at least find a *temporary* arrangement that takes into account both of your needs as best as possible. With large discrepancies in sexual desires, this will likely not be a permanent solution, but it will be a start. When couples are at a stalemate, they often disengage. Avoidance of these types of discussions can contribute to the pain of sexual discrepancies; avoidance causes greater pressure and works against you.

So just reengaging in the sexual conversation is a significant success. When the commitment to work on the sexual relationship is made explicit, each spouse then has permission to bring the topic up for discussion as frequently as needed. Frequently addressing the issue with a tone of problem-solving and charity can diffuse a lot of negative energy.

If you are unsure of how to negotiate this discussion because of the deep pain and seeming impossibility of satisfying both of you, please see our discussion on navigating perpetual issues at the end of chapter 7 for a step-by-step guide on how you can have this conversation without hurting each other.

Appropriate Sexual Behavior

In a highly sexualized culture in which anything goes, it does us well to consider what type of sexual behavior is appropriate relative to honoring the eternal purposes of sex in marriage. To do this, we first look at the official Church policy, which states: "The Lord's law of chastity is abstinence from sexual relations outside of lawful marriage and fidelity within marriage. Sexual relations are proper only between a man and a woman who are legally and lawfully wedded as husband and wife. Adultery, fornication, homosexual or lesbian relations, and every other unholy, unnatural, or impure practice are sinful."[29]

Disorders

A sexual difficulty can arise in the desire, arousal, or orgasm phases of the sexual-response cycle. Common problems include:

- Male erectile disorder is characterized by difficulty achieving and maintaining an erection during sexual contact.[35] This is the main sexual disorder for which men seek treatment.[36]

- Female orgasmic disorder is characterized by marked delay in, marked infrequency of, or absence of orgasm in almost all or all occasions of sexual activity.[37]

- Premature (early) ejaculation is characterized by a persistent pattern of ejaculation during intercourse within approximately one minute following vaginal penetration and before the individual wishes it.[38] This is the most prevalent male sexual difficulty (21 percent).[39]

The phrase "every other unholy, unnatural, or impure practice" is the guiding principle for appropriate sexual activity in an eternal marriage. Specific sexual practices are defined relative to this standard by each couple with the guidance of the Holy Ghost. If a couple feels by the guidance of the Spirit that certain sexual behaviors are unholy, unnatural, or impure, they should avoid such behavior.

The Church and prophets have offered some additional guidance. To be sure, pornography use in marriage constitutes an "unholy practice" and is unacceptable. The Church defines pornography as "any material depicting or describing the human body or sexual conduct in a way that arouses sexual feelings."[30] Viewing pornography ourselves or encouraging our spouse to view it with us in the belief that it would enhance our sexual relationship is inaccurate, inappropriate, and sinful. Relative to other sexual practices, President Howard W. Hunter counseled:

> Tenderness and respect—never selfishness—must be the guiding principles in the intimate relationship between husband and wife. Each partner must be considerate and sensitive to the

other's needs and desires. Any domineering, indecent, or uncontrolled behavior in the intimate relationship between husband and wife is condemned by the Lord.[31]

Couples should consider such counsel when questions about the acceptability of sexual practices arise. Speaking about the importance of unselfishness, Elder Neil A. Anderson taught, "The happiness of our spouse is more important than our own pleasure."[32]

Each partner's personal feelings should be considered, keeping in mind the eternal purposes of sex as we have discussed them here and seeking the guiding influence of the Holy Ghost. If you have differing opinions—so that one spouse feels a certain sexual practice is acceptable, while the other spouse feels it is not appropriate—the more conservative spouse's opinion should be honored in respect of their spiritual feelings. A summary of this principle is found in a book discussing the presidency of President Spencer W. Kimball: "Dr. Homer Ellsworth once asked what sexual conduct was acceptable for a married couple. Spencer replied that in his view anything mutually pleasurable and satisfying was acceptable, but neither should ask for conduct the other found offensive."[33]

Reflections

My wife has orgasm problems. We have sought out several avenues for help over the years, such as medications and therapy, but to no avail. It is discouraging for both of us. There are times when she will turn away and cry after sex because her needs are not met. I am sure I lack in my efforts, but I do my best to comfort and soothe her. It has been a tricky balance. I have curbed my sexual desires so that we are not having sex as often. I naturally want to be fulfilled, but I have a strong desire to see that she is also fulfilled. She feels guilty for not having sex with me as often as I would prefer, but this has helped relieve her of some of her emotional pain of continually feeling discouraged and unsatisfied sexually. Yet if I do this too much, I have noticed that she can also feel unwanted if I don't approach her for sex. So right now we just do our awkward best to work with and be sensitive to each other. To be honest, her attitude and continual efforts to still please me and make sure that my sexual desires are not neglected is a testimony to me of how amazing and selfless she is.

Sexual Dysfunction

As we've been discussing, the sexual relationship is complex, with varying contextual issues contributing to its function or dysfunction. In its complexity, the experience does not occur as our modern media would care to script it; it doesn't always go smoothly and it doesn't always create orgasm or sense of pleasurable ecstasy for each spouse every time. A classic study from the 1970s examined one hundred well-educated, happily married couples and found that more than 80 percent of the couples reported happy and satisfying sexual relations; yet 40 percent of the men reported occasional erectile and ejaculatory difficulties, and 63 percent of women reported occasional difficulties surrounding arousal and orgasm. This study found that in spite of these occasional difficulties, the overall sexual satisfaction of the couples studied was not reduced.[34]

Yet for some couples, difficulties with the sexual relationship go beyond normal, occasional setbacks. In these cases the sexual difficulties may cause impairment in the sexual relationship or create a great deal of distress.

Indeed, sexual dysfunction constitutes the most prevalent class of psychological disorders in the US. Most disorders discussed in abnormal-psychology courses have a prevalence rate of about 1 percent (i.e., 1 of every 100 people will have the disorder); whereas, among sexual disorders the prevalence rates are estimated at 31 percent for men and 43 percent for women.[40] In other words, many couples find that they will struggle with one or more sexual difficulties at various points in their marriage, with about 3 out of every 10 men and 4 out of every 10 women meeting diagnostic criteria for a sexual disorder. In some cases, penile-vaginal intercourse may not be possible for some couples, most common in those struggling with vaginismus or dyspareunia, thus requiring alternative scripts for their sexual activity.

These sexual difficulties can impact the marital relationship. For example, researchers examining women with orgasmic disorder found that when couples discussed intercourse with each other, men and women both reported feeling greater responsibility for the sexual problem (compared to control groups that did not struggle with sexual dysfunction). When these same couples discussed the topic of direct genital stimulation of the women, the men manifested greater blame, assigning responsibility for their wives' orgasmic problems to themselves. The researchers also found that women tended to be less receptive during these discussions—they were less likely to engage in listening behaviors (such as attentiveness and eye contact) and offer verbal indicators (such as acceptance and acknowledgment of their partner's viewpoint and incorporation of their partner's perspective into their own communication).[41] Blame and a failure to be open and receptive during sexual discussions will most certainly create negativity in the relationship and are likely to undermine efforts to resolve the sexual problem.

However, open communication about these issues, without blame, can mitigate some difficulties by addressing critical issues and honoring the expression of feelings. Researchers studying patients struggling with prostate cancer found that those couples who reported high levels of mutual constructive communication reported better marital adjustment than those with less healthy communication, regardless of their level of sexual dysfunction.[42]

Seeking treatment for a sexual difficulty is important, just as is seeking treatment for any other psychological disorder, such as anxiety or depression. When we seek treatment for problems with our knee, shoulder, or other such problem, the doctor does an assessment and then suggests treatment. We have found in our experience that since we go to the doctor in recognition of our ignorance and need for help, and in recognition of their expertise on the issue, we usually accept the treatment recommendations the doctor prescribes. However, we advise thoughtful prayer and consideration of all treatments prescribed relative to sexual difficulties, and if you feel it necessary, counsel with priesthood leaders.

Treatments such as education about basic sexual response, couple-reinforcing activities or exercises, or medications are commonly used in sex therapy with great success. However, be advised that some treatments prescribed by therapists may not always be in line with one's personal religious views about sexuality or with the general doctrines of the Church. For example, with sexual difficulty in areas of desire or arousal, the current psychological treatments often include the viewing of pornography. Likewise, one of the most common treatment recommendations for women experiencing difficulty achieving orgasm is masturbatory training. Counsel from Church leaders prohibiting the viewing of pornography and masturbation may make these treatments areas of concern. Thus, thoughtful and prayerful consideration would be appropriate.

Conclusion

The sexual relationship in marriage has been given to us by a loving Father in Heaven to enjoy physical pleasure, procreate, express love, and learn deeper spiritual truths. We learn more about His role as Creator and are able to gain greater unity with Him. We are able to more fully come to understand Christ's relationship with the Church, a relationship that also teaches us about how we should interact with our spouse. These great truths are available to us if we seek them, and by so doing we learn more about charity and service in meeting the needs and desires of our spouse. Through the sexual relationship we can therefore gain greater unity and intimacy with our spouse. The paradoxical truth is that as we are willing to forget ourselves in the true spirit of love, we are actually blessed with the satisfying of our own sexual pleasures.

Notes

1. David A. Bednar, "The Divinely Designed Pattern of Marriage" (address, Humanum Colloquium, New York City, 9 March 2017), http://www.mormonnewsroom.org/article/elder-bednar-transcript-the -divinely-designed-pattern-marriage.

2. Barry R. Komisaruk, Carlos Beyer-Flores, and Beverly Whipple, *The Science of Orgasm* (Baltimore, MD: John Hopkins University Press, 2006).

3. "Birth Control," The Church of Jesus Christ of Latter-day Saints, https://www.lds.org/topics/birth-control?lang=eng.

4. Neil L. Andersen, "Children," *Ensign*, November 2011, 28.

5. Jeffrey R. Holland, "Of Souls, Symbols, and Sacraments" (devotional address, Brigham Young University, Provo, UT, 12 January 1988), http://www.familylifeeducation.org/gilliland/procgroup/Souls.htm.

6. Vaughn Call, Susan Sprecher, and Pepper Schwartz, "The Incidence and Frequency of Marital Sex in a National Sample," *Journal of Marriage and Family* 57, no. 3 (August 1995): 639–52.

7. Ed Wheat and Gaye Wheat, *Intended for Pleasure: Sex Technique and Sexual Fulfillment in Christian Marriage* (Grand Rapids, MI: Revell, 1977), 138.

8. Wheat and Wheat, *Intended for Pleasure*, 136.

9. Laurie Mintz, *Becoming Cliterate: Why Orgasm Equality Matters—And How to Get It* (New York: HarperCollins, 2017), 46.

10. Wheat and Wheat, *Intended for Pleasure*, 137.

11. Denise A. Donnelly, "Sexually Inactive Marriages," *The Journal of Sex Research* 30, no. 2 (1993): 171–79; and Ted L. Huston and Anita L. Vangelisti, "Socioemotional Behavior and Satisfaction in Marital Relationships: A Longitudinal Study," *Journal of Personality and Social Psychology* 61, no. 5 (1991): 721–33.

12. Benjamin R. Karney and Thomas N. Bradbury, "The Longitudinal Course of Marital Quality and Stability: A Review of Theory, Methods, and Research," *Psychological Bulletin* 118, no. 1 (1995): 3–34.

13. Wheat and Wheat, *Intended for Pleasure*, 33.

14. Wheat and Wheat, *Intended for Pleasure*, 16; emphasis in original.

15. Holland, "Of Souls, Symbols, and Sacraments"; emphasis in original.

16. Gina Ogden, *Expanding the Practice of Sex Therapy: An Integrative Model for Exploring Desire and Intimacy* (New York: Routledge, 2013), 50.

17. Linda S. Reeves, "Protection from Pornography—A Christ-Focused Home," *Ensign*, May 2014, 15; emphasis added.

18. Ogden, *Expanding the Practice of Sex Therapy*, 14.

19. Ogden, *Expanding the Practice of Sex Therapy*, 14.

20. Linda J. Waite and Maggie Gallagher, *The Case for Marriage* (New York: Doubleday, 2000), 89.

21. Stephen E. Lamb and Douglas E. Brinley, *Between Husband and Wife: Gospel Perspectives on Marital Intimacy* (Salt Lake City: Covenant Communications, 2000), 170.

22. John Bytheway and Kimberly Bytheway, *What We Wish We'd Known When We Were Newlyweds* (Salt Lake City: Bookcraft, 2000), 87.

23. Wheat and Wheat, *Intended for Pleasure*, 121; emphasis in original.

24. Stacy Tessler Lindau and Natalia Gavrilova, "Sex, Health, and Years of Sexually Active Life Gained Due to Good Health: Evidence from Two US Population Based Cross Sectional Surveys of Ageing," *BMJ* 340:c810 (2010).

25. Jennifer Berman, Laura Berman, and Elisabeth Bumiller, *For Women Only: A Revolutionary Guide to Reclaiming Your Sex Life*, 2nd ed. (New York: Henry Holt, 2005).

26. Lindau and Gavrilova, "Sex, Health, and Years."

27. David H. Barlow and V. Mark Durand, *Abnormal Psychology: An Integrative Approach*, 6th ed. (Belmont, CA: Wadsworth, 2012), 348.

28. Jennifer Finlayson-Fife, *Female Sexual Agency in Patriarchal Culture: The Case of Mormon Women* (Ann Arbor, MI: UMI, 2002), 177.

29. The Church of Jesus Christ of Latter-day Saints, "Selected Church Policies and Guidelines," in *Handbook 2: Administering the Church* (Salt Lake City: The Church of Jesus Christ of Latter-day Saints, 2010), 179–97.

30. *True to the Faith: A Gospel Reference* (Salt Lake City: The Church of Jesus Christ of Latter-day Saints, 2004), 117–18.

31. Howard W. Hunter, "Being a Righteous Husband and Father," *Ensign*, November 1994, 50.

32. Neil L. Andersen, "Overcoming the World," *Ensign*, May 2017, 60.

33. Edward L. Kimball, *Lengthen Your Stride: The Presidency of Spencer W. Kimball* (Salt Lake City: Deseret Book, 2005), 172.

34. Ellen Frank, Carol Anderson, and Debra Rubenstein, "Frequency of Sexual Dysfunction in Normal Couples," *New England Journal of Medicine* 299, no. 3 (1978): 111–15.

35. American Psychiatric Association, *Diagnostic and Statistical Manual of Mental Disorders*, 5th ed. (Arlington, VA: American Psychiatric Publishing, 2013), 426.

36. Barlow and Durand, *Abnormal Psychology*.

37. American Psychiatric Association, *Diagnostic and Statistical Manual*, 429.

38. American Psychiatric Association, *Diagnostic and Statistical Manual*, 443.

39. Barlow and Durand, *Abnormal Psychology*.

40. Barlow and Durand, *Abnormal Psychology*.

41. Mary P. Kelly, Donald S. Strassberg, and Charles M. Turner, "Behavorial Assessment of Couples' Communication in Female Orgasmic Disorder," *Journal of Sex & Marital Therapy* 32 (2006): 81–95.

42. Hoda Badr and Cindy L. Carmack Taylor, "Sexual Dysfunction and Spousal Communication in Couples Coping with Prostate Cancer," *Psycho-Oncology* 18 (2009): 735–46.

CHAPTER 7

"The Spirit of Contention Is Not of Me"

Working through Differences

Just as couples can build intimacy in their relationship through purposeful efforts, as we have discussed in chapters 5 and 6, they can also undermine and damage it through high levels of conflict or destructive behaviors. In essence, the emotional bank account we discussed in chapter 5 can become completely bankrupt. Conflict undermines trust and loyalty, creates self-doubt, and brings an abrasive tone into the relationship that will make it difficult for the Spirit of the Lord to reside in a couple's relationship. Herein we will discuss causes of marital conflict, factors that can either escalate or minimize those causes, and ways to repair and prevent those stressful moments of conflict in marriage. We will also address how to work through perpetual issues so that couples can become more self-aware of these repeating cycles of destructive behavior and stop hurting each other again and again.

Marital Conflict and Resolve

There are many behaviors that can be destructive to relationships. John Gottman's research on marital conflict has identified four destructive behaviors in marriage: criticism, contempt, defensiveness, and stonewalling. According to Gottman and colleague, the chronic presence of these forces can predict divorce with 82 percent accuracy.[1] Due to these factors' highly destructive nature in the marital relationship, we will explore their full meaning here. Following, we will also discuss the impact of negative affectivity on conflict.

Criticism

Criticism in marriage is destructive; it hurts our spouse and undermines trust and love, thus weakening the marital relationship. However, it doesn't mean we can never make a complaint to our spouse. Gottman makes a clear distinction between a criticism and a complaint. When difficulties arise, a complaint about something your spouse has done focuses on a specific behavior and how that behavior was problematic.[2] This is generally a healthy option by which couples may address conflict.

For example, in the Book of Mormon, Alma had significant reason to confront his son Corianton, who had forsaken his ministry and sought after the harlot Isabel. In his address to his son in Alma 39, we see that in spite of the severe nature of the transgression, Alma issued a complaint to Corianton (and taught him doctrine) while avoiding criticism: "Now this is what I have against thee; thou didst go on unto boasting . . . and this is not all, my son. Thou didst do that which was grievous unto me" (verses 2–3). A basic complaint common in many marriages might include the following: "There's no gas in the car. Why didn't you fill it up like you said you would?" or "I've noticed your side of the closet is messy again. Would you please keep it clean?"

Reflections

When I was six years old, my parents would put me to bed at night and then begin to argue, argue, argue. I could hear them. I would think to myself, "I wonder if they're going to get a divorce." I swore to myself then, even at that young age, that I would never argue with my husband where the children could hear us. I am now eighty-six years old and fighting has always bothered me. Once I was married, my husband and I got along pretty well. We had disagreements but never big hollering, crying, and blaming fights like my parents had. When we did disagree, we would try to work it out wherever we happened to be working together at the time, such as in the pigpen, but not in the bedroom or the living room, where the children could hear us. We would sometimes let it work itself out over a couple of days after we pouted for a little bit. In time one of us would decide the other person was right, such as, "That was a good idea you had." We just didn't like to fight with each other. It always seemed to work out without hollering or fussing.

Contrast this process to that of criticizing our spouse; criticism takes a specific behavior that has bothered you and layers on top of it blame and general insult of one's character.[3] For example, criticisms of the situations involving the gas tank and closet might look like this: "Why can't you ever remember anything? I reminded you several times to fill up the tank, and you said you would. You couldn't even manage to get that right!" or "You are such a slob! No matter what I say, you can't seem to keep your side of the closet clean!" We read in James 3:10: "Out of the same mouth proceedeth blessing and cursing. My brethren, these things ought not so to be." In many cases the difference between a complaint and a criticism has a lot to do with the tone and delivery of the statement. And as James counsels, it can bless or curse the marriage relationship. Thus, a complaint may be necessary or justified in marriage in order to address pertinent issues, but criticism, never.

Contempt

Disgust with one's partner constitutes contempt. Contempt often arises out of resentment that a spouse allows to build up inside. It tends to be communicated through sarcasm, cynicism, name-calling, eye-rolling, sneering, mockery, and hostile humor. Contempt tends to be fueled by long-simmering negative thoughts about one's spouse.[4]

If we find ourselves talking negatively about or bad-mouthing our spouse to our other family members or friends, what is the attitude by which we do so? Upon honest reflection we may discover that the bad-mouthing originates from our contemptuous attitude. This attitude is devoid of respect for, or loyalty to, our spouse. Furthermore, because of the severe nature of this attitude—there is no hiding it!—the lack of respect and loyalty is clearly communicated not only to those to whom we vent but to our spouse as well. It is guaranteed that if we feel contempt for our spouse, our spouse knows it.

In contrast, let's consider the example of our Savior, Jesus Christ, as given to us in Isaiah 53. Regardless of being "despised," "rejected" (verse 3), "stricken," "smitten," "afflicted" (verse 4), "wounded," "bruised" (verse 5), and "oppressed" (verse 7)—all feelings we may likely feel at times relative to our relationship with our spouse, feelings that often can build resentment inside us—the scriptures report that "neither was any deceit in his mouth" (verse 9). We can work toward the ability to do this. If we keep the foundation of our marriage relationship steady, such as by utilizing the spirit of forgiveness discussed in chapter 4 and by building up our emotional bank account as discussed in chapter 5, then when we feel wounded in our marriage we can fairly easily resist resorting to a contemptuous attitude. Gottman and colleague teach, "Fondness and admiration are antidotes for contempt."[5] When we focus on the positive aspects of our spouse, we will build respect for them rather than contempt and will be "less likely to act disgusted with him or her when [we] disagree."[6]

Defensiveness

Defensiveness is an act of justifying oneself for poor behavior (or maybe for behavior we thought was just fine but for some reason we find out was hurtful to our spouse and they are letting us know). Although criticism and contempt are clearly damaging to a relationship, defensiveness may be a bit trickier to understand as a destructive force. It seems natural and understandable to be defensive, especially if one is feeling attacked or simply trying to "save face." However, in reality, defensiveness serves only to escalate the conflict, never resolve it, because it attaches blame to one's partner, promoting the attitude "The problem isn't *me*; it's *you*."[7]

The Book of Mormon story of Lehi and Sariah illustrates the positive influence that comes when we choose humility and meekness rather than defensiveness. It also provides us with a step-by-step process of how we can diffuse accusation within our own marital relationship without resorting to defensiveness. In 1 Nephi 5:2–3, we see that Sariah has been mourning the perceived loss of her sons after they have gone to recover the brass plates from Laban and have failed to return yet. In her distress, she lays upon her husband severe accusations, including that the death of her sons is *his* fault: "She also had complained against my father, telling him that he was a visionary man; saying: Behold thou hast led us forth from the land of our inheritance, and my sons are no more, and we perish in the wilderness. And after this manner of language had my mother complained against my father."

Although Sariah has some legitimate complaints within this exchange, this would qualify as a criticism because she attempts to lay blame and attack Lehi's character. Let's read Sariah's criticism in modern lingo: "Oh, great visionary man! You always have these grand ideas and think you're following God. But, because of this, we've lost our dream home, my sons are dead, and now the rest of us are going to die too!"

Let's just imagine for a moment how this intense scenario might have played out had Lehi jumped to acting in a defensive manner when the criticism came. Sariah makes the observation to Lehi that he is a "visionary man," and he immediately and defensively retorts, "No, I'm not! You are just so negative all the time! If you would just . . ." Most of us have made this mistake at one time or another, and, frankly, we've probably made it many times, so it is probably pretty easy to play out in our minds how quickly that interaction would completely fall apart.

Instead, we know from the scriptural account that continues that Lehi chose to honestly look at what Sariah had said and found that there *was* truth in what she had spoken. He then validated her

SCOTT SNOW, *Lehi's Family Leaving Jerusalem.*

by acknowledging that truth (which will always serve to diffuse a hostile combatant!): "And it had come to pass that my father spake unto her, saying: I know that I am a visionary man," or, in other words, "You know, Honey, you are right." After diffusing her negative energy, Lehi continues by explaining how his being a "visionary man" was actually a good thing for them and their family (verses 4–5). Again, in modern lingo, with a few embellishments for fun: "If I didn't see the things of God, I would not have the strong testimony of Him that I have, and, therefore, we *all* would have died already if we had stayed in Jerusalem. But, look, Sweetheart, we will get a new dream home, and it will be even better than the last one!"

Now, after offering this explanation as to the positive benefits of his visionariness, Lehi continues on the positive vein in verse 5 and shares his faith and testimony about the power of the

Lord to comfort his wife: "Yea, and I know that the Lord will deliver my sons out of the hands of Laban, and bring them down again unto us in the wilderness." Lehi's efforts to soothe his wife were masterfully successful! We learn in verses 6–8 that Sariah was comforted. Later, when her sons returned, just as Lehi had testified they would, Sariah's joy was full, and she was additionally comforted so that she was then prompted to offer her own newly strengthened testimony not only of the Lord but of her husband's role as a prophet—in essence, she embraced the great blessing that her husband was a visionary man (see verse 8). This great transformation in Sariah was possible only because Lehi chose not to become defensive when a criticism from his spouse came his way.

In some couples, defensiveness may be a pervasive problem, rather than one that occurs only on occasion when one spouse is attacking another. Sometimes, a spouse gets defensive about almost everything—a chronic defensiveness, if you will. If we find that we get upset at the slightest suggestion from our spouse or even the slightest hint of disagreement or any other such minor stressor, we may fall into this category. Has your spouse ever told you that you get mad at everything they say? If so, you are likely displaying a more chronic defensiveness that is indicative of deeper emotional or psychological wounds, perhaps even stemming from childhood.

DEBRA: *For example, one client I worked with was never good enough for his parents while he was growing up. He was often picked on. He was not allowed to join with his father in his favorite hobby because he wasn't "good enough" at the activity. Now, as an adult, he felt intense insecurity in his relationship with his wife, feeling often that he was not good enough for her too. Thus, many times when she would say things to him, he would interpret the situation through the lens of his childhood, feeling that she was now attacking his competency and value because she, too, must have been thinking he was not good enough for her. He would raise his voice and get defensive. This was a chronic problem for them, and after ten years of marriage she was very unhappy. They entered therapy to try to work through the process.*

If you have been wounded, it makes sense that you would try to protect yourself at even the slightest hint of danger. The problem comes when you have grown so accustomed to doing so that you are now trying to protect yourself even when you are *not* in danger. Overgeneralizing this protective instinct is pathological. Being defensive with your spouse when they make benign suggestions through the course of daily living creates a tense environment in which your spouse feels like they are walking on eggshells.

If you feel frequently that your ego or sense of self is threatened by your spouse (i.e., you do not feel the suggestions they make to you are benign but instead feel they are implying something deeper about your competence, value, intelligence, etc.), it may be helpful to examine on a deeper level the wounds that necessitate your feeling a need for continued protection. Have courage to go there and find healing. You and your spouse may benefit significantly from an openness and willingness to talk through the issues together, seeking the Lord for guidance. You may also consider attending therapy.

Stonewalling

Stonewalling involves tuning out and turning away from one's spouse.[8] Failing to respond in an argument, hanging up on someone when having an argument on the phone, or giving one's spouse the silent treatment are clear examples of stonewalling. Two subtle and unfortunately common forms of stonewalling today are consistently staying up late after your spouse has gone to bed, and hiding out with your smart phone or being on the computer for hours on end; both can be done for the purpose of avoiding as much interaction with one's spouse as possible. One study examining recently married LDS couples found that unregulated, habitual Internet use among wives was negatively related

Challenge

Stonewalling can become very easily accomplished if spouses get in the habit of going to bed at different times. For example, one spouse goes to bed while the other stays up surfing the Internet or watching movies. Going to bed at different times will exacerbate any felt emotional distance by increasing the physical distance between spouses and the temporal distance of being on different schedules. It will nix any opportunities to reconcile, talk, or have any other interaction that could foster intimacy. It may also create additional problems, such as putting someone at risk for getting involved with pornography. Make a commitment to go to bed together if at all possible.

to marital satisfaction from both the wives' and husbands' perspectives. The researchers proposed that this finding was possibly due to the wives using the Internet for mood-altering purposes, such as to avoid negative feelings and emotions.[9]

When we stonewall, we are giving our spouse the silent treatment. Stonewalling is not only a way of avoiding arguments, it is a way of avoiding the marriage relationship altogether.[10] And if we give our spouse the silent treatment for days or weeks on end, we are stonewalling in a *really* big way.

Criticism and contempt tend to lead to defensiveness, which escalates the negativity, leading to more contempt and more defensiveness. This toxic cycle gets intense enough that eventually one partner tunes out and stonewalls. Thus, stonewalling tends to be seen later in the marriage conflict process than the other three.[11]

Negative Affectivity

The destructive processes of criticism, contempt, defensiveness, and stonewalling can be caused by and exacerbated through a spouse's negative affective style. Negative affectivity includes the tendency to be emotionally reactive, such as responding to distressing situations by being intensely critical or expressing anger, anxiety, disgust, embarrassment, helplessness, or sadness.

By definition, this is a difficulty in emotional regulation (ways to improve this were discussed in chapter 3), and it affects how people perceive and resolve conflict. Negative affectivity has been shown to be significantly related with poor marital quality and risk for divorce.[12]

Research examining newlywed couples that had been married for five years or less found that for all spouses, negative affectivity was associated with a tendency to engage in more dysfunctional conflict styles. The research also found that the wives' negative affectivity was significantly associated with lower perceptions of marital satisfaction both from their own perspectives as well as from their husbands' perspectives; whereas, the study found that the husbands' negative affectivity was associated with only their own lower marital satisfaction.[13] Thus, negative affectivity will significantly decrease the quality of the marital relationship, particularly so if it is the wife that struggles to regulate her emotions.

Reflections

I have been married for twenty-two years, and the early years were the hardest. But now, to tell you the truth, I can't even remember the last time we had an argument. We are too busy to argue. But those early years the littlest things would set me off, and I would pick fights or arguments with my husband. At first he would argue back, but one day he just stared at me and then scooped me up into a big bear hug. At first I thought, "Oh, no! He is trying to snuff me out!" But then he caressed my head and whispered, "Everything is going to be okay." I instantly started crying and felt peace. He has done this many times in our marriage over the years. It's amazing how a simple hug can do so much. Now I have a married daughter, and I remember the call from her husband one night telling me that my daughter was crying and unreasonable. I told him to not argue but instead to go and hug her. He was amazed at how wonderfully that worked. Now they too have a peaceful way to calm down and talk reasonably.

Repair Attempts

Even in our best efforts to get along and to resolve conflict, we will sometimes fall short in our interactions with our spouse. We may fall prey to one of the difficulties we have just discussed or make other relationship mistakes. Because of this, we need to understand how to make repair attempts to try to recover from our mistakes and promote healing within the relationship. A repair attempt is any effort made by a partner to try to reduce negativity or increase positivity during a conflict.

Gottman and colleagues have studied repair attempts. In a study of newlywed couples that had been married six months or less, they found that the most effective repair attempts were *preemptive* repairs, which occurred in the first three minutes of a conflict. These types of repairs primarily sought to establish emotional connection, such as shared humor, affection, self-disclosure, expressions of understanding, empathy, acceptance of personal responsibility for a part of the issue being discussed, and messages of "we're okay." Repairs that took a logical, rational, or cognitive problem-solving approach were not as effective. The effectiveness of the repair attempt was also largely influenced by the reaction of the recipient. Thus, this study shows us that regardless of who actually initiates the repair attempt, both spouses have the ability to turn a tough situation around.[14]

As a note, these researchers did not find repair attempts to be very effective at the tail end of a conflict—it was just too late. So, as we consider making repair attempts in the midst of our own marital conflict, it's best to use them earlier, when negative emotion has not gotten too intense and the course of the conflict not gone too far awry.[15]

Process Commentary

A very helpful repair attempt or communication skill is to be able to shift the focus of a hostile interaction away from specific content and onto the process of the moment. For example, an unhappy spouse may offer criticism on a myriad of topics, sometimes within only a matter of minutes, not necessarily because those issues (such as filling up the gas tank, emptying the trash, paying the bills, etc.) are so very important at that moment but just because they are angry, hurt, or grumpy. If we try to discuss the issues they are criticizing, we may get lost in strange pathways, with no hope of finding our way out without causing a lot of pain and damage to the marital relationship. Instead, we can focus on the process of the interaction (i.e., what is happening in the room at that very moment) to avoid getting sucked into the specific content of the criticism. This also serves to make a more personal, emotional connection as a repair attempt.

When stonewalling occurs in our marital relationships, efforts to break the ice with a joke or other interaction may occasionally work but may just as often fail. A more direct and effective route requires a brave spouse to confront the stonewalling spouse, not with more negativity but with a loving process commentary. A comment such as "I know you are avoiding me because you are hurting and you don't know how to resolve the issue" can go a long way in softening hearts and initiating a

Reflections

I feel apologizing to my wife is a priesthood responsibility. Our eternal love for and commitment to each other far outweigh any disagreement or argument we may have. I remember a disagreement my wife and I had with each other that of course turned into an argument. We kind of gave each other the silent treatment for the better part of the day. I remember walking upstairs to our bedroom and finding my wife on her knees, praying. I was very humbled by this beautiful sight. I went downstairs to the bathroom, closed the door, and got on my knees and prayed. I felt an overwhelming feeling that I needed to humble myself and go to her and tell her that I was sorry and how much I loved her. She was very receptive and also apologized to me, with a nice hug. It is my experience and strong belief that any argument is caused by misunderstanding and pride. My remedy for that is to always humble myself by going to the Lord in prayer and asking for His help. It is then that He always reminds me to go to her with a kind attitude and apologize, no matter how much I am right or wrong. It is amazing how well that works.

discussion that has the potential for real healing. Another process commentary in this scenario could sound like this: "I know you are hurting. I am sorry I have hurt you. I want to move past this. What can I do to help you feel more comfortable interacting with me?"

In our own relationship, we have practiced using process commentary so much that we do it almost automatically now when there is tension. Our most commonly used observations are very simple but effective: "We don't seem to be communicating very well" or "We don't seem to be getting along right now." When one of us makes these no-brainer statements to the other, we usually get a chuckle out of it because by the time we feel prompted to make one of these comments it is clearly obvious to both of us that we are at odds with each other. Although these are simple process commentaries, just by *labeling what is actually going on in the moment*, we are almost always successful at shifting the tone of the interaction away from the tension and what may have previously become a downward spiral of negativity to a slightly lighter or even more productive discussion. In this way these process commentaries become repair attempts because they attempt to deescalate rising tension.

Other examples of process-focused commentary include the following:

"You seem to be really upset with me. No matter what I do, you seem displeased. Why are you grumpy?" "What is happening right now? What are you really trying to say? I don't think this is really about . . . " "What is this conversation like for you?" As we have learned, you also may be surprised at how quickly a process commentary can soften the feeling of hostility in the room and promote a deeper relationship discussion that can be therapeutic, instead of continuing destructive patterns.

RICHARD: *Here is an example of process commentary from our marriage. One evening we were both testy and short with each other; it was nothing serious, but we were both tired and a bit cranky from a long day. We kind of let things cool down until the next day, when we tried to move on and did pretty well at interacting, but just to make sure the air was fully clear Debra made a playful repair attempt that evening during dinner: "We need to be nice to each other," to which I enthusiastically responded, "I agree!" This was a subtle yet effective process commentary because Debra implicitly labeled what had been going on with us earlier—that we had not been nice to each other—with the explicit statement of how we should now choose to act moving forward.*

The Power of an Apology

An apology is also a type of repair attempt. We must never forget the power that comes by offering a genuine apology to our spouse when we have caused them pain. "Confess your faults one to another, and pray one for another, that ye may be healed" (James 5:16). Wendy Ulrich,

LDS psychologist and public speaker, has outlined steps to an effective apology.[16] First, we admit our mistake or empathically acknowledge the hurt our spouse is feeling because of our actions. Second, we tell our spouse what we can do to fix the situation (or what we will do differently in the future to prevent it). Third, we can ask our spouse what else we could do to make things right. As we seek their feedback, it may bring up other issues we were not aware of or other such feedback we had not anticipated. If we also accept this new information with Christlike grace and humility, the process of apologizing itself will create a greater sense of closeness and trust in each other that will not only resolve the difficulty at hand but increase bonds of love and tenderness.

Researchers have examined the role of an apology, and other efforts to make amends, in romantic relationships. One study has shown that a partner that was hurt by the other felt more forgiving of them when they apologized by extending a sincere apology, offering compensation, sincerely accepting responsibility, and conveying remorse and regret for the hurtful action. Being sincere in offering an apology to our spouse is vital. In this study sincerity in the apology was found to be a very important mediating factor because the partner that had been hurt perceived that the offender understood and validated their experience of the hurtful event.[17] Unfortunately, some may utter the words "I'm sorry" without really being thoughtful about the situation or without great sincerity in wanting to resolve the current issues. In these times, they expect the spouse to accept this token and "clear the air" emotionally. For many, this type of apology not only fails to perform its intended function but also exacerbates an already tense situation.

Prevention against Destructive Conflict

We have discussed these destructive forces and have offered means by which we can work to resolve them when they occur in our relationship. But how do we avoid falling prey to these destructive dynamics in our marital relationship in the first place? Let's take a look at some important behavioral and theoretical principles of prevention that provide couples with valuable interpersonal tools.

Learn to Pause

One effective behavioral strategy we can employ in our efforts to prevent destructive communication and infuse positive qualities into our interaction is a simple one: learn to pause before responding. Just pause. When we get caught up in the heat of an argument, we often begin to say things very quickly without thinking. In this rash manner much of our communication tends to violate our Christian values and falls into the realm of destructive communication. Yet we will find that if we can slow down the interaction of a tense moment, we can be thoughtful about our response and then respond in a way that will generally be more in line with our personal values and love for our spouse.

For example, before retorting critically or contemptuously to an accusation laid upon us by our spouse, we can pause, take a breath, and collect our thoughts in order to speak them in peace. As we pause, we can also ask ourselves additional questions to check the content of what we are about to say. Questions such as "Is what I am about to say kind?" "Will this help resolve tension or escalate it?" and "Is it even important?" can cause us to completely alter the words that will next come out of our mouths. We may be surprised at how often a simple check on what we are about to say will change the whole tone of an interaction. So try this simple strategy: when tempted to respond negatively, pause with a deep breath before speaking. That pause can offer bounteous protection from destructive forces and help us preserve our own Christianity.

Timing

Another practical conflict-prevention strategy is to consider the timing of a discussion that holds the potential for conflict. First, some couples believe that they should never go to bed without resolving an argument. We have heard of some couples staying up until the early hours of the morning, working to resolve their problems. We applaud any and all who work this hard. If this is an effective strategy for you in your efforts to resolve marital conflict, please continue.

Yet this has not been a good approach for us. Trying to follow this principle at various times, we have found that the conversation and our feelings toward each other deteriorate rapidly as the clock ticks later and later. And then we struggle the next day from fatigue and lack of sleep. Instead, we have found that much of the work of the argument is accomplished peacefully with a good night's sleep, a fresh day, and a new perspective. We tend to be much more humble in the mornings once we are both engaged in our respective duties and we have both had time to think things through independently. We will generally call each other a couple of hours later and, with a spirit of love, express remorse and a desire to reconnect.

In marriage therapy, therapists often encourage couples *not* to engage in conflict resolution, discuss topics with the potential for conflict, or air grievances after 9:00 p.m. This standard is understood when we acknowledge that many of us are unable to think clearly or that we have little desire to be humble or resolve conflict when we are both upset *and* exhausted. So, in considering the timing of a conflict-potential discussion, waiting until morning might be an option that may serve your marital relationship.

Second, as we consider issues of timing, we would also do well to keep a careful eye on the context surrounding our spouse. For example, if we want to discuss a perpetual issue that has risen to the surface again and yet we know our spouse is overly burdened by other current stressors (such as a deadline at work or fatigue from taking care of sick children), it would be better to hold off. With the extra stress, our spouse is likely unable to tolerate a difficult discussion the same way they would if they were feeling stronger, thus increasing the likelihood of conflict.

Third, we need to consider when to bring up issues for discussion when we have multiple complaints we'd like to discuss with our spouse. Don't bring them up all at the same time. There is a tendency for some spouses to think that if they are already arguing about one issue, they might as well throw all of their complaints into the mix.

DEBRA: *Admittedly, earlier in our marriage, Richard at times brought up multiple complaints during our efforts to work through a difficult issue. He thought that, since we were already arguing, by bringing up his other complaints, it would minimize conflict later by just getting it all out on the table. However, this approach proved unwise. It took energy away from the issue already at hand and directed it to other issues that were unrelated. When Richard did this, it immediately exploded the dynamic: we were then not arguing about one thing, but we were arguing about four, and I was steaming! The exponential increase in negative energy was significantly more destructive to our relationship than the smaller discussions to address the other issues would have ever been. Although these types of interactions were relatively rare, to date they have been the most heated arguments of our marriage. He has since learned better.*

Lastly, as we think about timing, we may need to consider taking a time-out from conflict resolution that has already begun when it becomes apparent nothing will actually be resolved. The attitude with which each of us goes into the conflict-resolution process becomes an important player here. If the discussion begins with criticism and contempt, with the spouses feeling negative or accusatory, Gottman and colleague indicate that we are likely to have a negative outcome to the discussion. They have reported that for a fifteen-minute discussion between spouses, they can predict the outcome of the interaction with 96 percent accuracy by examining only the first three minutes.[18] In other words, if the discussion starts badly, we would do well to put it on hold and try again another time, rather than continuing a process that may increase the problems and further undermine feelings of security or trust. (Time-outs are not just for children. They work great for adults too.)

The ultimate goal of any conflict-resolution process is to resolve the interpersonal difficulty quickly and allow the Spirit to be restored within the relationship. We want an eternal relationship in both duration and quality. We should be thoughtful, use wisdom and personal restraint, and make the choices that will encourage the greatest probability of peaceful resolution.

Principles and Preferences

A theoretical concept that will prevent conflict and destructive forces in our marriage before they even start and limit them if they do appear is to learn and apply the difference between principles and preferences. Sometimes we create unnecessary conflict because we wrongfully view the actions of our spouse as some major offense against God or His commandments or simply against us. In these cases, we need to ask, "Is the issue based on a principle or is it a preference?" Principles are eternal; their application makes a difference in our eternal well-being. A preference, on the other hand, is only about the here and now; it has nothing to do with eternal consequences. Far too many conflicts in marriage are because couples fail to recognize this distinction. The husband or wife thinks their spouse's behavior is a significant threat, but in fact it is only a behavior of preference that is of little consequence.

A blogger's story illustrates this concept:

> My "Aha Moment" happened because of a package of hamburger meat. I asked my husband to stop by the store to pick up a few things for dinner, and when he got home [I] realized he'd gotten

the 70/30 hamburger meat—which means it's 70% lean and 30% fat. I asked, "What's this?"

"Hamburger meat," he replied, slightly confused.

"You didn't get the right kind," I said.

"I didn't?" He replied with his brow furrowed. "Was there some other brand you wanted or something?"

"No. You're missing the point," I said. "You got the 70/30. I always get at least the 80/20."

He laughed. "Oh. That's all? I thought I'd really messed up or something."

That's how it started. I launched into him. I berated him for not being smarter. Why would he not get the more healthy option? Did he even read the labels? Why can't I trust him? Do I need to spell out every little thing for him in minute detail so he gets it right? Also, and the thing I was probably most offended by, why wasn't he more observant? How could he not have noticed over the years what I always get? Does he not pay attention to anything I do?

As he sat there, bearing the brunt of my righteous indignation and muttering responses like, "I never noticed," "I really don't think it's that big of a deal," and "I'll get it right next time," I saw his face gradually take on an expression that I'd seen on him a lot in recent years. It was a combination of resignation and demoralization. . . . I suddenly felt terrible. And embarrassed for myself. He was right. It really wasn't anything to get bent out of shape over.[19]

Perhaps many of us have found ourselves in a similarly painful interaction over something so trivial. President Dieter F. Uchtdorf defined for us more clearly the differences between principles and preferences:

> While the Atonement is meant to help us all become more like Christ, it is not meant to make us all the same. Sometimes we confuse differences in personality with sin. We can even make the mistake of thinking that because someone is different from us, it must mean they are not pleasing to God. This line of thinking leads some to believe that the Church wants to create every member from a single mold—that each one should look, feel, think, and behave like every other.
>
> As disciples of Jesus Christ, we are united in our testimony of the restored gospel and our commitment to keep God's commandments. But we are diverse in our cultural, social, and political preferences.

Reflections

My wife and I approach some things in life in completely different ways. I have a deep need to have order and cleanliness in my home and life because of the intense chaos of my childhood. My wife struggles in these areas. She is more of a creative personality that flits from project to project, most often without what I would consider "finishing" the job and cleaning up the mess. These two very different styles, of course, tend to create conflict in our family life. Many times our house is a wreck and I am stressed as a result, to say the least! It is hard for me, especially when my need for the other way—what I would consider the better way—is so great. Yet I have learned that my wife is more important than order, the house, or anything else.

The Church thrives when we take advantage of this diversity and encourage each other to develop and use our talents to lift and strengthen our fellow disciples.[20]

DEBRA: *We have successfully navigated several principle-preference issues throughout our marriage. Yet we have also gotten caught up in principle-preference confusion at times. Richard's personality style is to remain fairly even-keeled. He is steady, looks for solutions to problems, continues to move forward in spite of difficulties, and has faith that things will always work out. He doesn't get riled up very often. This is a strength in our relationship, especially in high-intensity moments that are caused by external sources. Yet, as part of this style, he tends to minimize himself; he does not draw attention to himself, if at all possible. This has created some problems for us.*

For example, early in our dating and marriage, Richard believed this personal preference to minimize himself was a principle relative to gospel teachings on pride. So, when he overheard me say something about myself or my daughters to friends, he chastised me for trying to draw attention to myself, being self-focused, or being prideful. I did not feel I was being self-focused, but in conversations with friends, I did spend time sharing about myself, just as my friends spent time sharing about themselves. On one occasion, while I was teaching a university class, I briefly mentioned the blessing that my education was in my life. I intended the disclosure to encourage the students and impress upon them the importance of continuing their education so they could have more stable, fulfilling lives. Richard, who happened to be in attendance, saw my comment as an effort to promote myself and later sought to correct me. Accusations such as these from Richard were frequent in those early years, were very painful, and created conflict as I felt unrighteously judged and completely misunderstood.

RICHARD: *Over time the pressure on this issue eased. In full irony I recognized that my corrective attitudes toward Debra were illustrative of my own self-righteous pride. I began to see that my minimizing style was my preference and that I had skewed my interpretation of what constituted the problem of pride. I also came to realize that connecting with people in a personable manner is one of Debra's great strengths and allows others to feel she is a trusted friend, teacher, and therapist. It became a powerful and important lesson to me that self-righteousness in marriage can be more damaging than any other type of pride. We both now seek to find ways to celebrate each other's preferences rather than judge them.*

Marriage gives us the task of learning to respect and support each other's principles and preferences. When we do so, *we simply will have fewer conflicts.* Period. Our general approach for marital navigation is that principles are worth discussing so that partners can attempt to become unified in those areas. Preferences are also worth discussing, but with a different aim—to ultimately recognize that there is strength in

Reflections

About a year and a half after my husband of twenty years died, I met my current husband. In time, as our relationship grew and I started having feelings for him, fear began to overtake me. I had only ever loved one man in all my life. Also, my new love was no longer Mormon, and he and his children had a different lifestyle than my girls and I did. Many of my favorite family members and friends are not Mormon, and I have tremendous respect for them, but this was different, or so I thought. As I prayed and contemplated these things, I received a powerful answer: "Just love him." Loving someone who is like me is easy, but loving someone who is different from me—truly loving that person, without judgments or assumptions—is what I believe expands my capacity to love and is the very thing that makes me more like Christ. The feeling I had was that I was trying to make sense of heavenly things with a mortal mind and that I should just let go and love him. I felt incredible peace in this. After I made my decision to let myself fall in love, I learned quickly that focusing on our differences always brings confusion and fear, but when I focus on what we have in common, we experience incredible joy and power. I've learned that our belief systems are fundamentally in alignment. We both believe that the most important things in life are love, kindness, forgiveness, service, honesty, and light. He's been a tremendous influence for good in our home. He continually inspires and empowers me. Recognizing his profound goodness allows me to let go and not feel the need to change him but, instead, to just love him.

diversity and use the discussion to promote and encourage personal preferences.

Sometimes it may be the case that our spouse *is* struggling to obey *principles* of the gospel. If we feel something is vital to the welfare of our marriage or our family and we decide a discussion with our spouse is warranted, it is necessary to always remember seeking to behave in a Christlike manner, particularly employing the principle of charity and remembering the gift of agency. President Dallin H. Oaks has counseled: "In so many relationships and circumstances in life, we must live with differences. Where vital, our side of these differences should not be denied or abandoned, but as followers of Christ we should live peacefully with others who do not share our values or accept the teachings upon which they are based. The Father's plan of salvation, which we know by prophetic revelation, places us in a mortal circumstance where we are to keep His commandments. That includes loving our neighbors of different cultures and beliefs as He has loved us."[21]

Our spouse may be this neighbor. This teaching becomes particularly relevant in marriages where spouses are not unified in gospel living or even Church membership. Rupertus Meldenius, a Lutheran theologian and educator, called for unity and the practice of charity. In time his teaching shortened to read, "In the essentials, let there be unity. In the non-essentials, let there be liberty. In all things, let there be charity."[22] Without charity, the pure love of Christ, we *all* have the potential to become self-righteous jerks.

When these types of sensitive discussions occur, we each must remember the Savior's mandate to avoid contention—even when we and our spouse have different opinions over points of principle: "There shall be no disputations among you, as there have hitherto been; neither shall there be disputations among you concerning the points of my doctrine, as there have hitherto been. For verily, verily I say unto you, he that hath the spirit of contention is not of me" (3 Nephi 11:28–29). Rather than live in contention, it is the Savior's will that we love one another: "And he commanded them that there should be no contention one with another, but that they should look forward with one eye . . . having their hearts knit together in unity and in love one towards another" (Mosiah 18:21). As we do this and remember the glorious gift of agency that we all enjoy, we will be able to have discussions when our principles differ without resorting to destructive means, thus drawing our hearts closer. It is only under these circumstances that perspectives on the principle we are discussing may draw nearer together as well.

On the other hand, if a particular issue of conflict represents an issue of preference, ask the following question: "What *principle* is illustrated by my spouse's preference?" Identifying the answer to this question is very important for reducing moments of conflict. Our preferences may reveal our valued principles. If we identify our spouse's values in a moment of potential conflict, we may be able to shift our attention to the good intentions of our spouse. This inevitably will produce a more respectful feeling towards them.

Reflections

Being an extrovert married to an introvert has its challenges. While I need to have friends and be able to visit with them, my husband needs small groups for short periods. In the beginning of our marriage, I thought I needed to force social gatherings on my spouse and that he should just be able to get used to it. When going to events, our nights would always end at about 9:00 p.m., which is ordinarily when he had enough and would want to go home. Having been taught that I should always leave an event with my spouse, I would leave, which meant our nights ended with at least one of us being very unhappy. After some struggling and even depression, we finally figured out that through communication, understanding, and love, there was a solution. We have found that it is very important to be together at social gatherings most of the time, but not all the time. Now, when we go out and my loving introvert has had enough, he will often head home and relieve our son from babysitting, while I stay with our friends for a little longer. While this is not always the case—as sometimes I will still go home with him, and sometimes he'll even stay with me—we have recognized that there are times when we have different needs. Our love grows from this understanding.

Reflections

My wife and I were married earlier this year. Since then we've learned to be better at kindly but openly communicating how we feel when there is a difference of opinion. Going into a discussion about a conflict, we both try to acknowledge that our feelings may be the result of a misinterpretation of the other's words or actions, or of ineffectively communicating our expectations. We try to have conversations at a time and place that we can both be comfortable and then show respect by waiting, listening, and taking turns. We have found that all of these things together bring us closer to the root of the conflict and serve as the foundation for compromise.

For example, if you are feeling irritated because your spouse is talking too much, you can ascertain that their style of interpersonal interaction is a preference. If you went on the attack at the smallest irritation or provocation, you might say something like this: "Gosh, I can't even hear myself think. Can you just stop talking for even a moment?" A rant such as this will inevitably provoke conflict. However, if you take the time to consider the *principle* that is illustrated by your spouse's talking-a-lot preferential behavior, you may, perhaps, realize that your spouse talks a lot because they value feeling connected with you and want to feel closer to you. Realizing that they are trying to feel closer to you would make it fairly difficult to continue to feel irritated in that moment and could entice you toward feelings of affection.

There will be times when we feel prompted to discuss issues of preference relative to how they influence the marital relationship. Sometimes, in discussions of preferences we can, through loving gentleness, persuade our spouse to adopt our preferences over time. Yet this is *not* necessary for a couple to be unified in principle and to have a strong and fulfilling relationship. A marriage will be magnified and strengthened when spouses recognize that in principles there is strength in unity, and in preferences there is strength in diversity. When spouses are unified in principles and yet have diversity in preferences, the marriage gains great strength and richness.

Being unified in principle helps us work together to apply gospel principles and build an

eternal marriage. Being diverse in preferences helps us enjoy different views in
life and to specialize in interests that bring
individual personality and flavor to the
relationship. Our Heavenly Father loves
and promotes both.

"Lord, Is It I?"

In the New Testament, during the Last
Supper, Jesus Christ announced to the
Apostles that one of them would betray
Him. Rather than pointing fingers at each
other, the responses of the Apostles were
acts of humility: "They were exceedingly
sorrowful, and began every one of them
to say unto him, Lord, is it I?" (Matthew
26:22). John Bytheway discussed the principle of meekness relative to this scripture:

> If someone were to ask whether com-
> munication skills or meekness is most
> important to a marriage, I'd answer
> meekness, hands down. You can be a
> superb communicator but still never
> have the humility to ask, "Is it I?" *Com-
> munication skills are no substitute for Christlike
> attributes.*[23]

Humility and meekness play a far
greater role in minimizing and even elim-
inating marital conflict than any other
characteristics. One writer observed:

> Without . . . theological perspec-
> tives, . . . secular exercises designed
> to improve our relationship and our
> communication skills (the common

Reflections

*Several years ago, I noticed
something in my own mar-
riage that began to bother me.
I wished I could blame this
problem on my wife, but I
knew that I was the problem.
I became aware that each
time my wife would question
a decision I had made or take
another approach or angle to
an idea I had, I began to be
defensive. I would immediately counter back with, "Why
don't you ever like my ideas?"
or "Do I get a say on this?"
or "How come you never like
the way I do things?" The
more I defended myself, the
more angry and resentful I
became. Then, one day, with
sudden clarity, I realized that
I was not being meek. Instead,
I was being proud, selfish,
and defensive. After all, my
wife's ideas were not a direct
attack on me—she was simply
trying to help me improve my
business, our lawn, or the
ward where I was serving as
bishop. And frankly, her ideas
were very good. I recognized
that had I been meek and
humble, I would have received
her counsel and wisdom as
revelation from heaven.*

tools of counselors and marriage books) will never work any permanent change in one's heart: *they simply develop more clever and skilled fighters!*[24]

DEBRA: *In marital therapy it is common to teach I-statements to help couples improve communication. An I-statement is one in which one spouse expresses to the other how they feel—their experience in the moment—rather than making statements that are accusatory and hostile, for example, "I felt hurt that I didn't hear from you while you were away" or "I felt unloved when you were sarcastic last night." Someone who has not sought the spirit of meekness in the moment of confrontation might still feel justified in their hostility if they seek to only apply communication skills and fail to implement fundamental Christlike attributes. To make the point with therapy clients about how we can inappropriately manipulate communication skills if we don't have the right spirit in our hearts, I have joked with them as I have counseled: "I feel like you are a jerk!" is not an I-statement!*

Yet, as we seek humbly to ask, "Lord, is it I?" we may still be tempted to hold on to a deeper-level belief that even though we have some things we need to change, our spouse's problems are *really* at the heart of the issue. Holding onto this belief can be especially tempting if our spouse is struggling with something quite glaring and obviously pathological or problematic. In these circumstances, we must make the Olympic effort to dig deep within ourselves in the search for Christlike humility and meekness and refocus ourselves upon this all-important question: "Lord, is it I?"

In a priesthood session of general conference, President Dieter F. Uchtdorf addressed the need to ask, "Lord, is it I?" and spoke of the humility needed to accept the answer: "And if the Lord's answer happens to be 'Yes, my son, there are things you must improve, things I can help you to overcome,' I pray that we will accept this answer, humbly acknowledge our sins and shortcomings, and then change our ways by becoming better husbands, better fathers, better sons."[25] The ability to accept the answer to this question requires sincere humility and determination to follow our Savior in all things.

A powerful example of this principle comes from LDS, *New York Times* best-selling author Richard Paul Evans, as he candidly shared a blog post entitled "How I Saved My Marriage":

> For years my wife Keri and I struggled. Looking back, I'm not exactly sure what initially drew us together, but our personalities didn't quite match up. And the longer we were married the more extreme the differences seemed. . . . We were on the edge of divorce and more than once we discussed it.
>
> I was on book tour when things came to a head. . . . I had reached my limit. That's when I turned to God. . . . I don't know if you could call it prayer—maybe shouting at God isn't prayer, maybe it is—but whatever I was engaged in I'll never forget it. I was standing in the shower of the [hotel] yelling at God that marriage was wrong and I couldn't do it anymore. As much as I hated the idea of divorce, the pain of being together was just too much. . . . Why had I married someone so different than me? Why wouldn't *she* change?
>
> Finally, hoarse and broken, I sat down in the shower and began to cry. In the depths of my despair powerful inspiration came to me. *You can't change her, Rick. You can only change yourself.* At that moment I began to pray. If I can't change *her*, God, then change *me*. I prayed late into the night. I prayed the next day on the flight home. I prayed as I walked in the door. . . . That night, as we lay in our bed, inches from each other yet miles apart, the inspiration came. I knew what I had to do.
>
> The next morning I rolled over in my bed next to Keri and asked, "How can I make your day better?" . . .
>
> The next day I asked the same thing. . . .
>
> The next morning came. "What can I do to make your day better?" . . .
>
> The next morning I asked again. And the next. And the next. Then, during the second week, a miracle occurred. As I asked the question Keri's eyes welled up with tears. Then she broke down crying. . . .
>
> I continued asking for more than a month. And things did change. The fighting stopped. Then Keri began asking, "What do you need from me? How can I be a better wife?"
>
> The walls between us fell. We began having meaningful discussion on what we wanted from life and how we could make each other happier. No, we didn't solve all our problems, I can't even say that we never fought again. But the nature of our fights changed. Not only were they becoming more and more rare, they lacked the

energy they'd once had. We'd deprived them of oxygen. We just didn't have it in us to hurt each other anymore.

Keri and I have now been married for more than thirty years. I not only love my wife, I like her. I like being with her. I crave her. I need her. Many of our differences have become strengths and the others don't really matter. We've learned how to take care of each other and, more importantly, we've gained the desire to do so.[26]

Following Christ's Example

Ultimately, following the example of Jesus Christ will provide the greatest inoculation against marital conflict. James 3:13, 17–18 states:

> Who is a wise man and endued with knowledge among you? let him shew out of a good conversation his works with meekness of wisdom. . . .
>
> The wisdom that is from above is first pure, then peaceable, gentle, and easy to be entreated, full of mercy and good fruits, without partiality, and without hypocrisy.
>
> And the fruit of righteousness is sown in peace of them that make peace.

Seeking to employ the principles of the gospel of Jesus Christ with a genuine heart, thus working to become more Christlike in character, will inoculate our marriage against destructive processes. Being Christlike doesn't mean there will never be disagreement, but it will protect us from causing greater damage to the eternal quality of our relationship while we try to resolve the disagreement. In other words, we will be able to disagree without being disagreeable.

President Wilford Woodruff spoke of protection from the destroying angels and other destructive influences: "If you do your duty, and I do my duty, we'll have protection, and shall pass through the afflictions in peace and safety. Read the scriptures and the revelations. . . . It's by the power of the gospel that we shall escape."[27] On another occasion, President Woodruff spoke again of how we may obtain protection from the destroying angels: "Wherever the eternal, everlasting and holy priesthood or its influence dwells, there is protection and salvation."[28] The more common destroying angels in our marriages, against which we can secure protection, are criticism, contempt, defensiveness, stonewalling, and affective negativity.

President Woodruff spoke of the "power of the gospel" and the "holy priesthood or its influence" as means of protection against these destructive angels. These may be summarized with several verses from Doctrine and Covenants (see D&C 121:41–46) which not only speak of destructive forces we need to remove from our characters but also highlight the necessity of infusing a variety of positive qualities into our interactions with others: persuasion, long-suffering, gentleness, meekness, love unfeigned (i.e., being genuine and sincere), kindness, pure knowledge, faithfulness, charity, and virtue. In order to employ these qualities in our relationship, we have to internalize these qualities within our own hearts. The presence of positive qualities—such as simple kindness, meekness, and humility—will provide protection against destructive forces

Reflections

A principle that has made an impression in my life stems from the scripture Ephesians 5:25, which says, "Husbands, love your wives, even as Christ also loved the church, and gave himself for it." For nineteen years growing up at home, and the subsequent times over the past twenty-six years I have been back to visit, I have never heard my father raise his voice to my mother. I am grateful to say that my father's example has made a profound impression on my marriage too. For twenty-two years, I can say my voice has not been raised to my beautiful princess, nor her voice to me. It isn't to say that we have not disagreed on things. But we committed to each other while we dated that working out differences would never occur with raised voices. I know this principle of loving each other as Christ loved the Church has blessed and strengthened our marriage in countless ways.

and lead to harmony, joy, and happiness within the marriage relationship.

Navigating Perpetual Issues

This chapter would be incomplete without a discussion of how to address those irksome recurrent, or perpetual, issues that cause conflict in marriage. Perpetual issues are ongoing relationship dynamics or specific reoccurring behaviors that cause marital frustration, annoyance, or even conflict over and over again in a variety of contexts. Each of us that has been married for more than a couple of months has experience with perpetual issues.

In spite of the honest and even effective efforts we may make to resolve conflict in any given moment, we generally find that because of the weakness of the flesh, the same or similar difficulties come up again and again—and again—over many years. We often see a difficulty as something our spouse does that drives us nuts. It may be a problem we seem to resolve for a time, but then we soon find it back again. Each time *that* problem comes up, we confront and discuss and negotiate and attempt to solve, feeling a bit empowered with renewed hope in the relationship; and each time the problem arises again we feel deflated and defeated, even feeling discouraged that we really haven't made any progress in our marriage at all.

In his work, John Gottman indicates that perpetual issues generally stem from life dreams that are hidden or not being respected in the marriage. This creates a lot of emotion that tends to lead to conflict. Gottman and colleague have counseled: "One good indicator that you're wrestling with a hidden dream is that you see your spouse as being the sole source of the marital problem. . . . It may indicate that you don't see your part in creating the conflict because it has been hidden from view."[30] Openly acknowledging the deeper meanings behind the issue can expose unacknowledged dreams. Examples of hidden dreams may include "I want to feel connected to my extended family" or "I want to feel that my life is meaningful" or "I want to feel stable financially so I have energy for other things."

So what can be done about these sticky, ongoing problems? As we have indicated throughout this chapter, our first step is always to turn to our Savior, Jesus Christ. The Apostle Paul struggled with a perpetual problem in his life. Relative to the purpose of the problem, his efforts to eradicate it from his life, and the Lord's response to his efforts, he records:

> And lest I should be exalted above measure through the abundance of the revelations, there was given to me a thorn in the flesh, the messenger of Satan to buffet me, lest I should be exalted above measure. For this thing I besought the Lord thrice, that it might depart from me. And he said unto me, My grace is sufficient for thee: for my strength is made perfect in weakness. Most gladly therefore will I rather glory in my infirmities, that the power of Christ may rest upon me. (2 Corinthians 12:7–9)

The word sufficient means "enough." Christ assures Paul that His grace is enough for the Apostle. We must remember that He can sustain and support us, even when a problem remains ongoing. Are you feeling overwhelmed by a "yet again" situation? Pull out the scriptures and read what our Savior would say to you. There is great power in His word and His assurances (see chapter 9). In John 16:33, the Savior says, "These things I have spoken unto you, that in me ye might have peace. In the world ye shall have tribulation: but be of good cheer; I have overcome the world."

Even as we try to draw near to our Savior, we would do well to also increase our ability to navigate these issues more productively with our spouse. Thus, we also need to work directly with our spouse through purposeful and effortful discussion. Gottman and colleague indicate that in these types of problems the goal is *not* to solve the problem but to "move from gridlock to dialogue. The gridlocked conflict will probably always be a perpetual issue in your marriage, but one day you will be able to talk about it without hurting each other."[31]

Gottman and colleague suggest five steps we can take to navigate the gridlock of a perpetual issue in our marital relationship:

1. Discover the dream that is not being honored in the marriage. Did you bury a dream, thinking you needed to do so to make the marriage work?

2. Write about your side of the dream, while your spouse writes about their side. Each of you explains where your dream came from and why it is meaningful to you. Then dialogue with your spouse, each of you taking fifteen minutes to speak while the other listens. The goal is not to problem solve or offer rebuttals to each other but to achieve understanding about why each of you feels the way you do about the issue.

3. Offer support to each other through this stressful process by soothing or calming each other.

4. Begin to work through accepting the differences between you and coming to an initial compromise that will allow you to continue discussion without the issue being so painful. This can be done by identifying core aspects of the issue on which you feel you cannot compromise and aspects for which you feel you can be more flexible. Use these lists to guide the compromise process and then practice those positions for a few months before revisiting the discussion. Although it is not expected that this will solve the problem, it will allow some peace to surround the issue.

5. Express gratitude to your spouse for all that you have together and for the effort you both went through in working to build up your relationship by addressing the perpetual issue. Tell your spouse three things you appreciate about them. This will help you end the discussion on a positive note.[32]

This process gets to the heart. It takes energy and commitment, but it will pay handsome dividends. Gottman and colleague have counseled, "Keep working on your unresolvable conflicts. Couples who are demanding of their marriage are more likely to have deeply satisfying unions than those who lower their expectations."[33]

Over the course of our marriage, we have found greater acceptance and peace relative to many of our perpetual issues. Discrepancy in desires and needs on a variety of fronts used to be cause for many a strong discussion early in our marriage. In one flavor or another, over a variety of issues, a similar dynamic would emerge again and again that would leave us feeling unloved, misunderstood, and dissatisfied. Over time we have learned that this process does not occur because we are trying purposely to fail each other but because we just *can't* meet 100 percent of each other's needs. As we have come to recognize and accept this truth without feeling threatened by it, we have found peace and stability within our relationship even though we are still not meeting each other's needs as we would prefer. So now, instead of conflict around these issues, there is flexibility.

Conclusion

Throughout this chapter we have discussed the necessity of being meek and humble, following the Savior's example in all things—even when there is conflict. The antithesis of any destructive force in marriage is meekness.

Avoiding or minimizing conflict in marriage requires hard work and ongoing, purposeful efforts. There really are no shortcuts. We need to look to God to discover what we can change about ourselves rather than placing blame on our spouse. Avoiding destructive behaviors, gaining a clearer perspective, and building personal Christlike characteristics will help each spouse in their ongoing efforts to be peacemakers rather than marriage wreckers.

Notes

1. John M. Gottman and Nan Silver, *The Seven Principles for Making Marriage Work* (New York: Three Rivers Press, 1999), 40.
2. Gottman and Silver, *Seven Principles*, 27–29.

COMMITMENT TO THE COVENANT

3. Gottman and Silver, *Seven Principles*, 28.

4. Gottman and Silver, *Seven Principles*, 29–31.

5. Gottman and Silver, *Seven Principles*, 65.

6. Gottman and Silver, *Seven Principles*, 65.

7. Gottman and Silver, *Seven Principles*, 31–33; emphasis in original.

8. Gottman and Silver, *Seven Principles*, 33.

9. John J. Davies et al., "Habitual, Unregulated Media Use and Marital Satisfaction in Recently Married LDS Couples," *Western Journal of Communication* 76, no. 1 (2012): 65–85.

10. Gottman and Silver, *Seven Principles*, 33.

11. Gottman and Silver, *Seven Principles*, 33.

12. Alesia Hanzal and Chris Segrin, "The Role of Conflict Resolution Styles in Mediating the Relationship Between Enduring Vulnerabilities and Marital Quality," *Journal of Family Communication* 9 (2009): 150–69.

13. Hanzal and Segrin, "Role of Conflict Resolution."

14. John M. Gottman, Janice Driver, and Amber Tabares, "Repair During Marital Conflict in Newlyweds: How Couples Move from Attack-Defend to Collaboration," *Journal of Family Psychotherapy* 26, no. 2 (2015): 85–108.

15. Gottman, Driver, and Tabares, "Repair During Marital Conflict."

16. Wendy Ulrich, "'Stop it' and Forgive," 5 June 2012, http://www.ksl.com/index.php?sid=20705426&nid=481.

17. Carolina Pansera and Jennifer La Guardia, "The Role of Sincere Amends and Perceived Partner Responsiveness in Forgiveness," *Personal Relationships* 19 (2012): 696–711.

18. Gottman and Silver, *Seven Principles*, 27.

19. MissFranJanSan, "I Wasn't Treating My Husband Fairly, and It Wasn't Fair," *Sunny Skyz*, 28 December 2014, http://www.sunnyskyz.com/blog/610/I-Wasn-t-Treating-My-Husband-Fairly-And-It-Wasn-t-Fair; story originally posted on Reddit.

20. Dieter F. Uchtdorf, "Four Titles," *Ensign*, May 2013, 59.

21. Dallin H. Oaks, "Loving Others and Living with Differences," *Ensign*, November 2014, 28.

22. Philip Schaff, *History of the Christian Church* (Grand Rapids, MI: W. M. Eerdmans, 1910), 7:650–53.

23. John Bytheway, *When Times are Tough: 5 Scriptures That Will Help You Get through Almost Anything* (Salt Lake City: Deseret Book, 2004), 42.

24. Douglas E. Brinley, *Toward a Celestial Marriage* (Salt Lake City: Bookcraft, 1986), 7.

25. Dieter F. Uchtdorf, "Lord, Is It I?," *Ensign*, November 2014, 58.

26. Richard Paul Evans, "How I Saved My Marriage," 9 February 2015, http://www.richardpaulevans.com/saved-marriage/#6FgOUXBlJxdj TGrf.01.

27. Wilford Woodruff, "The Temple Workers' Excursion," *Young Woman's Journal* 5 (August 1894): 512–13.

28. Wilford Woodruf, quoted in Donald W. Parry, *Angels: Agents of Light, Love, and Power* (Salt Lake City: Deseret Book, 2013), 159.

29. Jack Kornfield, *The Wise Heart: A Guide to the Universal Teachings of Buddhist Psychology* (New York: Bantam Books, 2008), 262–63.

30. Gottman and Silver, *Seven Principles*, 224.

31. Gottman and Silver, *Seven Principles*, 217.

32. Gottman and Silver, *Seven Principles*, 225–41.

33. Gottman and Silver, *Seven Principles*, 224.

CHAPTER 8

FOR RICHER OR FOR POORER

Working Together on Finances

DEBRA: *No couple, regardless of income level, can escape the management and negotiation of finances. Like most couples, we have had to negotiate different approaches to finances, particularly during our first years of marriage. Richard, as a longtime bachelor, was accustomed to having money at his own disposal for spending as he saw fit. He was a frequenter of fast-food restaurants, and he spent his money on a variety of hobbies, such as golfing, biking, and skiing. The circumstances of my family of origin and my time as a single mother led me to a frugal financial style of counting every penny and continually distinguishing between needs and wants—and usually not buying the wants. In our first years of marriage, Richard's purchase of real butter or BYU Creamery ranch dressing irked me because I saw these more expensive items as luxury items. Admittedly, I would complain to Richard that he was wasting our money.*

Although I did not value the items Richard valued, I did value decorating my home to create a comfortable environment in which I could feel the Spirit. Richard would never have chosen to use his money to purchase home décor and was satisfied with mismatched furniture. He could not understand why I would be upset by his trips to McDonald's and Krispy Kreme Doughnuts for relatively minuscule purchases when I might desire to spend a much larger amount of money on a piece of furniture.

We had to conscientiously work through these and other issues relative to our finances. Some issues were resolved fairly smoothly, while others continued to crop up repeatedly over many years. Yet we now enjoy unity. We continue to have real butter and BYU Creamery ranch dressing in the refrigerator, Richard enjoys his doughnuts and fast food, and we also have a comfortably decorated home. When larger financial issues arise, we are now able to work through them without competition and argument.

*F*inancial habits or beliefs are a cultural issue, rooted largely in our family of origin. Perhaps you come from an affluent family and your spouse comes from a middle-class or lower socioeconomic-status family. Perhaps you come from a large family that was always struggling financially, while your spouse comes from a small family in a comfortable middle-class setting. Or perhaps you and your spouse both come from lower-income households, but your parents accepted long-term Church assistance or government welfare, while your spouse's parents worked three jobs to make ends meet, never taking any financial assistance from outside sources. These cultural differences, and the myriad of other financial constellations within marriage, require a great deal of sensitive attention because they affect our ability to *come to agreement* about how to generate income and manage our expenditures.

Specific dollar amounts do not generally cause the difficulty in marital unity; the difficulty lies in how we make decisions together about those dollar amounts. For those who do not learn how to negotiate this vital aspect of their marriage in a healthy way, severe trouble often comes. Finances represent one of the strongest predictors of marital unhappiness and eventual divorce. In a 2012 study examining finances and divorce, researchers analyzed longitudinal data from more than 4,500 couples as part of the National Survey of Families and Households. They found that arguing about money was *the top predictor of divorce* regardless of income, debt, or net worth. The research also found that, rela-

tive to marital conflict, arguments about money were longer and usually more intense than other types of marital disagreements.[1] Thus, the trouble that comes for couples who do not work well together financially may very well endanger the long-term survival of the marriage. In order to avoid such difficulty, we now discuss several principles that will assist couples as they seek stability and marital unity in finances.

Finances Belong to the Couple

It is critical that *both* husband and wife be informed and actively involved in the family finances. Although one partner may hold the task of paying the bills for simplicity's sake, both partners

Reflections

When we got married, equally sharing a student account with about $500 in it was not too tough. But after graduation, when we actually had some money, it was not always easy to relinquish 50 percent of the control as the sole breadwinner. I grew up in an extremely frugal home, and I like to save. And, yes, my wife also values saving, but she also believes that money is a tool, and it's okay to spend some of it. Well, for many years, I would cringe at the grocery bill, especially when she came home with treats or other "expensive" things that I thought we could do without. I knew that my wife had also grown up in a frugal home, so I was quite puzzled. I thought, "Why does she have to spend so much?" But after many years and many discussions, it finally penetrated my brain that it was just as hard, if not even harder, for her to spend that money, not knowing for sure if I, as the breadwinner, would be able to replenish it. I am not sure what the exact catalyst was, but I now trust her completely. She knows what our children need, and I know that she is weighing each purchase very carefully. And now when she comes home with the occasional box of doughnuts, I allow myself to enjoy every single bite.

should be equally aware at all times of what is going on with the money. Paying bills or loans, making investments, and the like should be openly discussed on a frequent basis.

In a booklet published by the Church on finances, Elder Marvin J. Ashton indicates: "Management of family finances should be mutual between husband and wife in an attitude of openness and trust. Control of the money by one spouse as a source of power and authority causes inequality in the marriage and is inappropriate. Conversely, if a marriage partner voluntarily removes himself or herself entirely from family financial management, that is an abdication of necessary responsibility."[2]

Unfortunately, far too often women have taken a back seat in this area—either of their own choosing by leaving everything financial to their husbands or by being strong-armed by their husbands, who have unilaterally taken everything upon themselves. Financial expert Suze Orman explains to all women, "Your becoming involved with the finances is not about him giving up power or questioning his abilities. It is about your need to be knowledgeable and involved. To *share* responsibility with him."[3]

For couples that live on the income of the husband alone, there needs to be a particular sensitivity to the issue of finances relative to their respective roles. Many stay-at-home moms "equate a paycheck with power"[4] and thus feel they have no or limited power in their relationship since their work is not financially compensated. Orman strongly declares to these women:

> Listen up and listen good: The job of the stay-at-home mother is equal to the job of the breadwinner. Please read that again. Your job is important, as vital, and as necessary as that of your husband who earns a paycheck. . . .
>
> . . . No stay-at-home mom should ever have to ask for money or feel guilty about spending money. To behave that way presumes that the money coming in is "his." It is not his, it is yours. Both of yours.[5]

Let us remember the counsel from the Church's family proclamation that we are obligated to help each other in our relative stewardships "as equal partners."[6] In an eternal relationship, no one holds 51 percent of the authority, while the other holds only 49 percent. In an eternal marriage, each partner has equal authority, equal power, and equal say-so, for the partners are absolutely, unequivocally equals. If there is a power differential in your marriage, you will likely recognize the difficulties this creates not only in your financial relationship but throughout your relationship in general. Financial decisions should be discussed and then pursued only when there is agreement between both partners. This too will strengthen the quality of the marital relationship, as feelings of shared purpose and partnership are bolstered.

RICHARD: *Debra and I have always worked together on our finances. It has been a tremendous blessing both to our marriage and also in the building of financial stability. Debra's financial discipline has rubbed off on me, and because of this cooperative pattern, we have been able to be far more financially efficient than if we had tried to make financial decisions separately. In addition, there have been a number of occasions when we have felt that because we have pondered and consulted together, the Lord has directed and protected us financially as well. We*

Reflections

As a young, struggling college-student family, my wife and I were faced with one of the hardest decisions in our early marriage—pay tithing and fast offerings or go without food. With a one-year-old son, the decision was even harder. We had twenty dollars to get us to the next paycheck, one week and a half away. We struggled with the thoughts "The Lord will understand" and "He knows we will make it up later." After prayerful counsel we both felt that we should trust in the Lord—and so we paid our offerings to the Lord, leaving us with twelve dollars to get us through. We were very new to the ward; no one knew of our situation or even our names. We attended our Sunday meetings and quietly gave our offering to the Lord. After, we drove home, filled with both happiness and concern. When we approached our doorstep, we were shocked to find a box that contained some milk, food, and supplies with a note: "We just felt you might need some things—welcome to the neighborhood." We knew that it was a gift from heaven because they had misspelled our names; they did not know our names, but the Lord did. He has always promised, "Prove me now herewith . . . if I will not open you the windows of heaven."

will share one of these experiences in chapter 9 when we discuss the value of pondering together as a couple over financial decisions.

Principles of Provident Living

Over the years, the Church has promoted several basic financial principles of provident living. Five of these principles are specifically helpful when applied to marriage; they include paying tithes and offerings, avoiding debt, using a budget, building a reserve, and teaching family members. We will now examine each of these principles and discuss how they might help in strengthening and protecting marriage.

Pay Tithes and Offerings

The foundational principle of financial security, whether you are married or not, is to pay tithes and offerings. "To tithe is to freely give one-tenth of one's income annually to the Lord through His Church."[7] The Lord offers a promise to those who trust Him with their finances. We read in Malachi 3:10, "Bring ye all the tithes into the storehouse, that there may be meat in mine house, and prove me now herewith, saith the Lord of hosts, if I will not open you the windows of heaven, and pour you out a blessing, that there shall not be room enough to receive it." We firmly believe in this promise.

Although paying tithing is a fundamental practice in and of itself, paying a generous fast offering can sometimes be overlooked. President Spencer W. Kimball said the following in reference to the idea of making a liberal donation:

> Sometimes we have been a bit penurious and figured that we had for breakfast one egg and that cost so many cents and then we give that to the Lord. I think that when we are affluent, as many of us are, that we ought to be very, very generous. . . .
>
> I think we should be very generous and give, instead of the amount we saved by our two meals of fasting, perhaps much, much more—ten times more where we are in a position to do it.[8]

Let us consider generous offerings when we discuss with our spouse the budgeting of our tithes and offerings.

It seems paradoxical that living with less money can bless us with both temporal and spiritual surplus. Yet God blesses those who faithfully obey this commandment. Indeed, it is "God that giveth the increase" (1 Corinthians 3:7). Although we use our income to pay tithing, it is much more than that. It has been said that "we pay tithing with faith and not with money."[9] Many couples can testify of Malachi's promise that as they give, the windows of heaven open up. We have personal witness that the Lord fulfills His promises: "For he will fulfil all his promises which he shall make unto you, for he has fulfilled his promises which he has made unto our fathers" (Alma 37:17). He has truly blessed us not only temporally but also spiritually because we have put Him first in this commandment.

Perhaps one of the most fascinating findings in recent years that confirms the blessings of giving comes from the research of Arthur Brooks, a well-known economist and president of the American Enterprise Institute. Brooks found that charitable giving has a strong relationship to personal wealth and health

Reflections

I learned a very unexpected lesson associated with the Lord's promises with tithes and offerings. I had just arrived in my hotel room. The phone rang and the voice said, "You have an urgent call." All I can remember of that call is, after verifying my identity, the police officer saying, "Your entire family has been involved in a car accident, and you need to come to the hospital as soon as you can." My wife and all five kids were hit from behind, and the van had rolled three times, ejecting two of my children. They were in an emergency room six hundred miles away, and I could not get a flight out that night. I fell on my knees in both panic and pain—suffering, worrying. I knelt and begged, I pleaded, and I promised. The voice of the Spirit overcame me and spoke to the center of my soul, "Return unto me, and I will return unto you." These words shocked me. I was praying for my family, and the Lord took my mind directly to His promises in Malachi, then to a reference to a promise I had never before understood in this way. "And I will rebuke the devourer for your sakes, and he shall not destroy the fruits of your ground" (Malachi 3:11). The Lord indeed blessed and protected the fruits of my ground—my family received only minor cuts (just needing some stitches) and minor concussions. Even our one-year-old son, who had been ejected from the car, was sitting in his car seat on the lawn with no injuries. Angels attended us; prayers were heard. I will forever be grateful unto the Lord.

and that an increase in wealth is directly related to how much one gives. This seems counterintuitive. Yet, over the course of several types of research studies, Brooks found that same answer again and again—giving leads to receiving. Brooks explained: "If you have two families that are exactly identical—in other words, same religion, same race, same number of kids, same town, same level of education, and everything's the same—except that one family gives a hundred dollars more to charity than the second family, then the giving family will earn on average $375 more in income than the nongiving family—and that's statistically attributable to the gift."[10]

We love it when science catches up with revealed truth! The Lord will truly bless us financially as we faithfully trust him with the first 10 percent of our finances. Yet, as many can attest, the blessings of paying tithes and offerings may not always be financial; they may come in the form of physical or spiritual protections or blessings. The Spirit has at times whispered to us and to others that certain nonfinan-

cial blessings were directly linked to the discharge of tithes and offerings. Brooks offered this summary of his research, which highlights both the temporal and spiritual blessings of financial giving: "Givers are healthier, happier, and richer."[11]

The bottom line is this: Paying our tithing and giving generous offerings are the best investments we can make, not only for our family finances but for our spiritual and physical protection as well. God has given us everything. He asks us to give back to Him 10 percent for tithing, plus more for offerings. He then lets us keep the rest. He magnifies what remains and blesses us, especially in our marriage.

Avoid Debt

Some years ago, a short skit was produced on the television show *Saturday Night Live* with Steve Martin, Amy Poehler, and Chris Parnell called "Don't Buy Stuff You Can't Afford." The skit is full of satire, as Parnell teaches Martin and Poehler about a "revolutionary" plan to get out of debt by introducing a book titled *Don't Buy Stuff You Can't Afford*. Martin and Poehler act dumbfounded and shocked at the idea. Millions of *Saturday Night*

Live viewers laughed and laughed, and each time we watch the skit again, as silly as we think it is, we laugh. As one reviewer put it:

> We all have a good laugh at how ridiculous it is, but we're all kind of guilty of doing the very things we are laughing about—which is why we laugh. . . .
>
> How to buy expensive things using money you save—a common sense principle that so many of us struggle to grasp.
>
> How many of us buy things we cannot afford? . . .
>
> We laugh at the stupidity of the question, "I don't have enough money to buy something, should I buy it anyway?" . . .
>
> While the video is a good laugh, it teaches the most basic concept in personal finance, living on less than you make and not buying things you can't afford."[12]

Like the comedic skit portrays, avoiding debt is one of the great challenges of our time and is a pressure point, particularly in marriage.

We have sought to adhere to the principle taught in this skit. We plan ahead in anticipation of a significant purchase and begin to save. As we anticipated having more children, we realized we would need to move up from our sedan and purchase a larger vehicle. Minivans are pricey, so we began saving several years before we actually needed to make the purchase. When the time came to purchase the vehicle, we wanted to be very careful about using this hard-earned and hard-saved money wisely. We did a lot of homework on what to buy and where to buy. In the end, although it took a lot of research and it caused inconvenience (we had to travel from our home in Utah across state lines to California), we were able to find a used van with very low miles for about half of the cost of a new one and purchased it with saved money. No debt. No monthly payments. And since we found such a good deal, we had extra money left over to use for other desired purchases.

Avoiding debt is easier when married couples consider their finances sacred and seek to "appeal unto the Lord for all things whatsoever [they] must do with them" (Alma 37:16). One piece of counsel we were given during our temple sealing ceremony was to beware of getting preoccupied trying to "stay up with the Joneses" and to be modest in our purchases. We have sought to follow this counsel and have explicitly prayed over the years that our Father in Heaven would help us to "be wise stewards of our financial resources." This prayer is in line with a teaching from Elder Joe J. Christensen of the Seventy: "Our resources are a stewardship, not our possessions. I am confident that we will literally be called upon to make an accounting before God concerning how we have used them to bless lives and build the kingdom."[13] We believe that we have been blessed as we have purposefully sought our Heavenly Father's help to be wise financial stewards. We have been prompted to seek frugality as best we can in order to avoid debt and remain financially sound. This has required the sacrifice of some things we have wanted. However, through patience, financial discipline, and God's assistance, we have been able to obtain not only the things we need but sometimes the things we want: "Wherefore, let my servant . . . appoint unto this people their portions, every man equal according to his family, according to his circumstances and his wants and needs" (D&C 51:3).

RICHARD: *Sometimes God does make it possible for us to get what we want. When Debra and I first met, I had been house hunting; I was longing to live where the houses were further apart, where I could have some land and a beautiful view. When we got engaged, the practicalities of becoming a husband and instant father compelled me to set that dream aside for a few years. However, my dream continued, and there were times when I would fantasize by looking online for available houses in desirable areas. In time, I found a house and location that I loved. It was not unusual for me to take a little side tour after work and drive past the house "on my way home"—thirty minutes each direction out of my way.*

Based on the housing market at that time, purchasing the house would have been a big stretch financially. I pondered how the house could be afforded, and I gathered all of the information I could on what it would cost us to make the move. I contacted the city to inquire about taxes and utilities, I calculated gasoline costs for the extra distance I would have to commute to work, and I talked to people who lived in the area to find out about other costs I had not yet anticipated. Debra and I discussed and pondered all of these things together. Yet, when all was said and done, the only conclusion was that we could not afford, nor justify, making the move. I sadly made the difficult decision to walk away from the house and my dream.

Over the course of the next two years, the economy and housing market dropped. I continued to watch the house's activity in the housing market from a distance, having a silent hope that the price would drop. I watched as the house went on and off the market and then back on again under contract. Yet, unnoticed to me, it later went back on the market. One day I got online to look at houses in the area, and I was shocked to discover the same house was still unsold. And to my pleasant surprise, its price had dropped significantly—over 25 percent from its original price two years earlier. I couldn't believe it! I quickly recalculated our finances with the new asking price and found this time that the purchase would fit comfortably within our budget.

Things moved quickly after that. Within two months we had put an offer on the house, negotiated an even lower purchase price (which ended up being the same price we had paid for our then–current smaller home five years earlier at the top of the market), and moved our family into the new home. We felt Heavenly Father had blessed us for having had the self-discipline to walk away from what would have been a heavy and very lengthy financial burden. Yet through patience, homework, couple discussions, pondering, and prayer, we were able to finally purchase the same home, saving a significant amount of money.

This is one of our more dramatic personal financial stories; we have had many smaller experiences in which we walked away from something we wanted because it was not financially wise and never looked back. Most often, when we exercise self-denial, we will *not* get the desired item, but we are then blessed with greater spiritual or temporal blessings, blessings that are more desirable than the original sacrifice.

DEBRA: *Another example of exercising self-denial came before I met Richard and soon after I became a single mom. I needed to sell my old two–seater car to purchase a car for myself and two daughters. It didn't sell for very much. Family members offered to lend me money so I could purchase a newer, more expensive car. I was very tempted to accept their offers, but in the end I felt very strongly I needed to follow prophetic counsel to avoid debt. I made the decision to find a car for the same amount I received from the sale of my older car. I did. The car I purchased was reliable, requiring only some minor adjustments over the years I owned it. It met my needs as a single mom, and once Richard and I were married we continued to use the car for some years until it became necessary to purchase our minivan. The blessing I received from denying myself the nicer vehicle was that, in my already-strained financial circumstances as a single mom, I enjoyed the freedom of having my car paid for in full, with no monthly payments to create an additional burden. Then, when we married, Richard and I were free to purchase a home without additional debt to weigh us down.*

Prophets have long cautioned us about the discharge of financial stewardships. In the Book of Mormon, we have been counseled by Jacob to "not spend money for that which is of no worth, nor [our] labor for that which cannot satisfy" (2 Nephi 9:51). President Heber J. Grant stated: "If there is any one thing that will bring peace and contentment into the human heart, and into the family, it is to live within our means, and if there is any one thing that is grinding, and discouraging and disheartening it is to have debts and obligations that one cannot meet."[14] More recently President Thomas S. Monson said this concerning debt:

> My brothers and sisters, avoid the philosophy that yesterday's luxuries have become today's necessities. They aren't necessities unless we make them so. Many enter into long-term debt only to find that changes occur: people become ill or incapacitated, companies fail or downsize, jobs are lost, natural disasters befall us. For many reasons, payments on large amounts of debt can no longer be made. Our debt becomes as a Damocles sword hanging over our heads and threatening to destroy us.
>
> I urge you to live within your means. One cannot spend more than one earns and remain solvent. I promise you that you will then be happier than you would be if you were constantly worrying about how to make the next payment on nonessential debt.[15]

With this conservative counsel in mind, we might then ask ourselves the question "Is debt ever okay?" According to financial expert Suze Orman, there is actually "good debt." She explains, "Good debt is money you borrow to finance an asset.

An asset is something that has value today and is expected to rise in value over time."[16] In today's world, examples of good debt include such things as a mortgage (as your home is expected to rise in value) or a student loan (as your income will expect to rise with the additional education). She contrasts this to "bad debt," which is "any money you borrow that is not used to finance an asset."[17] Examples of bad debt include credit card debt and car loans (remember that the value of your car never rises but always falls). Orman counsels us "to keep the good/bad debt strategy in mind when you are contemplating taking on new debt. Always ask yourself: Is it good debt, or is it bad?"[18]

Use a Budget

There are many budgeting plans that are available with a simple keyword search on the Internet. They all do the same thing: they help us organize and discipline our finances. A budget is a valuable exercise for all couples, regardless of income level. It is especially important for couples with debt, as developing and holding to a budget is one of the ways to work your way out of debt. A useful financial tool is what is commonly called a debt-elimination calendar. This is, in effect, a budgeting method. It establishes a monthly amount of income to go to each debt, starting at the smallest debt and progressing to the largest. Once the smallest debt is paid off, then that amount is carried over to the next-smallest debt until it is paid off. Each time this happens more money is allocated to the next-highest debt, which helps pay it off faster, until all of the debts are finally cleared. For many couples this method has literally saved their marriage. They have been able to get out from underneath what was a heavy financial burden, learning the principle of discipline and planning. We read in Doctrine and Covenants 19:35, "Pay the debt. . . . Release thyself from bondage."

Debt-Elimination Calendar				
	Credit Card 1	Credit Card 2	Car Loan	Education Loan	Monthly Total
January	$120	$60	$200	$50	$430
February	$120	$60	$200	$50	$430
March	$120	$60	$200	$50	$430
April	$120	$60	$200	$50	$430
May		$180	$200	$50	$430
June		$180	$200	$50	$430
July		$180	$200	$50	$430
August			$380	$50	$430
September			$380	$50	$430
October			$380	$50	$430
November				$430	$430
December				$430	$430

AN EXAMPLE OF A BASIC DEBT-ELIMINATION CALENDAR.

DEBRA: *Early in our marriage we set up a budget. This took some time and effort and serious negotiation, as we had different approaches to budgeting and using money. Having been single for so many years, Richard rarely had a formal budget. He knew approximately how much money he had in the bank, and he knew it was enough for him to have what he wanted. He easily purchased what he wanted or spent his money on valued activities. On the other hand I was accustomed to being on a very tight budget. I chronically sacrificed wants in order to cover basic necessities; it was an exercise in continual self-denial. So when we sat down to discuss finances, we had to negotiate each other's beliefs about money and where that money should or shouldn't go. There was no questioning the basic categories of budgeting, such as tithing, fast offerings, mortgage, food, clothing, fuel, and utilities. But I really struggled to put optional things into our budget—like money for treats, hobbies, dates, family vacations, and the like—when I felt like we couldn't afford them. It was a patient effort to finish the budget; I had to be much more open to Richard's thoughts and desires.*

RICHARD: *One of the specific budgeting areas we struggled to negotiate when we were first married was allowing for a personal budget for each of us. I wanted a monthly allowance that I could use for whatever I wanted. I wasn't asking for much, but I wanted personal spending money for things like fast-food lunches or a doughnut when I felt like it. This was hard for Debra, as she saw those purchases as wasteful and felt that I was not being respectful of her efforts to be frugal for our family's welfare. So, initially, Debra resisted. However, eventually, she came to see that making such a concession was important to me and my personal satisfaction.*

With this agreement, Debra also received a personal budget equal to the one we had agreed to for me, although she rarely used it during the early years. More recently, however, when Debra finished having children and lost weight, she started using her personal budget to buy a new wardrobe; I didn't feel the least concern about her spending when all the new clothes started showing up because I had been using mine for years.

So, through patient and respectful negotiation, we were able to build a budget that included a small personal allowance or "fun money" budget. In this we were able not only to maintain the overall financial control of our income as a couple but also to provide personal spending money. This gave us some autonomy and flexibility and freed us from feeling a need to micromanage one another's certain purchases. This helped us both avoid unnecessary conflict.

We like the idea that couples should have a personal budget or allowance set up for each spouse. Whether the budget allows for $10 per month per person, $100 per month per person, $1,000 per month per person, or more, we feel strongly that this arrangement creates a needed feeling of independence within the interdependence of the couple's finances. It also saves a lot of nitpicking or nagging over minor personal purchases. Some couples leave the money in their account and just keep track of the personal-allowance expenditures, some couples cash out the personal allowance so each person has cash in hand, and others transfer money into a personal checking account. We think the arrangement you choose should work with your lifestyle and comfort level.

However, as we speak of setting up a personal allowance, we do not mean that spouses should set up personal bank accounts into which they put the money they personally earn for their own use. When couples do this, generally spouses divvy up the domestic bills for which they will be responsible (for example, "I pay the mortgage/rent, while you pay for utilities, medical expenses, clothing, and food"). This approach tempts spouses to not disclose their earnings and, after paying the allocated bills, gives them all the remaining money. We do not recommend doing this. If the purpose of marriage is to become unified, separate bank accounts appear to be antithetical to that purpose. Indeed, in some cases it fosters a this-is-mine-and-this-is-yours attitude toward spending.

We have talked with those in this arrangement and have heard resentments. Some have felt responsible to pay more than their fair share of the bills, while others have had bad feelings toward their spouse for withholding money for luxury expenditures when they themselves are struggling to pay for basic necessities simply because there is a discrepancy in earnings. We believe it is important that both spouses have access to and use a central bank account. This places spouses into a position of partnership that will build unity and make them both accountable to each other financially. On his finance show, financial expert Dave Ramsey once responded to the question of separate bank accounts for married couples:

> I don't believe in separate checking accounts in a marriage. I don't think you need to be independent when you're married. That's why they call it married. Independent is called single. If you want to be married, the preacher says, "And now you are one." Having a single checking account forces you to make your financial decisions together and to be in heavy communication about all aspects of your life. . . .
>
> When someone wants a separate checking account, that is a danger sign not to your money but to your relationship. . . .
>
> One checking account in your marriage forces you to cooperate, forces you to communicate, forces you to be of one mind, and creates a level of unity that is just plain weird. By the way, you will quit writing as many checks when you do this.[19]

We discussed in chapter 6 how the sexual relationship not only is important for marital unity but also is a type and shadow for our relationship with Christ. Here too the same principles of unity with Christ are relevant in the financial relationship we share with our spouse. Working to establish a budget and then honoring that budget will create a strength and sense of unity that will be an asset to our marriage and assist us in creating an eternal quality therein. This type of eternal financial relationship will teach us valuable principles about the relationship we share with Christ; as we become one with Him, we take on His great assets, He absorbs our great liabilities, and we become perfected in Him.

Build a Reserve

Building a reserve, or saving money, is another practice that will bless our marriage. Elder Joseph B. Wirthlin counseled:

> Remember the lesson of Joseph of Egypt. During times of prosperity, save up for a day of want. . . .
>
> The wise understand the importance of saving today for a rainy day tomorrow. They have adequate insurance that will provide for them in case of illness or death. Where possible, they store a year's supply of food, water, and other basic necessities of life. They set aside money in savings and investment accounts. They work diligently to reduce the debt they owe to others and strive to become debt free.
>
> Brothers and sisters, the preparations you make today may one day be to you as the stored food was to the Egyptians and to Joseph's father's family.[20]

Building a reserve will require a team effort of consistent self-discipline as a couple. In order to prepare for major setbacks such as unemployment or unexpected medical bills, Orman recommends a savings account that can serve as an emergency cash fund and is sufficiently large enough to cover eight months of living expenses.[21] We have heard others counsel a reserve of six months of living expenses. If these recommendations seem daunting, apply the spirit of the counsel and make a more modest savings plan that seems practical for you. Even if you are saving only a few dollars a month, that effort will add and even multiply; saved money can provide a way to easily pay for an unexpected expense or emergency. When a spouse then loses a job or a car repair becomes necessary, rather than panicking and scrambling to find some money, which often results in relying on a high-interest loan or credit card for cash, a couple can feel peace. As we read in Doctrine and Covenants 38:30, "If ye are prepared ye shall not fear."

There are several ways to save money. Of course, the most obvious is to designate an amount of savings into your monthly budget. Setting aside a certain amount each month into a savings or retirement account is an important beginning. Couples who consistently add money to one or both accounts will truly reap more than what they sow and will be happy when that rainy day comes.

DEBRA: *Besides saving money from one's income, there are other less obvious yet successful practices for building a reserve. One of these is to do house projects or car repairs yourself, rather than hiring out labor or services. The saved money can then be put in reserve. Richard was raised on a farm and learned creative handyman skills. He has been willing to utilize those skills to do work around our home in order to save money. Yet he has also been willing to extend his comfort zone to learn how to do things he didn't already know how to do; he spends time watching how-to videos on the Internet, talking to workers at home-improvement stores, and consulting with others who have done the type of work before. This has been a great effort on Richard's part because he often works on projects at the end of the day, after a full day's work, or on a Saturday rather than recreating. Yet he has saved us substantial labor fees. As a result, we have been able to do many home-improvement or car-maintenance projects that we otherwise would not have been able to afford. He also is able to enjoy the satisfaction of a job well done and the pride of knowing he did that.*

Another way to build savings is to spend less for the items you need to purchase. At the grocery store, we have been vigilant at price matching, saving significant amounts of money each year, particularly on produce. When we have nonfood item needs, Debra will first try to buy the item from a thrift store, buy it from a yard sale, or buy it used online at a reduced price before purchasing it at full price from a retail store. When Debra needed an entirely new wardrobe after having our children, she was able to purchase previously owned yet like-new brand-name clothing online for about a third of the retail price. In addition, Richard began to purchase his eyeglasses from an online store at a quarter of the price that he would pay at the optometrist's office. He has also found ways to save money on our monthly bills, such as refinancing the mortgage to get a better interest rate, saving on cell phone contracts and home phone bills by using online services, and choosing not to have cable television. All of these practices keep money from leaving our bank account and thus becomes saved money.

We have felt very blessed by our Father in Heaven in our efforts to save money as we have found these and additional opportunities for doing so. We also feel these financial practices have brought us closer together in our marriage. Being business partners in running our family brings great satisfaction that has unified us.

Teach Family Members

Following the above financial principles will bring great peace into our marriages, but all is not done until we teach our children their value. Teaching our children can be done naturally through daily interactions and family councils. Orman teaches that "your children's real education about money will take place all through their childhood, in the way you talk about money, in the way you present what working is all about, in the way they learn what they have a right to hope for in this world."[22] Elder Robert D. Hales explained how he and his family worked together on family finances:

> When our boys were young, we had a family council and set a goal to take a "dream vacation" down the Colorado River. When any of us wanted to buy something during the next year, we would ask each other, "Do we really want to buy that thing now, or do we want to take our dream trip later?" This was a wonderful teaching experience in choosing provident living. By not satisfying our every immediate want, we obtained the more desirable reward of family togetherness and fond memories for years to come.[23]

One of the most effective ways to teach our children about finances is to practice what we preach. Orman counsels parents to include the children in the formal financial process; this will ensure that they learn to not only live the principles but also value them. She recommends involving children in the family finances once they turn age twelve or so: "Have them sit with you as you pay the bills—not to make them feel grateful for what you provide, but so they have an understanding of what life costs."[24] She then suggests that as part of having your child involved in the paying of the bills, let them guess the family's monthly electric bill, and when they see what it actually is "you might find that he or she will think twice before leaving lights on or the TV on after leaving the room."[25]

We learned principles of financial responsibility in our young adult years. Our parents assisted us with the payment for our LDS missions, which was a great blessing to each of us. Beyond that, we were responsible ourselves to find our way financially as young adults.

RICHARD: *After my mission my father presented me with an old family car that I used as I went off to attend college at BYU. I received no other financial help from my parents. In fact the old family car only lasted one month, and then I had to use money from my fast-food job to purchase another old used car. I used grants, student loans, and part-time jobs to support myself through my college years. I learned never to spend more money than I earned.*

DEBRA: *I also attended school at BYU. Since I moved into dorms with a kitchen as a freshman, my parents took me to the grocery store and offered the groceries as a gift as I began my new life as a college student. I paid for my college tuition, books, housing, and food by taking out student loans and working part-time (glamorous kitchen and bathroom) jobs at the university. When my friends who had their tuition and housing paid for by their parents went out on the weekends, I assessed the cost of the activity and often thought to myself, "Do you know how much bread and milk I could buy with that money?" or "Do you know how many hours I had to work to earn the money for that?" I usually did not go with them. These were difficult times learning to be financially independent, but to this day I attribute much of my financial conscientiousness to this hard-knocks training in early adulthood.*

Transferring this type of teaching to our children will not only help them but will protect us as a couple from financial burdens imposed by our own children later. Our children's financial practices can come back to haunt us, creating a great deal of strain on our finances and our marital relationship. For example, some adult children have learned they can sponge off of parents without accepting their own financial responsibility. Of course there are times when it is entirely appropriate to assist adult children with their financial difficulties. However, in some families this has become a rule rather than an exception. In a BYU devotional, Elder Neal A. Maxwell discussed: "A few of our wonderful youth and young adults in the Church are unstretched—they have almost a free pass. Perks are provided, including cars complete with fuel and insurance—all paid for by parents who sometimes listen in vain for a few courteous and appreciative words. What is thus taken for granted . . . tends to underwrite selfishness and a sense of entitlement."[26]

DEBRA: *I have worked with several clients in the situation described by Elder Maxwell and have seen how the overly liberal giving of parents only continues to feed the dysfunction of the child. Despite the financial safety nets offered by the parents, the unhealthy children generally continue to sink lower and lower into dysfunction because the parents have maintained accountability for the child's finances without transferring responsibility to them in adulthood. I have unashamedly counseled parents in this situation, "Shower your child with love and support, but close your pocketbook." Through this process, the child can become responsible to make or break their own financial life. This type of intervention also allows parents to be able to influence and teach even adult children the importance of financial responsibility.*

How can we decide when it may be appropriate to financially help our needful adult children, without it putting a strain on our marriage? In the area of your adult children's finances, this becomes most complicated, fraught with powerful emotions and parental instincts. Of course we seek to be generous in our offerings to the Lord and to others, yet some practical guidance about generosity may also prove helpful as we consider trying to teach our family members about financial responsibility. Orman counsels, "It is very important that you understand that *true generosity is as much about the one who gives as it is about the one who receives*. If an act of generosity benefits the receiver but saps the giver, then it is not true generosity in my book."[27] She then provides six rules to follow relative to honest giving:

1. You give to say thank you and out of pure love. Not to get something back.
2. Whether it is a gift of time, money, or love, you must feel strongly that your gift is an offering.
3. An act of generosity must never adversely affect the giver. [And Debra would add here that it also must never adversely affect the receiver—such as enabling irresponsible or immature behavior.]
4. An act of generosity must be made consciously.
5. An act of generosity must happen at the right time.
6. An act of generosity must come from an empathic heart.[28]

Thus, giving to our adult children should be a win-win, injuring neither party.

It then follows that, in teaching our children, sometimes we will need to say, "No." This can be difficult to do, but when we feel it is appropriate to do so it can be done in a loving way: "I love you and support you, but if I were to help you financially right now it would actually limit your ability to become independent. I need to let you work this one out for yourself." If you have made a habit of rescuing your adult children financially, it will be difficult to change course, yet even one courageous moment in which you choose to do things differently can set your child on a new path. So as not to appear punishing when initially making the shift, you can take the issue upon yourself: "I can't help you financially this time. I know I have always said 'yes' before, but I feel I have actually hurt you by doing so. I apologize for limiting your growth and hope you'll forgive me. From now on I need to let you become more responsible for these things." This type of true generosity will allow love to flourish, as well as teach your adult children financial values.

There may be occasions when an adult child needs to move back into a parent's home. Regardless of the reason, this cannot become a free-for-all. The parents need to ask the child, "What is your plan? What is the timeline?" Establishing expectations is a very important part of helping our child. By doing this, we eliminate or reduce the potential stressors that might come between us and our child as well as between us and our spouse.

Teaching family members proper financial habits will establish proper boundaries, encourage fiscal responsibility, and provide tools for financial survival. Yet, more importantly for our purposes here, it will also immeasurably bless our marriage. When children come to us with a sense of entitlement that we fund their personal wants or even fix their perpetual financial problems, those circumstances can create a great deal of stress and even interpersonal tension in our marriage. At those times, the drama may often become all-consuming as we try to negotiate the best way to handle the situation. That strain

Reflections

When my adult son had financial problems, I offered financial help to him. He accepted my help, and I gave him access to my credit card to buy the things we had discussed. I hadn't told my husband—I was keeping a secret from him because in my heart I knew from the beginning he wouldn't have allowed me to do it. Then it got out of hand. My son started buying things I had not said I would pay for. I told him he would need to pay me back, and I trusted him to do so, but then it never happened. I would be upset each month when I didn't get any payments from my son. Finally, when I told my husband, he was disappointed in me and I didn't like that. My husband began to accuse me, asking, "Why did you even let him do it?" It caused conflict between us because things my husband said hit a nerve and made me feel guilty. I realized I had been wrong. I didn't like him reminding me about it. All this stress played on everything else I had going on in my life, and I began to feel depressed and suicidal. I decided I couldn't do it anymore; it scared my husband. In talking to a therapist I realized that my suicidality was not about my life as a whole but that my situation with my son was putting me over the edge. I called my son in to talk, and we set up some pretty clear boundaries and expectations. I feel much better, and it has relieved pressure with my husband.

can significantly drain the positive energy we need for our relationship, siphoning our energies away from our relationship to focus on the problems of the child. And in some cases our adult children's financial dependence becomes a frequently repeated endeavor that over many years becomes dysfunctional and taxing at ever-increasing levels. When we teach our family members principles of financial responsibility, we preserve precious time and positive energy for us as a couple.

Conclusion

Deuteronomy 2:6 reads, "Ye shall buy meat of them for money, that ye may eat; and ye shall also buy water of them for money, that ye may drink." Thus, managing finances is imperative to take care of our living needs. In marriage the task of managing our finances falls upon both of us as a couple. As we do this, we must learn how to work peacefully with each other while honoring each other as equal partners. If we do not, our marriage will be in severe jeopardy, as financial arguments are one of the strongest predictors of divorce. Yet couples who communicate often about their finances, work together, respect each other for their unique marital contributions (regardless of financial compensation), and show flexibility will be more likely to succeed in marriage not only interpersonally but financially as well.

Applying the five principles outlined in this chapter will provide a good foundation for financial solvency. Maintaining a disciplined effort to pay tithes and offerings will bring the acceptance and blessings of heaven. Avoiding debt protects a marriage from the heavy burdens of interest and bankruptcy. Budgeting provides a couple with a financial roadmap, saving money makes it possible for a reserve when that rainy day comes, and teaching children appropriate money practices protects couples from future financial burdens.

Couples will have to work hard, discipline themselves, and be patient with each other over financial decisions and practices. In the end, temporal blessings will come as we navigate finances together. We will also receive spiritual blessings and strength to our marital relationship as we improve unity, respect, and trust between spouses.

Notes

1. Jeffrey Dew, Sonya Britt, and Sandra Huston, "Examining the Relationship Between Financial Issues and Divorce," *Family Relations* 64, no. 4 (October 2012): 615–28.

2. Marvin J. Ashton, *One for the Money: Guide to Family Finance* (Salt Lake City: The Church of Jesus Christ of Latter-day Saints, 1992), 3.

3. Suze Orman, *Women and Money: Owning the Power to Control Your Destiny* (New York: Spiegel and Grau, 2007), 220.

4. Orman, *Women and Money*, 221.

5. Orman, *Women and Money*, 221.

6. "The Family: A Proclamation to the World," *Ensign*, November 2010, 129.

7. "Tithing," The Church of Jesus Christ of Latter-day Saints, 2015, https://www.lds.org/topics/tithing?lang=eng.

8. Spencer W. Kimball, in Conference Report, April 1974, 184.

9. G. Q. Morris, "Perfection through Obedience," *Improvement Era*, June 1953, 435–36.

10. Arthur C. Brooks, "Why Giving Matters" (devotional address, Brigham Young University, Provo, UT, 24 February 2009), https://speeches.byu.edu/talks/arthur-c-brooks_giving-matters-2/.

11. Brooks, "Why Giving Matters."

12. Mark, "What I Learned from an SNL Skit," *Debt-Free Mormon* (Blog), 14 March 2014, http://www.debtfreemormon.org/learned-snl-skit/.

13. Joe J. Christensen, "Greed, Selfishness, and Overindulgence," *Ensign*, May 1999, 11.

14. Heber J. Grant, *Gospel Standards: Selections from the Sermons and Writings of Heber J. Grant*, ed. G. Homer Durham (Salt Lake City: Deseret Book, 1976), 111.

15. Thomas S. Monson, "True to the Faith," *Ensign*, May 2006, 19.

16. Orman, *Women and Money*, 95.

17. Orman, *Women and Money*, 95.

18. Orman, *Women and Money*, 96.

19. Dave Ramsey, "Dave's Take on Separate Checking Accounts," 2015, http://www.daveramsey.com/index.cfm?event=askdave/&intContentItemId=120524.

20. Joseph B. Wirthlin, "Earthly Debts, Heavenly Debts," *Ensign*, May 2004, 42.

21. Orman, *Women and Money*, 76.

22. Suze Orman, *The 9 Steps to Financial Freedom: Practical and Spiritual Steps So You Can Stop Worrying* (New York: Three Rivers Press, 2000), 298.

23. Robert D. Hales, "Becoming Provident Providers Temporally and Spiritually," *Ensign*, May 2009, 9–10.

24. Orman, *Women and Money*, 226.

25. Orman, *Women and Money*, 226.

26. Neal A. Maxwell, "Sharing Insights from My Life" (devotional address, Brigham Young University, 12 January 1999), https://speeches.byu.edu/talks/neal-a-maxwell_sharing-insights-life/.

27. Orman, *Women and Money*, 50; emphasis in original.

28. Orman, *Women and Money*, 51.

PART 3

The *Thee* in Marriage

THE *THEE* IN MARRIAGE

*Marriage is the foundry for social order, the fountain of virtue, and
the foundation for eternal exaltation. Marriage has been divinely designated as an eternal and everlasting covenant. Marriage is sanctified
when it is cherished and honored in holiness. That union is not merely
between husband and wife; it embraces a partnership with God.*
—*President Russell M. Nelson*[1]

As couples, we can create good marriages through our own
efforts. The *Me* and the *We* contributions to building marriage are effective and powerful. However, alone, we cannot
access all that marriage has to offer us for our journey toward
perfection—we must look to God. Therefore, we now turn to
the *Thee* in the covenant of marriage, examining the extrapersonal ("extra" meaning "outside" or "beyond") contributions
to building marriage: How is God using our marriage to perfect us? His contribution elevates us above and beyond what
our intra- and interpersonal efforts can provide, perfecting
and exalting us together as husband and wife into the eternities. We discuss herein how marriage is positively influenced by
the practice of scripture study, prayer, pondering, and recording; heeding the Lord's prophets; and applying the principles
and sacred ordinances of the gospel.

CHAPTER 9

"Holding Fast to the Rod of Iron"

God's Word in Marriage

RICHARD: *Before I was married, I would from time to time theoretically consider how certain scriptures or words of the prophets would someday help me to be a faithful, righteous husband. Once Debra and I were married, things went from theoretical to practical very fast! I can't tell you how many times over our married life I have gone to the word of God to help me figure out how to be a more humble, sensitive, thoughtful, and engaged husband. My connection to God has been my lifeline and road map for my marriage to Debra. His words have encouraged me when I was discouraged. They have revealed to me the course I should take to lift Debra when she has been down. They have guided important decisions we have needed to make as a couple.*

Doctrine and Covenants 84:85 has comforted us: "Neither take ye thought beforehand what ye shall say; but treasure up in your minds continually the words of life, and it shall be given you in the very hour that portion that shall be meted unto every man." This scripture represents an ongoing pattern in our marriage: as we have studied the scriptures and been immersed in the word, God has brought to our minds "at the very hour" the ideas and thoughts that we have needed to make choices that would bless our marriage and family. Such experiences bring us closer to Him and to each other.

*S*trengthening the *Thee* in marriage refers to learning how to more fully invite the presence and influence of God the Father; His Son, Jesus Christ; and the Holy Ghost into our marriage. In a study examining LDS marriage, some participants spoke of their marriage in terms of a triangle, with God, their spouse, and themselves connected through a covenant relationship.[2] Indeed, illustrations, such as the one to the right, are commonly used in marital counseling with religious couples. As each spouse focuses on God and moves closer to Him, not only do they become more like Him, but the distance between husband and wife naturally narrows. They grow closer and become more unified. To maximize our opportunities for marital success, we must allow God to be partnered with us in all aspects of our marital relationship.

Elder Dale G. Renlund of the Quorum of the Twelve Apostles discussed this principle in a Facebook post and illustrated it with his own marriage to his wife, Sister Ruth Lybbert Renlund:

> Recently I have had the opportunity to officiate in the temple sealing of four wonderful couples. As I prepared for these wonderful experiences, I found myself pondering 1 Corinthians 11:11, "Nevertheless neither is the man without the woman, neither the woman without the man, in the Lord."
>
> I have found myself thinking about what "in the Lord" means within a marriage relationship. This is a question that each husband and wife would benefit from pondering.
>
> For me, it means that Ruth and I will be stronger as we center our relationship on the teachings, example, and love of Jesus Christ. As we each work to become more like the Savior, we will learn to love each other more and become more unified. It is a lifelong goal—it is actually an eternal goal—and it is well worth the effort.[3]

Thus, it is imperative that we as individuals and as couples keep ourselves connected to His words every day. This is foundational—critical—to keeping our marriages strong and safe. Elder Ronald A. Rasband of the Quorum of the Twelve Apostles said, "If we are casual or complacent in our worship, drawn off and

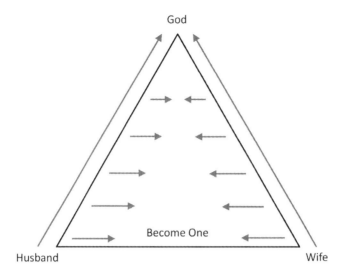

MARRIAGE AS A TRIANGLE.

desensitized by worldly pursuits, we find ourselves diminished in our ability to feel [the Spirit]."[4] Yet, as we keep ourselves tethered to the word of God, we will be able to more easily and clearly receive and interpret the promptings of the Holy Spirit, which will guide us as we navigate our marital relationship. What can I do to be a better spouse? How can I show love to my spouse today? What do we need to do together to strengthen our relationship? How can we more fully protect our marriage and our family? The answers to these questions come as gifts of the Spirit from a loving Heavenly Father, who is devoted to our safety, growth, and happiness.

The marital power and protection of bringing the *Thee* into our marriage is corroborated by research. Studies have consistently found that an individual's or couple's religious attendance, beliefs, experiences, and rituals are positively correlated with greater marital satisfaction, cohesion, and consensus (agreement

Reflections

My husband and I have strived to put our Savior first and foremost in our lives, and the natural consequence has been for us to draw nearer to each other as a couple. We understand the importance of commitment, selflessness, and forgiveness in having a successful marriage, trusting these qualities will see us through every difficult situation. We experience great joy as we build our lives together. We are very different people, the way Heavenly Father intended it to be, yet we are best friends.

on relationship issues). Researchers found that prayer and religious beliefs were linked to marital satisfaction and also buffered effects of marital risk factors, such as previous divorce, high stress in marriage, and premarital cohabitation.[5] Researchers studying Latter-day Saint marriages and religiosity have shown similar findings. Richard, working with Bruce Chadwick, found that religious behaviors like personal scripture study, private prayer, family scripture study, family prayer, and temple-worthy actions are each positively associated with both marital happiness and satisfaction.[6]

In this chapter we will focus on the personal and marital worship that develops our ability to bring God into our lives through revelation. This revelation will guide us as we seek to strengthen our marital relationship.

We will particularly discuss studying the scriptures, praying, pondering, and recording our sacred impressions as individuals and as a couple. It's interesting that each of these practices is found in the very first chapter of 1 Nephi. Father Lehi is given special revelation to protect himself, his wife, and his family because he reads the scriptures (verses 12–14), prays (verses 5–6, 14–15), ponders (verse 7), and records (verse 16). We encourage couples to follow each of these practices in both individual and marital capacities, as Lehi did. We testify that the Lord will bless us, as he did Lehi, with personal and marital revelations that will protect individuals, couples, and families.

Scripture Study

Searching the word of God is vital to maintaining a healthy marriage because it increases our ability to receive revelation as individuals and as a couple. Many members of the Church believe that when we pray we tell God what we want Him to know, and that when we read our scriptures we give God the opportunity to tell us what He wants us to know. The Prophet Joseph Smith declared, "Search the Scriptures, search the prophets and learn what portion of them belongs to you."[8]

The scriptures are our lifeline securing us to our Father in Heaven and His Son, Jesus Christ. The answers to life's challenges, and especially marital challenges, are found within the scriptures. Have you ever gone to the scriptures for assistance with your marital difficulties? The answers are there. Elder Gary E. Stevenson of the Quorum of the Twelve Apostles provided a powerful promise of the influence the Book of Mormon can have in our lives: "Within the book's pages, you will discover the infinite love and incomprehensible grace of God. As you strive to follow the teachings you find there, your

Practice

Here is a journaling exercise you can do to evaluate the values and goals you have surrounding your spirituality:

- Write down the type of spiritual relationship you want to have with both your Father in Heaven and His Son, Jesus Christ, as well as with your spouse. This may be as simple as communing with nature or engaging in personal or private worship or as formal as participating in church or church-related activities. Write about how you want this part of your life to look.

- Rate this value in terms of importance. Scale 1–10. 1 (not at all important), 10 (extremely important) _____.

- Now, ask yourself, "How consistent is my life currently (past week or two) in making this value a realization?" Scale 1–10. 1 (not at all consistent), 10 (completely consistent) _____.

- Subtract consistency number from importance number =_____.

- Look at this number. A high score means you have a large discrepancy between what you value as important and how you are honoring or enacting that value in your day-to-day life. A large discrepancy is not desirable. A small number indicates that you are living your life more closely consistent with your stated values. This is ideal. How are you doing? What are the obstacles, if any? Make a plan to overcome any obstacles.[7]

Reflections

Some years ago our bishop introduced the "Morning Five" to the youth in the ward. I was the Young Men president at the time. The Morning Five is this: (1) read the Book of Mormon every morning—it has to be in the morning—to please your spirit; (2) pray every morning to please Heavenly Father and to invite the Spirit to be with you throughout the day; (3) make your bed to please your mother; (4) eat breakfast to please your body; and (5) brush your teeth to please your friends. A few months after the bishop gave us the Morning 5, I was visiting with him, and he asked if I was doing the Morning 5. I told him that I wasn't, that I thought it was only for the youth. He then looked me straight in the eye and gave me a bishop's promise. He said that if I would do the Morning 5 every day, my relationship with my wife would be better than it had ever been and we would grow closer together than ever before. I testify that it worked and that it is true.

joy will expand, your understanding will increase, and the answers you seek to the many challenges mortality presents will be opened to you. As you look to the book, you look to the Lord."[9]

If we read with discerning eyes and hearts, the scriptures explicate many teachings regarding how couples can strengthen their marriage in spite of trials. We have referenced many such scriptures throughout the chapters of this book; thus, hearkening and holding fast in faith through study and personal application, the scriptures will bring many answers to the issues for which we seek relief.

Nephi felt strongly about the importance of clinging to the word of God. Indeed, he spoke of the spiritual power created by so doing. When his brothers asked him what the "rod of iron" meant in their father's dream, he answered that those who "hearken" unto and "hold fast" onto the word of God will "never perish" (1 Nephi 15:24). And, extending that promise, we testify that if both spouses are holding fast and hearkening to the word of God, there should be little reason why their marriage should ever perish as well.

Principles of Effective Scripture Study for Individuals and Couples

Individuals and couples approach their scripture study in a variety of ways; however, there are more effective ways than others. Speaking to seminary and institute teachers about their students, Elder Henry B. Eyring observed that many of the young people who are struggling are praying and studying their scriptures, but "they are not doing it the way that works."[10] We as couples need to make sure we are practicing personal and couple scripture study in the way that works. Specific scheduling will, of course, be based on personal circumstances and family timing. Yet the following provides some guiding principles from prophets and apostles on effective ways to fortify ourselves and our marriages through these practices.

While a member of the Quorum of the Twelve Apostles, Elder Howard W. Hunter taught that studying the scriptures daily is more effective than studying sporadically for long periods of time. He encouraged us to set aside a regular study time that allows our focus to remain undisturbed and uninterrupted. He indicated that we should have a plan for our study rather than just reading randomly. He also encouraged setting aside a specific time each day to study rather than reading a set number of chapters or pages. This would allow us time to ponder and give the Spirit the freedom to guide us. He explained that by doing this, perhaps we might spend our entire study time on a single verse.[11]

Accordingly, *effective* scripture study is best done daily, during a regularly scheduled time, for a predetermined amount of time, rather than attempting to cover a certain number of pages or chapters. One of the main purposes of scripture study is to open the way for the Lord to reveal His truths to us. If we are reading the scriptures in an effort to cover a certain number of pages, we may likely be focused on finishing our set number of pages or chapters rather than allowing the impressions of the Spirit to guide or teach us as we go. Setting a time aside rather than trying to cover a number of pages tells the Lord that we are willing to let the Holy Ghost guide us through our study time. Some days we may read only one verse because we are pondering and recording insights that the Lord gives us during that time.

In essence, we believe scripture study should not just be considered reading time but rather devotional time. We want to allow the Spirit to lead our study. Some days the Spirit will guide us through each of the practices we discuss in this chapter—reading, praying, pondering, and recording—all within the time we set aside for our worship. Some days the Spirit may lead us through only one or two of these elements. Yet if we listen, He will teach us things we need to know. That revelation will speak to things about our life, marriage, family, profession, Church calling, friendships, etc.

In our own marriage, we have set aside some time in the evening right before going to sleep for scripture study together. For us this time includes reading scriptures, reading or listening to general conference talks, reading from the *Ensign*, listening to something from the Mormon Channel, or engaging in other such activities. Sometimes we are very tired at night and only spend a few minutes, not able to quite give our full energy to our study and discussion. Other times, we get quite active in discussing what we have studied, and we end up spending much longer than planned. Those types of discussions are always full of positive energy and are some of our favorite times together, even when the specific topic at hand might be quite serious. Such moments create a great sense of closeness and intimacy, strengthening our marital relationship. They also provide the space to discuss and receive revelation on how the doctrinal principles we are studying relate to our marriage and family.

RICHARD: *One of my favorite memories of our couple scripture study time is when Debra and I spent several months reading together* Daughters in My Kingdom: The History and Work of Relief Society *when it was first published. We read and talked about the stories and doctrines in the book. It was a special time for me. I felt a special connection with Debra learning together about the love that God has for His daughters and the amazing history of this special organization. Reflecting back, I am not sure why this had such a powerful effect on me in terms of bringing me closer to Debra, but I think a lot of it had to do with realizing that I was blessed to be married to a choice daughter of God and that I belonged to a Church that elevates and reverences God's daughters.*

The Book of Mormon

Although all the scriptures from the standard works are valuable to us and we should be studying from each of them regularly, the Lord has emphasized the importance and preeminence of the Book of Mormon in our latter-day study. President Ezra Taft Benson gave several talks in the 1980s admonishing us as Church members to make the Book of Mormon the center of our scripture study. On one occasion, President Benson counseled: "There is a book we need to study daily, both as individuals and as families, namely the Book of Mormon. I love that book. It is the book that will get a person nearer to God by abiding by its precepts than any other book. (See Book of Mormon, Introduction.) President Romney recommended studying it half an hour each day. I commend that practice to you. I've always enjoyed reading the scriptures and do so on a daily basis individually and with my beloved wife."[12]

More recently, President Thomas S. Monson reaffirmed the salience of daily study of the Book of Mormon when he declared:

> This morning I speak about the power of the Book of Mormon and the *critical* need we have as members of this Church to study, ponder, and apply its teachings in our lives. The importance of having a firm and sure testimony of the Book of Mormon cannot be overstated.
>
> We live in a time of great trouble and wickedness. What will protect us from the sin and evil so prevalent in the world today? I maintain that a strong testimony of our Savior, Jesus Christ, and of His gospel will help see us through to safety. If you are not reading the Book of Mormon each day, please do so. . . .
>
> My dear associates in the work of the Lord, I *implore* each of us to prayerfully study and ponder the Book of Mormon *each day*. As we do so, we will be in a position to hear the voice of the Spirit, to resist temptation, to overcome doubt and fear, and to receive heaven's help in our lives. I so testify with all my heart in the name of Jesus Christ, amen.[13]

When a prophet uses words such as "critical" and "implore," we would be wise to listen. This wonderful book will preserve us and protect us if we heed counsel from the prophets.

As we study the Book of Mormon, we can connect to the Spirit and more fully deepen our testimony of the Savior as we seek Him. We can ask questions such as "What have I learned about the Savior from what I have read today?" or "What have I learned about the Atonement of Jesus Christ from what I read today?" We can also extend these types of questions to our marriage as well: "What have I learned about my relationship with my spouse from what I read today?"

As we have studied the Book of Mormon individually, as a couple, and as a family, we have been blessed. We will discuss these instances each in turn.

First, personal study of the Book of Mormon has strengthened us *individually*. It has strengthened, and continues to strengthen, our testimonies of Jesus Christ. Our individual resolve and commitment to live the gospel, including the principles of marriage we have shared throughout this book, is bolstered when we read the Book of Mormon. Such principles taught in the Book of Mormon have prepared us for, and continue to remind us of, the seriousness of the marital covenant and teach us about the Christlike characteristics we need to adopt to make our marital relationship thrive. Ultimately, as we each individually adopt Christlike qualities, we become better spouses to each other.

Second, couple study of the Book of Mormon has strengthened our *marriage relationship*. It has taught us about how to resolve marital conflict, such as the story of Lehi and Sariah shared in chapter 7. The Book of Mormon additionally teaches us about how we should be managing our financial stewardships and other aspects of provident living. We learn how we can protect our home

Reflections

We joined the Church in the 1960s as a family of five. A few weeks after baptism it was not going well with our marriage. My husband had an "intelligent" conversion, and I had more of a spiritual conversion. He knew and believed the Church was the true church, but he looked at it differently than I did. As a result we had some real heated discussions about things we should do, such as family home evening, scripture reading, family prayer, etc. We decided to separate for a while. During the separation I began reading the Book of Mormon. With a prayer in my heart as I read, I received the answers to so many questions. I realized that my place was with my husband and that our family needed to be together for eternity. I realized that I needed to have more patience and honor my husband. There was a lot of conversation. We took one step at a time. Scripture reading became a serious part of our lives. Approximately two years later, we were sealed in the temple as a family. Later in life, we both served as temple workers for many years. When my husband passed away, we had been married for fifty-seven years.

and marriage from Satan's worldly influences (those war chapters were written for us). Reading the Book of Mormon as a couple grants us the space and energy to think together about our current life events and how we can apply our testimonies of the gospel of Jesus Christ to those circumstances. As we do so, we get along with each other easily and have a greater sense of peace and harmony.

Third, Book of Mormon study has strengthened our *family*. As we read with our children, the Book of Mormon provides opportunity not only to teach them basic gospel doctrines but also to discuss how these doctrinal issues are relevant to our current societal challenges. We are able to present scenarios to our children that require them to think about how they would handle a situation at school or with friends. Thus, we are able to fortify our children and prepare them in advance to know how to respond to particular temptations or cunning sophistry so they don't get tricked. While we read and discuss the Book of Mormon with our children, we, as a couple, feel a greater sense of unity as we teach the gospel together. This sense of unity bolsters our relationship and strengthens our marriage.

Thus, the Book of Mormon has brought the spirit of protection and love into our home and into our hearts. The following promises from Elder Marion G. Romney, as a member of the Quorum of the Twelve Apostles, have come to pass in our home:

> I feel certain that if, in our homes, parents will read from the Book of Mormon prayerfully and regularly, both by themselves and with their children, the spirit of that great book will come to permeate our homes and all who dwell therein. The spirit of reverence will increase; mutual respect and consideration for each other will grow. The spirit of contention will depart. Parents will counsel their children in greater love and wisdom. Children will be more responsive and submissive to that counsel. Righteousness will increase. Faith, hope, and charity—the pure love of Christ—will abound in our homes and lives, bringing in their wake peace, joy, and happiness.[14]

Prayer

Another salient practice that will strengthen individuals and couples and facilitate the receipt of revelation is that of prayer. As we said earlier, Richard and Bruce Chadwick found that couples who pray privately and together have significantly higher rates of marital happiness.[15] The old saying that "Couples who pray together, stay together" is statistically true. There are many studies that have shown that individuals who pray for their spouse in personal prayer or in couple prayer have significantly higher levels of marital well-being.[16] We are taught about prayer in the LDS Bible Dictionary: "Prayer is the act by which the will of the Father and the will of the child are brought into correspondence with each other. The object of prayer is not to change the will of God but to secure for ourselves and for others blessings that God is already willing to grant but that are made conditional on our asking for them. Blessings require some work or effort on our part before we can obtain them. Prayer is a form of work and is an appointed means for obtaining the highest of all blessings."

We are further taught about prayer in the Book of Mormon when Alma implores us to

> cry unto God for all thy support; yea, let all thy doings be unto the Lord, and whithersoever thou goest let it be in the Lord; yea, let all thy thoughts be directed unto the Lord; yea, let the affections of thy heart be placed upon the Lord forever. Counsel with the Lord in all thy doings, and he will direct thee for good. (Alma 37:36–37)

As we see the word "let" four times in these verses, we are reminded that prayer is a matter of will and agency; it shows our willingness to humbly turn our hearts and choose our Father in Heaven. As we seek to ever turn our hearts toward our loving Father in Heaven in continual prayer, we are given tender blessings. Elder Richard G. Scott taught that "prayer is the source of comfort, relief, and protection, willingly granted by our loving, compassionate Heavenly Father."[17]

Many of us have great testimonies of the power of personal prayer and make it a daily habit. How blessed we are when we spend time communing directly with our Father in Heaven! We should seek to always maintain the practice of personal prayer. Sometimes, in the busyness of family life, personal time becomes limited, and the time spent in personal prayer is truncated or even neglected. Let us remember always to say our prayers.

In this section we focus on how the gift of prayer plays out in our marital relationships. We have three emphases in this section: pray for your spouse, pray with your spouse, and pray for your spouse with your spouse.

Pray for Your Spouse

When we say our personal or individual prayers, we can strengthen our marriage by including our spouse in our prayers. Does your husband have an important deadline at work? Is your wife overwhelmed with extended family responsibilities? Pray for your spouse's happiness, health, and success and invite the powers of heaven to bless their life. President Henry B. Eyring detailed: "I give counsel to husbands and wives. Pray for the love which allows you to see the good in your companion. Pray for the love that makes weaknesses and mistakes seem small. Pray for the love to make your companion's joy your own. Pray for the love to want to lessen the load and soften the sorrows of your companion."[18]

Praying for our spouse can strengthen and confirm positive, warm feelings in a strong, vibrant, and loving marital relationship. This can strengthen feelings of emotional closeness to them. As we pray for them, may we also remember to express gratitude to a loving Father in Heaven for bringing them into our lives and hearts.

Praying for our spouse can also be therapeutic in healing hearts and warming up feelings in a difficult moment, especially when struggling with a chronically difficult relationship. When there are dark feelings over our marriage, we may not feel like we want to connect emotionally or spiritually with our spouse, and it may feel impossible to send warm, positive feelings up into the heavens on behalf of our spouse. Yet if we will humble ourselves and choose to be willing to pray for our spouse in a personal prayer, the Lord will bless our efforts and bless our marriage. This concept of willingness is vital: we can choose to be willing even when we are *not* wanting to be.

Bruce Chadwick illustrates the great power of personal prayer in soothing pained marital relationships. During a BYU devotional, he told this story of a struggling couple who came to him for help. He had worked with the couple for several weeks with no progress relative to reducing marital anger and conflict. After reading in Matthew 5:43–44 about praying for one's enemy, he felt inspired to have the spouses pray for each other:

> When the couple arrived, I had the husband wait in the living room while I met with the wife in the family room. When I asked her if we could kneel and pray for her husband, she looked at me like I was crazy. When I explained that I . . . wanted her to sincerely pray for the Father to bless her husband with those things that would bring him true happiness, she simply replied, "I can't do it." I had anticipated this response. . . . I asked if we could kneel and pray that she be given the compassion, mercy, and love necessary to do so. We both took turns voicing a prayer, and after she shed a few tears she informed me she was ready to pray for her husband. She then offered a beautiful

prayer for him. A remarkable change in her demeanor toward her husband was immediately obvious. This was real progress.

I ushered her into the living room and invited the husband into the family room. We repeated the same sequence of events. His initial reaction to my request was one of shocked dismay. But later, after offering a sincere prayer for his wife, his attitude and his feelings toward her changed, and some of the earlier love reappeared. I could see it in his countenance, and he could feel it in his heart.

This was our last counseling session. I think the story had a happy ending for the couple. I haven't seen them for several years, but the last time we had contact they were still happily married.[19]

As this story shows, praying for our spouse can change hearts in a difficult and painful marital relationship. If we do not feel positive emotions toward our spouse and we cannot sincerely pray for our spouse to be happy, healthy, and successful, then let's begin by praying to our Father in Heaven to ask Him to help us to want to pray for them.

Pray with Your Spouse

In addition to praying for our spouse, the blessings of prayer will be more fully realized when we pray with our spouse. Many couples may not have a great testimony of couple prayer and may not make it a daily habit. Yet there is a special power and unity that comes into our lives and into our marriages when we choose to humbly pray together as spouses. It inoculates our relationship from the hazards of daily living,

Reflections

Many times while praying with my wife, I have experienced the very strong and overwhelming feeling of how blessed I am to have her as my wife. When we pray together, I feel our faith in the Lord is stronger, our love for our Heavenly Father grows, and our commitment and responsibilities to each other are very clear. I am reminded how deeply I love this amazing woman kneeling next to me and holding my hand. To me this is very humbling and heartwarming. I fall more in love with her in these few minutes each day. We have been having some very difficult times with our son, and we may have different opinions and ideas on how to handle those problems. After kneeling in prayer together, we always come together and agree on how we will work side by side to help our son. The revelation and love from our Heavenly Father is powerful when we pray together!

it elevates us above the mundane, and it helps us find the eternal happiness we desire. Elder Ezra Taft Benson, as a member of the Quorum of the Twelve Apostles, taught, "The differences and irritations of the day melt away as families approach the throne of heaven together. Unity increases. The ties of love and affection are re-enforced and the peace of heaven enters."[20]

The type of humble petition that elicits these blessings from a loving Heavenly Father also brings love and unity into the hearts of spouses. While a member of the Quorum of the Twelve Apostles, Elder Gordon B. Hinckley spoke extensively about the effect of couple prayer on a marital relationship:

> I know of no single practice that will have a more salutary effect upon your lives than the practice of kneeling together as you begin and close each day. Somehow the little storms that seem to afflict every marriage are dissipated when, kneeling before the Lord, you thank him for one another, in the presence of one another, and then together invoke his blessings upon your lives, your home, your loved ones, and your dreams.
>
> God then will be your partner, and your daily conversations with him will bring peace into your hearts and a joy into your lives that can come from no other source. Your companionship will sweeten through the years; your love will strengthen. Your appreciation for one another will grow. . . .
>
> The destroying angel of domestic bitterness will pass you by and you will know peace and love throughout your lives which may be extended into all eternity.[21]

Each of us can secure these blessings if we use our will and our agency to choose to turn our relationship ever toward God through couple prayer.

RICHARD: *In addition to praying together, the practice of simply kneeling together can also be a unifying experience. Often, while I am kneeling to say my individual prayer at the end of the day, Debra will come and kneel next to me at the side of the bed and just link her arm with mine and begin her personal prayer while I continue mine. I love it when she does that! Those quiet moments are tender and comforting, while also reinforcing the importance of the* Me, We, *and* Thee *of our marriage simultaneously. When we are both done with our individual prayers, it is then an easy transition to saying a prayer together arm in arm. This minor practice has been a special blessing to us.*

Elder Jeffrey R. Holland made a practical suggestion regarding couple prayer by sharing a personal story from his own marriage. Speaking of the early years of his marriage to his beloved wife, Sister Patricia Holland, he said:

> We were young . . . and we were very busy. We were finding ourselves having our evening prayer at the close of the day. We were exhausted. She had been raising children, I had been off to school or work. . . . We could hardly stay awake. We just decided there was no requirement that this has to be a prayer at 11 o'clock at night when we can hardly form the words. We just moved it up. We just took a time and said we are going to pray together earlier and it won't be flopped against the bed or almost asleep by the time [we] get into the conversation with the Lord just out of fatigue. It really materially changed our lives and our ability to make that evening prayer a meaningful experience with the Lord.[22]

Since we heard Elder Holland share this story, we have sought to implement this in our relationship as well. We saw the truth—that when we wait until we are half-asleep to pray together, our attitudes are not very positive and the prayers are certainly less effective.

These principles and practical suggestions can be encouraging when feelings between spouses are good and the relationship is strong. Yet when things are difficult—when we are not feeling

Very early in our married life, my wife and I began to pray together, kneeling before our Heavenly Father and praying out loud. Although it was uncomfortable at the beginning because we had not done this before, the practice quickly became some-thing we just did every morning and night. We have loved hearing each of us pleading for the other and for our chil-dren, family, friends, and neighbors. It has become a blessing to us in so many instances. As we pray we have a sense that our Heavenly Father is intimately involved in our lives and watches out for us as we heed the guidance of the Holy Ghost.

unified as spouses, such as when there has been conflict or when there is chronic interpersonal strain—it can be very difficult to want to pray together. And yet that is exactly what we need to do. In such difficult times, Elder David B. Haight counseled:

> If, as husband and wife, you are having serious misunderstandings or if you feel some strain or tension building up in your marriage, you should humbly get on your knees together and ask God our Father, with a sincere heart and real intent, to lift the darkness that is over your relationship, that you may receive the needed light, see your errors, repent of your wrongs, forgive each other, and receive each unto your-selves as you did in the beginning. I solemnly assure you that God lives and will answer your humble pleas.[23]

Pray for Your Spouse with Your Spouse

Praying for our spouse in our individual prayers draws our hearts to them, and praying with our spouse creates a sense of unity, but praying for our spouse while they are listening is particu-larly powerful.

RICHARD: *There is a sweetness and tenderness that comes into our relationship when we kneel together in prayer and hear the other petition the throne of God on our behalf. I feel at peace when I hear Debra pray for me that I might be successful and happy at work, that my projects will go smoothly so that I don't have to spend a lot of time and energy troubleshooting, and that I will receive the promptings necessary to effectively serve in my callings. When I pray for Debra in her presence, I know she really appreciates it. She senses my deep care for her when she hears me pray for her professional success, her Church calling, her personal health and welfare, and her strength to work with our children.*

Let Us Pray

Let us pray individually, pray for our spouse in our personal prayers, pray together with our spouse, pray for our spouse with our spouse, pray in times of peace and unity, and pray in times of conflict. Prayer will soothe our hearts, strengthen our relationship, increase our marital satisfaction, and open a conduit for receipt of personal and marital revelation through the Holy Spirit. If it is not our habit to have individual and couple prayer, may we begin now to establish these routines and allow the influence of the Holy Spirit more fully into our hearts and into our marriage. President M. Russell Ballard prescribed:

> There is great power in prayer. . . . I'm wondering if many of you parents, you couples, have lost that essential moment of kneeling together at the end of the day, just the two of you, holding hands and saying your prayers. If that has slipped away from your daily routine, may I suggest you put it back—beginning tonight![24]

Pondering

In addition to scripture study and prayer, we should dedicate ourselves to taking time to ponder or meditate, both individually and as a couple. In his postmortal visit to the Nephites, Jesus Christ taught us and them about the important role of pondering when he instructed them, "Go ye unto your homes, and ponder upon the things which I have said, and ask of the Father, in my name, that ye may understand, and prepare your minds for the morrow" (3 Nephi 17:2–3). As mortals we are weak and cannot initially understand many things of the Spirit. Yet taking the time

ROBERT T. BARRETT, *The Brother of Jared Seeing the Finger of the Lord.* © 2015 BY INTELLECTUAL RESERVE, INC.

to prepare to receive the word into our hearts will allow us to more fully receive and interpret the whisperings of the Spirit.

President David O. McKay counseled, "We pay too little attention to the value of meditation, a principle of devotion. . . . *Meditation is one of the most secret, most sacred doors through which we pass into the presence of the Lord.*"[25] Meditation, or pondering, can bring us into the presence of the Lord.

The scriptures provide several examples of those that have received great knowledge and visions after a period of individual or personal pondering. We will discuss three such stories herein: accounts of Lehi and Nephi, the brother of Jared, and President Joseph F. Smith.

The Book of Mormon prophet Lehi saw a pillar of fire in which he "saw and heard much" (1 Nephi 1:6). The record tells us that after the vision he "cast himself upon his bed, being overcome with the Spirit and the things which he had seen. And being thus overcome with the Spirit, he was carried away in a vision, even that he saw the heavens open" (verses 7–8). We believe as Lehi "cast himself upon his bed," he lay pondering on the vision he had just seen. As he did so, he received further light and truth through another vision. His pondering was an effective conduit to revelation, as we also learn later of another vision by this great prophet-leader, the vision of the tree of life (1 Nephi 8). Additionally, Nephi learned from his father and had a desire to know for himself the things his father had seen, and through pondering he received a vision. He recorded that while he "sat pondering in [his] heart [he] was caught away in the Spirit of the Lord, yea, into an exceedingly high mountain" (1 Nephi 11:1). It was there that the Spirit of the Lord gave him a personally guided tour of the things his father saw.

Many years earlier in the Book of Mormon chronology, as the Jaredites prepared to travel to the promised land, the brother of Jared discovered a few complications that the newly built barges would create during their journey: the need for air, the inability to steer, and the necessity of light. He prayed for help (Ether 2:19). The Lord gave him the answers to his questions about the need for air (verse 20) and how to steer (verses 24–25). Yet the brother of Jared did not so quickly or easily provide the answer relative to the need for light. The Lord, instead, instructed the brother of Jared to ponder upon the dilemma of traveling the ocean in darkness (verses 23, 25). He did so and derived a solution he then proposed to the Lord. As we learn from the narrative, the Lord honored this proposal.

As we see with the Brother of Jared, there may be times the Lord grants us answers to our prayers easily, without much more than the work of belief on our part. However, more often, as with the brother of Jared's question of how to travel the ocean with light, the Lord wants us to do our part in the revelatory process and exercise faith. He wants us to ponder, which includes examining our options (doing our research), making a decision, and then inquiring of Him if our decision be right (see D&C 9:7–9).

As a final scriptural example, in Doctrine and Covenants 138, President Joseph F. Smith illustrated the power of pondering on the word through his experience receiving revelation on the redemption of the dead:

> I sat in my room pondering over the scriptures; And reflecting upon the great atoning sacrifice that was made by the Son of God. . . . While I was thus engaged, my mind reverted to the writings of the apostle Peter. . . . I opened the Bible and read . . . , and as I read I was greatly impressed, more than I had ever been before. . . . As I pondered over these things which are written, the eyes of my understanding were opened, and the Spirit of the Lord rested upon me, and I saw the hosts of the dead, both small and great." (D&C 138:1–11)

His pondering, intermingled with and informed by his scripture study, opened the door for him to see the Lord's visit to those beyond the veil soon after His Resurrection.

RICHARD: *Pondering is one of my favorite things to do. Many times inspiration has come to me in the early hours of the morning, while I am still in bed, reflecting on decisions I need to make about my Church calling or family matters. I ponder often throughout the day while driving, walking, or sitting in my office, not just during scripture study, prayer, or sacrament meeting.*

Personal pondering is also a blessing in helping us get along in our marriage. There have been times when I have walked away from a moment of marital conflict feeling that I was right and feeling determined to stubbornly hold onto my position. Then, as I pondered the situation over several hours, my spirit would soften and I would ask, "Would you rather be right or would you rather have a marriage?" Humbled, I would then go and apologize to Debra (regardless of whether I felt I was right or not). This effort, brought about specifically by several hours of pondering, has always facilitated a path to more quickly resolve a disagreement. When Debra is considering a particular issue in her life, it is not uncommon for her to read and reread the same verses or chapters of scriptures for several days or more to create greater focus for her pondering. This type of pondering has led her to make many trajectory shifts, including changes that positively influenced our relationship.

As shown by these examples, pondering can bring small and simple, yet powerful, revelations. Through pondering the Lord leads us by the Holy Spirit's voice. Although pondering can be done anytime throughout the day or night, sometimes nighttime can be an especially important time for the Lord to send us messages. In a meeting for new mission presidents and their wives, President Gordon B. Hinckley shared the following regarding counsel he had received from President Harold B. Lee, then a member of the Quorum of the Twelve Apostles: "I remember only one thing he said: 'Listen for the whisperings of the Spirit in the middle of the night, and respond to those whisperings.' I don't know why revelation comes sometimes in the night, but it does. It comes in the day as well, of course. But listen to the whisperings of the Spirit, the gift of revelation, to which you are entitled."[26]

Pondering Together

Pondering together as a couple is also very powerful. When we ponder together, it generates tremendous power to reveal the line-upon-line revelations we so desperately need to navigate our personal lives and our marriages.

RICHARD: *Often, Debra and I will ponder about our marriage, finances, or other decisions. For example, one time we were seeking to make a financial decision and were struggling to come to resolution about how to proceed. For several days we were stuck, so I just decided to move full steam ahead on what I deemed the right course of action. Debra still struggled to feel good about it. She couldn't articulate her feelings well and wasn't quite sure why she felt as she did. I explained everything from my position, which seemed very logical and which Debra fully understood, yet she still couldn't get on board. When I pushed ahead, Debra grew panicked, and she determined to talk to me one more time about her concerns. I had to leave for a Church meeting just at that time.*

While driving to my meeting, I continued to ponder about the decision. The Spirit came clearly into my mind with a strong rebuke: "Richard, you're not listening to your wife." It was very still, yet very powerful and forceful. I knew I had to listen to that counsel. When I got back home, Debra was anxiously waiting in the driveway to meet me as I arrived. She said, "I need you to humor me to have one more conversation on the issue." You can imagine Debra's surprise when I immediately agreed to change course on the plan and get on the phone to pull the plug on the deal without even having the discussion!

As we continued later to explore other options, we realized that the Spirit— who knows the truth of all things (see Moroni 10:5)—had communicated through Debra that my original assumption about how to proceed in this situation was not in our best interest. By pondering together and respecting each other's insights, we were able to establish another plan that we both felt good about and that had the potential to save us a significant amount of money. Marriage naturally provides the law of two witnesses (see D&C 6:28; 8:2; 9:8). When we both, as spouses, ponder, pray, and counsel together, the Spirit can guide us to a unanimous decision that will lead to wise decision making.

DEBRA: *Richard and I spend a lot of time pondering together. The consequences of one particular pondering session have had a widespread positive impact in my personal life and on our marriage at large.*

Shortly after the birth of our fifth child, I felt overwhelmed, as I have shared with you already in chapter 3, but I also felt dramatically understimulated intellectually. I was home all day with three babies, aged two and under, and then in the afternoons, after school let out, I had the addition of our two older daughters. I felt like I had "mommy mush brain." I was working professionally at that time, but it amounted to no more than a few hours a week and just wasn't enough to offset the massive amount of time I spent alone with my children and doing domestic chores. As a couple we spent an evening pondering and counseling on how we could provide me with more professional engagement without compromising my role as a stay-at-home mom.

We had recently completed writing a chapter together on commitment in marriage for a book focused on marriage and family,[27] and working on that project during our babies' nap times and such had been quite a positive for me. So Richard had the idea that we could expand that book chapter into a presentation for BYU's Education Week. I responded, "I thought you had to be invited to present at Education Week?" to which Richard replied with a wry smile, "Oh, I can find someone to invite us." He did.

Prepping for the Education Week presentation gave me more time in my professional brain, allowing me to feel less like I had mommy mush brain. I felt much happier at home. When Education Week came along, we gave four one-hour lectures on commitment in marriage. We felt the blessings of service as we shared the content of our presentation with those in attendance. The process was a great boost to our marriage too. We saw each other shine in our professional areas of strength and felt proud of each other. Also, speaking about marriage strengthened our marriage intellectually and romantically, and the positive sentiment from that experience had a palpable influence within our relationship for several months. It was a wonderful growing experience for us!

After one of our lectures during Education Week, I was approached by someone about the possibility of writing a book. Richard and I felt prompted to pursue the opportunity; this book is the result.

Writing this book while my three youngest children were still so very small was crazy, but it actually did a tremendous amount of good for me personally. Since I had very few therapy clients at the time we started the book and I was home all day by myself with the kids, it gave me something to think about while I was doing mundane tasks that didn't use much brain power, such as folding the laundry. Over the years of writing, the "Babies 3" became the "Toddlers 3," and my days got even crazier, with all three of them walking, none of them reliable, and all of them screaming, crying, and making demands for one reason or the other. Nevertheless, working on this project gave me a sense of accomplishment as I saw ideas become paragraphs and paragraphs become chapters—

and no one undid my work afterwards (unlike my work sweeping the floor, cleaning up after meals, doing the dishes and laundry, or changing diapers). I also felt the blessings of service come into my heart as I got outside of myself and thought about how this material might bless others.

Writing this book was also a miracle in our marital relationship, as we previously shared in chapter 5. Our good marriage is now a great marriage! We more fully prioritize our relationship. We spend more time thinking of each other and what we can do to bless each other. We express lots of gratitude to one another. Our efforts to be sensitive or generous are more concerted. In other words, we do our marriage more fully on purpose. All of these blessings have come to us as a result of a simple pondering discussion one evening as a couple, trying to help me—as a frazzled, understimulated stay-at-home mother—find an avenue to get a mental break from my kiddos.

Writing and Recording Spiritual Promptings

When we receive impressions and ideas from the Lord, there is great value in learning to write them down or record them. Elder Richard G. Scott has said: "Knowledge carefully recorded is knowledge available in time of need. Spiritually sensitive information should be kept in a sacred place that communicates to the Lord how you treasure it. This practice enhances the likelihood of your receiving further light."[28] Following this counsel has been a great blessing for us. Writing our impressions in our scriptures and scripture journals has allowed the Lord to give us more ideas and directions. It helps us ponder upon the revelations He gives us with more clarity; seeing them written on the page enhances them. It helps us remember what we have received of the Lord when perhaps we tend to forget. It allows us to go back and review. There have been many times when we have gone back to our scripture journals and have been amazed at what we had previously learned, thinking, "This is good stuff!"

In fact, our scripture journals have become great reference books for us. Many of our sacrament meeting talks or church lessons are laced with ideas or insights the Spirit has given us, sometimes even years earlier, that we are able to access because we have recorded them. In other words, the revelations we personally receive and record remain available not only to bless us and our marriage but to bless others as well.

DEBRA: *As an example, one Easter Sunday I was asked to speak in sacrament meeting. I had spoken on Easter Sunday only two years earlier in our previous ward and had planned to largely rely on the talk I had given then. As I pondered and edited the talk, I felt it was not the message I needed to give and worked to write a new one. Easter morning I again felt that what I had prepared was not the talk I was supposed to give and that I needed to write the talk for a third time. With urgency I searched my scripture journal. I soon found the Easter-appropriate ideas I was supposed to share. This experience confirmed something Elder Richard G. Scott taught, that when you record spiritual promptings, "the knowledge you gain will be available throughout your life."*[30]

The Easter talk I gave was a message about Christ and His ability to heal us. After sacrament meeting I was approached by a brother who thanked me for the talk and said that I had tied some things together for him that he had never thought of before. Richard, who was bishop at the time, informed me that the man was not a baptized member of the congregation but attended meetings regularly with his wife. Later in the meeting block, a sister—the wife of the same man that had approached me earlier—came up to me and thanked me for the message and told me that I had taught her something new. I can only imagine the discussion this couple may have had together after church about what they learned that day, perhaps creating a bonding and growing moment for their marriage. This experience was made possible by insights the Holy Spirit had shared with me during my scripture study and that I had taken the time to honor by recording—years earlier.

RICHARD: *There are a variety of approaches we can choose to record our gospel insights. My approach to recording my spiritual impressions has evolved over time. I initially began by going beyond highlighting a verse to also writing notes or related quotes in the margins. I began extending those efforts into recording my impressions in a physical journal after my stake president began to emphasize scripture journals. I used small pocket-sized notebooks that I would carry with my scriptures so they would be available and convenient at all times. I would jot down anything that struck me as meaningful, without regard to any particular kind of organization in the notebook.*

Sometimes I would copy a poignant scripture word for word into the notebook, following Nephi's pattern of first recording a scripture and then making commentary (see 2 Nephi 12–25). I benefitted by following this pattern; I learned that by physically writing the scripture word for word, I saw words I did not previously notice when reading it because writing it down focused my attention differently.

As the Church began to more fully support digital formats, I began reading my scriptures on my laptop, iPad, and smartphone. The digital format allows me to highlight a particular verse and then write impressions, thoughts, and other notes about it directly into the scriptures as a pop-up note. These recordings automati-

cally save to my copy of the digital scriptures as well as to a notes file which becomes available to me digitally at all times through all of my various electronic devices.

DEBRA: *Richard introduced me to the idea of a scripture journal while we were dating. I have always chosen to use a simple electronic document on my computer as my scripture journal. I study with my laptop nearby so I can record impressions, or I will jot ideas on a piece of paper and then type them into my scripture-journal document at a later time. I like this format because it is easy for me to find previously written ideas in the electronic document later.*

I have taken three various approaches to recording my impressions during scripture study over the years. First, at times when I have studied a particular topic, I have grouped scriptures into my own topical guide and written notes about the verses, definitions of words, and quotes from Church leaders. For example, when I struggled earlier in our marriage to forgive Richard for hurts he had caused, I took this approach to study the topic of forgiveness. Below, I show you my work. The original work was very lengthy, but I have truncated it here, as my purpose is to show you the general structure of my work in the scripture journal rather than focus on the content.

1. *Frankly forgive. 1 Nephi 7:21, "And it came to pass that I did frankly forgive them all that they had done." Luke 7:42, "When they had nothing to pay, he frankly forgave them both." Frankly = freely, openly, plainly, candidly. I need to do better at this.*

2. *Do not bring up past misdeeds. Ezekiel 18:22, "All his transgressions that he hath committed, they shall not be mentioned unto him: in his righteousness that he hath done he shall live." If I still bring up Richard's misdeeds against me, it is evidence that I have not yet forgiven him.*

3. *I must forgive!—it is a commandment. Matthew 6:12, "Forgive us our debts, as we forgive our debtors." Substitute the word "like" for "as" to bring a clearer impression of the message of this scripture.*

4. *Be patient when I am hurt in the present day. Forbearance = refraining from something (anger, offense): forbearing conduct or quality, patient endurance; self-control; abstaining from enforcing a right; a creditor's giving of indulgence after the day originally fixed for payment (e.g., even after I think he should've already learned what not to say). Matthew 18:21–22, "How oft shall my brother sin against me, and I forgive him? till seven times? . . . Not . . . seven times; but . . . seventy times seven." Joseph Smith manual p. 393 about this scripture: "We have not*

(yet) forgiven them seventy times seven, as our Savior directed; perhaps we have not forgiven them once."

5. *Seek healing of hurt and wounds through the Atonement of my Savior, Jesus Christ. Alma 7:11–12, "He will take upon him the pains and the sicknesses of his people . . . that he may know according to the flesh how to succor his people according to their infirmities." Exodus 15:26, "For I am the Lord that healeth thee."*

6. *Blessings come by forgiving. Not only will I be forgiven if I forgive (see #3; Matthew 6:14–15; Luke 6:37; D&C 82:1), but I will be further blessed: D&C 132:56, "Let mine handmaid [Debra] forgive my servant [Richard] his trespasses; and then shall she be forgiven her trespasses, wherein she has trespassed against me; and I, the Lord thy God, will bless her, and multiply her, and make her heart to rejoice." The joy I seek comes from Christ—knowing Him, emulating Him, having gratitude for what He has done. That will overshadow everything else of the world that may bring me sorrow.*

Second, and most commonly, I have recorded an insight on a common gospel principle or familiar verse that I gained by a unique coupling of ideas, verses, or such. I have found this approach to recording to be the most useful to me in gaining spiritual insights. In one scripture–journal entry, as I began to record a new insight gained by familiar verses, I recorded by way of introduction, "The 'Liahona' of the Book of Mormon changed its writings to me today." In this particular instance, I had read Alma 37:13–17, in which Alma gives specific counsel to his son Helaman to care for the plates, of which he has been given stewardship, and to care for the sacred things of God according to His commandments. As I read these verses, I received personal revelation relative to our children. Even though I had read Alma 37 many times, I had never previously thought of these scriptures relative to our children or my role as a mother. Yet I had experienced some significant events with some of our children only the day before, turning my thoughts to them and, thus, affecting my view of the familiar verses to allow me to receive new insights. I now understood that our children were spoken of within those verses—they were the "sacred things"—and I received specific instructions from the verses regarding

RIGHT: JOSEPH BRICKEY, *Lehi and the Liahona.*

God's mandate that I "appeal unto the Lord for all things whatsoever ye must do with them" (see Alma 37:16). I recorded what I learned in my scripture journal.

Third, there have been times when I have taken a particular verse or idea that has prompted me and then used that idea as a springboard to journal about the personal, marital, and gospel insights I received. For example, the following entry was taken from my scripture journal I kept during our first year of marriage, when adjustment issues, particularly relative to Richard having been a longtime bachelor, were rampant:

> *Richard and I are still battling because I perceive he is making judgment that my way of interacting with the world (my personality and the feelings I have as a woman) is wrong, and that I "should" do it his way. So, as I came across this scripture today it was very meaningful: Acts 5:38 "And now I say unto you, Refrain from these men, and let them alone; for if this counsel or this work be of men, it will come to nought." I don't have to prove he is wrong, I don't have to persuade him that he is wrong; as we live together over time, I believe he will start to see the value of being married to someone who is not his emotional clone. He has already come to say that many of the other things he nit-picked me on historically were wrong . . . , and he doesn't say them anymore. Be patient; . . . it's a developmental process.*

Not only does this type of journal entry show that we are trying to honor the principle to "liken all scriptures unto us, that it might be for our profit and learning" (1 Nephi 19:23), but it certainly becomes a great piece of personal history. Many happily married years later, it is also amusing to be reminded of where we had first been and how much we struggled to become unified in contrast to where we are today.

How do you prefer to record your impressions? Whether it be one of the ways we have mentioned or your own unique way, it does not matter—it only matters that you do it.

Conclusion

To strengthen and bring the *Thee* into our marriage, we need to spend time with the Lord through personal and couple worship. Effective scripture study is done on a daily basis during a regularly scheduled time for a predetermined amount of time. A primary purpose of our scripture study is to open the way for the Lord to give us revelation. Then our study becomes a devotional with the Lord. In tandem with scripture study time, our worship will more fully invite the Spirit of revelation as we include praying, pondering, and writing directed by the Holy Ghost.

When we pray individually, as well as with our spouse, we invite not only the spirit of revelation but a soothing, loving spirit into our marital relationship. Prayer can be particularly powerful in helping us overcome dark feelings and in enticing us to want to have the desire to draw nearer to each other.

Since we often cannot understand many things of the Spirit when we first receive them, we will also be blessed with a greater level of understanding and a deeper connection with the Spirit when we take the time to ponder the word in our hearts. As we ponder individually, we can often understand more fully what we can do individually to improve our marital relationship in various circumstances. As we ponder with our spouse, including counseling with them, we can be more clearly directed in the choices we need to make regarding our lives and our marriage.

Writing down our spiritual promptings contributes to our ability to ponder on them with more clarity, helps remind us of what we have learned when we tend to forget, and allows us to access them at a later date. It invites the Lord to give us more revelation as we show Him that we honor the revelations he provides to us.

When we make our personal and couple worship a priority, we invite God to be more fully involved in our marriage and life. He will teach us what we need to know and do to help our marriage thrive. We cannot go wrong with His influence.

Notes

1. Russell M. Nelson, "Nurturing Marriage," *Ensign*, May 2006, 36.
2. Michael A. Goodman, David C. Dollahite, and Loren Marks, "Exploring Transformational Processes and Meaning in LDS Marriages," *Marriage and Family Review* 48, no. 6 (2012): 555–82.

3. Dale G. Renlund's Facebook Page, 21 May 2017, https://www.facebook.com/DaleGRenlund/posts/1907337372876436.

4. Ronald A. Rasband, "Let the Holy Spirit Guide," *Ensign*, May 2017, 94.

5. Samuel L. Perry, "Spouse's Religious Commitment and Marital Quality: Clarifying the Role of Gender," *Social Science Quarterly* 97, no. 2 (June 2016): 476–90; Jonathan R. Olson et al., "Shared Religious Beliefs, Prayers, and Forgiveness as Predictors of Marital Satisfaction," *Family Relations* 64, no. 4 (October 2015): 519–33; Christopher G. Ellison, Amy M. Burdette, and W. Bradford Wilcox, "The Couple That Prays Together: Race and Ethnicity, Religion, and Relationship Quality Among Working-Age Adults," *Journal of Marriage and Family* 72, no. 4 (August 2010): 963–75.

6. Richard J. McClendon and Bruce A. Chadwick, "Latter-day Saint Families at the Dawn of the Twenty-First Century," in *Helping and Healing Families: Principles and Practices Inspired by "The Family: A Proclamation to the World,"* ed. Craig H. Hart et al. (Salt Lake City: Deseret Book, 2005), 32–43.

7. Adapted from Kelly G. Wilson, Emily K. Sandoz, Jennifer Kitchens, and Miguel Roberts, "The Valued Living Questionnaire: Defining and Measuring Valued Action within a Behavioral Framework," *Psychological Record* 60 (2010): 249–72.

8. Joseph Smith Jr., "To the Honorable Men of the World," *The Evening and the Morning Star*, August 1832, 22.

9. Gary E. Stevenson, "Look to the Book, Look to the Lord," *Ensign*, November 2016, 47.

10. Henry B. Eyring, "'And Thus We See': Helping a Student in a Moment of Doubt" (address to CES religious educators, 5 February 1993), https://si.lds.org/bc/seminary/content/library/talks/evening-with/and-thus-we-see_helping-a-student-in-a-moment-of-doubt_eng.pdf.

11. Howard W. Hunter, "Reading the Scriptures," *Ensign*, November 1979, 64.

12. Ezra Taft Benson, "A Sacred Responsibility," *Ensign*, May 1986, 78.

13. Thomas S. Monson, "The Power of the Book of Mormon," *Ensign*, May 2017, 86–87; emphasis added.

14. Marion G. Romney, in Conference Report, April 1960, 110–13.

15. McClendon and Chadwick, "Latter-day Saint Families," 37, 42.

16. Olson et al., "Shared Religious Beliefs." See also Ellison, Burdette, and Wilcox, "The Couple That Prays Together."

17. Richard G. Scott, "Using the Supernal Gift of Prayer," *Ensign*, May 2007, 8.

18. Henry B. Eyring, "Our Perfect Example," *Ensign*, November 2009, 71.

19. Bruce A. Chadwick, "Hanging Out, Hooking Up, and Celestial Marriage" (devotional address, Brigham Young University, Provo, UT, 7 May 2002), https://speeches.byu.edu/talks/bruce-a-chadwick_hanging-hooking-celestial-marriage/.

20. Ezra Taft Benson, in Conference Report, April 1949, 197–98.

21. Gordon B. Hinckley, "Except the Lord Build the House . . . ," *Ensign*, June 1971, 72.

22. Jeffrey R. Holland, "Face to Face with President Eyring and Elder Holland" (worldwide youth broadcast, 4 March 2017), https://www.lds.org/broadcasts/face-to-face/eyring-holland?lang=eng.

23. David B. Haight, "Marriage and Divorce," *Ensign*, May 1984, 14.

24. M. Russell Ballard, "The Sacred Responsibilities of Parenthood," *Ensign*, March 2006, 33.

25. David O. McKay, *Teachings of Presidents of the Church: David O. McKay* (Salt Lake City: The Church of Jesus Christ of Latter-day Saints, 2003), 29; emphasis added.

26. Gordon B. Hinckley, *Teachings of Presidents of the Church: Gordon B. Hinckley* (Salt Lake City: The Church of Jesus Christ of Latter-day Saints, 2016), 117.

27. Richard J. McClendon and Debra Theobald McClendon, "Commitment to the Covenant: LDS Marriage and Divorce," in *By Divine Design: Best Practices for Family Success and Happiness*, ed. Brent L. Top and Michael A. Goodman (Salt Lake City: Deseret Book, 2014), 93–116.

28. Richard G. Scott, "Acquiring Spiritual Knowledge," *Ensign*, November 1993, 86.

29. David V. Clare, "Attaining, Accessing, Using Priesthood Power" (address, BYU Women's Conference, Provo, UT, 2 May 2014), https://womensconference.byu.edu/sites/womensconference.ce.byu.edu/files/david_clare.pdf.

30. Richard G. Scott, "To Acquire Knowledge and the Strength to Use It Wisely" (devotional address, Brigham Young University, Provo, UT, 23 January 2001), https://speeches.byu.edu/talks/richard-g-scott_acquire-knowledge-strength-use-wisely/.

CHAPTER 10

"Safety in Counsel"

Heeding Prophets and Apostles

Another way to bring the *Thee* into our marriage is by following God's modern oracles. We have the privilege to live in a time when God speaks to us through living prophets and apostles; he gives us continual counsel and commandments through them. President M. Russell Ballard of the Quorum of the Twelve Apostles said, "It is no small thing to have a prophet of God in our midst. Great and wonderful are the blessings that come into our lives as we listen to the word of the Lord given to us through him."[1]

This chapter will first look at the doctrine of prophets to help us understand the seriousness with which we must heed their counsel in our lives and marriages. God the Father gives prophets and apostles special keys and authority to represent Him here on earth. Understanding how He does this and why He does this is important in bringing God into our marriage. We will then look at specific counsel that modern-day prophets and apostles have given relative to marriage to help it thrive and be successful.

The Doctrine of Prophets

Since the days of Adam, the Lord has established a pattern and plan to direct His work here on the earth. He has called special, faithful men throughout the ages to be prophets by communicating with them and giving them authority and keys to direct His work.[2] This pattern was also followed in this final dispensation with the calling of the Prophet Joseph Smith. As a young boy, he went to a grove of trees to inquire of the Lord which church he should join. In answer to that humble question, God the Father and His Son, Jesus Christ, appeared to him. Throughout the rest of his life, Joseph was continually visited by angels and even Christ Himself. During several of these visits, Heavenly Father sent angels to physically confer priesthood keys and authority upon Joseph. Joseph, in turn, conferred these keys and authority upon other men who were called as Apostles. This pattern continues within the Church today.

The prophets serve as a liaison between God the Father and His children, leading us and giving us what we need in our daily lives. In the Book of Mormon, Nephi gave a thorough discourse to his rebellious brothers, Laman and Lemuel, on the role of prophets. He taught his brothers using the familiar story of Moses leading the children of Israel out of Egyptian slavery. Nephi explained to his brothers that the slavery of the children of Israel could not have ended without a decision by the people to listen to the Lord through His prophet, Moses. He outlined the miracles God performed on their behalf through His prophet: He split the waters of the Red Sea so the children of Israel could escape (1 Nephi 17:23–26), He fed them with manna (verse 28), He blessed them with water after Moses split a rock (verse 29), and He blessed them with guidance in the wilderness (verse 30).

DEL PARSON, *The First Vision*, COURTESY OF INTELLECTUAL RESERVE, INC.

We see here that everything of importance to the children of Israel was provided by the living prophet: deliverance, food, water, and guidance through the desert. When the people were righteous and followed the prophet, they were blessed; when they were not righteous, they failed to prosper. This example illustrates how God uses His divinely called prophet to do His work among His children. This is true in our day as well.

The doctrine of prophets teaches us that we cannot separate ourselves from the prophets without also separating ourselves from Heavenly Father and Christ. Doctrine and Covenants 1:38 explains, "What I the Lord have spoken, I have spoken, and I excuse not myself; and though the heavens and the earth pass away, my word shall not pass away, but shall all be fulfilled, whether by mine own voice or by the voice of my servants, *it is the same*" (emphasis added). Some members of the Church have struggled to accept specific counsel from the prophets and instead of humbly seeking confirmation from the Lord, they have sought to resolve their disagreeable feelings by shifting away from Church leadership to focus exclusively on their relationship with Christ. This strategy may provide temporary soothing, but at some point this stance will whittle away at their testimony and faith and likely lead to apostasy. The Lord warned of this when He declared that "the day cometh that they who will not hear the voice of the Lord, neither the voice of his servants, neither give heed to the words of the prophets and apostles, *shall be cut off from among the people*" (D&C 1:14; emphasis added).

There may be times when what a prophet speaks is a challenge to follow. In these circumstances, the Lord requires our faith, which will lead us to be humble and seek confirmation. The Book of Mormon is full of stories that contrast those who meekly follow the prophet and are blessed, and those who rebel and fall. Take for example the story of the prophet Lehi and his family when he left his riches and property back in Jerusalem. Naturally, everyone was a bit shocked and upset by the declarations of their prophet-father. Laman and Lemuel murmured and simply did nothing to seek spiritual understanding. This failure to be humble and faithfully seek the Spirit's witness contributed to even greater hardening of their hearts, as they later became angry and murderous. By contrast, Nephi chose to be meek and teachable. "And it came to pass that I, Nephi, . . . having great desires to know of the mysteries of God, wherefore, I did cry unto the Lord; and behold he did visit me, and did soften my heart that I did believe all the words which had been spoken by my father; wherefore, I did not rebel against him like unto my brothers" (1 Nephi 2:16).

In this story, Nephi illustrates for us the spiritual work we must do to receive confirmation of prophetic counsel and admonition. Elder Harold B. Lee stated: "It is not alone sufficient for us as Latter-day Saints to follow our leaders and to accept their counsel, but we have the greater obligation to gain for ourselves the unshakable testimony of the divine appointment of these men and the witness that what they have told us is the will of our Heavenly Father."[3]

Prophets and Apostles are Seers

In addition to serving as liaisons between God and the people for their present needs, the prophets and apostles have also been called of God to serve as seers: "A seer can know of things which are past, and also of things which are to come, and by them shall all things be revealed . . . ; therefore he becometh a great benefit to his fellow beings" (Mosiah 8:17–18).

In today's world there are many dangers particularly targeting our marriages. These seers are called to serve as watchmen on the tower to warn us of these dangers. In ancient civilizations, watchtowers were vital to implementing a military's defensive strategy. With watchtowers in place, watchmen could see their enemy's movements and provide timely alerts for the inhabitants of their city so they could prepare for battle. Captain Moroni used this strategy to protect his people. He had towers built and then put "places of security" atop the towers. This approach allowed them to elude the stones and arrows of the Lamanites as well as be prepared to mount an offense against enemies if they came near the city walls (Alma 50:4–5).

President M. Russell Ballard explained:

> Often in the scriptures the Lord speaks of watchmen on the towers and of watchtowers themselves (see, for example, D&C 101:12, 43–60). A watchtower is generally raised so that someone can climb to the top and see a greater distance. In this way they are alerted to the danger or threat much sooner than they would otherwise be.
>
> The same principle holds true in our lives. We can raise watchtowers which help us deal with threats before they actually descend upon us.[4]

A MAN STANDING IN A STONE WATCHTOWER OVERLOOKING A VALLEY.
PHOTO BY JAMES ILIFF JEFFERY.

In 1833 the Lord gave a parable to the Saints in Missouri concerning the redemption of Zion which included striking imagery about the importance of establishing a watchtower for protection: "The watchman upon the tower would have seen the enemy *while he was yet afar off* and then ye could have made ready and kept the enemy from breaking down the hedge thereof and saved my vineyard from the hands of the destroyer" (D&C 101:54; emphasis added). Using watchtowers to see the enemy while he is *yet afar off* takes away one of Satan's most important strategies—the element of surprise. Satan delights in ambush, taking us out before we realize what happened. Consequently, the Lord has provided us with watchmen (our Church leaders, particularly the prophets and apostles) on the watchtower (the Church's structure and organization).

The watchmen receive relevant and timely alerts about Satan's current and future plans of attack. Their warnings come often, especially during general conference. Elder Bruce R. McConkie explained, "In their capacity as elders, prophets, ambassadors, and ministers, the Lord's agents are *watchmen* upon the tower. Their obligation is to raise the warning voice so that the sheepfold of Israel shall stand secure from the dangers and evils of the world."[5]

One of the great challenges in today's culture and society is to become aware of and expose Satan's subtle and unseen ways of deception. He often masks destructive influences or lifestyles and makes them look not only innocent but even desirable (see the discussion on commitment and culture in chapter 2).

In modern warfare, the watchtowers and watchmen of old have been replaced by high-tech satellites that lie in orbit above the earth. These satellites are able to see what we as mortals upon the ground are unable to see.

RICHARD: *I once watched a PBS program called* Earth from Space, *produced by NOVA. The program explained how hundreds of satellites that circle the earth expose unseen events that transpire on the earth. The video posed the question "How can a dust storm in the Sahara Desert in Africa affect the Amazon in South America?" In an amazing display seen only by satellites, mineral-rich dust particles are swept up into the jet stream during daily dust storms in the Sahara Desert. These microscopic particles then make a two-thousand-mile journey across the Atlantic Ocean and are deposited onto the rainforests of the Amazon, thus providing them with nutrient-rich fertilizer. Scientists have known for many years that the soil in the Amazon itself has been leached and has not been able to produce its own fertilized soil, but they did not know how it continued to grow plants. Satellites have revealed the mystery. Nutrients from the other side of the world are miraculously deposited like clockwork into the Amazon to feed it. This unseen process is now seen by way of these marvelous satellites.*

I began to ponder this idea of the unseen, relative to prophets serving as our satellites. Just as there are unseen forces in the physical environment, there are many unseen events and influences in our spiritual or moral environment; they occur all around us and we remain unaware of their presence. Yet the prophets and apostles see. They are our satellites, here to discern for us that which we cannot discern for ourselves. They see the big picture and are closer to the heavens than we are.

CREDIT: 123RF

LIKE SATELLITES, PROPHETS HELP US SEE THE BIG PICTURE.

Elder Boyd K. Packer related a discussion between President Harold B. Lee and Elder Charles A. Callis of the Quorum of the Twelve Apostles in which Elder Callis asserted that as Church leaders they are able to "see clearly what is ahead." He said that to "see clearly what is ahead and yet find members slow to respond or resistant to counsel or even rejecting the witness of the apostles and prophets brings deep sorrow."[6]

We have many evidences of the future-focused vision of Church leaders. One example is their 1995 publication of "The Family: A Proclamation to the World." This proclamation defines and establishes the preeminent and proper role of gender and the family in society and provides guiding principles of success for spouses, parents, and children. It teaches that "marriage between man and woman is essential to [God's] eternal plan" and that "happiness in family life is most likely to be achieved when founded upon the teachings of the Lord Jesus Christ."[7] It also includes this very important declaration about marriage: "Successful marriages and families are established and maintained on principles of faith, prayer, repentance, forgiveness, respect, love, compassion, work, and wholesome recreational activities."[8]

This proclamation was sent to the world when there was yet relatively little organized societal opposition to the familial principles declared therein. Times have changed in the decades since. The truths of this document are not so clear to the world. As the world is in crisis and confusion relative to gender, the roles of men and women, and the family, *the Church is not!* Decades earlier modern prophets, as seers, were able to foresee our day and thoroughly prepare. For that, we are exceedingly grateful; we feel comfort knowing that we are in good hands. President M. Russell Ballard declared: "These are difficult times. Is there one clear, unpolluted, unbiased voice that we can always count on? Is there a voice that will always give us clear directions to find our way in today's troubled world? The answer is *yes*. That voice is the voice of the living prophet and apostles."[9] Like watchtowers and watchmen of old and like our modern-day satellites, the words of the living prophets expose these unseen tactics of the enemy, and, if we heed them, their counsel will protect us, our marriages, and our families.

Reflections

When my dear companion and I were married in 1974, we were both desirous to obey the commandment to "multiply and replenish the earth," but after a few years of marriage we were not blessed with children. We met with a fertility specialist but were told there was no medical reason why we couldn't have children. So after prayerful consideration we decided we should apply for adoption. A few years later we were finally blessed with a beautiful little baby boy. When we met with the social worker to pick up our new baby boy, he said, "The mother told me she saw you both in a dream, and knew you were to raise this sweet little boy." At last we finally understood why this great blessing was held back for so many years, and even though it was initially difficult for us to understand the will of the Lord, over time it became clear why we had needed to wait for our family to come. We were so grateful for the blessing to raise this sweet son. Our marriage was strengthened through this trial, as we learned to trust in the Lord. Our prayers became less focused on our desires and more focused on accepting the Lord's will for us.

Marriage Is Blessed When We Give Heed to the Prophets

We are promised blessings for following the prophets. Doctrine and Covenants 124:25 promises us, "If my people will hearken unto my voice, and unto the voice of my servants whom I have appointed to lead my people, behold, verily I say unto you, they shall not be moved out of their place." To this, President Boyd K. Packer added, "Remember this promise; hold on to it. It should be a great comfort to those struggling to keep a family together in a society increasingly indifferent to, and even hostile toward, those standards which are essential to a happy family."[10] Thus, couples who commit themselves to following the living oracles of God will find added protection in their lives, family, and marriage.

To us this is very comforting doctrine; God is invested in helping us to focus our time and energy on principles and practices that truly make a difference and will bring success into our marriage. In a modern world that often gets caught up in pop culture or alternative fads, following the counsel of leaders is vital to help us avoid getting deceived by Satan and his trends in society that go counter to the commandments of God. It is also important to keep us from wasting precious resources—such as our time, energy, or money—on ideas or programs or causes that will not bear fruit (see John 15:16). President Boyd K. Packer taught:

> The ministry of the prophets and apostles leads them ever and always to the home and the family. . . .
>
> The ultimate purpose of all we teach is to unite parents and children in faith in the Lord Jesus Christ, that they are happy at home, sealed in an eternal marriage, linked to their generations, and assured of exaltation in the presence of our Heavenly Father.

He later continued: "The great plan of happiness (see Alma 42:8, 16) revealed to prophets is the plan for a happy family. It is the love story between husband and wife, parents and children, that renews itself through the ages."[11]

JAMES JOHNSON, *Widow of Zarephath*. COURTESY OF INTELLECTUAL
RESERVE, INC.

Prophetic Counsel May Challenge Us

Although blessings come from following the prophets, sometimes giving heed to their counsel is not always easy. Sometimes
the application becomes painful as that counsel pushes up against
our own wants and desires.

We see in the story of Elijah and the widow of Zarephath
(1 Kings 17:10–13) the excruciating decisions that are sometimes
required to follow a prophet of God, yet we also see the blessings that come as a result of doing so. Elijah called to the woman
as she gathered sticks and asked her to bring him some water to

drink. As she left to get a container for the water, he also asked her to bring him some bread. She replied to him that she did not have any bread, but only some meal and oil. She then explained that she was currently gathering sticks in order to build a fire so that she and her son could cook what little meal and oil they had so they could then eat it and die. Elijah then said to her, "Fear not; go and do as thou hast said: but make me thereof a little cake first, and bring it unto me, and after make for thee and for thy son" (verse 13).

In general conference, Sister Carol F. McConkie, first counselor in the Young Women General Presidency, implored us to think about this story: "Imagine for a moment the difficulty of what the prophet was asking a starving mother to do." She then continued:

> But Elijah also promised a blessing for obedience. . . .
>
> In a world threatened by a famine of righteousness and spiritual starvation, we have been commanded to sustain the prophet. . . .
>
> We heed prophetic word even when it may seem unreasonable, inconvenient, and uncomfortable. According to the world's standards, following the prophet may be unpopular, politically incorrect, or socially unacceptable. But following the prophet is always right. . . .
>
> The Lord honors and favors those who will heed prophetic direction. For the widow of Zarephath, obedience to Elijah saved her life and ultimately the life of her son.[12]

Following the prophet will indeed save our marriage and our family. As in this story, we have also felt the burden of faith as we have sought to follow the prophet when it has been difficult, yet we have also experienced the blessings.

DEBRA: *My example that follows involves my personal efforts to follow one particular piece of counsel that has been very difficult and painful for me over many years. The purpose of this story is to illustrate the sometimes–difficult and occasionally complex process of submitting our will to our Father by following His appointed servants.*

I spent eight long years working on what should have been a five-year PhD program. In that time I went through pregnancy illness, the delivery of two daugh-ters, a divorce, dating as a single mother, and remarriage. I sacrificed in many areas to get my professional training and have the other experiences the Lord had inspired me to pursue, while personally caring for my daughters as much as possible during these difficult life circumstances.

The last year of my PhD training required a full-time internship, which mandated that my daughters spend a full day in daycare five times a week for a year. Just prior to the beginning of that internship, I was personally recruited to apply for what I felt would be my dream job postgraduation—a university teach-ing job for which I felt I had been groomed. I was so honored to be personally recruited that I bounded through the house, squealing with delight. It was at that time, one day in the summer of 2008, while Richard and I were doing couple scripture study, that we found a First Presidency Message by President Henry B. Eyring called "Safety in Counsel." He clearly taught that the only sure path of safety in life is to humbly follow prophetic counsel even when it is difficult, without justification or rationalization.

President Eyring's message took a generalized approach to discussing fol-lowing prophetic counsel. Yet within his discussion he highlighted one example of specific prophetic counsel that has been given to the general body of the Church:

In our own time we have been warned with counsel on where to find safety from sin and from sorrow. One of the keys to rec-ognizing those warnings is that they are repeated. For instance, more than once in general conferences, you have heard our prophet say that he would quote a preceding prophet and would therefore be a second witness and sometimes even a third. Each of us old enough to listen heard President Spencer W. Kimball (1895–1985) give counsel on the importance of a mother in the home and then heard President Ezra Taft Benson (1899–1994) quote him, and we have heard President Gordon B. Hinck-ley . . . quote them both.[13]

The only specific example of general prophetic counsel in the entire message was about the importance of mothers in the home. This stung me painfully, partic-ularly because my instinct and desire was to think that since God had given me very

Reflections

clear personal revelation about the need to obtain my professional training and had clearly helped me forge through very difficult personal circumstances in order to do so, I must somehow be exempt from the counsel. I wanted to believe that God had slated me to be an exception and that I was called to work professionally while my children were young. Yet President Eyring addressed the danger of seeking to make ourselves "an exception to the counsel."[14]

Richard and I were profoundly struck by this message, and we pondered and discussed it at length together. Whereas I had received very clear, unmistakable, and powerful revelation that I was supposed to do the PhD, that personal revelation was not present in this circumstance. In the end, in a fiercely determined move to try to submit my will to the Lord's and to follow His prophets, I chose not to apply for the job. It was a very painful decision.

As I worked in my required full-time internship that year, I learned two practical lessons that strengthened my faith that I had made the right choice to follow prophetic counsel and not apply for the postgraduation full-time teaching job. First, for our daughters' sake I was glad I had not already committed to work full-time once the internship concluded. Working full-time was exceedingly difficult on our daughters, then preschool and kindergarten aged. Our younger daughter cried every time she was dropped off for daycare for the first eight months. Second, I found a great deal of satisfaction and fulfillment in my internship work in a university counseling center and decided that the previously offered job was not really my dream job.

Yet, in the years that have followed since, I have learned, and am continuing to learn, broader and deeper lessons about following the counsel of our leaders. I have come to believe that instead of making a sacrifice to not work full-time outside of the home with small children, my choice has represented a wise and fruitful investment.

For example, God has supported me in finding other ways to contribute professionally and feel personally fulfilled with my contributions, such as in giving presentations, seeing private-practice therapy clients during my kids' preschool and school hours, and writing this book (as we discussed in chapter 9) without compromising my role as a stay-at-home mom. I have had fulfilling professional opportunities that I would not have had the time to pursue had I been engaged in full-time employment elsewhere.

Through these experiences I have come to believe that God is giving me the most rewarding professional opportunities I could desire, which I never would have been able to create of my own accord. I believe God is making more of my career than I could have, because I was willing to submit to and follow Him. Additionally, our children know that Mom is there for them. They are securely attached, they are learning from me the values that we as parents espouse, and they have been afforded miraculous protections.

That difficult personal decision of 2008 has been retested many times since then. My desire to return to work in the university counseling center of my internship remained strong for many years. Whenever I heard of a job opening or I was directly asked if I was interested in applying, I grimaced with intense yearning and excitement and simultaneous pain and regret, knowing I needed to let it pass while I raised our children. I always called Richard on the phone with the painful announcement: "Guess what? The counseling center has an opening." I would wistfully talk about how much I wanted to be there and how happy I was when I was working there, and would ask if there would be any way we could work it out. Richard was always supportive and told me we would work it out if we needed to do so.

We had many of these discussions over the years; this script played out again and again and again. At the end of each discussion, I would submissively end with, "But I know it is not time yet." I would then go grab my well-worn, marked-up copy of President Eyring's article and read it repeatedly over the next few days to remind myself of what I was purposely seeking to do. In doing so, I always felt reinforced by the Spirit for my decision.

Reflections

Years ago I heard President Ezra Taft Benson [counsel] us to do all we could to get out of debt and stay out. He mentioned mortgages on houses. He said that it might not be possible, but it would be best if we could pay off all our mortgage debt.

I turned to my wife after the meeting and asked, "Do you think there is any way we could do that?" At first we couldn't. And then by evening I thought of a property we had acquired in another state. For years we had tried to sell it without success.

. . . We placed a phone call Monday morning to the man in San Francisco who had our property listed to sell. I had called him a few weeks before, and he had said then, "We haven't had anyone show interest in your property for years."

But on the Monday after conference, I heard an answer that to this day strengthens my trust in God and His servants.

The man on the phone said, "I am surprised by your call. A man came in today inquiring whether he could buy your property." In amazement I asked, "How much did he offer to pay?" It was a few dollars more than the amount of our mortgage.

. . . Our mortgage was paid off.[18]

President Eyring speaks of following counsel "when it is hard to do."[15] *This has been* very hard *doctrine for me, yet I have felt the blessings of obedience. I know that the Lord has accepted my offering. I testify that we have seen marital and family blessings and protections.*

RICHARD: *Debra's commitment to put the counsel of the Lord's prophets ahead of her own desires not only has blessed her professionally and blessed our children but has positively influenced our marriage. It has strengthened my confidence and trust in her, knowing that she has faith in God's anointed servants, not only in word but in (sometimes painful) deed. Because I have the same love for and commitment to those who hold priesthood keys, her ongoing efforts to follow the prophet, even when tempted repeatedly to do otherwise, have generated a peace and assurance in me that has increased my desire to be close to her. I have felt greater trust and confidence in her spiritual promptings. I have also felt closer to her because of her diligence in nurturing and training our children in the home. It has reminded me that we are unified in how we want to raise our children, and that strengthens our general feelings of unity. These blessings have brought increased positive sentiment to our relationship, thus strengthening our marriage by increasing the loving bonds between us.*

At times, submitting our will to God's by being willing to follow prophetic counsel becomes an ongoing process of committing and recommit-ting as we are tempted to move toward the world. We testify that as we submit in faith, we are blessed.

Prophetic Counsel on Marriage and Family

Prophetic counsel regarding marriage has been presented throughout this book. Yet here we offer in a single presentation salient quotes from each of the prophets about the marriage relationship. This arrangement strikes us powerfully—there is no denying the continuous concern our Father in Heaven has for our marriages, as He prompts our prophets again and again throughout every age.

From the Prophet Joseph Smith, we learn of course the doctrine of eternal marriage, as revealed in D&C 132. The promise that a man and woman can be sealed together forever into the eternities is the most fundamental, yet glorious, doctrine of all. It is the doctrine of doctrines.

Joseph Smith has also taught:

> It is the duty of a husband to love, cherish, and nourish his wife, and cleave unto her and none else [see D&C 42:22]; he ought to honor her as himself, and he ought to regard her feelings with tenderness, for she is his flesh, and his bone, designed to be an help unto him, both in temporal, and spiritual things; one into whose bosom he can pour all his complaints without reserve, who is willing (being designed) to take part of his burden, to soothe and encourage his feelings by her gentle voice.[17]

President Brigham Young has testified:

> [Eternal marriage] is without beginning of days or end of years. . . . We can tell some things with regard to it[;] it lays the foundation for worlds, for angels, and for the Gods[;] for intelligent beings to be crowned with glory, immortality, and eternal lives. In fact, it is the thread which runs from the beginning to the end of the holy Gospel of Salvation—of the Gospel of the Son of God; it is from eternity to eternity.[19]

Reflections

After about eleven years of marriage, I was serving on the high council. A member of the Seventy was visiting our stake to interview potential candidates for the new stake presidency, and because of my position I was interviewed. One question that he asked me was if I took my wife to the temple regularly. I told him that both of us attended the temple each month, but because of young children and babysitting, we had developed the practice of mostly attending the temple separately. He counseled me to attend the temple regularly with my wife, a practice that we implemented immediately. We now dedicate one night each month to attending the temple together. While our relationship has always been good, I noticed a sweetness that developed in our relationship that came from following this counsel. Our marriage has been blessed with a greater love for each other as we serve in the temple together. Communication lines remain strong, and the desire to serve and strengthen each other has grown.

President John Taylor counseled:

Husbands, do you love your wives and treat them right, or do you think that you yourselves are some great moguls who have a right to crowd upon them? . . . You ought to treat them with all kindness, with mercy and long suffering, and not be harsh and bitter, or in any way desirous to display your authority. Then, you wives, treat your husbands right, and try to make them happy and comfortable. Endeavor to make your homes a little heaven, and try to cherish the good Spirit of God. . . . If you do, we will have peace in our bosoms, peace in our families, and peace in our surroundings.[20]

President Wilford Woodruff expressed his concern that

the blessing that God has revealed to us in the patriarchal order of marriage—being sealed for time and eternity—is not prized by us as it should be." He also counseled, "We should prize our families, and the associations we have together, remembering that if we are faithful we shall inherit glory, immortality and eternal life, and this is the greatest of all the gifts of God to man [see D&C 14:7].[21]

President Lorenzo Snow taught:

Wives, be faithful to your husbands. I know you have to put up with many unpleasant things, and your husbands have to put up with some things as well. Doubtless you are sometimes tried by your husbands, on account perhaps of the ignorance of your husbands, or perchance at times because of your own ignorance. . . . I do not say but that your husbands are bad—just as bad as you are, and probably some of them are worse; but, never mind: try to endure the unpleasantnesses which arise at times, and when you meet each other in the next life you will feel glad that you put up with those things. To the husbands, I say: Many of you do not value your wives as you should. . . . Be kind to them. When they go out to meeting, you carry the baby at least half the time. When it needs rocking, and you have not much to do, rock it. Be kind when sometimes you have to make a little sacrifice to do so; feel kind anyway, no matter what the sacrifice.[22]

President Joseph F. Smith explained:

The lawful union of man and woman [is] the means through which they may realize their highest and holiest aspirations. To the Latter-day Saints, marriage is not designed by our Heavenly Father to be merely an earthly union, but one that shall survive the vicissitudes of time, and endure for eternity, bestowing honor and joy in this world, glory and eternal lives in the worlds to come.[23]

The man and his wife who have perfect confidence in each other, and who determine to

Reflections

We learn from the prophets and in the temple that the Lord desires us "to build up my church, and to bring forth Zion" (D&C 39:13). During my first pregnancy, my husband was called to serve in a bishopric, the first of many succeeding calls to ward and stake leadership positions during the forty years we shared together before his death. He was away many evenings as the children were growing up, and I sometimes felt overwhelmed. But I knew that my husband and I had made covenants to help build the Lord's kingdom, and my feelings were that He would help us build our little "family kingdom" if we helped Him build His. As I gave my husband to the Lord, He gave me things that I did not naturally possess to help me in my husband's absence to meet the physical and emotional needs of the children. As a result, the blessings I received then as a mother and wife were commensurate with (and probably greater than) our covenant offerings of time spent in the Lord's service—a truth that I treasure and wish I could share with every faithful young mother. Now that our children are grown, it's even easier to see that great truth, as they show by their actions or choices their love of Heavenly Father, His gospel, and His Church. My heart is touched. The harvest is even more generous and abundant from our early plantings than we could have anticipated as the seeds were sown.

follow the laws of God in their lives and fulfil the measure of their mission in the earth, would not be, and could never be, contented without the home. Their hearts, their feelings, their minds, their desires would naturally trend toward the building of a home and family and of a kingdom of their own; to the laying of the foundation of eternal increase and power, glory, exaltation and dominion, worlds without end.[24]

We all have our weaknesses and failings. Sometimes the husband sees a failing in his wife, and he upbraids her with it. Sometimes the wife feels that her husband has not done just the right thing, and she upbraids him. What good does it do? Is not forgiveness better? Is not charity better? Is not love better? Isn't it better not to speak of faults, not to magnify weaknesses by iterating and reiterating them? Isn't that better? and will not the union that has been cemented between you and the birth of children and by the bond of the new and everlasting covenant, be more secure when you forget to mention weaknesses and faults one of another? Is it not better to drop them and say nothing about them—bury them and speak only of the good that you know and feel, one for another, and thus bury each other's faults and not magnify them; isn't that better?[25]

President Heber J. Grant testified:

I believe that no worthy young Latter-day Saint man or woman should spare any reasonable effort to come to a house of the Lord to begin life together. The marriage vows taken in these hallowed places and the sacred covenants entered into for time and all eternity are [protection] against many of the temptations of life that tend to break homes and destroy happiness. . . .

The blessings and promises that come from beginning life together, for time and eternity, in a temple of the Lord, cannot be obtained in any other way and worthy young Latter-day Saint men and women who so begin life together find that their eternal partnership under the everlasting covenant becomes the foundation upon which are built peace, happiness, virtue, love, and all of the other eternal verities of life, here and hereafter.[26]

President George Albert Smith implored:

Let us be examples of righteousness to our children, have our family prayers and ask the blessing upon the food. Let our children see that as husbands and wives we are affectionate with one another. While there is yet time take the opportunity as husbands and wives to bless each other with your love, with your kindness and your helpfulness in every way. Take opportunity while there is yet time to teach your sons and daughters how to live to be happy. . . . Let our homes be sanctuaries of peace and hope and love.[27]

President David O. McKay recommended the following:

I should like to urge *continued courtship*, and apply this to grown people. Too many couples have come to the altar of marriage looking upon the marriage ceremony as the end of courtship instead of the beginning of an eternal courtship. Let us not forget that during the burdens of home life—and they come—that tender words of appreciation, courteous acts are even more appreciated than during those sweet days and months of courtship. It is after the ceremony and during the trials that daily arise in the home that a word of "thank you," or "pardon me," "if you please," on the part of husband or wife contributes to that love which brought you to the altar. It is well to keep in mind that love can be starved to death as literally as the body that receives no sustenance. Love feeds upon kindness and courtesy. It is significant that the first sentence of what is now known throughout the Christian world as the Psalm of Love, is, "Love suffereth long, and is kind." [See 1 Corinthians 13:4.] The wedding ring gives no man the right to be cruel or inconsiderate, and no woman the right to be slovenly, cross, or disagreeable.[28]

President Joseph Fielding Smith preached:

If a man and his wife were earnestly and faithfully observing all the ordinances and principles of the gospel, there could not arise any cause for divorce. The joy and happiness pertaining to the marriage relationship would grow sweeter, and husband and wife would become more and more attached to each other as the days go by. Not

Reflections

President Hinckley taught, "I am satisfied that a happy marriage is not so much a matter of romance as it is an anxious concern for the comfort and well-being of one's companion."[37] I have taken this advice to heart. While I am not perfect, I do seek out ways to show my husband that I am anxiously concerned for his comfort and well-being. As I prepare meals, I take into account his likes and dislikes, and fix foods I think he will enjoy. I try to keep up on his laundry so that he has clean clothes as he is getting ready for work in the morning. I encourage him to pursue his hobbies and interests. But it is more than just attending to details. Truly caring about his comfort and well-being affects how I handle conflict. Instead of focusing on being right, I sincerely try to understand his point of view. I listen respectfully. I avoid using hurtful language. I apologize when I do say something that offends. And I have discovered that as I focus on caring for my husband, he reciprocates with equally caring actions.

only would the husband love the wife and the wife the husband, but children born to them would live in an atmosphere of love and harmony. The love of each for the others would not be impaired, and moreover the love of all towards our Eternal Father and his Son Jesus Christ would be more firmly rooted in their souls.[29]

President Harold B. Lee taught:

If [young people] would resolve from the moment of their marriage, that from that time forth they would resolve and do everything in their power to please each other in things that are right, even to the sacrifice of their own pleasures, their own appetites, their own desires, the problem of adjustment in married life would take care of itself, and their home would indeed be a happy home. Great love is built on great sacrifice, and that home where the principle of sacrifice for the welfare of each other is daily expressed is that home where there abides a great love.[30]

President Spencer W. Kimball counseled:

A marriage may not always be even and incidentless, but it can be one of great peace. A couple may have poverty, illness, disappointment, failures, and even death in the family, but even these will not rob them of their peace. The marriage can be a successful one so long as selfishness does not enter in. Troubles and problems will draw parents together into unbreakable unions if there is total unselfishness there. . . .

Love is like a flower, and, like the body, it needs constant feeding. The mortal body would soon be emaciated and die if there were not frequent feedings. The tender flower would wither and die without food and water. And so love, also, cannot be expected to last forever unless it is continually fed with portions of love, the manifestation of esteem and admiration, the expressions of gratitude, and the consideration of unselfishness.

Total unselfishness is sure to accomplish another factor in successful marriage. If one is forever seeking the interests, comforts, and happiness of the other, the love found in courtship and cemented in marriage will grow into mighty proportions. Many couples permit their marriages to become stale and their love to grow cold like old bread or worn-out jokes or cold gravy. Certainly the foods most vital for love are consideration, kindness, thoughtfulness, concern, expressions of affection, embraces of appreciation, admiration, pride, companionship, confidence, faith, partnership, equality, and interdependence.[31]

Ezra Taft Benson emphasized the importance of serving our spouse:

The secret of a happy marriage is to serve God and each other. The goal of marriage is unity and oneness, as well as self-development. Paradoxically, the more we serve one another, the greater is our spiritual and emotional growth.[32]

President Howard W. Hunter cautioned, "Tenderness and respect—never selfishness—must be the guiding principles in the intimate relationship between husband and wife."[33]

President Gordon B. Hinckley taught, "If you will make your first concern the comfort, the well-being, and the happiness of your companion, sublimating any personal concern to that loftier goal, you will be happy, and your marriage will go on through eternity."[34] He also indicated that "marriage, in its truest sense, is a partnership of equals, with neither exercising dominion over the other, but, rather, with each encouraging and assisting the other in whatever responsibilities and aspirations he or she might have."[35]

He also counseled, "Be loyal in your family relationships. . . . I have long felt that the greatest factor in a happy marriage is an anxious concern for the comfort and well-being of one's companion. In most cases selfishness is the leading factor that causes argument, separation, divorce, and broken hearts."[36]

President Thomas S. Monson gave this counsel to a body of priesthood holders:

> If you choose wisely and if you are committed to the success of your marriage, there is nothing in this life which will bring you greater happiness. . . .
>
> Choose a companion carefully and prayerfully; and when you are married, be fiercely loyal one to another. Priceless advice comes from a small framed plaque I once saw in the home of an uncle and aunt. It read, "Choose your love; love your choice." There is great wisdom in those few words. Commitment in marriage is absolutely essential.
>
> Your wife is your equal. In marriage neither partner is superior nor inferior to the other. You walk side by side as a son and a daughter of God. She is not to be demeaned or insulted but should be respected and loved.[38]

President Russell M. Nelson declared:

> Marriage brings greater possibilities for happiness than does any other human relationship. Yet some married couples fall short of their full potential. They let their romance become rusty, take each other for granted, allow other interests or clouds of neglect to obscure the vision of what their marriage really could be. Marriages would be happier if nurtured more carefully. . . .
>
> When you as husband and wife recognize the divine design in your union—when you feel deeply that God has brought you to each other—your vision will be expanded and your understanding enhanced.[39]

We feel a great sense of peace and security as we seek to follow the words of these prophets. The themes here, as echoed throughout the chapters of this book, focus on expressing loving kindness, being selfless, forgiving, sharing time and purpose, expressing gratitude, and the like.

Conclusion

Prophets have been provided to us from a loving Heavenly Father. They have been called with authority from God to speak His word and guide us in our present circumstances. These prophets and apostles are also seers—watchmen upon the tower, or satellites—to warn us in advance of approaching dangers. Following the words of the modern prophets will save our marriages and allow them to thrive. We must be meek and teachable, always ready to hear and heed their words. Those words, no matter how easy or hard for us to follow, will in the end offer us great blessings, including protection and peace.

President Eyring gave a deeply thoughtful and inspired analogy as a witness to this principle:

> Sometimes we will receive counsel that we cannot understand or that seems not to apply to us, even after careful prayer and thought. Don't discard the counsel, but hold it close. If someone you trusted handed you what appeared to be nothing more than sand with the promise that it contained gold, you might wisely hold it in your hand awhile, shaking it gently. Every time I have done that with counsel from a prophet, after a time the gold flakes have begun to appear, and I have been grateful.[40]

We testify that God has sent prophets to protect marriage, because the gospel plan is a marriage plan. The words of the prophets and apostles will promote thriving within the interpersonal context of our marriages and provide protection from outside (extramarital) worldly influences. As we live and apply the words and warnings of the prophets, the gold flakes will appear and we will realize we are indeed rich beyond measure.

Notes

1. M. Russell Ballard, "Follow the Prophet," *New Era*, September 2001, 4.

2. *Preach My Gospel: A Guide to Missionary Service* (Salt Lake City: The Church of Jesus Christ of Latter-day Saints, 2004), 32–34.

3. Harold B. Lee, in Conference Report, October 1950, 130.

4. M. Russell Ballard, "Be Strong in the Lord, and in the Power of His Might" (devotional address, Brigham Young University, Provo, UT, 3 March 2002), https://speeches.byu.edu/talks/m-russell-ballard_strong-lord-power-might/.

5. Bruce R. McConkie, *Mormon Doctrine*, 2nd ed. (Salt Lake City: Bookcraft, 1966), 832.

6. Boyd K. Packer, "The Twelve Apostles," *Ensign*, November 1996, 8.

7. "The Family: A Proclamation to the World," *Ensign*, November 2010, 129.

8. "The Family," 129.

9. Ballard, "Follow the Prophet," 4; emphasis in original.

10. Packer, "The Twelve Apostles," 8.

11. Boyd K. Packer, "The Shield of Faith," *Ensign*, May 1995, 8–9.

12. Carol F. McConkie, "Live According to the Words of the Prophets," *Ensign*, November 2014, 78.

13. Henry B. Eyring, "Safety in Counsel," *Ensign*, June 2008, 6.

14. Eyring, "Safety in Counsel," 6.

15. Eyring, "Safety in Counsel," 8.

16. Carol F. McConkie, "Live According to the Words," 79.

17. "Elders' Journal, August 1838," 61, The Joseph Smith Papers, http://www.josephsmithpapers.org/paper-summary/elders-journal-august-1838/13.

18. Henry B. Eyring, "Trust in God, Then Go and Do," *Ensign*, November 2010, 72–73.

19. Brigham Young, *Discourses of Brigham Young*, comp. John A. Widtsoe (Salt Lake City: Deseret Book, 1925), 302.

20. John Taylor, *The Gospel Kingdom,* sel. G. Homer Durham (Salt Lake City: Deseret Book, 1943), 284.

21. Wilford W. Woodruff, "Remarks," *Deseret News*, 26 June 1867, 202.

22. Lorenzo Snow, "The Grand Destiny of Man," *Deseret Evening News*, 20 July 1901, 22.

23. Joseph F. Smith, "Official Declaration," *Millennial Star* 69, no. 16 (18 April 1907): 245.

24. Joseph F. Smith, "The Great Teacher," *Juvenile Instructor*, November 1916, 739.

25. Joseph F. Smith, "Sermon on Home Government," *Millennial Star* 74, no. 4 (25 January 1912): 49–50.

26. Heber J. Grant, "Beginning Life Together," *Improvement Era* 39, no. 4 (April 1936): 198–99.

27. George Albert Smith, in Conference Report, October 1941, 101.

28. David O. McKay, in Conference Report, April 1956, 8–9; emphasis in original.

29. Joseph Fielding Smith, in Conference Report, April 1965, 11.

30. Harold B. Lee, *The Teachings of Harold B. Lee*, ed. Clyde J. Williams (Salt Lake City: Bookcraft, 1996), 239–40.

31. Spencer W. Kimball, "Oneness in Marriage," *Ensign,* March 1977, 4, 5.

32. Ezra Taft Benson, "Fundamentals of Enduring Family Relationships," *Ensign*, November 1982, 60.

33. Howard W. Hunter, "Being a Righteous Husband and Father," *Ensign*, November 1994, 51.

34. Gordon B. Hinckley, quoted in "Nurturing a Love That Lasts," *Ensign*, February 2000, 70.

35. Gordon B. Hinckley, "I Believe," *Ensign*, August 1992, 6.

36. Gordon B. Hinckley, "Loyalty," *Ensign*, May 2003, 59.

37. Gordon B. Hinckley, "What God Hath Joined Together," *Ensign*, May 1991, 73.

38. Thomas S. Monson, "Priesthood Power," *Ensign*, May 2011, 67–68.

39. Russell M. Nelson, "Nurturing Marriage," *Ensign*, May 2006, 36, 38.

40. Eyring, "Safety in Counsel," 9.

CHAPTER 11

"We Are a Covenant-Making People"

Gospel Principles and Ordinances in Marriage

The fourth article of faith declares, "We believe that the first principles and ordinances of the Gospel are: first, Faith in the Lord Jesus Christ; second, Repentance; third, Baptism by immersion for the remission of sins; fourth, Laying on of hands for the gift of the Holy Ghost." These first principles and ordinances, along with higher ordinances that are administered in the holy temple, may not be commonly associated with marriage in general discourse. Yet we testify that these are vital in bringing God into our marriage.

As we have discussed throughout the previous chapters, the relationship with our spouse is inseparable from our journey through the plan of salvation, for we cannot reach the highest degree of glory without our spouse. President Brigham Young taught, "No man can be perfect without the woman, so no woman can be perfect without a man."[1] We read in Doctrine and Covenants 131:1–3, "In the celestial glory there are three heavens or degrees; and in order to obtain the highest, a man must enter into this order of the priesthood [meaning the new and everlasting covenant of marriage]; and if he does not, he cannot obtain it."

Thus, our marital relationship requires our sober attention, which we commit by giving it priority status in our lives and devoting our time and energy to its growth and development. This careful attention is necessary to bring the great joy and happiness that comes from a relationship which is eternal in quality.

Connecting marriage to covenant making, particularly to the first principles and ordinances of the gospel and priesthood ordination, as well as the temple ordinances, is critical in more fully understanding the role of our marriage—its fundamental role—in our salvation and exaltation.

Faith in the Lord Jesus Christ

Faith in the Lord Jesus Christ is the founding principle of our personal lives; it must also be the founding principle in our marriage. Elder Neil L. Andersen of the Quorum of the Twelve Apostles described: "Faith in the Lord Jesus Christ is not something ethereal, floating loosely in the air. . . . It is, as the scriptures say, 'substance . . . , the evidence of things not seen.' . . . Your faith is either growing stronger or becoming weaker. Faith is a principle of power, important not only in this life but also in our progression beyond the veil.[2]

When we think about it, marriage in and of itself is an extraordinary act of faith: faith in our spouse, faith in our self as a spouse, faith in an unknown future together, and faith that Christ will somehow help us make it all work. Sometimes marriage is called a leap of faith because it is an exciting jump into the unknown—in sickness and in health, for better or for worse. Yet we do it! Every day thousands joyfully begin their journey of faith together. No one knows what the future will hold, but when a man and a woman make sacred vows, it is an exercise of extraordinary faith.

Why is faith such a necessary part of marital success? How can faith in Jesus Christ help us strengthen and enrich our marital relationship? The Apostle Paul says that "faith is the substance of things hoped for, the evidence of things not seen" (Hebrews 11:1). In Alma 32:21 we read, "Faith is not to have a perfect knowledge of things; therefore if ye have faith ye hope for things which are not seen, which are true." When we live by faith, we exercise a belief in God and His plans for us, without having a full knowledge. We place our hopes in Him and His Son, Jesus Christ, and the future they promise us. We believe and act in accordance with His directions, commandments, and counsel because we believe that He and His plans are sure and unshakable. Our future becomes secure because He is secure and faithful Himself. Thus, faith is the substance that must be present for the successes of this life as well as the next.

Reflections

For me it took a huge leap of faith to commit to a temple marriage. Although I was raised in the Church, all around me I saw temple marriages full of emotional abuse and dysfunction. I had a difficult time trusting that my marriage could be different. Faith played an important part in the beginning of our marriage, too—faith that we would find a job, find an apartment we could afford, learn to live within our means, and finish school without debt. A bit later, faith was necessary to begin a family when our other newlywed friends chose to wait until it was more convenient. Faith was needed to start graduate school with a young family, choose a job that allowed me to stay home with my new baby, and have more children before graduate school was over. Faith was essential to find jobs, to know where to move and when, and to know what career path to follow. Faith was an important part of our relationship as well. It helped me forgive, repent, and know when to be more humble and when to require more of our relationship. It helped me to help my husband when I didn't know what he needed and he didn't either. As our marriage has progressed, my faith has begun to be unshaken in God's hand in our lives. He truly knows what we need and is always there to help us when we ask. He knows what is best for us. Today, after twenty-three years of a wonderful life together, I am so grateful that I took the plunge, so grateful that I took that leap of faith.

Reflections

As a frightened young adult on the brink of the most import-ant decision of my life, if I could have glanced, just for a brief moment, down the path that lay before me, I would have shouted for joy at what awaited us in marriage. Hard decisions we have faced over the years have helped unify us, not divide us, through the gift of faith. Do we stay in this career path? Where do we live? Do we take out a loan for a vehicle after years of making expensive repairs? Do we have another baby? If so, when? Can we handle this many babies? No one else is having this many babies. Is this crazy? How do we help our children and teenagers find their testimonies? Are we doing enough? How do we make time for our marriage in the midst of such a busy life? Answers to all of these ques-tions and many, many more have been resolved together as we walked forward in faith in the Lord Jesus Christ. I am immensely thankful for the path the Lord has led us down together as we have turned to Him in faith.

The Prophet Joseph Smith taught this principle in the *Lectures on Faith*:

> Who cannot see, then, that salvation is the effect of faith? for, as we have pre-viously observed, all the heavenly beings work by this principle; and it is because they are able so to do that they are saved, for nothing but this could save them. And this is the lesson which the God of heaven, by the mouth of all his holy prophets, has been endeavoring to teach to the world. . . . These with a multi-tude of other scriptures . . . plainly set forth the light in which the Saviour, as well as the Former-day Saints, viewed the plan of salvation. That it was a *system of faith*—it begins with faith, and contin-ues by faith; and every blessing which is obtained, in relation to it is the effect of faith, whether it pertains to this life or that which is to come.[3]

Herein, Joseph Smith called the plan of salvation a "system of faith." What is a system? A system is an organization of parts put together in an object designed for a specific purpose. For example, a car motor is an example of a system. It is an object that is made up of several special-ized parts that work together as a whole to propel a car. However, once created, the car motor must have one additional com-ponent for it to work—it must have fuel. Most car motors run on gasoline. This is the *only* thing that it is built to run on. It cannot run on water or any other liquid.

So we say that the motor is a system of gasoline; it cannot run on anything else, or it will sputter and die.

In like manner, the Prophet Joseph Smith said that the gospel or plan of salvation is a system whose fuel is not gasoline, but faith. It cannot run on reason, science, intellectualism, or doubt. It can work only on faith, particularly faith in the Lord Jesus Christ. That is why faith is called the "first principle" of the gospel (see Articles of Faith 1:4). Thus, once we apply faith in our lives, the eternal effects of the Atonement of Jesus Christ and of His gospel begin to manifest themselves to us. Faith propels our personal plan of salvation: It blesses us with spiritual gifts and insights; it changes us and makes us like Christ, full of love and charity; we gain eternal knowledge and light; and we gain spiritual power and influence. No other fuel but faith will make this happen. Sometimes members of the Church try to utilize other fuels, but testimonies built on these replacements sputter and die. It is faith that brings and sustains light and life in us. Thus, "all the heavenly beings work by [faith]; and it is because they are able so to do that they are saved, for nothing but this could save them."[4]

From this analogy, faith's critical role in marriage should be apparent. Spouses must exercise faith in their marriage every day. Faith in the Savior's Atonement and His plan for us provides the fuel that will propel our marriage forward. When marital challenges come, spouses who exercise their faith receive heavenly help. Elder Jeffrey R. Holland declared: "You want capability, safety, and security . . . in married life and eternity? Be a true disciple of Jesus. Be a genuine, committed, word-and-deed Latter-day Saint. Believe that your faith has *everything* to do with your romance, because it does. . . . Jesus Christ, the Light of the World, is the only lamp by which you can successfully see the path of love and happiness for you *and* for your sweetheart."[5]

We have had many challenges in our marriage. Without faith in Jesus Christ and in each other, we could have allowed our marriage to fail when those times wrenched our souls. Yet we have not failed each other; faith in Christ has provided the light to help us see our way through times of darkness.

Repentance

Repentance is the companion to faith as a "first principle" of the gospel. Without applying it, we cannot really begin our journey back to God. When we think of repentance, we think of changing or turning away from sin. The Hebrew root word for repentance is the word *shuv* or *shub* (pronounced *shoob*), which means to turn back or return.[6] Both the implication and application of this Hebrew word is that we are not just to turn away from one particular sin but rather to turn our *whole life* around and begin returning to God, reconciling everything. We are to do a 180-degree turn from following the world to walking toward God.

In marriage, repentance—this turning toward God—must be an ongoing attitude in order for there to be interpersonal harmony. When both spouses are seeking to follow our Heavenly Father and His commandments, the spirit of unity, forgiveness, and love prevails. Sometimes we offend God, and we must repent before we can feel His Spirit again. Other times we offend our spouse, and it is necessary to reconcile with them before we can feel God's Spirit and restore a feeling of love and harmony in our marriage. There is a very close tie between marital harmony and the feelings we receive from the Holy Ghost. If there is a rift or contention in our marriage and no reconciliation or repentance, it is very difficult to feel love for our spouse or feel the Spirit and receive revelation.

Consider the following story of the Prophet Joseph Smith and Emma, as told by David Whitmer:

He [Joseph Smith] was a religious and straightforward man. He had to be; for he was illiterate and he could do nothing of himself. He *had* to trust in God. He could not translate unless he was humble and possessed the right feelings towards everyone. To illustrate, so you can see. One morning when [Joseph] was getting ready to continue the translation, something went wrong about the house and he was put out about it. Something that Emma, his wife, had done. Oliver and I went up stairs, and Joseph came up soon after to continue the translation, but he could not do anything. He could not translate a single syllable. He went down stairs, out into the orchard and made supplication to the Lord; was gone about an hour—came back to the house, asked Emma's forgiveness and then came up stairs where we were and then the translation went on all right. He could do nothing save he was humble and faithful.[7]

In other words, Joseph needed to have an ongoing spirit and attitude of repentance in order to feel close to God and his wife, Emma. David Whitmer's observation continues:

At times when Brother Joseph would attempt to translate . . . , he found he was spiritually blind and could not translate. He told us that his mind dwelt too much on earthly things, and various causes would make him incapable of proceeding with the translation. When in this condition he would go out and pray, and when he became sufficiently humble before God, he could then proceed with the translation. Now we see how very strict the Lord is, and how he requires the heart of man to be just right in his sight before he can receive revelation from him.[8]

There have been times over the years when this has happened to us, when we have found ourselves to be in an adversarial position with one another. Regardless of the reason for the conflict, we lack the Spirit's companionship until we have resolved the issue. And it has been very difficult to muster any positive energy for our daily lives without His guidance. That spiritual blunting has affected our ability to relate with each other, parent our children, fulfill our Church callings, or focus adequately in our professional activities. Yet when we humble ourselves, repent, and choose reconciliation, the light comes back into our hearts and we can move forward with our relationship in a positive manner, as well as with the other things required of us in our daily lives.

Baptism and the Sacrament

Baptism is the first ordinance of the gospel. It is also a saving ordinance. Saving ordinances include promises, or covenants, made between us and God. When we make and keep a covenant, God then extends His promise, which provides saving blessings. Covenants are powerful because they create a way for each of us to exercise our agency. When we do so, it places personal ownership and responsibility on us as we work on following through with our promises. This allows for each of us to personally grow and to show our Father in Heaven that we will obey Him and that He can trust us. So covenants that are made through ordinances are a way that we can bind ourselves to God and build our trust and relationship with Him. The promises we make in the ordinance of baptism are that we will take upon ourselves the name of Christ, keep His commandments, always remember Him, and serve others (see Mosiah 18:8–9). When we do this, our Father promises that He will pour out His Spirit upon us. These promises are renewed each time we partake of the sacrament.

It may seem strange to relate baptism and the sacrament to building and sustaining our marriage relationships, but the covenant we make in the ordinance of baptism, which is renewed weekly through the sacrament, has powerful implications for our marriages. Frankly, it has powerful implications for all of our interpersonal relationships. Partaking of the sacrament is a formal event in which we witness before God, our fellow Saints, and most importantly our spouse that we are seeking to reconcile our hearts with God and promising to follow Him.

Sister Cheryl Esplin, as second counselor in the Primary General Presidency, taught in general conference that "as we partake of the sacrament, we witness to God that we will remember

WALTER RANE, *In Remembrance of Me*. COURTESY OF INTELLECTUAL
RESERVE, INC.

His Son always, not just during the brief sacrament ordinance.
This means that we will constantly look to the Savior's example
and teachings to guide our thoughts, our choices, and our acts."[9]
Following His example builds trust and unity in marriage. If we
are continually remembering Jesus Christ and looking to Him
as our exemplar, particularly regarding our marriage relationship and how we treat our spouse, the behavior between us as
spouses will be supportive and loving and the bonds of intimacy
will increase. When we know our spouse is working at making and
keeping their baptismal promises with God, it helps us to have
more trust in them and more patience with their shortcomings,
and vice versa. Bringing God into our marriage by renewing the
baptismal covenant through the ordinance of the sacrament is a

sure way to remind each of us to support and sustain our spouse. When we keep the promises we make to the Lord during the ordinance of the sacrament, the Lord, in turn, sends to us His Spirit.

DEBRA: *During Richard's Church service as bishop of our congregation, I had the opportunity and privilege of more objectively observing him partake of the sacrament on a weekly basis as he sat up in the front of the chapel facing the congregation. A subtle yet powerful feeling of trust and stability came over me each time I watched Richard partake of the bread and water.*

I knew he did not partake of the sacrament lightly. I was reminded that Richard's first and foremost commitment was to his Father in Heaven by following His Son, Jesus Christ. I knew that all else regarding our life together would follow appropriately, as it should, with that priority recurrently affirmed. I knew that Richard would always try to do the right thing. I knew that he would continue to try to be a good husband and a good father. My confidence in his motives and desires was firmly in place because his personal determination to follow his Savior (made public for me—and for all—to see each week) continually reminded me of who he was at his core. In this stability, minor issues that came up throughout the course of daily living had less pull to become distractions in our relationship.

Beyond the formal witnessing of the sacrament ordinance, the specific covenants we make at baptism, those covenants that we renew weekly with the ordinance of the sacrament, are also critical to our marital relationships. If we humbly examine these covenants relative to building and strengthening our marriage, we realize that our spouse should be the main recipient of the covenants we make. We have committed to bear one another's burdens, mourn together, comfort our neighbor, etc. As mentioned previously, our spouse is our first neighbor for whom we should be doing these things, and we are bound by covenant to do so.

When relationships are close, supportive behaviors often occur naturally as spouses care for each other during the course of daily living. But during times of struggle or in strained relationships, we sometimes neglect this aspect of our baptismal covenant and shift our focus outward. For example, some will diligently serve others outside of the family while neglecting their spouse, who should be their priority, second only to God. It is understandable how this may occur, particularly if a spouse is hurtful, irritating, or neglectful. When a relationship causes us pain, the natural instinct is to pull away. Yet, by resisting the urge to pull away and by committing more deeply to fulfill our baptismal covenants, beginning first by serving and loving our spouse, great power can be brought to the marital relationship.

Honoring our baptismal covenants will reduce contention, help us see eye to eye, and knit our hearts together in unity and love (see Mosiah 18:21). By doing this we become unified and become "the children of God" (Mosiah 18:22), for we are taught, "Behold, thou art *one in me*, a son of God; and thus may all become my sons" (Moses 6:68; emphasis added).

The Gift of the Holy Ghost

Receiving guidance and comfort from the third member of the Godhead is perhaps the most literal manner by which we bring the *Thee* into our lives and marital relationship. To have a member of the Godhead as a companion in our marriage is truly a remarkable gift. Yet this gift may often be underutilized and unappreciated by many of us.

When we are baptized and confirmed members of The Church of Jesus Christ of Latter-day Saints, we are told to "receive" the Holy Ghost. The word *receive* is an action word that is a commandment rather than a passive suggestion. It places the responsibility on each of us to act and do things that will invite the Spirit into our life. Thus, it is incumbent upon us to build a close relationship with the Spirit so that He will always be with us as our companion.

Perhaps one of the most powerful illustrations of this principle comes from a dream that Brigham Young had a few years after Joseph Smith died. In his dream, Brother Brigham visited

ROBERT T. BARRETT, *Moses Parting the Red Sea*. COURTESY OF INTELLECTUAL RESERVE, INC.

with the Prophet Joseph and asked if he had any counsel for him. Brigham explained:

> Joseph stepped toward me, and looking very earnestly, yet pleasantly said, "Tell the people to be humble and faithful, and be sure to keep the spirit of the Lord and it will lead them right. Be careful and not turn away the small still voice; it will teach you what to do and where to go; it will yield the fruits of the kingdom. Tell the brethren to keep their hearts open to conviction, so that when the Holy Ghost comes to them, their hearts will be ready to receive it. They can tell the Spirit of the Lord from all other spirits; it will whisper peace and joy to their souls; it will take malice, hatred, strife and all evil from their hearts; and their whole desire will be to do good, bring forth righteousness and build up the kingdom of God. Tell the brethren if they will follow the spirit of the Lord

they will go right. Be sure to tell the people to keep the Spirit of the Lord; and if they will, they will find themselves just as they were organized by our Father in Heaven before they came into the world. Our Father in Heaven organized the human family. . . ."

Joseph then showed me the pattern, how they were in the beginning. This I cannot describe, but I saw it, and saw where the Priesthood had been taken from the earth and how it must be joined together, so that there would be a perfect chain from Father Adam to his latest posterity. Joseph again said, "Tell the people to be sure to keep the Spirit of the Lord and follow it, and it will lead them just right."[10]

Having the companionship of the Holy Ghost is critical in marriage. He provides guidance by supplying inspiration and revelation that sustains and protects the marriage. He is a partner who helps us make both general decisions about our life together and decisions about how we treat each other interpersonally. Over the years we have sought to be humble and sensitive to invite the Holy Ghost into our marriage. There have been important decisions we have needed to make in which we knew it was vital that we got the Spirit's input for fear of creating unforeseen negative circumstances years later via a wrong decision. In times such as these, we have done a lot of pondering and discussing together.

One of the keys we use in understanding how the Holy Ghost talks to us is found in section 2 of the Doctrine and Covenants, where the Lord says to Oliver Cowdery: "Yea, behold, I will tell you in your mind *and* in your heart, by the Holy Ghost, which shall come upon you and which shall dwell in your heart. Now, behold, this is the spirit of revelation; behold, this is the spirit by which Moses brought the children of Israel through the Red Sea on dry ground" (D&C 8:2–3; emphasis added). The idea that the Lord will tell us in our minds *and* in our hearts follows the law of two witnesses. When we get both our mind and heart together on a decision, it provides a double witness that the decision is correct. This is what the Lord calls the spirit of revelation, and as the example given by the verse indicates, this is the way He directed Moses in performing a miracle to save the children of Israel.

As we ponder and pray together about decisions in our marriage, we seek to get our minds and hearts together in unity as well. We ponder and pray about each of the options and seek to feel the rightness both in our minds and our hearts. Once this takes place, we gain confidence in moving forward. This process has blessed us in numerous circumstances in which we had to know the Lord's will and were ready to follow the Holy Ghost.

In addition to general decision-making guidance, the Holy Spirit blesses us with the ability to make good decisions about how we treat each other within the context of the marital relationship. Do we treat our spouse with patience, kindness, respect, and love? These attributes are only borne from the Spirit, and we must be worthy of His assistance. For example, if we are close to the Spirit, the split-second decision to be patient with our spouse could allow a moment of irritation to pass in peace and calm, quickly dissolving into the next moment; contrast this decision to impatiently accusing our spouse, damaging the relationship, and extending the moment of irritation exponentially with now-increased levels of anger and hurt.

RICHARD: *I remember a specific moment when I was irritated with Debra about something minor during an interaction one day. I had the strong impression at that very moment that if I followed the natural man and blurted out my frustration, it would lead to conflict. Instead, I let things pass. Even though Debra had been unaware of my irritation, a few minutes later, in simply an effort to reach out and be kind, she independently came and kissed me and expressed her love for me. It was a great lesson to me about the power and benefit of following the Spirit.*

If we are concerned about our relationship with our spouse and we are frustrated and uncertain about how to lessen or positively influence (what may be chronic) interpersonal strain, the Spirit can soften hearts and give us specific instruction relative to what we can say or do to repair damage and move forward.

Taking Counsel from the Holy Ghost Line upon Line

The scriptures provide us with an illustration of detailed revelation given in a line-upon-line manner. Through revelation,
the Lord gave Nephi a commandment to build a ship. However,
Nephi was not to build the ship his way; he was to build it the
Lord's way: "Thou shalt construct a ship, after the manner which
I shall show thee" (1 Nephi 17:8). Nephi did not know where to
begin and petitioned the Lord for help: "Lord, whither shall I go
that I may find ore to molten, that I may make tools to construct
the ship *after the manner which thou hast shown unto me*?" (1 Nephi 17:9;
emphasis added). The Lord then told Nephi where to go to find
the ore (see 1 Nephi 17:10). Nephi took time to make bellows in
order to make fire (see 1 Nephi 17:11), and he made tools (see
1 Nephi 17:16).

Each of the steps Nephi took required a great deal of energy
and time—yet note that he had not yet begun to build the ship.
As we receive instruction from the Spirit regarding how to
strengthen or heal our marital relationships, we must be patient
to follow the instructions of the Lord through the Holy Ghost—
even if some of the instructions may seem insignificant relative
to the larger building project; those beginning steps will prepare
us for more significant adjustments later.

Continuing with Nephi's experience, we learn that after he
took the time to make preparations, he did follow the Lord in
building the ship: "Now I, Nephi, did not work the timbers after
the manner which was learned by men, neither did I build the
ship after the manner of men; but I did build it after the manner
which the Lord had shown unto me" (1 Nephi 18:2).

If we will build our marriages after the manner which the Lord
has shown us rather than try to hastily construct them according
to our own style or desires, we will have the Holy Ghost as our
partner. The Bible teaches us similarly when it counsels, "Except

the Lord build the house, they labour in vain that build it" (Psalm 127:1).

So how can we allow the Spirit to guide us along the way so that our marriage can be built after the manner of the Lord? Let's use one common interpersonal example. Perhaps we have a tendency to get angry quickly, and our abrasive tone and high-volume level send our spouse into hiding. The Spirit may initially speak to our hearts about the importance of reducing our volume through a prompting such as "a soft answer turneth away wrath" (Proverbs 15:1). We may decide to work on reducing our volume even though we know that that one change will not miraculously cure every problem in our relationship.

Perhaps at a later occasion, during scripture study of the Book of Mormon, we may feel the spirit of caution as we read about Zeniff's experiences in being overzealous: "And yet, I being over-zealous to inherit the land of our fathers, collected as many as were desirous to go up to possess the land . . . ; but we were smitten with famine and sore afflictions; for we were slow to remember the Lord our God" (Mosiah 9:3). We may then realize as we ponder the scripture that it is has been not only our volume but also our strong and determined will that comes across as overzealous and intense which makes our spouse cower and withdraw from us during a disagreement. Even though we may have worked successfully to reduce our volume, we see that this additional intensity has continued to hinder our ability to peacefully work through conflict with our spouse, even though we had been previously unaware of it.

We may then begin to think about reducing our intensity from what had been a ten on a scale of one to ten (ten being the strongest) down to about a five or six. We may practice asking our spouse more frequently for their thoughts and opinions, hearing from them how they would solve a problem or what they would like to do in a particular situation.

As we continue to keep our volume low while practicing the skill of reducing our intensity, over time we may begin to see our spouse less anxious and more willing to voice their opinion and have a discussion with us when a difference of opinion arises. We may notice that this newfound ability to peacefully discuss a point of disagreement somehow allows more free-flowing positive energy to be present throughout other interactions as well. Over time, we may realize that the relationship we now have with our spouse is entirely new, having been miraculously changed for the better.

In this scenario, this marital miracle was allowed to occur because we were willing to take step-by-step counsel from the Lord through his Holy Spirit. We are then able to see, as did Nephi, "that after I had finished the ship, according to the word of the Lord, my brethren beheld that it was good, and that the workmanship thereof was exceedingly fine" (I Nephi 18:4).

The Oath and Covenant of the Priesthood

In addition to the first principles and ordinances of the gospel, the ordination to the priesthood is another gift the Lord has provided to bless our marriages. To understand the power and blessings that come to a marriage through this ordination, let's first look at the doctrine of the priesthood.

The Lord has established that all worthy male members of the Church, based on age and circumstance, may have either the Aaronic or Melchizedek Priesthood conferred upon them and be ordained to a respective office of that priesthood. The priesthood is defined as "the power of God delegated to man by which man can act in the earth for the salvation of the human family."[II] Although "the Lord has directed that only men will be ordained to offices in the priesthood," President Dallin H. Oaks explained that "men are not 'the priesthood.' Men hold the priesthood, with a sacred duty to use it for the blessing of all of the children of God."[12]

Each office in the priesthood has inherent rights, responsibilities, and obligations of service that are given to a boy or man when he is ordained. However, priesthood keys held by designated priesthood leaders direct the exercise of those rights and responsibilities. President Oaks further explained, "Every act or ordinance performed in the Church is done under the direct or indirect authorization of one holding the keys for that function."[13] Priesthood keys, then, direct priesthood authority. And priesthood authority is and has always been about service and salvation. The Lord has cautioned that ordination to the priesthood does not give any boy or man self-righteous power or authority to control or demean others (D&C 121:34–46).

The doctrine of the priesthood also teaches that priesthood authority, power, and blessings are accessible to women, as well as men. For example, when either a man or woman is set apart for a calling under the direction of a priesthood leader who holds keys, they receive priesthood authority to perform their duties of service in that calling. In addition, as each woman or man acts in faith and worthily seeks the Holy Ghost, she or he has the right to receive priesthood power to lead, teach, and strengthen those of whom she or he is called to serve. Finally, the blessings of the priesthood come to both women and men through faithful and righteous living.

How does all of this apply to marriage? First, although only men are ordained to priesthood offices in the Church, within a marriage *priesthood power* and *blessings* are shared between a husband and wife. The oath and covenant of the priesthood as found in Doctrine and Covenants 84:33–42 explains that only through "obtaining" and "receiv[ing]" the priesthood and "magnifying their calling" are men promised "all that the Father hath." Of course, the only way a man can receive this promise of eternal inheritance is by way of sharing it with his wife through a temple sealing in the house of the Lord. No husband can be exalted without his wife and no wife without her husband. So eternal marriage, then, is the catalyst that unlocks the promises found in the oath and covenant of the priesthood. President M. Russell Ballard taught, "Men and women have different but equally valued roles. Just as a woman cannot conceive a child without a man, so a man cannot fully exercise the power of the priesthood to establish an eternal family without a woman. In other words, in the eternal perspective, both the procreative power and the priesthood power are shared by husband and wife."[14]

Second, priesthood must be understood from the perspective that although a husband and wife have different roles, they are still equal in the sight of God. Sometimes there is misunderstanding about a husband's priesthood authority and how it works in a marriage. A husband who misunderstands the doctrine of the priesthood might think that his ordination to the priesthood gives him some type of self-privilege to "pull priesthood rank" on his wife. Nothing can be further from the truth. President Gordon B. Hinckley boldly proclaimed:

> The wife you choose will be your equal. . . . In the marriage companionship there is neither inferiority nor superiority. The woman does not walk ahead of the man; neither does the man walk ahead of the woman. They walk side by side as a son and daughter of God on an eternal journey. She is not your servant, your chattel, nor anything of the kind. . . . Any man in this Church . . . who exercises unrighteous dominion over [his wife] is unworthy to hold the priesthood.[15]

As equals, wives and husbands work together in priesthood power for the welfare of their family. We read in "The Family: A Proclamation to the Word": "By divine design, fathers are to preside over their families in love and righteousness and are responsible to provide the necessities of life and protection for their families. Mothers are primarily responsible for the nurture of their children. In these sacred responsibilities, fathers and mothers are obligated to help one another as *equal partners*."[16] What does it mean for a man to preside in love and righteousness and for a father and mother to be equal partners? President M. Russell Ballard stated, "Our Church doctrine places women equal to and yet different from men. God does not regard either gender as better or more important than the other. . . . When men and women go to the temple, they are both endowed with the same power, which is priesthood power."[17] The wise and faithful husband who understands the doctrine of the priesthood correctly knows that to preside in the home as an equal partner with his wife, he will always love and respect his wife's thoughts, revelation, opinions, and feelings. He would not move ahead on any decision without working together in unity with his wife, always in love and respect. When a husband presides, he is a humble servant, looking out for the welfare, respect, and tender feelings of his beloved eternal companion and children.

The Temple and Higher Ordinances

The word *temple* comes from the Latin root word *templum*, which represents a crossing point where two lines, one vertical and the other horizontal, meet or intersect. Spiritually speaking, it's the crossing point where heaven and earth meet and where we can go to get our spiritual bearings.[18] It is the perfect place to bring the *Thee* into our marriage. President Gordon B. Hinckley observed:

> Everything that occurs in that temple is of an uplifting and ennobling kind, and it speaks of life here and life beyond the grave. It speaks of the importance of the individual as a child of God. It speaks of the importance of the family as a creation of the Almighty. It speaks of the eternity of the marriage relationship. It speaks of going on to greater glory. It is a place of light, a place of peace, a place of love where we deal with the things of eternity.[19]

Researchers studying LDS marriages examined religious practices that increased couples' marital commitment. In qual-

itative interviews, the religious practice most often spoken about in relation to commitment was temple attendance. Interviewees referred to both their own temple sealings as well as to returning to the temple as a couple.[20] Richard and Bruce Chadwick found that being temple worthy had a significant relationship with marital happiness among active LDS couples.[21]

Latter-day temple builders have decorated the temples with symbols to help us remember the important role of the temple in receiving revelation from God. For example, the Salt Lake Temple has numerous sun, moon, star, and earth motifs etched throughout its exterior. All of these have been placed by the designers and builders to remind us that God is the Creator

Reflections

My wife and I seek to go to the temple often. Before we visit the temple each time, we pray that we will be taught and will feel the Spirit. The temple reminds us of our relationship to each other. We sit side by side, wearing white, as equals. I am not in front of her; she is not in front of me. We walk through the wilderness of life side by side, counseling together and making decisions together. Attending the temple also helps us connect with each other. We have had many sacred conversations in the celestial room, comparing notes on what we learned that day. I continue to learn so much from her. Our temple experiences together also help us keep things in our relationship in proper perspective; they remind us of the big picture, which helps us move past petty grievances.

Reflections

My husband and I served several years in the temple as ordinance workers and also served in a temple presidency. This service gave us a daily perspective of eternity and God's exquisite plan for us. Each day we were surrounded with sacred things. I would carefully walk through each room in the early morning hours, before anyone else was in the temple, and note the altars and the cloths covering them to make certain that they were straight. While there I would reflect on the covenants and promises made during the sealing ceremony. My husband and I would spend time sitting in the celestial room alone, sharing our thoughts, desires, and feelings. We were a team in our temple service. We came together to clean the temple. We read and studied together. We traveled together to outlying areas to speak. Whenever we spoke, we always shared our love for each other and for the temple. Each time I attend the temple with my sweetheart, I am overwhelmed with the love that I have for him. I look at him, dressed in white, across the room and feel reinforced in my desire to spend all eternity with him.

and Holder of both the heavens and the earth and that He directs His children on their mortal journey.

In addition, with careful eyes we can notice another cosmic pattern etched in the stone on the west wall of the Salt Lake Temple. It is Ursa Major, or the Big Dipper. Why would the designers and builders of the Salt Lake Temple place this constellation on the side of a sacred building? When travelers in the northern hemisphere look for direction at night, they will first find the Big Dipper to guide them to the North Star, or Polaris. It is there that they get their bearings in order to travel in the right direction and avoid getting lost. So it is with the temple; the temple is our North Star, the place where we get our spiritual bearings. It is the place where God comes down to meet us and give us direction and ordinances to help us progress. The higher ordinance of sealing couples together and binding them for eternity is the crowning ordinance in the temple and represents this divine meeting between husband, wife, and Deity.[22]

This type of marriage, an eternal marriage, begins at the altar, an altar that represents the Savior's place of sacrifice. As we are sealed, we are reminded that we are covenanting over the altar of Christ, and we thus symbolically invite Him into the covenant, while He promises that

He will be the cornerstone of our marital relationship. When we as couples truly understand this, it should make a significant difference in our daily lives relative to how we treat each other, as well as how we treat our marriage on the whole.

Learning from Temple Ordinances

As we make sacred covenants within the temple, our Father in Heaven teaches us directly and symbolically. The various temple ordinances are rich with instructions and symbolism, symbolism that ultimately leads our hearts to our Savior Jesus Christ. These ordinances include the washings and anointings (or initiatory ordinances), the endowment, and the sealing. Elder Boyd K. Packer taught that washings and anointings are "mostly symbolic in nature, but [promise] definite, immediate blessings as well as future blessings."[23] The endowment provides a series of instructions "relative to the purpose and plans of the Lord in creating and peopling the earth" as well as "what must be done . . . to gain exaltation."[24] We make covenants "to live righteously and comply with the requirements of the gospel."[25] The sealing ordinance, uniting man and woman as husband and wife for eternity, represents the crowning jewel of the temple ordinances.

Reflections

My wife and I have always had a goal to attend the temple at least monthly. This has not always been easy, and there were many times that it simply didn't work, especially during the years we had many young children or when I was in graduate school and working multiple jobs. However, when we first moved to Provo, Utah, our life was significantly different. Instead of eight children at home with us, we were down to just three. And my wife and I both had lighter Church callings. Since we lived so close to the Provo Temple, we decided we would attend weekly instead of monthly. It was during that time that I noticed a significant change in our marriage. Attending weekly seemed to make a significant difference in the way that we treated each other. We both seemed to have more patience with each other and our children; we seemed to be more humble and meek; we were not easily provoked; we had more control over our emotions; and we didn't get irritated as easily. We were able to demonstrate more kindness, love, and understanding in our marriage.

Within each of these ordinances, those with ears to hear and eyes to see will also learn about ways to strengthen their marriage. We read in the Doctrine and Covenants:

> And again, verily I say unto you, if a man marry a wife by my word, which is my law, and by the new and everlasting covenant, and it is sealed unto them by the Holy Spirit of promise, by him who is anointed, unto whom I have appointed this power and the keys of this priesthood; and it shall be said unto them—Ye shall come forth in the first resurrection; and if it be after the first resurrection, in the next resurrection; and shall inherit thrones, kingdoms, principalities, and powers, dominions, all heights and depths—then shall it be written in the Lamb's Book of Life . . . and shall be of full force when they are out of the world; and they shall pass by the angels, and the gods, which are set there, to their exaltation and glory in all things, as hath been sealed upon their heads, which glory shall be a fulness and a continuation of the seeds forever and ever. (D&C 132:19)

Referring to this scripture, Elder Robert D. Hales of the Quorum of the Twelve Apostles explained: "As taught in this scripture, an eternal bond doesn't just happen as a result of sealing covenants we make in the temple. How we conduct ourselves in this life will determine what we will be in all the eternities to come. To receive the blessings of the sealing that our Heavenly Father has given to us, we have to keep the commandments and *conduct ourselves in such a way that our families will want to live with us in the eternities.*"[26] Elder Hales gives

Reflections

Regular visits to the temple have been a stable influence in our lives and have blessed us as a couple. My wife and I have a strong testimony of the temple because we make it a priority to attend and we have seen how the temple has blessed our family. I have particularly noticed that the longer we are married, the nicer it is to attend the temple together. As we come out of the temple the world just seems clearer and brighter. As we take family names to the temple we have greater joy in our experiences together. Sealings of family members together in the sealing rooms have been especially sweet experiences. Last month we took several family names to be sealed together. As I knelt across the altar from my wife I noticed the mirrors that helped me see into the eternities. My love for my wife increased beyond description.

Reflections

My husband and I were married two weeks ago. As our sealer brought us to stand in front of the mirrors in the sealing room, our images reflected in the mirrors as eternal beings. We have eternal beginnings, and now after being sealed we will continue eternally together. He told us that the first mirror represented our ancestors. I thought of parents, grandparents, and others who were with me and had shaped me into the woman I am today. I felt strongly that my great-grandma and others who had gone before us were also there, proudly watching us make those sacred covenants. The sealer then brought us to the opposite side of the room and we stood in front of the mirror that represents our posterity. I was filled with joy as I thought of those who would shape my life in the future. Those precious spirits who would help me fulfill my role as a mother and who would now be born into the covenant. I looked around and joyfully realized that we are all connected and sealed as part of God's family. We are His children. Knowing that gives me strength in my identity but also courage that when I do become a mother, God will help me care for my children because they are His children first.

us here a simple yet profound idea to ponder: We may love our spouse with a deep commitment and conviction relative to our testimonies of family and our efforts to honor the temple sealing, but do we also *like* our spouse? Does our spouse *like* us? (See chapter 5, particularly the section "Build or Enhance Friendship, Fondness, and Admiration.") When our mortal probation has come to an end, will we *want* to be together forever? The temple can assist us in receiving the personal answers to those questions.

Elder Royden G. Derrick, then a member of the First Quorum of the Seventy and the president of the Salt Lake Temple, wrote the following:

> In the temple, through the power of the Holy Spirit, knowledge is transformed into virtues. A person who attends the temple more regularly grows more patient, more long-suffering, and more charitable. He becomes more diligent, more committed, and more dedicated. He develops a greater capacity to love his wife and children and to respect the good qualities and the rights of others. He develops a greater sense of values, becoming more honorable and upright in his dealings and less critical of others.[27]

The power the temple can have to transform our marriage, even when there is significant conflict, is represented in the following story by President Thomas S. Monson:

Many years ago in the ward over which I presided as the bishop, there lived a couple who often had very serious, heated disagreements. I mean real disagreements. . . .

One morning at 2:00 a.m. I had a telephone call from the couple. They wanted to talk to me, and they wanted to talk right then. I dragged myself from bed, dressed, and went to their home. They sat on opposite sides of the room, not speaking to each other. The wife communicated with her husband by talking to me. He replied to her by talking to me. I thought, "How in the world are we going to get this couple together?"

I prayed for inspiration, and the thought came to me to ask them a question. I said, "How long has it been since you have been to the temple and witnessed a temple sealing?" They admitted it had been a very long time. . . .

I said to them, "Will you come with me to the temple on Wednesday morning at 8:00? We will witness a sealing ceremony there."

In unison they asked, "Whose ceremony?"

I responded, "I don't know. It will be for whoever is getting married that morning."

On the following Wednesday at the appointed hour, we met at the Salt Lake Temple. The three of us went into one of the beautiful sealing rooms, not knowing a soul in the room except Elder ElRay L. Christiansen. . . . Elder Christiansen was scheduled to perform a sealing ceremony for a bride and groom in that very room that morning. . . . My couple were seated on a little bench with about a full two feet (0.6 m) of space between them.

Elder Christiansen began by providing counsel to the couple who were being married, and he did so in a beautiful fashion. He mentioned how a husband should love his wife, how he should treat her with respect and courtesy, honoring her as the heart of the home. Then he talked to the bride about how she should honor her husband as the head of the home and be of support to him in every way.

I noticed that as Elder Christiansen spoke to the bride and the groom, my couple moved a little closer together. Soon they were seated right next to one another. What pleased me is that they had both moved at about the same rate. By the end of the ceremony,

SEALING ROOM IN THE OQUIRRH MOUNTAIN UTAH TEMPLE. CHRISTINA SMITH, © INTELLECTUAL RESERVE, INC.

my couple were sitting as close to each other as though *they* were the newlyweds. Each was smiling.

We left the temple that day, and no one ever knew who we were or why we had come, but my friends were holding hands as they walked out the front door. Their differences had been set aside. I had not had to say one word. You see, they remembered their own wedding day and the covenants they had made in the house of God. They were committed to beginning again and trying harder this time around.[28]

We feel we have been particularly blessed with a spirit of love and unity as we have attended temple sealing sessions together, whether they be for the sealing ordinance for those couples among our family and friends or for the vicarious work we perform for those who have passed on. It is there that we are reminded of the covenants we made when we first knelt across the altar to be married. We also remember the instructions we were given during our sealing ceremony by our temple sealer. It sparks a feeling of closeness, it sparks a feeling of unity, and it sparks loving feelings as we ponder upon our journey together. Regardless of our trials and stresses, in that moment we are where the Lord would have us be, and we are there together, and that recognition brings a feeling of stability and strength to our relationship.

Temple Mirrors and the Crown of Eternal Life

After a man and woman receive the sealing ordinance over the altar of God, they are often invited to look at themselves together as husband and wife for the first time by looking into one of two large mirrors hanging on opposite walls of the sealing room. Those of us who have already received the sealing ordinance can also take the opportunity to do this when we do proxy sealings for those who have passed on before us.

On these occasions, when we stand facing one of the mirrors, side by side, an interesting phenomenon occurs. We can see our own reflection, as we do in any ordinary mirror hanging on the wall in our own home—we see one level, one plane, one image. But when we glance to look at the reflection of our dear spouse, we become quickly aware that our view in the mirrors has changed. We not only see the first reflection of our spouse, as we did our own, but we also see level beyond level, plane beyond plane, image beyond image of our spouse—continuing on forever.

Such a phenomenon suggests at least a couple of thoughts. First, if we think about our marriage from an interpersonal perspective, if we focus only on ourselves and are concerned only about taking care of ourself, our needs, and our desires, then our development in the eternities will stop abruptly; we will not be able to progress. Yet if we focus with charity and serviceable intention on our spouse—as would our Savior, Jesus Christ—on what they need, on what they desire, making sure they are happy and comfortable, then our development as husband and wife will continue for the eternities. The way to grasp this type of eternal relationship is quite simply by consistently focusing on the other.

DEBRA: *Doctrinally, it may be difficult with our mortal minds in our finite state to comprehend the immensity of the eternal promises of the sealing ordinance. In one of our visits to perform vicarious sealing ordinances in the temple, I took particular time to look into the mirrors while other couples knelt across the altar to participate as proxies in the sealing session. I became overwhelmed with the enormity of it all. For all of my intent staring and straining to look as far as I could into the mirrors as the images got smaller and smaller, I could not see the end of those reflections. As I peered into those eternities while listening to the sacred ordinances being performed, I received the strong impression that the doctrine of the sealing, and all that is accomplished through performing the sealing ordinance, goes* way *beyond what I could even begin to understand.*

In a BYU documentary on the mission of Jesus Christ, Marcus H. Martins, professor of Religious Education at BYU–Hawaii, reminds us of the expansive nature of this gospel plan:

> In the Pearl of Great Price . . . we learn, that not only Jesus Christ was God even before this life, but that He being the creator of

worlds without number, was not a beginner. That this earth where we live and these experiences that we have here are really nothing new in the eternities and that The Lord is not experimenting with us and hoping that something good comes out of this plan of Salvation. No, he has done this countless times.[29]

When we reach the limits of our mortal understanding, the temple helps extend our understanding beyond those limits and carries our vision into the eternities. The temple brings heaven to earth, it brings God into our marriage, and it brings us into God's presence. Its ordinances teach us of the plan of salvation and show us the way back to Him.

Learning in the temple is most critical in our relationship with our spouse, for it reminds us that exaltation is a couple's affair. As we make temple covenants and faithfully endure to the end, we "shall have a crown of eternal life" (D&C 66:12), which is "the greatest of all the gifts of God" (D&C 14:7). The temple reminds us that eternal life represents God's life—to live forever as spouses and families in God's presence.

At the beginning of this book, we talked about how marriage is a journey in which two imperfect people strive together toward perfection. The temple sealing promises perfection if we remain true and faithful to God, His priesthood, and each other. We then will be crowned as kings and queens, priests and priestesses in the kingdom of our Father. President Joseph Fielding Smith wrote: "The main purpose for our mortal existence is that we might obtain tabernacles of flesh and bones for our spirits that we might advance after the resurrection to the fullness of the blessings which the Lord has promised to those who are faithful. They have been promised that they shall become sons and daughters of God, joint heirs with Jesus Christ, and if they have been true to the commandments and covenants the Lord has given us, to be kings and priests and queens and priestesses, possessing the fullness of the blessings of the celestial kingdom."[30] As kings and priests, queens and priestesses in His kingdom, we receive from our Father His life, eternal life, to rule and reign side by side as spouses throughout the eternities. It is the holy temple and the priesthood ordinances found therein that establish and solemnize these blessings in marriage.

> And they shall pass by the angels, and the gods, which are set there, to their exaltation and glory in all things, as hath been sealed upon their heads, which glory shall be a fulness and a continuation of the seeds forever and ever.
>
> Then shall they be gods, because they have no end; therefore shall they be from everlasting to everlasting, because they continue; then shall they be above all, because all things are subject unto them. Then shall they be gods, because they have all power, and the angels are subject unto them. . . .
>
> This is eternal lives—to know the only wise and true God, and Jesus Christ, whom he hath sent. I am he. Receive ye, therefore, my law. (D&C 132:19–20, 24).

And this glorious sharing of heavenly power, promised to us as we remain true and faithful to our spouse and the covenants of our Father, is most lovingly and generously "the greatest of all the gifts of God" (D&C 14:7).

Conclusion

Marriage is significantly connected to the first principles and ordinances of the gospel even though it is not generally thought of in this way. Yet when we take time to reflect on this connection, there is a rich well of understanding to help our marriages thrive. Further, pondering upon the temple and its higher ordinances can also make our marriage better. Our Father has built His gospel and has provided principles and ordinances in order to bind couples and families to Him. Exercising our faith, repenting, and making covenants at baptism and in holy temples bring the Holy Ghost into the marital relationship, guiding spouses from above on their journey together here on earth.

THE SALT LAKE TEMPLE, COURTESY OF ELLE STALLINGS/PIXABAY.

Notes

1. Brigham Young, "Speech Delivered by President B. Young, in the City of Joseph, April 6, 1845," *Millennial Star* 6, no. 8 (1 October 1845): 121.

2. Neil L. Andersen, "Faith Is Not by Chance, but by Choice," *Ensign*, November 2015, 65.

3. Joseph Smith Jr., *Lectures on Faith* (Salt Lake City: Deseret Book, 1985), 79–80; emphasis added.

4. Smith, *Lectures on Faith*.

5. Jeffrey R. Holland, "How Do I Love Thee?" (devotional address, Brigham Young University, Provo, UT, 15 February 2000), https://speeches.byu.edu/talks/jeffrey-r-holland_how-do-i-love-thee/; emphasis in original.

6. *Strong's Hebrew Concordance*, s.v. "שׁוּב (shub)," http://biblehub.com/hebrew/strongs_7725.htm.

7. David Whitmer, quoted in "Letter from Elder W. H. Kelley," *Saints' Herald*, 1 March 1882, 68.

8. David Whitmer, *An Address to All Believers in Christ: By a Witness to the Divine Authenticity of the Book of Mormon* (Richmond, MO: David Whitmer, 1887), 30.

9. Cheryl A. Esplin, "The Sacrament—A Renewal for the Soul," *Ensign*, November 2014, 12.

10. Brigham Young, *Manuscript History of Brigham Young, 1846–1847*, comp. Elden J. Watson (Salt Lake City: Smith Secretarial Service, 1971), 529–30.

11. Joseph F. Smith, *Gospel Doctrine*, 5th ed. (Salt Lake City: Deseret Book, 1939), 139.

12. Dallin H. Oaks, "The Keys and Authority of the Priesthood," *Ensign*, May 2014, 51.

13. Oaks, "Keys and Authority," 49.

14. M. Russell Ballard, "'This Is My Work and Glory,'" *Ensign*, May 2013, 19.

15. Gordon B. Hinckley, "Personal Worthiness to Exercise the Priesthood," *Ensign*, May 2002, 54.

16. "The Family: A Proclamation to the World," *Ensign*, November 2010, 129; emphasis added.

17. M. Russell Ballard, "Men and Women in the Work of the Lord," *New Era*, April 2014, 4.

18. Hugh Nibley, *Temple and Cosmos*, vol. 12 of the Collected Works of Hugh Nibley (Salt Lake City: Deseret Book, 1992).

19. Gordon B. Hinckley, "Excerpts from Recent Addresses of President Gordon B. Hinckley," *Ensign*, September 1997, 72–73.

20. Michael Goodman, David Dollahite, and Loren Marks, "Exploring Transformational Processes and Meaning in LDS Marriages," *Marriage and Family Review* 48, no. 6 (2012): 555–82.

21. Richard J. McClendon and Bruce A. Chadwick, "Latter-day Saint Families at the Dawn of the Twenty-First Century," in *Helping and Healing Families: Principles and Practices Inspired by "The Family: A Proclamation to the World,"* ed. Craig H. Hart et al. (Salt Lake City: Deseret Book, 2005), 32–43.

22. See Gordon B. Hinckley, "New Temples to Provide 'Crowning Blessings' of the Gospel," *Ensign*, May 1998, 88.

23. Boyd K. Packer, *The Holy Temple* (Salt Lake City: Bookcraft, 1980), 154.

24. Packer, *Holy Temple*, 154.

25. *True to the Faith: A Gospel Reference* (Salt Lake City: The Church of Jesus Christ of Latter-day Saints, 2004), 171.

26. Robert D. Hales, "The Eternal Family," *Ensign*, November 1996, 65; emphasis added.

27. Royden G. Derrick, *Temples in the Last Days* (Salt Lake City: Bookcraft, 1988), 53.

28. Thomas S. Monson, "Priesthood Power," *Ensign*, May 2011, 68–69.

29. Marcus H. Martins, quoted in "Messiah Script: Episode 1, Part 2," 19 April 2011, http://messiahjesuschrist.org/messiah-the-narrative/messiah-script-2/messiah-script-episode-1-part-2.

30. Joseph Fielding Smith, *Answers to Gospel Questions* (Salt Lake City: Deseret Book, 1963), 61.

In Sickness and in Health

Mental Health Issues and Access to Treatment

What Is Mental Illness?

*M*ental illness is complex. It is not always easy to understand how it develops, and it is not always easy to define.
We will briefly address these two complexities and then discuss
defining mental illness, or *psychological disorders*.

Understanding the development of mental illness (including addiction) involves examining many intersecting factors
coming from a variety of sources, including genetics, childhood
development, current and ongoing stressors, the availability of
supportive resources, and the ability or inability to use adaptive
coping skills. Even with the best assessment techniques available, psychologists may not always be able to explain the origins
of certain difficulties. For example, among the most heritable
disorders, such as schizophrenia, genetics can only account for
up to 50 percent of the contribution to the disorder.[1]

Defining mental illness is also challenging. Even though the professional psychological community attempts to categorize and define mental illness in standard terms so that researchers may contribute to the development of effective treatments, those categorizations have changed, and continue to change over time, as the culture changes. For example, homosexuality was considered a mental disorder in 1980 in the third edition of the *Diagnostic and Statistical Manual of Mental Disorders,*[2] yet this is no longer the case.

Thus, for our purposes here, we will define mental illness with a broad-stroke definition that captures its essence without getting tangled up in the details of competing arguments or political correctness that can change over time. In general, mental illness is the presence of all three of the following elements: dysfunction, distress, and atypical cultural response.[3] Let's take a look at each of these. We will then provide a brief list of disorders that have been classified as mental illness.

Dysfunction

A psychological dysfunction refers to a breakdown of normal functioning in the cognitive, emotional, or behavioral areas.[4] Experiencing uncontrollable crying and grief, restricted emotional reactions (i.e., appearing to have only one emotion, such as anger), memory problems, chronic fear when situations are nonthreatening, and such are all examples of a psychological dysfunction. In this manner, addiction to substances, pornography, gaming, and the like also qualify as mental illness because compulsive behaviors override peoples' ability to regulate themselves despite consequences. An example of this is someone with substance abuse problems who continues to use drugs in spite of knowing they will lose custody of their children—and then continues to use the drugs once they have lost custody of their children even though they are well aware that they cannot regain custody of their children until they are clean.

How do you know if you or your spouse has experienced a breakdown in normal functioning? Many symptoms (such as fear, agitation, hopelessness, insomnia, obsessions) contribute to the type of dysfunction we are describing. Here are some examples of dysfunction: If you or your spouse cannot seem to get out of bed, take care of basic personal hygiene, or attend required activities—such as work, school, or church activities—there is a problem. If you or your spouse is restricted emotionally so that there seems to be only one emotional response to every situation, there is a problem. If previously enjoyed activities or hobbies provide no interest or excitement and you or your spouse consistently turns down invitations to participate or socialize in order to stay home in isolation, there is a problem. If compulsive behaviors or activities are taking over life so that there is no time or mental space for meaningful interactions and relationships with loved ones, there is a problem. If you or your spouse is seeing or hearing things that others do not seem to see or hear (hallucinations), there is a problem.

Distress

Personal distress is also a required factor in defining mental illness and generally accompanies the breakdown in functioning. This is understandable from a commonsense perspective.

People may suffer from a host of symptoms throughout their life for which they may never seek treatment because the symptoms don't distress them. In other words, when there is no distress there is no problem. Many symptoms are just a transient part of normal life and nothing to worry too much about (such as an occasional headache or nervousness before trying something new). A common maxim Debra shares with clients is "Normal is not symptom free." For example, it is possible to have an isolated panic attack that does not lead to continued anxiety problems. In this case an individual would not be given a panic disorder diagnosis because they are not experiencing ongoing distress.

Yet if there is distress, there is a problem. The symptoms which cause us a great deal of concern are the ones that take us to a doctor to seek a diagnosis in hopes of getting treatment. In our panic attack example, when a person has had a panic attack and is very distressed about it, that individual may begin to worry excessively about having another panic attack. With that worry they may then begin to alter and restrict their life and thoughts according to that fear. That type of distress contributes to the possible diagnosis of a panic disorder.

Every disorder has its own flavor of distress. For example, those with depression or bulimia nervosa (vomiting or other purging of their food after eating) are generally very distressed by their symptoms, even experiencing self-hatred. Or those with posttraumatic stress disorder (PTSD) have chronic, extreme fears that keep them continuously on edge, which sucks energy away and keeps them agitated. Yet, while those with various disorders all experience distress differently, generally they hate how they feel and what they are doing but are paralyzed and stuck, not knowing how to change it because of the severity of their dysfunction.

However, our definition of mental illness does not necessarily require the individuals suffering from a psychological dysfunction to experience distress. Rather, their behavior can create distress for others. Indeed, it may be an individual's spouse, family members, or friends that are distressed by their dysfunctional behavior. For example, those with the eating disorder anorexia nervosa starve themselves. As they lose weight and become emaciated, they feel good; they are happy to be skinny and like the attention it may get them. Often, they will not claim they are distressed. Yet family members and friends may become quite distressed as they watch their loved one restrict healthy eating options and become weak and unhealthy, even (rightfully so) fearing for their life in some extreme cases.

Another (trickier) example is when someone has a personality disorder. Personality disorders represent personality types that are rigid, making it very frustrating and difficult to get along with these individuals. Personality disorders develop as an individual develops, line upon line, and their presence may often be very subtle to those who do not know the person well and have limited contact with them. The intensity and pathology of the disorder may not be fully understood by the one with the disorder, as they may respond to those with concerns with an uninterested shrug of their shoulders: "I've just always been this way." In other words, they are not bothered or distressed by their dysfunction. Yet, for loved ones interacting with this person on a daily basis, a personality disorder flavors almost every interaction with deep pathology, such that it makes day-in and day-out interactions very difficult and at times almost unbearable. The loved ones' distress becomes the red flag that there is a problem, even if the one with the problem doesn't register it.

Atypical Cultural Response

In defining mental illness, it also becomes important to look at how commonly the problem occurs. Even if there is dysfunction and distress, if the individual's experience is just like everybody else's, we just don't diagnose mental illness. A diagnosis at that point would become meaningless. Instead, the problem is atypical or not culturally expected if it is a *deviation from the norm*. Generally, most psychological disorders have a prevalence rate of 1 percent, meaning that only one person out of one hundred people has this problem. This represents an atypical cultural response. However, the problem may also be considered atypical for the culture if it is a *severe* violation of social norms.[5]

Disorders

Here are some classification groups for mental illness:[7]

- Schizophrenia spectrum and other psychotic disorders, which include disorders such as delusional disorder and schizophrenia;
- Bipolar and related disorders, which include disorders such as bipolar I and bipolar II disorders;
- Depressive disorders, including major depressive disorder and persistent depressive disorder (dysthymia);
- Anxiety disorders, such as social anxiety disorder (social phobia), panic disorder, and generalized anxiety disorder;
- Obsessive-compulsive and related disorders, including obsessive-compulsive disorder, body dysmorphic disorder, hoarding disorder, and the like;
- Feeding and eating disorders, such as anorexia nervosa, bulimia nervosa, and binge eating disorder;
- Sexual dysfunctions, such as erectile disorder and female orgasmic disorder;
- Neurocognitive disorders, such as delirium and major neurocognitive disorder (formerly known as dementia);
- Personality disorders, such as paranoid personality disorder, narcissistic personality disorder, and obsessive-compulsive personality disorder.

Mental Illness Labels and Diagnoses

The *Diagnostic and Statistical Manual of Mental Disorders* is now in its fifth edition, with 697 pages dedicated to the current perspectives of the American Psychiatric Association regarding defining and describing each mental disorder.[6] These disorders are classified into groups that share common features. As can be seen in the truncated list to the side, the scope of possible mental health problems extends well beyond the more ubiquitous problems of depression and anxiety or the rarer but commonly known problems of bipolar disorder or schizophrenia. Therefore, we have chosen to keep our discussion of mental illness herein at a broad, introductory level, presented in a question and answer format, so as to allow applicability to as many couples as possible.

If you need additional support for a particular mental health challenge, please consult more specialized treatment materials through Internet resources and available books, or seek personalized individual or couple treatment through a licensed mental health professional.

How Do I Know If My Spouse or I Need Professional Help?

If you wonder whether you or your spouse needs professional intervention, we encourage careful consideration of our discussion above. Are all three elements of our definition (dysfunction, distress, and atypical cultural response) present? Perhaps you are not quite sure. If that is the case, we offer three tips on what mental illness is *not* in order to help you clarify how your particular issues may or may not necessitate professional intervention.

First, mental illness is not the same as struggling with the difficulties of life. We all struggle, and life is hard for the majority of us much of the time. We are taught in the scriptures that "it must needs be, that there is an opposition in all things" (2 Nephi 2:11). Indeed, this opposition is what enables us to become strong. Ralph Parlette has said: "Strength and struggle go together. The supreme reward of struggle is strength. Life is a battle and the greatest joy is to overcome."[8] Sometimes a person who appears to be struggling with mental illness concerns may be *cured* with simple changes made to their problematic lifestyle. Such changes can include getting a babysitter for a few hours a week to help with the kids, changing majors at school, changing jobs, getting appropriate medication to assist with chronic medical difficulties, getting enough sleep, improving nutrition, etc.

Second, mental illness is not having particular little quirks, habits, or beliefs that may be a bit extreme or compulsive.

DEBRA: *For example, I laugh at myself over my obsessive quirk of wanting all the books I purchase from the same author, or as part of the same series, to match as they line up on the bookshelf. I will only buy printings from the same publisher and with the same cover design. I will not buy paperback books if the other books I own from the series are hardback.*

Once, I ordered a particular copy of a book online for our older daughters specifically because the cover was supposed to match a set I already had at home on the bookshelf. This book was a popular book that the girls were excited to read, and

I ordered it without the girls knowing so that I could offer it as a surprise. When it arrived in the mail, it was the right book but did not have the right cover on it. I am embarrassed to admit it, but I was unwilling to give the girls the book. In fact, I did not give the book to them for many months, waiting in hopeful expectation of finding the particular printing I wanted at a local thrift store. It was only after writing about it in this chapter, and laughing at how silly I was, that I finally gave our daughters the book. However, even now, when I look at that series of books on the bookshelf, it still bothers me that that book doesn't match the others from the same author.

Admittedly, this is quite obsessive, but as my urge for book matching does not interfere with my general ability to function in life and since I have no other extreme obsessive symptoms, we can chalk it up to a silly quirk and simply laugh at it.

Third, mental illness is not struggling with common spiritual struggles of unrepentance, which may bring guilt or emotional fear. A person experiencing significant guilt over unresolved sin may display many of the symptoms of mental illness, particularly those of depression; however, this doesn't mean they are depressed. In the Book of Mormon, Alma described the state of his soul as he recognized the reality of his guilt:

> I was racked with eternal torment, for my soul was harrowed up to the greatest degree and racked with all my sins.
>
> Yea, I did remember all my sins and iniquities, for which I was tormented with the pains of hell. . . .
>
> Oh, thought I, that I could be banished and become extinct both soul and body, that I might not be brought to stand in the presence of my God, to be judged of my deeds. (Alma 36:12–13, 15)

Yes, these symptoms and feelings can be extremely distressing. But when the sin is confessed and dealt with through a bishop or other ecclesiastical leader with appropriate priesthood keys, the symptoms dissipate. Alma also illustrates this miracle of light returning to him when he turned his thoughts to the Savior: "And now, behold, when I thought this, I could remember my pains no more; yea, I was harrowed up by the memory of my sins no more.

And oh, what joy, and what marvelous light I did behold; yea, my soul was filled with joy as exceeding as was my pain!" (Alma 36:19–20).

Therefore, if we reflect on these three considerations and remain true to our definition of mental illness—the presence of impairment or dysfunction, distress, and atypical cultural response—the question as to the necessity of treatment for ourselves or our spouses becomes easier to answer. In each of these areas (common life struggles, obsessive quirks, or spiritual trials resultant from unrepentant sin), mental illness would *not* be considered as a contributing factor to the mental health difficulties.

Ecclesiastical Leader or Mental Health Professional?

In a quick note here about the difference between ecclesiastical leaders and mental health professionals, we look to Elder Alexander B. Morrison, who has given specific attention to mental illness in large measure because of his own experiences trying to help his daughter, Mary, with long-term panic attacks and depression.[9] In an *Ensign* article, he carefully outlined the respective roles of bishops and professionally trained mental health workers:

> Those who, like Alma, experience sorrow during the repentance process are not mentally ill. If their sins are serious, they do require confession and counseling at the hands of their bishop. As part of his calling, each bishop receives special powers of discernment and wisdom. No mental health professional, regardless of his or her skill, can ever replace the role of a faithful bishop as he is guided by the Holy Ghost in assisting Church members to work through the pain, remorse, and depression associated with sin. . . .
>
> We must understand, however, without in any way denigrating the unique role of priesthood blessings, that ecclesiastical leaders are spiritual leaders and not mental health professionals. Most of them lack the professional skills and training to deal effectively with deep-seated mental illnesses and are well advised to seek competent

Reflections

Healing through the power of the Atonement of Jesus Christ was paramount in dealing with the baggage I carried into marriage. I'm so thankful for a kind and merciful Savior. As I sought healing, I felt inspired to seek counseling. I made sure to choose a counselor that supported marriage and our gospel standards. I had a wonderful professor while attending BYU who commented that we don't hesitate to see a doctor when we have a knee injury or some other physical problem, but for some reason we are embarrassed to go to a therapist for issues that may be even more detrimental to our lives, our emotional health, and family relationships. I didn't ask for the issues that I carried due to my upbringing, and I was able to overcome them, or at least deal with them, through the Atonement of Christ and through counseling.

professional assistance for those in their charge who are in need of it. Remember that God has given us wondrous knowledge and technology that can help us overcome grievous problems such as mental illness. Just as we would not hesitate to consult a physician about medical problems such as cancer, heart disease, or diabetes, so too we should not hesitate to obtain medical and other appropriate professional assistance in dealing with mental illness. When such assistance is sought, be careful to ensure, insofar as possible, that the health professional concerned follows practices and procedures which are compatible with gospel principles.[10]

RICHARD: *As a second witness to what Elder Morrison has said here, may I say that during my time as a bishop I found that the Lord helped guide me in knowing the difference between a spiritual matter and a mental health problem regarding a member of my ward. Often I could help support them and teach them about spiritual things, but I knew that my abilities were limited when it came to counseling about a mental health challenge either for them or a family member. In these cases, I directed them to a mental health professional, who could assist them in ways that I could not. It was truly satisfying to see how, after a few weeks or months of treatment, they were able to improve and manage their life in a much healthier way.*

Mental Health Symptoms and Related Factors

So what types of behaviors *do* indicate that you or your spouse may need professional mental health intervention? In addition to considering our earlier discussion about dysfunction, distress, and atypical cultural responses, warning signs include such things as extreme spending or erratic behavior, loss of interest in sex, sloppy grooming and housekeeping, chronic insomnia, aggressive or violent behavior, and the like. Particularly concerning are issues relative to personal safety, such as frequent suicidal ideation or fantasy, self-harm or self-mutilative behaviors (e.g., cutting, burning, and hair pulling), or outright suicidal behaviors (such as overdosing on pills and then going to the emergency room to get their stomach pumped).

As mentioned earlier, the frequency and longevity of problems are also factors in deciding if treatment is necessary. If mental health difficulties are infrequent or transient, it is not likely necessary to seek treatment; those types of issues are common and mostly indicative of the heightened stress typical of life's challenges. If those same symptoms, however, come and go over a lengthy period of time, masquerading as transient problems but wielding their ugly heads repeatedly, they may be indicative of deeper issues. In that case, treatment from a qualified mental health professional would be useful to improve quality of life, but it may

Reflections

By the time I realized I needed professional help, I was in pretty big trouble. I had no appetite and would eat only because I wanted to stop my stomach from disturbing me. I hardly left the house. I was sedentary and lethargic. I had horrible insomnia and no energy or motivation. The only emotion I could feel was anger, and it colored every thought and action in my life. I isolated myself. I had no desire to go to school despite enjoying learning. I was manipulative with acquaintances. Somewhere I looked at myself in the mirror and didn't recognize what I saw, and it scared me. My life felt out of control. If you were able to look at me now and compare me to where I was when I started therapy, you would probably see two different people. Therapy didn't just make me feel better; it helped me regain control of my life. Instead of coasting through my schooling, I find myself enjoying learning and eagerly awaiting going to class. I'm making long-term goals and achieving them. Instead of simply being active, I find I'm pushing myself to try difficult things and am in better shape than I have ever been. In short, I'm a better "me" now than I was even before my problems started.

not necessarily be required if the individual shows good levels of resilience and if normal functioning is maintained. But if those same symptoms largely take over one's life by causing difficulty in functioning in day-to-day activities, thus making the individual incapable of engaging appropriately in life or unable to bounce back after even small setbacks, treatment would be highly recommended—if not considered mandatory. Additionally, if a problem is severe, such as a suicidal gesture, one instance may be enough to warrant seeking professional mental health treatment.

Also important in considering the necessity of treatment is taking inventory of one's coping capacities. A person with little stress tolerance and few coping skills will generally require treatment at an earlier stage than will a person with a high tolerance for distress and a cornucopia of resources to assist them in maintaining adaptive functioning.

A word of caution may be useful here. The assumption could be made that someone who is functioning externally in life does not need treatment. Many depressed clients are severely emotionally impaired—with suicidal ideation or engaging in self-harm behaviors—even though they still succeed in school or excel in their professional endeavors. Outward functioning does not necessarily equate with level of dysfunction. To have a better idea of what the level of dysfunction is, you or your loved one should reflect on the following questions: How do you feel you or they are coping? What is your or their quality of life? Do you feel you or they are out of control? Are you or they in control, but the effort required to retain that control is an exhausting, constant struggle?

Finally, the onset of mental health symptoms is another important consideration relative to the necessity to seek professional mental health treatment. A common adage used in abnormal psychology is "The earlier the onset, the poorer the prognosis." Early onset of mental illness is, therefore, generally indicative of a more severe disorder that will be more difficult to treat and have a poorer outcome. For example, if your spouse begins having memory difficulties in their early fifties, even if symptoms appear mild you would be wise to get them assessed and involved in treatment as soon as possible, as this could be an early onset of neurocognitive disorder, formerly known as dementia.

How Do We Get the Right Treatment for Our Needs?

Initial efforts to seek treatment will be specific to the difficulties you or your spouse are experiencing. For some psychological symptoms that mimic symptoms of common physical ailments, the first trip to the doctor may be to a physician's office. For example, people with panic disorder often go to the emergency room of the hospital, as the symptoms of panic mimic symptoms of a heart attack. Sometimes, after several emergency room visits and test results assuring a patient that there is no medical problem with their heart, a doctor may suggest the problem could be psychological, offer a prescription of some sort of tranquilizer to help with the anxiety, and make a referral to a mental health professional. For others who know the issue to be of a psychological nature—such as a person who is struggling with deep, complicated grief following the death of a loved one—the first appointment they make may be to see a psychologist.

Be aware that the medical and psychological communities operate from different perspectives and thus have different biases and treatments. Understanding this basic premise is critical to be informed consumers of treatment. If you or your spouse is struggling with depression, anxiety, or another such psychological difficulty and you go to a physician, the physician will likely recommend taking antidepressants, antianxiety medications, or other relevant medications. In a study examining primary care physicians' approach to treating depression, 72.5 percent of the doctors gave the patient an antidepressant medication prescription compared to only 38.4 percent that gave patients a referral to a mental health provider.[11]

On the other hand, psychologists have a bias that often leads them to avoid medications altogether, especially for those with mild or moderate problems. One meta-analysis, which compares the results of several research studies in order to examine overarching patterns, shows that antidepressants work no better than a basic placebo for most people and that these drugs are most helpful for those at the extreme level of depression only.[12] Thus, many clinicians tend to avoid recommending medications and will only do so for more severe cases. In the aforementioned panic scenario, panic attacks are easily treated with psychological treatment, and generally psychologists or other mental health professionals will not suggest that an antianxiety medication is needed due to the effective nature of panic treatment and the high relapse rates of medications.

Therefore, when faced with the decision of what types of treatments to secure, the best thing you can do is to do your homework; get opinions from both the medical and psychological communities and then make the decision that you feel would be best for you and your spouse in regard to treatment, taking into account your specific problems, long-term goals, and treatment objectives.

Types of Mental Health Professionals

In seeking psychological treatment, people often have questions regarding what type of mental health professional they should be seeing. First know that psychotherapy is a licensed profession and that all mental health professionals, regardless of type, should be currently licensed with their state. You can check the status of a clinician's license through online resources.

There are many types of licensed professionals that provide psychotherapy, yet their level of training, experience, and areas of focus vary widely, so it is important to be aware of the similarities and differences between them. Professional counselors, licensed clinical social workers, and marriage and family therapists are generally master's level (MA) clinicians with high levels of experiential hours. Professional counselors assist in general counseling and often in substance-abuse treatment. Licensed clinical social workers are social workers who have also received general counseling training to assist with mental health difficulties or daily living problems. A marriage and family therapist has training in general mental health issues and counseling interventions yet focuses their work on the family system and its role in perpetuating mental illness or other difficulties. A psychologist is a doctoral level (PhD or PsyD) clinician with expert training in mental illness (abnormal psychology) and its treatments, high levels of experiential hours, and experience in mental health research.

Research has suggested that therapist training is a relative factor; those with more training tend to produce better client outcomes.[13]

Psychotherapy, also referred to as simply *therapy* or *counseling*, is an effective process by which many people are strengthened, healed, and given valuable coping skills. Researchers who have studied the effectiveness of therapy have consistently found that it produces positive outcomes. They have found a range of therapeutic benefits by examining the results of many studies through meta-analysis and found moderate effect sizes of 0.60 to large effect sizes of 0.85.[14] This means, generally speaking, that the person who engages in psychotherapy treatment is better off than 60 to 85 percent of those who do not receive treatment.

Psychotherapy usually consists of individualized treatment sessions in which you visit alone with a mental health provider who then develops a personalized treatment plan and works with you on that plan throughout the treatment process. Psychotherapy can also be done with others, such as your spouse, a parent, a sibling, or others if familial relationships are problematic and

Reflections

As I attended BYU, the stress of school was too much, and I began the habit of cutting myself and entertaining suicidal fantasies. I was in a very dark place. Loving friends suggested that I seek professional help. I was nervous to see a therapist because in my mind you were "crazy" if you went to therapy. But I went anyways and will forever be grateful that I did. That decision changed—and probably saved—my life! I began my journey through therapy; it was hard and painful to work through things—hard things. I had been hurt as a young girl, and a lot of my issues seemed to stem from that experience. As my chapter at BYU closed, I felt I was in a better place, concluded therapy, and continued on in my life. A few years went by, and I began to feel like I'd benefit from therapy again. I once again began a journey, this time working on deeper feelings I had not previously discussed in therapy. I worked hard for many months. The darkness I felt was replaced with much light, peace, and joy. My mental health has been outstanding for years now, and I credit that to the work I did in therapy. It was work! But it was worth every effort.

contributing to the mental health difficulties.

Psychotherapy can also be done in groups. Group therapy is often used as an adjunct treatment for those already in individual treatment, but this is not necessarily the case and may also be used as a primary treatment. In group therapy, the dynamic relationships of group members become tools of therapeutic intervention, so one does not just benefit from insights and treatments from the therapist but learns from their fellow group members through the modeling of various behaviors, gaining a sense of not being uniquely alone in their problems (universality), and helping and supporting each other (altruism).[15]

Generally, psychotherapy treatment is done on an outpatient basis, in which you attend a session, perhaps once a week, as you continue living in your own home and engaging in your own activities, such as going to school or work. For those with more severe disorders that are interfering with daily functioning, more intensive treatments—such as day programs (living in the home but attending treatment for several hours a day), inpatient treatments (living in a hospital for a number of days to weeks), or even residential programs (living in a treatment facility generally for several months to years)—are available. In the more intensive programs, you will often receive a combination of individual, family, and group therapies to maximize outcomes.

Be aware that the higher the level of intensity, the greater the cost of the program. An average inpatient or residential treatment center is approximately $1,000 per day. Therefore, you always want to begin with the least invasive, less expensive treatment that will meet your treatment needs. If you find the treatment you have selected is not meeting your needs, you would be wise to increase the level of intensity with a more invasive treatment program.

Psychological treatment is a process that requires a varying number of treatment sessions: a few sessions for mild problems, a protracted process for more long-term or severe difficulties. It is not uncommon for many difficulties to be effectively treated in eight to fourteen sessions.[16] This is an important point—for many people who attend treatment, psychotherapy is a short-term process.

DEBRA: *As an example, I was contacted by the parents of a twenty-two-year-old young man suffering with obsessive-compulsive disorder complicated with depression and attention deficit problems. His distress was very high, his quality of life was poor, and his issues were creating problems in his new marriage relationship. He had tried medication for eight months and felt it made things worse. He was willing to attend therapy because he was tired of suffering and didn't want to destroy his new marriage. Due to the severe nature of his difficulties, treatment began with two sessions per week for the first five weeks. Within a few sessions, his distress levels dropped significantly, and he began thinking in different ways that allowed him to process reality in a healthy way again. His distress and symptom levels continued to drop, and within nineteen sessions (four and a half months) he was functioning well within the normal range. You can see data collected during his treatment sessions in figure 1. These data points are from the OQ-45 that was developed by BYU researchers.17 The OQ-45 is a measure that tracks symptom distress and functioning over the course of treatment. Please note that in this chart a score of 45 is the average score for someone not in therapy while a score of 63 is the clinical cutoff, meaning an individual warrants treatment if their distress score is higher than 63. This client's initial score was a high 94, whereas the last score shown on this chart is a 43.*

Although this client's level of functioning was well within normal range after four and a half months (as seen by his score of 45 plotted on the graph), we continued to meet to work on relapse prevention as well as to address some of the marital issues that had developed over the course of his illness. As you can see on the graph, he continued to stabilize in the normal range thereafter. He reported: "The speed at which I can process reality now averages within five seconds to five minutes. Don't get me wrong; there are occasionally a few setbacks where it takes me a day to recover, but that is very seldom. I would recommend therapy to everyone."

Although this client began treatment with two therapy sessions per week (whereas most people will generally begin treatment with one session per week), please note that this example is not unusual in regards to the speed by which he began to heal and regain his quality of life; many people have similar treatment outcomes after relatively brief therapeutic interventions.

Before I move on, it is important to note that this client's story has another side to it—how his healing blessed his wife and the quality of their marriage. In addition to regaining health and an improved quality of life, he also regained a positive relationship with his spouse.

My husband's crippling anxiety was plaguing our relationship. We were newlyweds, and our relationship was full of misunderstandings and unfounded accusations that made it difficult to perform well in school and work. Therapy didn't change him overnight; however, after months of hard work he overcame his challenges. Through therapy he gained improved communication skills, emotional intelligence, confidence, and empathy . . . in addition to learning to manage his anxiety. It has transformed our marriage! The difference is like going from night to day. I finally feel like I can be myself around him without worrying that he will interpret something I do or say the wrong way. He is now my biggest source of support and comfort, instead of a burden and source of angst. We trust each other more, treating ourselves as equal partners in the marriage. I will be forever grateful that my husband courageously sought the help he needed.

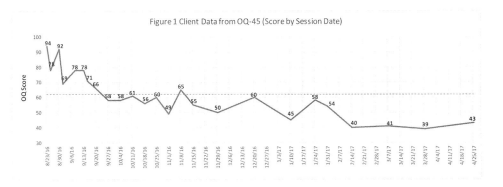

FIGURE 1. CLIENT DATA FROM THE OQ-45.

We hope the point we make here is clear: treatment will not only bless you but it will also bless your spouse and your marriage. If your own misery is not enough to spark a willingness to seek appropriate treatment for your mental health concerns, then please humbly seek the treatment you need for the sake of your spouse and your marriage. Allow that concern and welfare for them to encourage you to move toward health.

What to Expect in the Treatment Process

In the therapeutic community, the modal number of therapy sessions is one. This means that many people attend therapy once and never return. Debra was once told by a client whose husband resisted attending marital counseling that her husband might be willing to go to a therapist, *but only once*—that if the therapist was worth anything, they'd get the job done in one session. In this case the problems that led to the need for therapy had developed over a thirty-year period. If only mental health professionals had a magic wand! We hope to educate you enough about the treatment process here to understand that you will need to attend therapy more than one time.

When you meet with a therapist, the first session or two are actually assessment meetings in which the therapist is largely gathering information in order to develop a treatment plan. Generally, there is no official therapeutic intervention employed during this initial process other than the offering of hope and encouragement that things can improve for you in your particular difficulties as you commit to return and work the therapy process.

These assessment sessions are also important for you as the client. This is a time to get a feel for the therapist and assess goodness of fit. If there is not a feeling of connection to the therapist or a strong sense that they know how to assist you, consider seeking another treatment provider. If you or your spouse is not comfortable with a particular mental health counselor, it is likely that you will *not* feel comfortable allowing that person into the vulnerable or painful parts of yourselves that need healing, thus limiting the helpfulness of the therapy process.

In addition, researchers have identified therapist variables associated with creating better outcomes for clients. In the first couple of meetings, you will want to get a sense for "(1) the therapist's adjustment, skill, and interest in helping patients; (2) the purity of the treatment they offer; and (3) the quality of the therapist/ patient relationship."[18]

So shop for a therapist like you would shop for a car; test drive them before committing to one in particular. A good way to reduce the time, stress, and expense of this searching process is to get referrals from those you trust or to read reviews posted online by those who have met with that treatment provider.

Generally speaking, the therapist will assess your personal history and needs, set some therapy goals, and then work with you collaboratively to address each of those goals. You will be the expert on your life experience, the therapist will be the expert on how to enact therapeutic change on your behalf, and you will both bring your expertise to the table to create a wonderful partnership of healing and growth. Some of the therapeutic goals may be quickly addressed (such as improving sleep, diet, or hygiene), while some may take more substantial amounts of time (such as working through issues and trauma related to abuse, chronic depression, or personality difficulties).

DEBRA: *For example, one client struggling with severe depression came in to see me. As I assessed her symptoms, distress, and personal circumstances, I had an initial sense of where treatment should begin. However, as we talked together I asked her about her goals for therapy, what she wanted to accomplish. After she laid out her goals, I asked her which goal felt like the biggest priority to her—what was most strongly driving her depression at that time. Her answer was not what I expected. Instead of beginning treatment with what I thought, we began with what she thought was most important. She knew what she needed!*

Instead of immediately getting into deeper issues related to a negative cognitive style, difficult circumstances from her adolescence, insecurities about her professional competence, or the like—all important, and all topics we did eventually work with in therapy—we began with parenting issues for her young toddlers. The intensity of parenting two toddlers had ramped up the level of distress and her feelings so that she could not cope in her life. Within five sessions, her distress level had dropped significantly. We were then able to see more clearly how the deeper issues were playing into her depression and work with those issues without the feelings of desperation and crisis she had experienced initially because of feeling out of control with her children. Her treatment was very successful. We can see in figure 2 the OQ-45 scores for her first twenty sessions. Although this chart shows her distress level well within the normal ranges after twelve sessions (with a score of 33), we continued therapy for a time to address some deeper, long-standing painful issues from her adolescence. It is quite clear that her score shot up to a 96 on session thirteen. Confronting her deepest pains and torments terrified her and caused her a great deal of distress. Yet she bravely kept with therapy and did what she needed to do to get healthy. After that one difficult session when her fears were highly activated, her distress levels went back under the clinical cutoff, although the distress of that particular therapy content kept her distress score a bit higher than it had been previously for three more sessions. You then see her scores drop again, and her distress level was almost identical to where she was before we began the really tough stuff, dropping to her lowest scores yet, 26 and 34. This illustrates well the ups and downs of the therapy process on any given day but also shows the overall trajectory that occurs as one continues treatment.

The critical thing about this data is that these numbers represent real pain and distress. This client started with an exceedingly high score of 118. In just under five and a half months, her distress level registered a score of 34, well within the average range for someone not in therapy. The tremendous impact of this type of change in her life cannot be understated. The client said this about her change:

> It's amazing the baggage I was carrying that I wasn't even aware of. It's so much lighter being able to be a normal, functioning adult instead of one who is carrying all this unseen and very heavy baggage. At a score of 118—there aren't even words to describe it. I couldn't picture a future. I-didn't-think-I-would-be-there-to-see-my-kids-grow-up type of thing. It just wasn't feasible in that state of mind. It was just nothing and it was just so overwhelming. I could only do the bare minimum. At a score of 34—it's like being a different person. It allows me to be who I really am rather than being clouded by depression. I am actually enjoying being alive and actually enjoying being a mom and enjoying everything I never thought would be possible for me to enjoy ever again.

This type of change changes lives! This type of change is possible in your life or in the life of your spouse. Therapy works.

What you actually do in your therapy sessions will vary based on your particular needs, the therapy goals you and your therapist have established, and the style of your therapist. There are many *theoretical orientations* taken by clinicians. This means there are a variety of psychological theories that look at how mental illness develops and how to enact change in that illness in order to break through the "stuckness" that the dysfunction and distress are causing in the person's life. That theoretical orientation will influence the approach your therapist takes to your problems. In addition, the personality style of the therapist will also impact their approach in the therapy process.

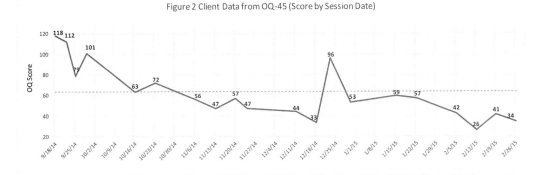

FIGURE 2. CLIENT DATA FROM THE OQ-45.

You may spend your time in therapy doing some of the following: working on starting healthier behaviors or working to quit problematic ones, talking about dynamics or events from your childhood, role-playing current interpersonal difficulties to learn more adaptive responses, learning new cognitive skills, journaling about past or present scenarios, filling out worksheets or other written exercises, and the like. Your therapy will be your personal process, and the course of your treatment will be determined together by you and your therapist. As seen with the client above, sometimes the work you do in therapy will elevate your distress because you are facing difficulties that you have spent many years trying to avoid. A metaphor I commonly use as I describe the therapy process is that of doing a really good deep cleaning of your bedroom. Deciding to do a thorough cleaning requires you to start pulling things out from under your bed, from the upper recesses of your closet shelf, and from behind the door. As you do this, you just throw it all in a massive pile on your bed or in the middle of the floor. Ten minutes into the cleaning process, your messy room is now completely trashed! Do you panic and say, "I better quit cleaning my room; it's making it worse"? No, because you understand what you are doing and you trust the process. You keep going. And, generally speaking, it doesn't take too long after that to start sorting and organizing and getting everything into its proper place in the room.

So too with the therapy process. It is understandable that you may not trust the therapy process because it is unfamiliar to you and you may not see how it can help you, but your therapist knows it. Trust your therapist to help see you through the process, and you, too, can enjoy the benefits that come—just as you enjoy the benefits of a clean and orderly bedroom when you do the work.

Sometimes, as part of the treatment process, you may need medication (you may hear the term *psychotropic medication*). If this is the case, you or your spouse would generally secure the assistance of a psychiatrist, which is a medical doctor (MD) who has done specialty training in mental illness and psychopharmacology (drugs). Psychiatrists generally do not conduct psychotherapy but meet with patients for brief appointments to discuss medications compliance, side effects, and needed medication adjustments. Thus, it is common for an individual to meet regularly with a mental health counselor for therapy and then meet with a psychiatrist once every few months for medication management. Psychotherapy providers, such as psychologists and master's-level clinicians, do not prescribe medication (although some states are making additional training available for what are termed *prescription privileges*).

Once treatment begins, it is critical that you or your spouse follow the treatment protocol established by your treatment providers. Haphazardly taking medication will not provide a therapeutic dose, and failing to attend therapy or to do planned interventions or assignments between therapy sessions limits the therapeutic benefit of psychotherapy.

How Do We Find a Therapist?

Finding a therapist usually starts with an assessment of the financial resources already available to you through insurance coverage if applicable. If you check a summary of your insurance plan's coverage, you can examine the mental health coverage listed for in-network and out-of-network providers. Some plans have excellent mental health benefits, but some have very poor coverage.

For individuals with mental health benefits, finding a therapist can be as simple as going to your insurance company's website and locating a list of contracted or in-network providers in your area. You then choose one of those based on location, recommendations or reviews, or other such criteria. In those circumstances, you will pay the co-pay established by your insurance company for each treatment session or service rendered.

If you have insurance coverage but choose a therapist outside of the insurer's contracted network, you may still be able to get your insurance company to reimburse you with a portion of the service fees if it so states in the insurance plan summary. In those cases you would choose a therapist (such as a local provider that has good reviews posted online or one for which you received a strong recommendation) and simply go to them and pay their standard treatment fee. The therapist will provide a receipt that you then submit personally to the insurance company. The company then

Reflections

I am in my midfifties, and I could still not talk about the abuse that happened in my adolescence without tearing up. I started going to therapy for help with my marriage, but it quickly turned to dealing with past abuse. I knew this was necessary, but I dreaded it. I had spent thirty years trying to forget my past, and now with therapy I was supposed to remember. I was very apprehensive. I could not see how this was going to help. I was so desperate that I had no choice but to try and trust the system. As I trusted the therapy process, shared openly my pain and vulnerability, and did all the homework assignments my therapist gave me, I started to feel a huge weight taken from me. I started to see the process work in my life. I even started to look forward to my therapy sessions because I knew each time I went I was letting go of the past more and more. I knew I was getting healthier and stronger.

reimburses you the amount established by your insurance plan for an out-of-network provider.

For those who do not have insurance coverage for mental health treatment but have access to sufficient financial resources, you may choose any therapist and pay their fee directly. Paying out of pocket may be a difficult decision for some, as it can be difficult financially and emotionally to commit to pay for therapy. This decision to pay for therapy (rather than foregoing treatment) may prove to be one of your best investments.

DEBRA: *One of my cash-paying clients had tight finances but, knowing she needed help, chose to enter therapy anyway. At the end of her treatment, which lasted ten sessions, this client said that it was "worth every penny." Three years later, she and I had a brief email exchange in which she strengthened her conviction and wrote to me, "It was definitely worth every penny!"*

For those who do not have access to sufficient financial resources, seeking out community clinics in your area may be a wise choice. If you attend school, counseling services are often included for free or for reduced fees on college and university campuses. If you live near a university, there are often training facilities in which graduate programs give their students supervised therapy experience by offering reduced-fee services to the general, nonstudent public. If your employer has an employee assistance program, it may be possible to receive therapy benefits. For example, some companies offer a certain number of therapy sessions for free each calendar year. LDS Family Services may also be a lower-cost option than seeking treatment from a private therapist.

Lastly, there are times when LDS bishops have intervened financially to help a ward member receive at least initial treatment intervention. As these financial helps use fast-offering funds, they should only be sought out as a last resort and with careful counseling with your bishop. A bishop may agree to pay for initial sessions but may contract with you to provide service or such in return for the financial assistance.

Do We Need an LDS Therapist?

It is common for Christians with high levels of committed religiosity to desire to see Christian therapists.[19] Likewise, many LDS individuals and couples may feel a desire to work with LDS therapists.

DEBRA: *When I first began seeing therapy clients, I lived in California. My clients generally had no religious orientation, and they never asked if I had a religious orientation. It was simply a nonissue. In an LDS community, it plays out very differently. Since I am now located in Utah, the majority of my clients have been LDS, and the fact that I am an active member of the LDS Church has been of paramount importance to them. Here are some thoughts on this issue from a few of my clients:*

> It was extremely important to me. I had seen another therapist previously who wasn't LDS, and even though she tried, we couldn't discuss spiritual things the way I wanted to.

> It was very important to be able to relate to someone who I thought shared my same values and standards . . . an understanding of my frame of reference in discussing my experiences. A solid LDS therapist has a much better idea of where I want to go. They are also better able to help me resolve issues where I think I'm out of balance with LDS values. I've been to a marginally active LDS therapist who was way too far into theories of self-actualization. It didn't work for me.

> I cared more about the therapist being Christian. I didn't want to have to spend therapy time defending or introducing my values. Also, I didn't want to have to spend session time to explain about the sex culture and other LDS cultural terms.

> It was important to me because some of the things I was struggling with were of a religious nature, specifically through LDS beliefs. I don't think another counselor outside of the LDS religion would have understood.

> In the beginning I was dealing a lot with feelings of returning home early from an LDS mission, and with therapy or opening up to any person, it's important for me to feel connected and understood.

> I didn't think I could achieve that with someone who was not LDS and didn't understand the mission aspect.

> There's a definite advantage to having an LDS therapist; they understand the stresses from the Church without encouraging you to just leave and find a new church.

For couples living in Utah, it is not difficult to find therapists from all professional areas of training who are members of The Church of Jesus Christ of Latter-day Saints if they so desire. For others this may become a problem, as LDS therapists may not be readily available in their area. For LDS couples in rural areas, the task of finding an LDS therapist may be virtually impossible. It is not uncommon to have members of the Church travel many hours each direction in order to be able to meet with an LDS therapist.

Is this necessary? We believe there are several points for consideration as you decide whether finding an LDS therapist is the right choice for you.

First, for what purpose are you seeking therapy? If you are seeking sex therapy, we would, as we recommended in chapter 6, encourage you to seek an LDS therapist if at all possible. An LDS therapist would be more likely to be sensitive to your sexual culture and the types of sexual interventions they will recommend during your treatment process. If you are seeking marital counseling relative to difficulties in the relationship that are faith based, such as issues around gender roles, priesthood, and the like, we believe it would be most useful to meet with an LDS therapist.

We do believe that a well-trained, more advanced therapist of any religious affiliation (or of no religious affiliation) will be sensitive to religious influences. They will encourage you to teach them about your religious belief and be respectful to those influences in your life. They will use interventions that will not violate your personal or religious beliefs. However, not being familiar with the tenets of the religion, or especially with its cultural nuances, could impose some limitations during the therapy process, as they may miss things or fail to provide insights an LDS therapist may readily see or provide that may prove critical to healing.

If you are seeking psychotherapy treatment for nonreligious issues—such as dealing with anger, money or time management, basic communication skills, substance abuse, or the like—we believe the religious orientation of the therapist may not need to be a major consideration in your selection of a therapist. In these cases, issues such as the therapist's level of training, area of expertise or the focus of their practice, and goodness of fit would likely be of greater importance than religious affiliation.

Second, as you consider whether to seek treatment with an LDS treatment provider, it is important to remember that not all LDS therapists are of equal training and competence. One of Debra's clients shared this feedback:

> I preferred an LDS therapist because I needed someone who would understand my faith and its part in the healing process and in my progress. I can't separate my faith and my therapy. They need to go hand in hand. But not just any LDS therapist would do. Therapists, even LDS ones, are not created equal. There are other factors as well, such as knowledge, experience, maturity, style, theoretical philosophy, and approach to diagnostic testing.

A good therapist will ask you what it means to you to be LDS, regardless of their religious orientation. We mentioned this above, but it is necessary to highlight the point that this is also important if your therapist *is* LDS. If you have a therapist that is highly trained, competent, and conscientious about providing good treatment, they will ask you questions rather than make assumptions. Therapists may make the mistake of assuming that because they share religious affiliation with you as a client, what it means to *them* to be LDS is what it means to *you*. This assumption can become a problem in your therapy if your meanings are indeed different.

If you find an LDS therapist who is not sensitive to this issue, the fact that you share your religious affiliation may not necessarily be useful in the therapeutic process and you may be better off with another therapist, even if that means meeting with someone who is not affiliated with the LDS Church. One research study supports this idea, indicating that religious similarity between the client and therapist did not necessarily produce the best therapeutic outcomes.[20]

A third consideration is the cost of seeking treatment from an LDS therapist, relative to money, time, and energy. If you find a great LDS therapist that seems ideal for your particular needs but meeting with them requires a three-hour drive each direction, you may want to rethink the plan. A lengthy drive each direction adds a great deal of money to the cost of the treatment process when taking into account transportation costs. It also adds significant stress to the therapeutic process by requiring a greater time and energy commitment and a dramatic rearrangement of your weekly schedule. This puts pressure on both therapist and client that does not allow the treatment process to unfold naturally (and therapy is already a lot of work, so the additional stress may be counterproductive).

For example, a client living a great distance from a particular LDS therapist may decide that they can only handle making the long drive a handful of times, so they would then limit the therapist to only a few sessions. Putting this type of arbitrary session limit on the therapeutic process is likely to only create disappointment and frustration for both of you. Instead, a therapist closer to your home, even if they do not share your LDS religious affiliation, may offer you a much better treatment experience because they have the space to provide treatment that can promote true healing.

Lastly, as you consider whether it is necessary to the success of your therapeutic process to have an LDS treatment provider, it may simply come down to your personal preference and comfort. It may simply be the case that you want an LDS therapist that understands doctrinal and cultural nuances, as it gives you more faith that the therapist will understand you and your specific needs. Comfort with the therapist is very important and may prove more important to you than the distance of the drive or other considerations.

DEBRA: *When all is said and done, if it is your preference to meet with an LDS therapist and you are unable to do so, please do not use the inability to locate an LDS therapist as a reason (or an excuse) to not go to therapy. One of my clients had this feedback about the importance of the therapist's religious orientation:*

> [Meeting with an LDS therapist] was not my priority. I wouldn't be able to talk about church stuff straight up [with a non-LDS therapist], but that was not a priority for me at the time. I was focused on getting healthy. Spiritual stuff could wait.

I want to underscore the importance of this point. If you prefer to work with an LDS therapist and an LDS therapist is not available, please make getting healthy your priority and go see a competent licensed professional in your area, regardless of religious orientation.

What Do I Do If My Spouse Refuses Treatment?

You may be more than willing to seek your own treatment, but what if it is your spouse that needs the mental health treatment or you need treatment as a couple and your spouse is not so inclined? Here are some considerations.

Some aspects of treatment may be more amenable to your spouse than others. Even if you feel strongly that your spouse needs a particular type of treatment that they are currently refusing, if there is any facet of therapy they are willing to engage in, go for it. As some healing occurs, their willingness to pursue additional treatment may increase. Allow time for the process to unfold. Take whatever your spouse is willing to put their energy into and support them in any way that you can. Yet be cautious that you do not micromanage them, causing resentment toward both you and the treatment process. Allow them stewardship over their own process and offer to be a support and comfort when needed.

Elder Jeffrey R. Holland reminds us: "Broken minds can be healed just the way broken bones and broken hearts are healed. While God is at work making those repairs, the rest of us can help by being merciful, nonjudgmental, and kind."[21]

Ultimately, your spouse has the power to exercise their agency and refuse treatment. In these cases, you can seek support for yourself through accessing online support groups, reading self-help books, or seeking personalized psychological treatment to learn how to cope with the difficulties the mental illness is producing for you and your relationship with your spouse. Family therapy operates on a basic premise that by changing one member of the family the whole family can change, since the habitual and dynamic patterns of interpersonal relationships by necessity change when one person is behaving differently. So the therapeutic community generally believes that if your spouse refuses treatment, *you* should still go. You can help your spouse by getting help yourself.

What Do I Do If My Spouse Is in Crisis?

Agency is a powerful gift from God. In the Pearl of Great Price we read, "In the Garden of Eden, gave I unto man his agency" (Moses 7:32). Thus, we should seek to support another's use of agency, that "every man may act in doctrine and principle pertaining to futurity, according to the moral agency which I have given unto him, that every man may be accountable for his own sins in the day of judgment" (D&C 101:78).

We seek to respect the agency of our spouse. Yet, in some isolated circumstances, you as a spouse must decide to act in a way that limits your spouse's exercise of agency. This will only occur

Reflections

A couple's story:

HUSBAND: *Living with a spouse with depression has been very difficult. My wife rarely feels good. She is reluctant to go anywhere or do anything, and she will not initiate activities such as making phone calls or writing letters. She won't drive and she won't cook. She needs constant companionship. She spends most of her time lying on the couch watching TV. Very few days go by when she doesn't say, "I don't want to do this anymore." She has already said it today and it is before 10:30 a.m. I have always felt getting more exercise would improve her outlook on life, so I have encouraged her to walk. I bought her a treadmill and set it up in front of a TV, but she has never used it with any consistency. She used to go for walks outside, but after we moved to an area with steep roads, she stopped. At the urging of one of our children, I called and made a therapy appointment to try to get her into treatment, but once I told her about it she made me cancel the appointment. If there is any perceived discomfort or anything that is going to take any effort, she shies away from it. I haven't done really well in trying to be patient with her. I still get upset at times when she is totally off-the-wall unreasonable about something. I have felt really overloaded.*

WIFE: *I have struggled with depression all of my adult life; I am now seventy-four years old. I have been to a psychiatrist many times, and I began trying antidepressants about thirty years ago. Whenever a new antidepressant would come on the market, I would be hopeful that this new thing would be my answer for depression relief. Each time I would try something, I would have side effects that I felt were more miserable than the depression itself. There were about three or four over the years that I actually stuck with for about a month, but I ultimately gave them all up. Some of them I even tried more than once. But they just made me feel too awful. I have also tried diet changes, over-the-counter herbal supplements and medications, and one session of hypnosis. I was always looking forward hopefully to something new that would be an answer to my prayers. I did not seek counseling, because I felt I needed some altering chemically, having a sister who has a severe combination of schizophrenia and bipolar depression. But even though the chemical interventions didn't work, I have just felt too bad to try to make the effort to go to therapy.*

Reflections

My twenty-year marriage has been very hard. After a particularly bad experience last year, I felt I was faced with three choices: stay unhappily married until my youngest child graduated from high school and then get divorced, stay unhappily married until we died, or— what I really wanted—stay married and be happy! But how could I accomplish my third option with someone who was controlling and undermining our relationship? I felt so beat down; I knew that I needed counseling. I was going to go so that I could make changes to be happy and learn some skills that would specifically help me communicate with my husband. I went to a therapist and invited my husband as well. He did go with me three times. My husband never practiced the skills that the therapist gave him or even remembered the exercises. He was resentful about me going to a therapist. He thought it was a waste of money and that I just needed to stop being "angry" and trust him more. I continued to see the therapist. The therapist showed me how to talk with less emotion and speak more logically, how to tell my husband exactly what I wanted or needed, and how to tell him if I disagreed and how not to take it personally when he disagrees with me, which can be a lot. I took notes and have been using them. I feel good and think my husband and I have a chance. Things have improved.

in rare circumstances and usually when there is a safety issue at play.

For example, if your spouse is struggling with dementia and they have repeatedly overdosed on their medications, you will likely make the choice to take their medications from them and only distribute them at the appropriate times to take them, even if your spouse protests.

In like manner, a person who becomes acutely suicidal does not have the mindset to be able to exercise their agency clearly, and you will likely need to take them to an emergency room, even if they attempt to physically resist you or verbally assault you in the process. In a circumstance such as this, if your spouse becomes physically aggressive, do not put yourself in danger, but call 911 and have a police officer escort them to the emergency room. Do not try to transport them yourself if they are in the middle of a psychotic episode, panic attack, or other extreme emotional meltdown.

If your spouse becomes verbally aggressive, insulting, or abusive, don't take it personally but don't back down. You can continue to assure them that you are trying your best to support them and keep them safe and that you love them. This will ultimately lead to a strengthening of marital ties when energies are calm and stability is reclaimed.

If you have to involve the police in an acute situation with a spouse who is mentally ill or under the influence of drugs or alcohol to maintain your safety, be aware that the authorities may hold an individual against their will (*involuntary commitment*) for a specified period of time (this varies from state to state but is often between three to five days). This time allows the authorities to conduct their own assessment to see if additional services, such as a hospitalization, may be warranted. If the state finds that additional treatment is required and the individual will not consent to treatment, a court order may be issued to continue to hold and treat the individual.

Conclusion

As you can see throughout this discussion of mental illness and treatment considerations, mental health issues are tricky and complicated. Taking a thoughtful approach is imperative to getting the appropriate assistance for you or your spouse. If you continue to be unsure about the need for mental health intervention, we would recommend a mental health assessment conducted by a licensed mental health professional. Let them tell you if they believe treatment is needed and how they see treatment will benefit you. Then you and your spouse can evaluate your circumstance from a more informed position.

Treatments are available—and they work in the large majority of cases! There is no need to continue to suffer and endure a poor quality of life. Be willing to work at therapy and to find the peace and stability of living with greater emotional resources and resilience and of living free of the debilitating effects of mental illness.

Notes

1. David H. Barlow and V. Mark Durand, *Abnormal Psychology: An Integrative Approach*, 6th ed. (Belmont, CA: Wadsworth, 2012), 34.

2. American Psychiatric Association, *Diagnostic and Statistical Manual of Mental Disorders*, 3rd ed. (Washington, DC: American Psychiatric Association, 1980).

3. Barlow and Durand, *Abnormal Psychology*, 1–2.

4. Barlow and Durand, *Abnormal Psychology*, 2.

5. Barlow and Durand, *Abnormal Psychology*, 2.

6. American Psychiatric Association, *Diagnostic and Statistical Manual of Mental Disorders*, 5th ed. (Washington, DC: American Psychiatric Association, 2013), 31–727.

7. American Psychiatric Association, *Diagnostic and Statistical Manual*, 5th ed., 87, 123, 155, 189, 235.

8. Spencer W. Kimball, *The Miracle of Forgiveness* (Salt Lake City: Bookcraft, 1969), 164.

9. Carrie A. Moore, "Elder Morrison Gets Service to Humanity Award," *Deseret Morning News*, 2 April 2004, http://www.deseretnews.com/article/595053229/Elder-Morrison-gets-Service-to-Humanity-Award.html.

10. Alexander B. Morrison, "Myths of Mental Illness," *Ensign*, October 2005, 33–34. See also Alexander Morrison, "Mental Illness in the Family," in *Helping and Healing Families: Principles and Practices Inspired by "The Family: A Proclamation to the World,"* ed. Craig H. Hart et al. (Salt Lake City: Deseret Book, 2005), 288–94.

11. John W. Williams Jr. et al., "Primary Care Physicians' Approach to Depressive Disorders: Effects of Physician Specialty and Practice Structure," *Archives of Family Medicine* 8, no. 1 (1999): 58–67.

12. Jay C. Fournier et al., "Antidepressant Drug Effects and Depression Severity: A Patient-Level Meta-Analysis," *JAMA* 303, no. 1 (2010): 47–53.

13. David M. Stein and Michael J. Lambert, "Graduate Training in Psychotherapy: Are Therapy Outcomes Enhanced?," *Journal of Consulting and Clinical Psychology* 63, no. 2 (1995): 182–196.

14. Michael J. Lambert, "The Efficacy and Effectiveness of Psychotherapy," in *Bergin and Garfield's Handbook of Psychotherapy and Behavior Change*, 5th ed., ed. Michael J. Lambert (New York: Wiley, 2004), 141.

15. Gary M. Burlingame and Debra Theobald McClendon, "Group Psychotherapy," in *Twenty-First Century Psychotherapies: Contemporary Approaches to Theory and Practice*, ed. Jay L. Lebow (Hoboken, NJ: John Wiley and Sons, 2008), 354.

16. Lambert, "Efficacy and Effectiveness," 156.

17. Michael J. Lambert et al., *Administration and Scoring Manual for the Outcome Questionnaire (OQ 45.2)* (Wilmington, DE: American Professional Credentialing Services, 1996); Michael J. Lambert et al., "The Reliability and Validity of the Outcome Questionnaire," *Clinical Psychology and Psychotherapy* 3, no. 4 (1996): 249–58.

18. Lambert, "The Efficacy and Effectiveness of Psychotherapy," 168.

19. Donald F. Walker et al., "Religious Commitment and Expectations about Psychotherapy among Christian Clients," *Psychology of Religion and Spirituality* 3, no. 2 (2011): 98–114.

20. L. Rebecca Propst et al., "Comparative Efficacy of Religious and Nonreligious Cognitive-Behavioral Therapy for the Treatment of Clinical Depression in Religious Individuals," *Journal of Consulting and Clinical Psychology* 60, no. 1 (1992): 102.

21. Jeffrey R. Holland, "Like a Broken Vessel," *Ensign*, November 2013, 42.

Bibliography

American Psychiatric Association. *Diagnostic and Statistical Manual of Mental Disorders*. 3rd ed. Washington, DC: American Psychiatric Association, 1980.

———. *Diagnostic and Statistical Manual of Mental Disorders*. 4th ed. Washington, DC: American Psychiatric Association, 1994.

———. *Diagnostic and Statistical Manual of Mental Disorders*. 5th ed. Arlington, VA: American Psychiatric Publishing, 2013.

Andersen, Neil L. "Children." *Ensign*, November 2011, 28–31.

———. "Faith Is Not by Chance, but by Choice." *Ensign*, November 2015, 65–68.

———. "Never Leave Him." *Ensign*, November 2010, 39–42.

———. "Overcoming the World." *Ensign*, May 2017, 58–61.

Anderson, Jana, and Rajeswari Natrajan-Tyagi. "Understanding the Process of Forgiveness after a Relational Hurt in Christian Marriages." *Journal of Couple and Relationship Therapy* 15, no. 4 (2016): 295–320.

Ashton, Marvin J. *One for the Money: Guide to Family Finance*. Salt Lake City: The Church of Jesus Christ of Latter-day Saints, 1992.

Badr, Hoda, and Cindy L. Carmack Taylor. "Sexual Dysfunction and Spousal Communication in Couples Coping with Prostate Cancer." *Psycho-Oncology* 18 (2009): 735–46.

Ballard, M. Russell. "Be Strong in the Lord, and in the Power of His Might." Devotional address, Brigham Young University, Provo, UT, 3 March 2002. https://speeches.byu.edu/talks /m-russell-ballard_strong-lord-power-might/.

——. "Follow the Prophet." *New Era*, September 2001, 4–6.

——. "Men and Women in the Work of the Lord." *New Era*, April 2014, 2–5.

——. "The Sacred Responsibilities of Parenthood." *Ensign*, March 2006, 26–33.

——. "'This is My Work and Glory.'" *Ensign*, May 2013, 18–21.

Barlow, David H., and V. Mark Durand. *Abnormal Psychology: An Integrative Approach*. 6th ed. Belmont, CA: Wadsworth, 2012.

Bartholomew, Brent H. "A Conversation on Spouse Abuse." *Ensign*, October 1999, 22–27.

Bednar, David A. "The Divinely Designed Pattern of Marriage." Address, Humanum Colloquium, New York City, 9 March 2017. http://www.mormonnewsroom.org/article/elder-bednar -transcript-the-divinely-designed-pattern-marriage.

——. "More Diligent and Concerned at Home." *Ensign*, November 2009, 17–20.

Benson, Ezra Taft. "Fundamentals of Enduring Family Relationships." *Ensign*, November 1982, 59–61.

——. "Our Homes Divinely Ordained." In Conference Report, April 1949, 194–99.

——. "A Sacred Responsibility." *Ensign*, May 1986, 77–78.

Benson, Harry, and Steve McKay. "Couples on the Brink." Marriage Foundation. February 2017. http://www.marriage foundation.org.uk/wp-content/uploads/2017/02/MF-paper -Couples-on-the-brink-FINAL-1.pdf.

Berman, Jennifer, Laura Berman, and Elisabeth Bumiller. *For Women Only: A Revolutionary Guide to Reclaiming Your Sex Life*. 2nd ed. New York: Henry Holt, 2005.

Braithwaite, Scott, Cindy M. Mitchell, Edward A. Selby, Frank D. Fincham. "Trait Forgiveness and Enduring Vulnerabilities: Neuroticism and Enduring Vulnerabilities: Neuroticism and Catastrophizing Influence Relationship Satisfaction via Less Forgiveness." *Personality and Individual Differences* 94 (2016): 237–46.

Brinley, Douglas E. *Toward a Celestial Marriage.* Salt Lake City: Bookcraft, 1986.

Brinley, Douglas E., and Mark D. Ogletree. *First Comes Love.* American Fork, UT: Covenant Communications, 2002.

Brooks, Arthur C. "Why Giving Matters." Devotional address, Brigham Young University, Provo, UT, 24 February 2009. https://speeches.byu.edu/talks/arthur-c-brooks_giving -matters-2/.

Brown, Brené. *Daring Greatly.* New York: Gotham Books, 2012.

Burlingame, Gary M., and Debra Theobald McClendon. "Group Psychotherapy." In *Twenty-First Century Psychotherapies: Contemporary Approaches to Theory and Practice*, edited by Jay L. Lebow, 347–88. Hoboken, NJ: John Wiley and Sons, 2008.

Burns, David D. *Feeling Good: The New Mood Therapy.* New York: William Morrow, 1980.

Bytheway, John. *When Times Are Tough: 5 Scriptures That Will Help You Get through Almost Anything.* Salt Lake City: Deseret Book, 2004.

Bytheway, John, and Kimberly Bytheway. *What We Wish We'd Known When We Were Newlyweds.* Salt Lake City: Bookcraft, 2000.

Call, Vaughn, Susan Sprecher, and Pepper Schwartz. "The Incidence and Frequency of Marital Sex in a National Sample." *Journal of Marriage and Family* 57, no. 3 (August 1995): 639–52.

Chadwick, Bruce A. "Hanging Out, Hooking Up, and Celestial Marriage." Devotional address, Brigham Young University, Provo, UT, 7 May 2002. https://speeches.byu.edu/talks/bruce -a-chadwick_hanging-hooking-celestial-marriage/.

Chapman, Gary. *The Five Love Languages: How to Express Heartfelt Commitment to Your Mate.* Chicago: Northfield, 1995.

Christensen, Joe J. "Greed, Selfishness, and Overindulgence." *Ensign*, May 1999, 9–11.

Christofferson, D. Todd. "Why Marriage, Why Family." *Ensign*, May 2015, 50–53.

The Church of Jesus Christ of Latter-day Saints. "Birth Control." Accessed 2015. https://www.lds.org/topics/birth-control ?lang=eng.

———. "Forgiveness." Accessed 2015. https://www.lds.org/topics /forgiveness?lang=eng.

——. "Hope." Accessed 2014. https://www.lds.org/topics/hope?lang=eng.

——. "Pornography." Accessed 2015. https://www.lds.org/topics/print/pornography?lang=eng.

——. "Provident Living." Accessed 2015. http://www.providentliving.org/.

——. "Tithing." Accessed 2015. https://www.lds.org/topics/tithing?lang=eng.

Clare, David V. "Attaining, Accessing, Using Priesthood Power." Address, BYU Women's Conference, Provo, UT, 2 May 2014. http://ce.byu.edu/cw/womensconference/pdf/archive/2014/David_Clare.pdf.

Clyde, Aileen H. "Charity Suffereth Long." *Ensign*, November 1991, 76–77.

Condie, Spencer J. "A Mighty Change of Heart." *Ensign*, November 1993, 15–17.

Cook, Quentin L. "Foundations of Faith." *Ensign*, May 2017, 127–31.

Daugherty, Jill, and Casey Copen. "Trends in Attitudes about Marriage, Childbearing, and Sexual Behavior: United States, 2002, 2006–2010, and 2011–2013." *National Health Statistics Reports* 92 (2016).

Davies, John J., Brittany Bird, Casey Chaffin, Joseph Eldridge, Angela Hoover, David Law, Jared Munyan, and Keri Shurtliff. "Habitual, Unregulated Media Use and Marital Satisfaction in Recently Married LDS Couples." *Western Journal of Communication* 76, no. 1 (2012): 65–85.

DePaulo, Bella. "What Is the Divorce Rate, Really?" Psychology Today. 2 February 2017. https://www.psychologytoday.com/blog/living-single/201702/what-is-the-divorce-rate-really.

Derrick, Royden G. *Temples in the Last Days*. Salt Lake City: Bookcraft, 1988.

Dew, Jeffrey, Sonya Britt, and Sandra Huston. "Examining the Relationship between Financial Issues and Divorce." *Family Relations* 64, no. 4 (October 2012): 615–28.

Dew, Sheri L. *Go Forward with Faith: The Biography of Gordon B. Hinckley.* Salt Lake City: Deseret Book, 1996.

DiBlasio, Frederick A. "Christ-Like Forgiveness in Marital Counseling: A Clinical Follow-Up of Two Empirical Studies." *Journal of Psychology and Christianity* 29, no. 4 (2010): 291–300.

Doherty, William J. *Take Back Your Marriage: Sticking Together in a World That Pulls Apart.* 2nd ed. New York: Guilford Press, 2013.

Donnelly, Denise A. "Sexually Inactive Marriages." *The Journal of Sex Research* 30, no. 2 (1993): 171–79.

Duckworth, Angela. *Grit: The Power of Passion and Perseverance.* New York: Scribner: Simon and Schuster, 2016.

Dyches, Timothy J. "Wilt Thou Be Made Whole?" *Ensign*, November 2013, 37–39.

Egbert, Nichole, and Denise M. Polk. "Speaking the Language of Relational Maintenance: A Validity Test of Chapman's (1992) Five Love Language." *Communication Research Reports* 23, no 1. (2006): 19–26.

Ellison, Christopher G., Amy M. Burdette, and W. Bradford Wilcox. "The Couple That Prays Together: Race and Ethnicity, Religion, and Relationship Quality among Working-Age Adults." *Journal of Marriage and Family* 72, no. 4 (August 2010): 963–75.

Esplin, Cheryl A. "The Sacrament—a Renewal for the Soul." *Ensign*, November 2014, 12–14.

Evans, Richard Paul. "How I Saved My Marriage." 9 February 2015. http://www.richardpaulevans.com/saved-marriage/#6Fg OUXBlJxdjTGrf.01.

Eyring, Henry B. "'And Thus We See': Helping a Student in a Moment of Doubt." 5 February 1993. https://si.lds.org /bc/seminary/content/library/talks/evening-with/and-thus-we -see_helping-a-student-in-a-moment-of-doubt_eng.pdf.

———. "Our Perfect Example." *Ensign*, November 2009, 70–73.

———. "Safety in Counsel." *Ensign*, June 2008, 5–9.

———. "To My Grandchildren." *Ensign*, November 2013, 69–72.

———. "Transcript: President Eyring Addresses the Vatican Summit on Marriage." 18 November 2014. http://www.mormon newsroom.org/article/transcript-president-eyring-addresses -vatican-summit-marriage.

———. "Trust in God, Then Go and Do." *Ensign*, November 2014, 70–73.

"The Family: A Proclamation to the World." *Ensign*, November 2010, 129.

Faust, James E. "Father, Come Home." *Ensign*, May 1993, 35–37.

Fife, Stephen T., Gerald R. Weeks, and Jessica Stellberg-Filbert. "Facilitating Forgiveness in the Treatment of Infidelity: An Interpersonal Model." *Journal of Family Therapy* 35 (2013): 343–67.

Fincham, Frank D., Ross W. May, and Marcos A. Sanchez-Gonzalez. "Forgiveness and Cardiovascular Functioning in Married Couples." *Couple and Family Psychology: Research and Practice* 4, no. 1 (2015): 39–48.

Fincham, Frank D., Steven R. H. Beach, and Joanne Davila. "Forgiveness and Conflict Resolution in Marriage." *Journal of Family Psychology* 18 (2004): 72–81.

Finlayson-Fife, Jennifer. *Female Sexual Agency in Patriarchal Culture: The Case of Mormon Women.* Ann Arbor, MI: UMI, 2002.

Fournier, Jay C., Robert J. DeRubeis, Steven D. Hollon, Sona Dimidjian, Jay D. Amsterdam, Richard C. Shelton, and Jan Fawcett. "Antidepressant Drug Effects and Depression Severity: A Patient-Level Meta-Analysis." *Journal of the American Medical Association* 303, no. 1 (2010): 47–53.

Frank, Ellen, Carol Anderson, and Debra Rubenstein. "Frequency of Sexual Dysfunction in Normal Couples." *New England Journal of Medicine* 299, no. 3 (1978): 111–15.

Frankl, Viktor E. *Man's Search for Meaning.* 1959. Reprint, New York: Washington Square Press, 1984.

Frederickson, Barbara L., and Marcial F. Losada. "Positive Affect and the Complex Dynamics of Human Flourishing." *American Psychologist* 60, no. 7 (2005): 678–86.

Gates, Susa Young. "The Temple Workers' Excursion." *Young Woman's Journal* 5, no. 11 (August 1894): 512–13.

Gillespie, Brigid M., Wendy Chaboyer, and Marianne Wallis. "Development of a Theoretically Derived Model of Resilience through Concept Analysis." *Contemporary Nurse* 25, no. 1–2 (2007): 124–35.

Glendon, Mary Ann. *Abortion and Divorce in Western Law: American Failures, European Challenges.* Cambridge: Harvard University Press, 1987.

Godoy, Carlos A. "The Lord Has a Plan for Us!" *Ensign*, November 2014, 96–98.

Goodman, Michael A., David C. Dollahite and Loren Marks. "Exploring Transformational Processes and Meaning in LDS Marriages." *Marriage and Family Review* 48, no. 6 (2012): 555–82.

Gottman, John M., Janice Driver, and Amber Tabares. "Repair during Marital Conflict in Newlyweds: How Couples Move from Attack-Defend to Collaboration." *Journal of Family Psychotherapy* 26, no. 2 (2015): 85–108.

Gottman, John M., and Nan Silver. *The Seven Principles for Making Marriage Work*. New York: Three Rivers, 1999.

Gottman, John Mordechai. *What Predicts Divorce: The Relationship between Marital Processes and Marital Outcomes*. New York: Lawrence Erlbaum, 1994.

Grant, Heber J. *Gospel Standards: Selections from the Sermons and Writings of Heber J. Grant*, edited by G. Homer Durham. Salt Lake City: Deseret Book, 1976.

———. *Teachings of Presidents of the Church: Heber J. Grant*. Salt Lake City: The Church of Jesus Christ of Latter-day Saints, 2002.

Hafen, Bruce C. "Covenant Marriage." *Ensign*, November 1996, 26–28.

Haight, David B. "Be a Strong Link." *Ensign*, November 2000, 19–21.

———. "Marriage and Divorce." *Ensign*, May 1984, 12–14.

Hales, Robert D. "Becoming Provident Providers Temporally and Spiritually." *Ensign*, May 2009, 7–10.

———. "The Eternal Family." *Ensign*, November 1996, 64–67.

Hanzal, Alesia, and Chris Segrin. "The Role of Conflict Resolution Styles in Mediating the Relationship between Enduring Vulnerabilities and Marital Quality." *Journal of Family Communication* 9 (2009): 150–69.

Hayes, Steven C., Kirk D. Strosahl, and Kelly G. Wilson. *Acceptance and Commitment Therapy: An Experiential Approach to Behavior Change*. New York: Guilford, 1999.

Herrman, Helen, Donna E. Stewart, Natalia Diaz-Granados, Elena L. Berger, Beth Jackson, and Tracy Yuen. "What Is Resilience?" *Canadian Journal of Psychiatry* 56, no. 5 (2011): 258–65.

Hinckley, Gordon B. "A Conversation with Single Adults." *Ensign*, March 1997, 58–63.

——. "Except the Lord Build the House . . ." *Ensign*, June 1971, 71–72.

——. "Excerpts from Recent Addresses of President Gordon B. Hinckley." *Ensign*, September 1997, 72–73.

——. "I Believe." *Ensign*, August 1992, 2–7.

——. "Loyalty." *Ensign*, May 2003, 58–60.

——. "New Temples to Provide 'Crowning Blessings' of the Gospel." *Ensign*, May 1998, 87–88.

——. "Nurturing a Love That Lasts." *Ensign*, February 2000, 70.

——. "Personal Worthiness to Exercise the Priesthood." *Ensign*, May 2002, 52–59.

——. *Teachings of Presidents of the Church: Gordon B. Hinckley.* Salt Lake City: The Church of Jesus Christ of Latter-day Saints, 2016.

——. "What Are People Asking About Us?" *Ensign*, November 1998, 70–72.

——. "What God Hath Joined Together." *Ensign*, May 1991, 71–74.

Holland, Jeffrey R. "Face to Face with President Eyring and Elder Holland." Worldwide youth broadcast, 4 March 2017. https://www.lds.org/broadcasts/face-to-face/eyring-holland ?lang=eng.

——. "How Do I Love Thee?" Devotional address, Brigham Young University, Provo, UT, 15 February 2000. https://speeches .byu.edu/talks/jeffrey-r-holland_how-do-i-love-thee/.

——. "Keeping Covenants: A Message for Those Who Will Serve a Mission." *New Era*, January 2012, 2–5.

——. "Lessons from Liberty Jail." Devotional address, Brigham Young University, Provo, UT, 7 September 2008. https:// speeches.byu.edu/talks/jeffrey-r-holland_lessons-liberty-jail/.

——. "Like a Broken Vessel." *Ensign*, November 2013, 40–42.

——. "Of Souls, Symbols, and Sacraments." Devotional address, Brigham Young University, Provo, UT, 12 January 1988. https://speeches.byu.edu/talks/jeffrey-r-holland_souls -symbols-sacraments/.

——. "'Remember Lot's Wife': Faith Is for the Future." Devotional address, Brigham Young University, Provo, UT, 13 January 2009. http://speeches.byu.edu/talks/jeffrey-r-holland _remember-lots-wife/.

———. "What I Wish Every New Member Knew—and Every Longtime Member Remembered." *Ensign*, October 2006, 10–16.

Hunter, Howard W. "Being a Righteous Husband and Father." *Ensign*, November 1994, 49–51.

———. "Reading the Scriptures." *Ensign*, November 1979, 64–65.

Huston, Ted L., and Anita L. Vangelisti. "Socioemotional Behavior and Satisfaction in Marital Relationships: A Longitudinal Study." *Journal of Personality and Social Psychology* 61, no. 5 (1991): 721–33.

Jensen, Marlin K. "Loving with the Spirit and the Understanding." Devotional address, Brigham Young University, Provo, UT, 28 March 1993. http://speeches.byu.edu/talks/marlin -k-jensen_loving-spirit-understanding/.

Jones, Gracia N. "My Great-Great-Grandmother, Emma Hale Smith." *Ensign*, August 1992, 30–39.

Joseph, Stephen. *What Doesn't Kill Us: The New Psychology of Posttraumatic Growth*. New York: Basic Books, 2011.

Karney, Benjamin R., and Thomas N. Bradbury. "The Longi-tudinal Course of Marital Quality and Stability: A Review of Theory, Methods, and Research." *Psychological Bulletin* 118, no. 1 (1995): 3–34.

Kelly, Mary P., Donald S. Strassberg, and Charles M. Turner. "Behavorial Assessment of Couples' Communication in Female Orgasmic Disorder." *Journal of Sex and Marital Therapy* 32 (2006): 81–95.

Kennedy, Sheela, and Steven Ruggles. "Breaking Up Is Hard to Count: The Rise of Divorce in the United States, 1980–2010."*Demography* 51, no. 2 (2014): 587–98.

Kimball, Edward L. *Lengthen Your Stride: The Presidency of Spencer W. Kimball*. Salt Lake City: Deseret Book, 2005.

Kimball, Spencer W. "Marriage and Divorce." Devotional address, Brigham Young University, Provo, UT, 7 September 1976. https://speeches.byu.edu/talks/spencer-w-kimball_marriage -divorce/.

———. "Marriage Is Honorable." Fireside address, Brigham Young University, Provo, UT, 30 September 1973. https://speeches .byu.edu/talks/spencer-w-kimball_marriage-honorable/.

———. *The Miracle of Forgiveness*. Salt Lake City: Bookcraft, 1969.

———. "Oneness in Marriage." *Ensign*, March 1977, 3–5.

Komisaruk, Barry R., Carlos Beyer-Flores, and Beverly Whipple. *The Science of Orgasm*. Baltimore: John Hopkins University Press, 2006.

Kornfield, Jack. *The Wise Heart: A Guide to the Universal Teachings of Buddhist Psychology*. New York: Bantam Books, 2009.

Lamb, Stephen E., and Douglas E. Brinley. *Between Husband and Wife: Gospel Perspectives on Marital Intimacy*. Salt Lake City: Covenant Communications, 2000.

Lambert, Michael J., and Benjamin M. Ogles. "The Efficacy and Effectiveness of Psychotherapy." In *Bergin and Garfield's Handbook of Psychotherapy and Behavior Change*, edited by Michael J. Lambert, 139–93. 5th ed. New York: Wiley, 2004.

Lambert, Michael J., Gary M. Burlingame, Val Umphress, Nathan B. Hansen, David A. Vermeersch, Glenn C. Clouse, and Stephen C. Yanchar. "The Reliability and Validity of the Outcome Questionnaire." *Clinical Psychology and Psychotherapy* 3, no. 4 (1996): 249–58.

Lambert, Michael J., Nathan B. Hansen, Val Umphress, Kirk M. Lunnen, John C. Okiishi, Gary M. Burlingame, Jonathan C. Huefner, and C. Reisinger. *Administration and Scoring Manual for the Outcome Questionnaire (OQ 45.2)*. Wilmington, DE: American Professional Credentialing Services, 1996.

Lange, Johann Peter, ed. *Lange's Commentary on the Holy Scriptures: An Exegetical and Doctrinal Commentary*. Vol. 8, *Galatians–2 Timothy*. Grand Rapids, MI: Zondervan, 1960.

LaRocque, Teresia. "Commitment Transforms a Promise into Reality!" *Erickson International* (blog). 7 March 2012. http://erickson.edu/blog/commitment-transforms-a-promise-into-reality/.

Laurenceau, Jean-Philippe, Lisa Feldman Barrett, and Michael J. Rovine. "The Interpersonal Process Model of Intimacy in Marriage: A Daily-Diary and Multilevel Modeling Approach." *Journal of Family Psychology* 19, no. 2 (2005): 314–23.

Ledermann, Thomas, Guy Bodenmann, Myriam Rudaz, and Thomas N. Bradbury. "Stress, Communication, and Marital Quality in Couples." *Family Relations* 59, no. 2 (April 2010): 195–206.

Lee, Harold B. In Conference Report, October 1950, 129–32.

———. *Teachings of Presidents of the Church: Harold B. Lee.* Salt Lake City: The Church of Jesus Christ of Latter-day Saints, 2000.

Lewis, C. S. *Mere Christianity.* New York: HarperCollins, 1952.

Lindau, Stacy Tessler, and Natalia Gavrilova. "Sex, Health, and Years of Sexually Active Life Gained Due to Good Health: Evidence from Two US Population Based Cross Sectional Surveys of Ageing." *BMJ* 340, no. 810 (2010).

Linehan, Marsha M. *Skills Training Manual for Treating Borderline Personality Disorder.* New York: Guilford, 1993.

Martins, Marcus H. "Messiah Script: Episode 1, Part 2." 19 April 2011. http://messiahjesuschrist.org/messiah-the-narrative/messiah-script-2/messiah-script-episode-1-part-2.

Maxwell, Neal A. *All These Things Shall Give Thee Experience.* Salt Lake City: Deseret Book, 1979.

———. "'Apply the Atoning Blood of Christ.'" *Ensign*, November 1997, 22–24.

———. "Hope through the Atonement of Jesus Christ." *Ensign*, November 1998, 61–63.

———. "Sharing Insights from My Life." Devotional address, Brigham Young University, Provo, UT, 12 January 1999. https://speeches.byu.edu/talks/neal-a-maxwell_sharing-insights-life/.

———. *Whom the Lord Loveth: The Journey of Discipleship.* Salt Lake City: Deseret Book, 2003.

McClendon, Richard J., and Bruce A. Chadwick. "Latter-day Saint Families at the Dawn of the Twenty-First Century." In *Helping and Healing Families: Principles and Practices Inspired by "The Family: A Proclamation to the World,"* edited by Craig H. Hart, Lloyd D. Newell, Elaine Walton, and David C. Dollahite, 32–43. Salt Lake City: Deseret Book, 2005.

McClendon, Richard J., and Debra Theobald McClendon. "Commitment to the Covenant: LDS Marriage and Divorce." In *By Divine Design: Best Practices for Family Success and Happiness*, edited by Brent L. Top and Michael A. Goodman, 93–116. Salt Lake City: Deseret Book, 2014.

McConkie, Bruce R. *Mormon Doctrine.* 2nd ed. Salt Lake City: Bookcraft, 1966.

McConkie, Carol F. "Live according to the Words of the Prophets." *Ensign*, November 2014, 77–79.

McCullough, Michael E. "Savoring Life, Past and Present: Explaining What Hope and Gratitude Share in Common." *Psychological Inquiry* 13, no. 4 (2002): 302–4.

McCullough, Michael E., William T. Hoyt, and K. Chris Rachal, "What We Know (and Need to Know) about Assessing Forgiveness Constructs." In *Forgiveness: Theory, Research, and Practice,* edited by Michael E. McCullough, Kenneth I. Pargament, and Carl E. Thoresen, 65–90. New York: Guilford, 2000.

McKay, David O. *Teachings of Presidents of the Church: David O. McKay.* Salt Lake City: The Church of Jesus Christ of Latter-day Saints, 2003.

Meichenbaum, Don. *Roadmap to Resilience: A Guide for Military, Trauma Victims and Their Families.* Clearwater, FL: Institute Press, 2012.

Mintz, Laurie. *Becoming Cliterate: Why Orgasm Equality Matters—and How to Get It.* New York: HarperCollins, 2017.

Monson, Thomas S. "The Power of the Book of Mormon." *Ensign,* May 2017, 86–87.

———. "Priesthood Power." *Ensign,* May 2011, 66–69.

———. "True to the Faith." *Ensign,* May 2006, 18–21.

Moore, Carrie A. "Elder Morrison Gets Service to Humanity Award." *Deseret Morning News,* 2 April 2004. http://www.deseretnews.com/article/595053229/Elder-Morrison-gets-Service-to-Humanity-Award.html.

Morris, George. "Perfection through Obedience." *Improvement Era,* June 1953, 435–36.

Morrison, Alexander B. "Mental Illness in the Family." In *Helping and Healing Families: Principles and Practices Inspired by "The Family: A Proclamation to the World,"* edited by Craig H. Hart, Lloyd D. Newell, Elaine Walton, and David C. Dollahite, 288–94. Salt Lake City: Deseret Book, 2005.

———. "Myths of Mental Illness." *Ensign,* October 2005, 31–35.

Murray, William H. *The Scottish Himalayan Expedition.* London: J. M. Dent, 1951.

Muth, Jon J. "A Heavy Load." In *Zen Shorts,* 30–33. New York: Scholastic Press, 2005.

Nelson, Russell M. "Decisions for Eternity." *Ensign,* November 2013, 106–9.

———. "Drawing the Power of Jesus Christ into Our Lives." *Ensign*, May 2017, 39–42.

———. "Joy and Spiritual Survival." *Ensign*, November 2016, 81–84.

———. "Lessons from Eve." *Ensign*, November 1987, 86–89.

———. "Nurturing Marriage." *Ensign*, May 2006, 36–38.

———. "Perfection Pending." *Ensign*, November 1995, 86–88.

Nibley, Hugh. *Temple and Cosmos.* Vol. 12 of *Collected Works of Hugh Nibley.* Salt Lake City: Deseret Book, 1992.

Oaks, Dallin H. "Divorce." *Ensign*, May 2007, 70–73.

———. "The Keys and Authority of the Priesthood." *Ensign*, May 2014, 49–52.

———. "Loving Others and Living with Differences." *Ensign*, November 2014, 25–28.

OECD. "The Decline in Crude Marriage Rates between 1970 and 2009." Graph illustration. In *SF3.1: Marriage and Divorce Rates.* 24 January 2014. http://www.oecd.org/els/family/SF3_1 _Marriage_and_divorce_rate_Jan2014.pdf.

Ogden, Gina. *Expanding the Practice of Sex Therapy: An Integrative Model for Exploring Desire and Intimacy.* London: Routledge, 2013.

Ogletree, Mark D. "Speak, Listen, and Love." *Ensign*, February 2014, 14–17.

Olson, Jonathan R., James P. Marshall, H. Wallace Goddard, and David G. Schramm. "Shared Religious Beliefs, Prayers, and Forgiveness as Predictors of Marital Satisfaction." *Family Relations* 64, no. 4 (October 2015): 519–33.

Orman, Suze. *Women and Money: Owning the Power to Control Your Destiny.* New York: Speigel and Grau, 2007.

Packer, Boyd K. *The Holy Temple.* Salt Lake City: Bookcraft, 1980.

———. "The Plan of Happiness." *Ensign*, May 2015, 26–28.

———. "The Shield of Faith." *Ensign*, May 1995, 7–9.

———. "The Twelve Apostles." *Ensign*, November 1996, 6–8.

Pansera, Carolina, and Jennifer La Guardia. "The Role of Sincere Amends and Perceived Partner Responsiveness in Forgiveness." *Personal Relationships* 19, no. 4 (2012): 696–711.

Parry, Donald W. *Angels: Agents of Light, Love, and Power.* Salt Lake City: Deseret Book, 2013.

Pelluchi, Sara, Giorgia F. Paleari, Camillo Regalia, and Frank D. Fincham. "Self-Forgiveness in Romantic Relationships: It Matters to Both of Us." *Journal of Family Psychology* 27, no. 4 (2013): 541–49.

Perry, L. Tom. "Becoming Goodly Parents." *Ensign*, November 2012, 26–28.

Perry, Samuel L. "Spouse's Religious Commitment and Marital Quality: Clarifying the Role of Gender." *Social Science Quarterly* 97, no. 2 (June 2016): 476–90.

Pew Research Center. "Marriage and Divorce Rates, 1867–2011." Graph illustration. In Paul Waldman, "Marriage Is What Brings Us Together Today." *American Prospect* (blog), 4 April 2013. http://prospect.org/article/marriage-what-brings-us-together-today.

Pratt, Parley P. *Autobiography of Parley P. Pratt*, edited by Parley P. Pratt Jr. Salt Lake City: Deseret Book, 1938.

Preach My Gospel. Salt Lake City: The Church of Jesus Christ of Latter-day Saints, 2004.

"The Privilege of Giving a Generous Fast Offering." *Ensign*, May 1986, 96.

Propst, L. Rebecca, Richard Ostrom, Philip Watkins, Terri Dean, and David Mashburn. "Comparative Efficacy of Religious and Nonreligious Cognitive-Behavioral Therapy for the Treatment of Clinical Depression in Religious Individuals." *Journal of Consulting and Clinical Psychology* 60, no. 1 (1992): 94–103.

Ramsey, Dave. "Dave's Take on Separate Checking Accounts." 2015. http://www.daveramsey.com/index.cfm?event=askdave/&intContentItemId=120524.

Rasband, Ronald A. "Let the Holy Spirit Guide." *Ensign*, May 2017, 93–96.

Reeves, Linda S. "Protection from Pornography—a Christ-Focused Home." *Ensign*, May 2014, 15–17.

Reid, Rory C., and Dan Gray. *Confronting Your Spouse's Pornography Problem*. Sandy, UT: Silverleaf, 2006.

Reis, Harry T., and Phillip Shaver. "Intimacy as an Interpersonal Process." In *Handbook of Personal Relationships*, edited by Steve Duck, 367–89. Chichester, England: Wiley and Sons, 1988.

Rohn, Jim. *The Seasons of Life*. Grapevine, TX: Jim Rohn International, 2011.

Romney, Marion G. In Conference Report, April 1960, 110–13.

Samuelson, Cecil O., Jr. "Testimony." *Ensign*, May 2011, 40–41.

Schaff, Philip. *Modern Christianity. The German Reformation*. Vol. 7 of *History of the Christian Church*. Grand Rapids, MI: W. M. Eerdmans, 1910.

Scott, Richard G. "Acquiring Spiritual Knowledge." *Ensign*, November 1993, 86–88.

———. "The Eternal Blessings of Marriage." *Ensign*, May 2011, 94–97.

———. "To Acquire Knowledge and the Strength to Use It Wisely." Devotional address, Brigham Young University, Provo, UT, 23 January 2001. https://speeches.byu.edu/talks/richard-g -scott_acquire-knowledge-strength-use-wisely/.

———. "Using the Supernal Gift of Prayer." *Ensign*, May 2007, 8–11.

"Selected Church Policies and Guidelines." In *Handbook 2: Administering the Church*, 179–97. Salt Lake City: The Church of Jesus Christ of Latter-day Saints, 2010.

Seligman, Martin E. P. "Building Resilience." *Harvard Business Review* 89, no. 4 (April 2011): 104–6.

Seligman, Martin E. P., Tracy A. Steen, Nansook Park, and Christopher Peterson. "Positive Psychology Progress: Empirical Validation of Interventions July–August 2005." *American Psychologist* 60, no. 5 (2005): 410–21.

Smith, George A. *Teachings of Presidents of the Church: George Albert Smith*. Salt Lake City: The Church of Jesus Christ of Latter-day Saints, 2011.

Smith, Joseph. *History of the Church of Jesus Christ of Latter-day Saints*. Vol. 5. Salt Lake City: Deseret Book, 1950.

———. In *Lectures on Faith*. Salt Lake City: Deseret Book, 1985.

———. *Teachings of Presidents of the Church: Joseph Smith*. Salt Lake City: The Church of Jesus Christ of Latter-day Saints, 2007.

Smith, Joseph F. *Gospel Doctrine*. 5th ed. Salt Lake City: Deseret Book, 1939.

———. *Teachings of Presidents of the Church: Joseph F. Smith*. Salt Lake City: The Church of Jesus Christ of Latter-day Saints, 2011.

Smith, Joseph Fielding. *Teachings of Presidents of the Church: Joseph Fielding Smith*. Salt Lake City: The Church of Jesus Christ of Latter-day Saints, 2013.

Snow, Lorenzo. *Teachings of Presidents of the Church: Lorenzo Snow*. Salt Lake City: The Church of Jesus Christ of Latter-day Saints, 2011.

Sorensen, David E. "Forgiveness Will Change Bitterness to Love." *Ensign*, May 2003, 10–12.

Stein, David M., and Michael J. Lambert. "Graduate Training in Psychotherapy: Are Therapy Outcomes Enhanced?" *Journal of Consulting and Clinical Psychology* 63, no. 2 (1995): 182–96.

Stevenson, Gary E. "Look to the Book, Look to the Lord." *Ensign*, November 2016, 44–47.

Tan, Siang-Yang. "Resilience and Posttraumatic Growth: Empirical Evidence and Clinical Applications from a Christian Perspective." *Journal of Psychology and Christianity* 32, no. 4 (2013): 358–64.

Taylor, John. *Teachings of Presidents of the Church: John Taylor*. Salt Lake City: The Church of Jesus Christ of Latter-day Saints, 2011.

ten Boom, Corrie. *The Hiding Place*. New York: Bantam Books, 1971.

Toussaint, Loren L., and Alyssa C. D. Cheadle. "Unforgiveness and the Broken Heart: Unforgiving Tendencies, Problems Due to Unforgiveness, and 12-Month Prevalence of Cardiovascular Health Conditions." In *Religion and Psychology*, edited by Michael T. Evans and Emma D. Walker, 107–21. New York: Nova, 2009.

Toussaint, Loren L., Amy D. Owen, and Alyssa Cheadle. "Forgive to Live: Forgiveness, Health, and Longevity." *Journal of Behavioral Medicine* 35, no. 4 (2012): 375–86.

Uchtdorf, Dieter F. "Continue in Patience." *Ensign*, May 2010, 56–59.

———. "Four Titles." *Ensign*, May 2013, 58–61.

———. "Grateful in Any Circumstances." *Ensign*, May 2014, 70–77.

———. "In Praise of Those Who Save." *Ensign*, May 2016, 77–80.

———. "Lord, Is it I?" *Ensign*, November 2014, 56–59.

———. "The Merciful Obtain Mercy." *Ensign*, May 2012, 70–77.

Ulrich, Wendy. "'Stop it' and Forgive." 5 June 2012. http://www.ksl.com/index.php?sid=20705426&nid=481.

Vaillant, George E. *The Triumphs of Experience: The Men of the Harvard Grant Study*. Cambridge: Belknap, 2012.

Vespa, Jonathan. *The Changing Economics and Demographics of Young Adulthood: 1975–2016*. Washington, DC: US Census Bureau, April 2017. https://www.census.gov/content/dam/Census/library/publications/2017/demo/p20-579.pdf.

Vieselmeyer, Julie, Jeff Holguin, and Amy Mezulis. "The Role of Resilience and Gratitude in Posttraumatic Stress and Growth Following a Campus Shooting." *Psychological Trauma: Theory, Research, Practice, and Policy* 9, no. 1 (2017): 62–69.

Vohs, Kathleen, Catrin Finkenauer, and Roy F. Baumeister. "The Sum of Friends' and Lovers' Self-Control Scores Predicts Relationship Quality." *Social Psychological and Personal Science* 2, no. 2 (2010): 138–45.

Wade, Nathaniel G., Donna C. Bailey, and Philip Shaffer. "Helping Clients Heal: Does Forgiveness Make a Difference?" *Professional Psychology: Research and Practice* 36, no. 6 (2005): 634–41.

Wade, Nathaniel G., and Everett L. Worthington. "Overcoming Unforgiveness: Is Forgiveness the Only Way to Deal with Unforgiveness?" *Journal of Counseling and Development* 81, no. 3 (2003): 343–53.

Waite, Linda J., Don Browning, William J. Doherty, Maggie Gallagher, Ye Luo, and Scott M. Stanley. *Does Divorce Make People Happy? Findings from a Study of Unhappy Marriages*. New York: Institute for American Values, 2002.

Waite, Linda J., and Maggie Gallagher. *The Case for Marriage*. New York: Doubleday, 2000.

Walker, Donald F., Everett L. Worthington Jr., Aubrey L. Gartner, Richard Gorsuch, and Evalin Rhodes Hanshew. "Religious Commitment and Expectations about Psychotherapy among Christian Clients." *Psychology of Religion and Spirituality* 3, no. 2 (2011): 98–114.

Wallerstein, Judith S., and Sandra Blakeslee. *The Good Marriage: How and Why Love Lasts*. New York: Grand Central Publishing, 1995.

Wheat, Ed, and Gaye Wheat. *Intended for Pleasure: Sex Technique and Sexual Fulfillment in Christian Marriage*. 3rd ed. Grand Rapids, MI: Revell, 1977.

Whitmer, David. *An Address to All Believers in Christ: By a Witness to the Divine Authenticity of the Book of Mormon*. Richmond, MO: David Whitmer, 1887.

Williams, John W., Kathryn Rost, Allen J. Dietrich, Mary C. Ciotti, Stephen J. Zyzanksi, and John Cornell. "Primary Care Physicians' Approach to Depressive Disorders: Effects of Physician Specialty and Practice Structure." *Arch Fam Med* 8, no. 1 (1999): 58–67.

Wilson, Kelly G., Emily K. Sandoz, and Jennifer Kitchens. "The Valued Living Questionnaire: Defining and Measuring Valued Action within a Behavioral Framework." *Psychological Record* 60, no. 2 (2010): 249–72.

Wirthlin, Joseph B. "Come What May, and Love It." *Ensign*, November 2008, 26–28.

———. "Earthly Debts, Heavenly Debts." *Ensign*, May 2004, 40–43.

———. "The Great Commandment." *Ensign*, November 2007, 28–30.

Woodruff, Wilford W. *Teachings of Presidents of the Church: Wilford Woodruff.* Salt Lake City: The Church of Jesus Christ of Latter-day Saints, 2004.

Wu, Hui-Ching. "The Protective Effects of Resilience and Hope on Quality of Life of the Families Coping with the Criminal Traumatization of One of Its Members." *Journal of Clinical Nursing* 20, no. 13–14 (2011): 1906–15.

Young, Brigham. *Manuscript History of Brigham Young, 1846–1847,* compiled by Elden J. Watson. Salt Lake City: Smith Secretarial Service, 1971.

———. "Speech Delivered by President B. Young, in the City of Joseph, April 6, 1845," *Millennial Star* 6, no. 8 (1 October 1845): 119–23.

———. *Teachings of Presidents of the Church: Brigham Young.* Salt Lake City: The Church of Jesus Christ of Latter-day Saints, 1997.

Index

A

abuse, 51, 52–57, 105, 109, 387. *See also* personal distress

acceptance, 46, 50–51, 73, 101, 316–17, 318

active constructive communication, 138–39

active destructive communication, 138–39

Adam and Eve, 132

addiction, 66, 110, 115–16, 364

adjustment period, 1–2, 44, 46–47, 294

admiration, 152–53, 197

adoption, 307

adult children, financial support for, 252–56

adversity. *See* opposition; resilience

age, and sexual relations, 176–77, 179

agency, 83–84, 273, 394–96

alcoholism, 66

allowances, personal, 245–46

Alma, 89, 133–34, 195

alone time, 146

Amazon, 305

Amulek, 89, 133–34

angels, protection from destroying, 222–23

anorexia, 366–67

antidepressants, 375–76, 395

anxiety, 1–2, 27, 117–18, 375, 376

apologizing, 101–4, 206, 207–8, 284

apostasy, 302

apostles. *See* prophets and apostles

arguing, 195, 204, 206, 207, 211

assets, 243–44

Atonement, 77, 85, 101, 108, 119, 372

attraction, 168

B

bad-mouthing spouses, 196–97

bank account, emotional, 147–49, 151

bank accounts, separate, 246–47
baptism, 334–37
Barua, Dipama, 43
bed and bedroom, uses of, 174
bed debt, 244
bedtimes, 201–2
Big Dipper, 348
biking, 159
bishops, and mental illness, 371–72, 388
Book of Mormon, 265–66, 269–72, 282–84, 333
Brooks, Arthur, 237–38, 239
brother of Jared, 283–84
budgeting, 244–48

C

car accident, 238
car repair, 249–50
cars, purchasing, 240, 242–43
celestial kingdom, 327–28, 357–58
charity, 53, 175–79, 318, 356
chastity, 183
children
    challenges of, 61–62, 63, 66–70, 80–81, 86–89, 90, 91
    difficulty conceiving, 307
    and family scripture study, 272
    financial education of, 251–56
    and power of creation, 169
    revelation concerning, 292–94
    serving as example for, 319
    teaching forgiveness to, 103
Christiansen, ElRay L., 353
Christmas gifts, 144, 251

chronically difficult marriages, 48–52, 275–77, 280
chronic defensiveness, 200–201
church activity, 159, 263–64. See also word of God
church callings, trials in, 61–62, 66–70, 80–81, 86–89, 90, 91, 134, 317
Clare, David V., 287
clean pain, 120–21
coexistence, 131–32
cognitive distortions, 74–75
cognitive theory, 74
cohabitation, 8, 12, 264
commitment
    in abusive marriages, 52–57
    and behavior, 35–40
    in chronically difficult marriages, 48–52
    cultural difficulties regarding, 30–32
    importance of, 322
    and LDS doctrine, 32–34
    in new marriages, 44–48
    patience in, 40–42
    principle of, 29–30
    selflessness in, 42–43
    temple attendance and, 345–46
    and trust, 34–35
    as work, 27–29
commitment for mental health treatment, 397
communication
    levels of, 139–40
    through listening, 140–43
    through love languages, 143–47
    through talking, 136–40
    types of, 138–39
compensation, for loss, 51–52

complaint(s)
  bringing up, 211
  versus criticism, 195–96
compulsive behavior, 369–70
concentration camps, 85, 107–8
conditional forgiveness, 101–3
conflict, 193, 227
  apologies in, 207–8
  causes of, 194–203
  contempt as cause of, 196–97
  criticism as cause of, 195–96
  defensiveness as cause of,
    197–201
  following Christ's example in,
    222–24
  humility in, 219–24
  and negative affectivity, 202–3
  pausing before responding
    in, 209
  and perpetual issues, 224–27
  pondering after, 284
  prayer through, 275–77, 280
  presence of Holy Ghost
    during, 332–34
  prevention against, 208–19
  principles versus preferences
    in, 212–19
  and process-focused
    commentary, 205–7
  regarding finances, 232–33
  repair attempts for, 204–8
  and showing concern for
    spouse's well-being, 320
  stonewalling as cause of,
    201–2
  temple attendance and
    overcoming, 352–55
  and timing of discussions,
    210–12
contempt, 196–97
contracts, breaking, 9–10
Corianton, 195

counsel, refusing, 139
counseling, 55–56, 57, 111, 372,
  376–86, 396
couple pondering, 285–88
couple prayer, 276, 277–81
couple scripture study, 268–69,
  271–72
courtship. See dates and dating
covenants, 334, 336
creation, through sexual
  relations, 169
crisis intervention, 54, 394–97
criticism, 195–96, 198, 318
culture, and commitment,
  30–32

D

dancing, 117–18
dates and dating, 154, 155–57,
  318–19
dead, redemption of, 284
debt, 239–44, 314
debt-elimination calendar, 244
defensiveness, 197–201, 219
dementia, 375
depression, 370–71, 374, 395
destroying angels, protection
  from, 222–23
difficult marriages, commitment
  in, 48–52
dirty pain, 120–21
disgust, 196–97
disposability of marriage, 31
distraction, and building
  resilience, 72
distress, and mental illness,
  365–67
diversity, 213–19
divine nature, sexuality and,
  167–68

divorce
  among Latter-day Saints,
    13–14
  choosing, 57
  finances and, 232
  happiness in, 10–11
  just causes for, 53–54
  as marriage example, 68
  present law and attitude
    toward, 11–12
divorce laws, no-fault, 8
divorce rates, 5–6, 7fig.
doctrine
  commitment and LDS, 32–34
  of priesthood, 343–44
  of prophets and apostles,
    300–303
domestic violence, 52–57
"Don't Buy Stuff You Can't
  Afford" skit, 239–40
dream(s)
  of author, 68–69
  of Brigham Young, 337–39
  hidden, 224–25, 226
  letting go, 73
drug abuse, 364
dyadic forgiveness, 100
dysfunction, psychological,
  364–65, 374

E

Easter talk, 289–90
education, funding, 252
Education Week, 286–87
Elijah, 309–10
emotional bank account, 147–
  49, 151
emotional intimacy, 131–32,
  162–63

emotional intimacy (continued)
  importance of, 135–36
  and love languages, 143–47
  and partnership and support,
    132–35
  through building friendship,
    152–53
  through building positive
    sentiment, 147–51
  through continued dating,
    155–57
  through creating shared
    meaning, 158–62
  through listening, 140–43
  through noticing positive
    efforts, 151–52
  through purposefully building
    your relationship, 153–54
  through talking, 136–40
emotional reasoning, 75
emotional regulation, 202–3
endowment, 349
entitlement, in children, 252,
  255–56
episodic forgiveness, 100
eternal life, 355–58
eternal marriage, 12, 32–34,
  308, 315, 318–19, 344–45,
  348–52. See also sealing
Evans, Keri, 221–22
Evans, Richard Paul, 221–22
exaltation, 33, 81–90, 349, 357
extroversion, 217

F

faith
  in accepting prophetic
    counsel, 302–3
  in Jesus Christ, 328–32

family
    prophetic counsel on, 315–22
    responsibilities in, 345–46
    Satan's attack on, 31
    as support, 66
"Family: A Proclamation to the
    World, The," 306–7, 345–46
family scripture study, 272
fast offerings, 236–39
fatherhood, 36, 345–46
finances, 231–33, 256–57. *See
    also* provident living
    and dating, 155
    pondering decisions
        regarding, 285–86
    as shared responsibility,
        233–36
First Vision, 300
fondness, 152–53, 197
forgiveness, 97–99, 125–26
    and avoiding offense, 109–11
    defined, 99–103
    fruits of, 123–25
    in marriage, 105–8
    offering, 103–4
    for ourselves, 118–19
    scripture journal entries
        concerning, 291–92
    withholding, 112–18, 119–21
    working together toward,
        111–12
Frankl, Viktor, 85
friendship, 152–53

G

generosity, 253–55
gifts, 144, 251
goals, achieving, 154
God. *See also* word of God
    as Creator, 169
    as partner in marriage, 262

God (*continued*)
    submitting to will of, 311–15
    trust in, 62
    unity with, 172–75
good, noticing, 151–52
good debt, 243–44
gospel principles and
    ordinances, 327–28, 358
    baptism and sacrament,
        334–37
    faith in Jesus Christ, 328–32
    gift of Holy Ghost, 337–43
    oath and covenant of the
        priesthood, 343–46
    repentance, 332–34
    temple ordinances, 345–58
Grant study, 135–36
gratitude, 78–80, 137, 226
group therapy, 378
growth. *See* posttraumatic growth

H

handyman skills, 249–50
happiness, 5, 10–11, 43–44, 135–
    36, 232, 273. *See also* joy
"happy list," 79
health. *See also* mental health and
    illness
    forgiveness's impact on, 123
    and sexual relations, 179
    unforgiveness's impact on,
        119–20
heart, listening with, 142–43
hidden dreams, 224–25, 226
hobbies, 73, 159–62
Holland, Jeffrey R., 279
Holland, Patricia, 279
Holy Ghost
    forgiveness and, 106–7
    gift of, 337–40

Holy Ghost (*continued*)
    and nighttime revelation, 285
    and pondering as couple,
        285–86
    recording promptings from,
        289–94
    repentance and, 332–34
    and scripture study, 267–68
    sexual relations and guidance
        of, 184
    step-by-step counsel from,
        341–43
home repair and improvement,
    249–50
hope, 76–78
house, buying, 241–42
household responsibilities, 36
hugs, 204
humility, 219–24, 302–3, 323

I

infertility, 307
infidelity, 100–101
insurance, for mental health
    treatment, 386–88
intentionality, 36–40
Internet use, and stonewalling,
    201–2
interpersonal process model of
    intimacy, 140–41
intimacy. *See* emotional
    intimacy; sexual relations
introversion, 217
involuntary commitment, 397
I-statements, 220

J

Jared, brother of, 283–84
Jensen, Marlin K., 97–98
Jesus Christ
    faith in, 328–32
    following example of, 50–51,
        52, 222–24
    and forgiveness, 108, 125
    hope in, 77–78
    lacks contempt for others, 197
    as priority, 264
    remembering, 334–35
    turning to, 225
Job, 64–66
Joseph of Egypt, 85–86, 248
journaling exercises, 38, 265
joy, 90–92, 171. *See also*
    happiness
justice, and withholding
    forgiveness, 113–14, 116

L

labeling, 75
Laman and Lemuel, 300, 302
Lehi, 198–200, 264, 282–83,
    302
Liberty Jail, 81–82
life, purpose of, 357
listening, fostering emotional
    intimacy through, 140–43
loss, compensation for, 51–52
love
    creating feelings of, 147–51
    expressing, 137, 143, 145–46,
        148, 276
    feeding, 321
    prayer for, 275

love languages, 143–47, 151–52
loyalty, 35, 196–97

M

magnification, 75
marriage(s)
abusive, 52–57
among Latter-day Saints,
12–14
chronically difficult, 48–52,
275–77, 280
current state of, 4–8
decline in, 5, 6–12
delay of first, 6–8, 9fig.
disposability of, 31
God as partner in, 262
influence of religious beliefs
and participation on,
263–64
new, 44–48
in plan of salvation, 3, 22–23,
32–34
preparing for successful, 64
present law and attitude
toward, 11–12
prophetic counsel on, 315–22
requirements for, 2–3
medications, for mental illness,
375–76, 386
meditation, 282. See also
pondering
meekness, 219–24, 302–3, 323
mental health and illness
classification groups for, 368
crises stemming from, 394–97
defining, 364–67
determining need for
professional help with,
369–71
labels and diagnoses for, 368
resilience and, 92

mental health and illness
(continued)
seeking treatment for, 375–
76, 379–81, 389–93
spouse's refusal of treatment
for, 393–94
symptoms of, 372–75
treatment process for, 381–86
understanding, 363
unforgiveness's impact on,
119–20
mental health professionals,
371–72, 376–79, 382, 386–93
mental rests, 73
minimization, 75
mirrors, in temple, 352, 355–58
missionary companionships,
133–34
monks, allegory of, 114
Monson, Thomas S., 352–55
monthly allowances, 245–46
Morning Five, 266
mortality, purpose of, 357
mortgage, paying off, 314
Moses, 300–301
Mosiah, sons of, 40–41
motherhood
lacking intellectual
stimulation in, 286–88
responsibilities of, 345–46
stay-at-home mothers, 235,
311–14
trials of, 61–62, 66–70,
80–81, 86–89, 90, 91
moving on, 114–15
mundane acts, 36–37

N

Naaman, 150
National Domestic Violence
Hotline, 54

negative affectivity, 202–3
Nephi, 32, 104, 266, 283, 300–301, 302, 341
Nephite culture, 32
neurocognitive disorder, 375
new marriages, 44–48
night, as time of revelation, 285
no-fault divorce laws, 8
North Star, 348

O

oath, of Nephi and Zoram, 32
oath and covenant of the priesthood, 343–46
offense, avoiding, 109–11
offense-specific forgiveness, 100
opposition, 48, 62. *See also* posttraumatic growth; resilience; trials
ordinances. *See* gospel principles and ordinances
overgeneralization, 75

P

pain
    clean and dirty, 120–21
    and withholding forgiveness, 113–18
panic disorder, 375, 376
passive constructive communication, 138, 139
passive destructive communication, 138, 139
past, dwelling on, 114–17
patience, 40–42, 141, 291, 340, 352
Paul, 124–25, 225
pauses, before responding, 209
perfection, 357

perpetual issues, 227. *See also* chronically difficult marriages
personal distress, 365–67. *See also* abuse
personality differences, 2, 213–19
personality disorders, 367
personal prayer, 275–76
personal revelation, 49–50
personal scripture study, 271
personal spending money, 245–46
physical attraction, 168
plan of salvation, 3, 22–23, 32–34, 308, 330–31
Polaris, 348
pondering, 281–88
pornography, 100, 115–16, 184
positive efforts, noticing, 151–52
positive psychology, 74, 148–49
positive sentiment, 147–51
positivity-to-negativity ratio, 50
posttraumatic growth, 80–81, 92–93. *See also* resilience
    exaltation and, 81–90
    joy and, 90–92
prayer, 273–75
    pondering and answers to, 283–84
    for your spouse, 275–77
    with your spouse, 277–80
    for your spouse with your spouse, 280–81
preemptive repairs, 204
preferences, versus principles, 212–19
pregnancy, and sexual relations, 179
prescription drugs, for mental illness, 375–76, 386, 395
prices, finding lower, 250
pride, 214–15, 219

priesthood, oath and covenant of, 343–46
priesthood authority, 344
priesthood keys, 344
principles, versus preferences, 212–19. *See also* gospel principles and ordinances
prison-temple experience, 81–90
privatization of marriage, 11
process-focused commentary, 205–7
prophets and apostles, 299–300. *See also* word of God
   blessings of heeding, 308, 323
   counsel of, on marriage and family, 315–22
   difficulty in heeding, 309–15
   doctrine of, 300–303
   as seers, 303–7
provident living. *See also* finances
   avoiding debt, 239–44
   budgeting, 244–48
   building up reserve fund, 248–51
   teaching family members, 251–56
   tithes and offerings, 236–39
psychiatrists, 386
psychological disorders. *See* mental health and illness
psychotherapy, 372, 376–86, 396
punctuality, 42
purposeful offense, 110–11

Q

quality time, 146
quirks, 369–70

R

rearview mirrors, 41
recreation, 73, 159–62
redemption of dead, 284
relationship, purposely building, 153–54
Renlund, Dale G., 262
Renlund, Ruth Lybbert, 262
repair attempts, 204–8
repentance, 100, 105–6, 332–34, 370–71
resentment, 111, 116, 117–18
reserve, building up, 248–51
resilience, 62–70, 92–93. *See also* posttraumatic growth
   factors influencing, 74
   gratitude in strengthening, 78–80
   hope in strengthening, 76–78
   joy and, 90–92
   mental health and, 92
   strategies for building, 70–76
   through trials, 61–62
respect, contempt and lack of, 196–97
revelation. *See also* word of God
   at night, 285
   opportunities for growth and, 81–82
   received line upon line, 341–43
   recording, 19, 289–94
   regarding difficult marital relationships, 49–50
   through Holy Ghost, 339–40
   through prayer, 278

S

sacrament, 174–75, 334–37
sacrament meeting, 36–37, 67

safety planning, 54

salvation, 330

same-sex attraction, 175

Sariah, 198–200

Satan

  attacks families, 31

  deception of, 305

  surprise as tactic of, 304

satellites, 305

Saturday Night Live skit, 239–40

Saul of Tarsus, 124–25, 225

saving money, 248–51

saving ordinances, 334

scripture journal, 290–92

scriptures. *See also* Book of
  Mormon

  examples of pondering in,
    282–84

  sexual relations in, 172–74

scripture study, 265–66

  Book of Mormon as center of,
    269–72

  principles of effective, 266–
    69

sealing, 33–34, 315, 318–19,
  344–45, 349–58. *See also*
  eternal marriage

seers, prophets and apostles as,
  303–7

self-control, 37–40

self-denial, 239–42

self-forgiveness, 118–19

selfishness

  in children, 252, 255–56

  effects of, 322

  and poor marital
    commitment, 9–12

  and sexual relations, 176,
    177–78

selflessness

  in commitment, 42–43

  in marriage, 9, 320–21

  and sexual relations, 177,
    184–85

self-soothing, 70–72

Seligman, Martin, 74, 80

separate bank accounts, 246–47

separation, 55, 56–57

service

  as aspect of baptismal
    covenant, 336–37

  and eternal life, 356

  listening as, 141

  as love language, 145–46,
    320, 321

sex therapy, 187–88, 390

sexual dysfunction, 177, 184–88

sexual relations, 167–68

  appropriate behavior in,
    183–85

  charity in, 175–79

  creation through, 169

  finding solutions in, 182–83

  scheduling, 180–82

  spiritual purposes of, 169–79

  timing and frequency of,
    179–80

  and unity between husband
    and wife, 170–72

  and unity with God, 172–75

shared meaning, creating,
  158–62

ship, Nephi commanded to
  build, 341

shuv / shub, 332

side mirrors, 41

silent treatment, 201–2, 205–6

single-income households, 235

single mothers, 64

small and simple things, 36–37, 149–51

Smith, Emma, 107, 158, 332–33

Smith, Jessie Evans, 149–50

Smith, Joseph
    appears to Brigham Young in dream, 337–39
    asks for wife's forgiveness, 107, 332–33
    as pattern for calling of prophets and apostles, 300
    resilience of, 66
    revelation given to, in Liberty Jail, 81–82
    shared meaning between Emma and, 158

Smith, Joseph F., 284

Smith, Joseph Fielding, 149–50

social gatherings, 217

soft heart, listening with, 142–43

sons of Mosiah, 40–41

specificity, in building positivity and friendship, 154

spending money, personal, 245–46

spirituality, evaluating values and goals concerning, 265

spiritual power, 89–90

sports, 159, 161–62

stay-at-home mothers, 235, 311–14

stonewalling, 201–2, 205–6

stress, dealing with, 65

T

talking, fostering emotional intimacy through, 136–40

temple attendance, 316, 347, 348, 349, 351, 352–55

temple ordinances, 346–49
    and eternal life, 355–58
    learning from, 349–55

ten Boom, Corrie, 107–8

therapy, 55–56, 57, 111, 372, 376–86, 396

thinking traps, 74–75

THRIVE self-help model, 75–76

time, quality, 146

time management, 42

time-outs, from conflict resolution, 211–12

timing, for discussions, 210–12

tithes and offerings, 236–39, 251

tolerance, 46, 50–51, 73, 316–17, 318

trait forgiveness, 100

transformation, 52

trials, and mental illness, 369. *See also* posttraumatic growth; resilience

trust, and commitment, 34–35

two witnesses, law of, 286, 339–40

U

unforgiveness, 112–18, 119–21

unity
    in finances, 246–48
    in sexual relations, 170–75

unrepentance, 370–71
unresolved issues, 117–18
Ursa Major, 348

V

vengeance, and withholding
  forgiveness, 113–14, 116

W

washings and anointings, 349
watchmen and watchtowers,
  303–5
weaknesses, patience with, 41–42
wealth, and charitable giving,
  237–38
widow of Zarephath, 309–10
will of God, submitting to,
  311–15
word of God, 261–64, 294–95.
  See also prophets and apostles;
  revelation
    pondering, 281–88
    prayer, 273–81
    recording spiritual
      promptings, 289–94
    scripture study, 265–72
work
  as priority, 39–40
  shared meaning in, 159–60
  and stay-at-home mothers,
    235, 311–14
  stress caused by, 65
World War II, 85, 107–8

Y

Young, Brigham, 337–39
young adult children, financial
  support for, 252–56

Z

Zarephath, widow of, 309–10
Zeniff, 342
Zoram, 32

About the Authors

DEBRA THEOBALD McCLENDON was born and raised in San Jose, California. She found her passions were helping individuals and families, and mentoring students through teaching. She received a bachelor's degree in family science, a master's degree in marriage and family therapy, and a PhD in clinical psychology. She has spent many years teaching in the LDS Church, worked as an adjunct psychology instructor for Utah Valley University and Brigham Young University, and given presentations at BYU Women's Conference and Education Week. She has coauthored book chapters and articles on outcome assessment and group therapy in the academic community. She works as a licensed psychologist in the state of Utah with individuals, couples, and families. She enjoys working out, doing puzzles, sitting on the deck in the evening with her husband, reading to her children, and eating mint dark chocolate.

RICHARD J. McCLENDON is an associate director of Institutional Assessment and Analysis at Brigham Young University. He taught in the Department of Sociology at BYU and was an adjunct professor in Religious Education. He spent several years teaching in CES as a seminary and institute instructor. He received his PhD in sociology from Brigham Young University, where his focus of study was on LDS returned missionaries, families, and education. He is the author and coauthor of several books and publications including *Shield of Faith: The Power of Religion in the Lives of LDS Youth and Young Adults*. He has also presented at BYU Education Week as well as professional conferences across the United States. He enjoys music, biking, basketball, and most outdoor recreational activities.